CRACKING TH

ASPECTS OF FIFTIES AMERICA

THE DOLPHIN

General Editor: Tim Caudery

23

CRACKING THE IKE AGE:

ASPECTS OF FIFTIES AMERICA

Edited by Dale Carter

AARHUS UNIVERSITY PRESS

Copyright: Aarhus University Press, 1992
Word-processed at the Department of English, Aarhus University
Printed in the UK by the Alden Press, Oxford
ISBN 87 7288 373 1
ISSN 0106 4487

The Dolphin no. 23, autumn issue 1992

Published with financial support from the Danish Research Council
for the Humanities

Editorial address:
The Dolphin
Department of English, Aarhus University
DK-8000 Aarhus C, Denmark

Distribution:
Aarhus University Press
Building 170, Aarhus University
DK-8000 Aarhus C, Denmark
Fax: + 45 86 19 84 33

Cover illustration: Demonstrators picketing School Board offices in protest at
continuing racial segregation in public schools in spite of the landmark *Brown
vs. Board of Education* Supreme Court decision of 1954. (American History Slide
Collection, Instructional Resources Corporation).

Contents

Preface

Over the past fifteen or twenty years, a number of general texts dealing with the decade of the 1950s as a whole have been published. Beginning with works like Charles Alexander's *Holding the Line: The Eisenhower Era* (1975) and Douglas Miller and Marion Nowak's *The Fifties: The Way We Really Were* (1977), subsequent studies have included Paul Carter's *Another Part of the Fifties* (1983), and J. Ronald Oakley's *God's Country: America in the Fifties* (1986). Another more recent contribution to the field, John Diggins' *The Proud Decades: America in War and Peace, 1941-1960* (1988), features an annotated bibliography which gives a good sense of the growth, not only in the general literature but also in the more specialized works upon which the broader-ranging texts necessarily depend.

Given their individual or dual authorship, it is hardly surprising that (even as they differ in their emphases) these volumes all seek in one way or another to synthesize a complex of information into an integrated, if not homogenized, narrative. The present work is slightly different in both its structure and purpose: more closely related, perhaps, to the collection of conference papers edited at the University of Copenhagen English Department by Anne Clauss, and published under the title *America in the Fifties* in 1978. Emphasizing the diversity and contentiousness of an era popularly conceived of as consensual and one-dimensional, *Cracking the Ike Age: Aspects of Fifties America* is distinguished by its breadth of subject matter, intellectual approach and interpretive voice. Bringing together work by leading authorities in their fields and some of the newest voices in American Studies, it ranges from up-to-date syntheses of the latest research on American cold war diplomacy to pioneering work on humour as social criticism; it offers novel interpretations of key developments in the civil rights movement and highlights less-publicized aspects of the San Francisco renaissance; it encompasses not only poetry, prose and drama but also the visual arts, film and popular music. In the process it provides, or so I hope, fresh perspectives on American culture, society and politics during the 1950s.

Even were agreement on definitions of such terms possible, a volume of this size would in any event be unable to encompass all significant or noteworthy developments of the decade. Under these circumstances, no attempt has been made to be comprehensive. While aspects of race receive attention in more than one of the essays, for example, questions of gender are dealt with in less detail. Even as some aspects of the visual arts are closely analysed, others are passed over in silence. In addition, although more space is devoted to Elvis

7

Presley and Dwight Eisenhower than to John Cage or Adam Clayton Powell, this collection places at least as much emphasis on the less-known or the scarcely-analyzed as on the familiar. The subject of the longest chapter is the little-known but significant story of KPFA radio in San Francisco; by contrast, the much-discussed life and work of Marilyn Monroe receive only passing attention. Finally, while established perspectives and scholarship are by no means ignored, a number of the contributors to this volume address the decade's events from innovative angles. Epochal developments in the field of race relations, for example, are presented as much as faltering extensions of the 'forgotten years' of the black struggle in the 1940s as triumphant preludes to the so-called revolution of the 1960s. In these and other ways, *Cracking the Ike Age* presents the familiar in new ways or enables the unfamiliar to be glimpsed for the first time.

While the authors were given more or less free range in deciding on the subject of their contributions, and even though an emphasis has so far been placed on the correspondingly variegated nature of the collection, the end products of their individual labours have more in common, I hope, than merely a shared decade. There are, in other words, certain patterns, if not some grand design, evident in the resulting collection. This belief (or hope) has, in any event, influenced the volume's organization. Insofar as it is possible to summarize this arrangement in broad terms, then, this is a book about various forms of security and insecurity whose focus shifts gradually from the top to the bottom. We proceed from the establishmentarian to the dissident; from the insiders to the self-appointed or involuntary outcasts; from the secure and the recognized to the venturesome, hazardous or vulnerable.

Callum MacDonald's opening chapter discusses the assumptions, objectives, and circumstances of the Eisenhower administration's efforts to develop new national security strategies in the light of the perceived shortcomings of those inherited from the previous administration of President Harry Truman. My own contribution takes up the concept of security but redefines it in somewhat broader terms, investigating the ways in which dreams of security constituted often self-defeating avenues of escape for a public embroiled in new and complex forms of conflict fought out in an unfamiliar no-man's-land between war and peace. Elsebeth Hurup's essay looks at the reconstruction of the decade in more recent Hollywood cinema. She points out that, while much of our mythology of the 1950s as an era of relative innocence and happy days is encoded through popular culture, the latter may offer critical analyses of such a vision even as it articulates it. In his study of the civil rights movement of the 1950s, Peter Ling addresses the struggles of the one group most obviously excluded from and victimized by the security programming of white, middle-class America and its various agents. His attention centres on contending interpretations of the movement's nature, strategy and tactics.

In the following chapters, the focus of the volume shifts increasingly from the social and explicitly political to the cultural and, in the first instance, literary. Sharing with Peter Ling a concern with matters of race, Marzia Balzani and Clive Bush discuss the responses of the distinguished American writer Paul Bowles to the *other* – not only the non-white but the non-American and non-Christian – via a comparison with those of French author Albert Camus. Karl-Heinz Westarp's contribution maintains the literary theme but returns attention directly to the United States through his analysis of Arthur Miller's artistic and political activities during the decade. Sharing with Bowles a concern for the ways in which individuals handle experiences of the feared, the unknown and the threatening, Miller analyses in his work and challenged in his own life a predatory and debilitating authoritarianism. While major artistic and political differences might have otherwise existed, something similar could be said of the figures Eric Mottram discusses in the first of his two essays in this collection. Although generalizations about the so-called 'San Francisco renaissance' can be misleading, he makes clear that during the fifteen or so years following World War Two the city by the bay provided a base for communities which together engendered a major cultural occasion – one which, at least temporarily, defied the pressures of a beseiging dominant commercial culture.

In the first of four chapters dealing with non-literary dimensions of the decade's culture, Allen Fisher offers an analysis of certain aspects of the era's painting which identifies a critical inventiveness analogous to that investigated by Eric Mottram across the arts. Drawing on, challenging and adding to a wide range of artistic theories and practices, as well as the resources of numerous other intellectual fields, painters like Motherwell and Rauschenberg produced work that adapted and analysed the very culture which at the time ridiculed (but which later invested in) them. Documenting in detail another aspect of the broader field investigated by Eric Mottram, John Whiting's contribution on the development of listener-sponsored radio broadcasting demonstrates, via the first-hand accounts of those directly involved, the potentials and achievements of individuals and groups willing to challenge established forms of public communication even at a time of reactionary dominance. In his chapter on the development of one of the decade's novel cultural forms, Jody Pennington discusses the ways in which rock'n'roll music (which would become one of the staple contents of commercial radio) thrived at the intersection of, and encoded the tensions between, a dominant commercialism, changing patterns of racial interaction, technological innovation, and popular need to counter the disabling securities being offered by established cultural authorities. Finally, in his second contribution to this volume Eric Mottram offers a pathbreaking probe into the humour of social criticism exemplified at the time by Mort Sahl, Dick Gregory and Lenny Bruce. Far from providing no more than risqué entertainment for metropolitan swingers or subject matter for establishment indignation, these and other comedians used satire to expose and (to varying degrees) analyse the nature of power. They did so to such an effect that, in Bruce's case at least, the authorities turned authoritarian and destructively vengeful.

Having begun this collection with an analysis of the ways in which the humourless communist monolith abroad was to be cracked open by federal authorities in the name of security, we thus conclude with a discussion of an American comedian who may have been cracked down on by state and local authorities in the name of decency – but whose own cracks, along with the breakthroughs of many others discussed in this volume, nevertheless helped advance the crack up of the security complex which has perhaps constituted one of this work's latent themes.

Most books are a product of collective effort and this is particularly so in the case of an essay collection. I would therefore like to thank the contributors to the volume, not only for their work but also for their tolerance of my periodic assaults (via letter, fax, phone or bulky package) on their time, texts, energy and patience. I am indebted, as well, to Tim Caudery, General Editor of the *Dolphin* series, who for no apparent reward has provided advice, filled in forms, carried out copy editing, and instructed me in the mysteries of the departmental laser printer; and to Signe Frits of the Department of English, who has maintained her characteristic cool and efficiency while retyping and setting up the contents in the teeth of my flexible deadline editing system. Appreciation is also due to Karen Kirk Sørensen and the Library of the United States Information Service in Copenhagen for help with the cover; to the galleries, private individuals and agents who helped furnish the illustrations; to the publishers, Aarhus University Press; and to the Danish Research Council for the Humanities, who have provided most generous financial support for the publication. Finally, I would like to thank Robert Creeley's typewriter for last minute support.

Dale Carter

The Paradox of Power: Eisenhower and the 'New Look'

Callum MacDonald

In January 1953 Dwight D. Eisenhower became the first Republican to enter the White House since Herbert Hoover over twenty years before. Early historical writing on Eisenhower's two terms was critical, portraying him as a do-nothing president, more interested in golf than in government, who left foreign policy to his Secretary of State John Foster Dulles, an inflexible moralist prepared to take the world to the edge of the nuclear abyss. In the past fifteen years, however, this view has been attacked by historians such as Robert Divine, John Lewis Gaddis and Stephen Ambrose.[1] The revisionist school offered a very different view of the period, presenting Eisenhower as a president fully in control of his administration with an acute understanding of the problems of war and peace in the nuclear age. In the process the old picture of John Foster Dulles was also subjected to some reinterpretation.[2] Eisenhower revisionism was shaped partly by the declassification of government papers which offered greater insight into the workings of the administration and partly by the turbulent experience of the United States at home and abroad after 1960. In retrospect the Eisenhower years could be regarded as an era of peace and stability: the 'good old days' before the trauma of Vietnam. In this respect Eisenhower's achievement in extricating the United States from Korea and avoiding involvement in any new war for the remainder of his presidency seemed particularly significant.[3] The revisionists concentrated on Eisenhower's skilled crisis management rather than on nuclear brinkmanship and emphasized his attempts to promote detente with the Soviet Union, arguing that US policy in the period was both more cautious and more subtle than suggested by the rhetoric of 'massive retaliation'.

Eisenhower and the American System

Eisenhower's approach to the cold war and containment can be understood only in the context of NSC-68, the national security programme inaugurated by the Truman administration in September 1950, three months after the Korean War began. NSC-68 was a reaction to the successful Soviet atomic bomb test in the early autumn of 1949 which broke the American monopoly of atomic weapons. Defining communism as an inherently expansionist system, implacably opposed by its nature to the values and interests of the United States, NSC-68 predicted an increased Russian threat and called for massive rearmament, both conventional and atomic, to contain and roll back Soviet power. It ruled out preventive war but called on the United States and its allies to establish positions of strength and prepare to meet the Russians at every level of conflict, conventional or atomic, global or limited: an approach defined by Gaddis as 'symmetrical containment'.[4] In June 1950 the Truman administration chose to reply to what it regarded as a communist probe in Korea by fighting a limited war while at the same time preparing to fight a global war with the Soviet Union by 1954, defined as the crisis year in which the Russians would have sufficient atomic weapons to risk attacking the United States. NSC-68 was based on a form of military Keynesianism derived from the experience of the Second World War which assumed that America could afford both guns and butter, arguing that an arms budget of up to $50 billion would expand and stimulate the economy. It denied that permanent semi-mobilization was a threat to American values, arguing that the 'integrity of our system will not be jeopardized by any measures, covert or overt, violent or non-violent, which serve the purposes of frustrating the Kremlin design'.[5]

NSC-68 became controversial almost as soon as it was adopted. In the crisis that followed Chinese intervention in the Korean War in November 1950, it was attacked by right-wing Republicans under Senator Robert Taft as strategically inept, economically disastrous and morally bankrupt. According to Taft, NSC-68 left the strategic initiative with the communists, allowing them to dictate the location, timing and rules of engagement as in Korea. It risked involving the United States in a series of limited peripheral wars in which American blood and treasure would be expended without any decisive result. Like the hero of the Republican right, General Douglas MacArthur, Taft favoured carrying the war to China to break the military stalemate, regardless of the repercussions on Western Europe and NATO, considered by the Truman administration the most important area in the cold war.[6] Economically, Taft believed that NSC-68 was disastrous because it allowed the communists to subvert the free enterprise system by bankrupting the United States. As he argued in *A Foreign Policy for Americans*, a book compiled with an eye to the presidential elections of 1952, there was 'a definite limit to what a government can hope to spend in peace and still maintain a free economy'.[7] Taft believed

12

that under Truman means were subverting ends, that national security policy was undermining the very structures and values it was meant to preserve. According to Taft, 'an unwise and overambitious foreign policy ... is the one thing which in the end might ... prove a real threat to the liberty of the people of the United States'.[8] Taft sought an alternative in air/atomic striking power, a solution also favoured by other figures on the Republican right such as ex-President Hoover, arguing that the threat of massive retaliation would restrain further communist probes along the lines of Korea. With the Kremlin thus placed on the defensive, the United States should seize the initiative in a psychological warfare campaign designed to subvert communist control over the satellite states. Containment would be replaced by liberation.[9]

According to Taft, this approach would be both cheap and effective, ruling out huge and destabilizing programmes of rearmament, preserving the American free enterprise system and allowing the United States to prevail in the cold war. Although sometimes described as neo-isolationism because of its distrust of collective security, the United Nations and US participation in the NATO alliance, right-wing Republican thinking was more properly defined as a form of unilateralism which sought a quick release from the frustrations of Korea and the wider stalemate of the cold war.[10] This deliberate rejection of both international and domestic consensus on the methods and goals of American foreign policy has been interpreted as the last stand of declining fractions of capital against the hegemony of the New Deal system based on structural reforms at home and the establishment of a world economy compatible with the operations of American multinationals, the form of American late capitalism which had emerged supreme from the inter-elite struggles of the 1930s.[11] In this respect it was significant that the Republican right demanded not only a unilateral exercise of American power, primarily in Asia, without regard for the repercussions on a European alliance system, NATO, which reflected economic as well as strategic priorities, but also an assault on the New Deal state at home. For this reason some historians have agreed with the description of the Republican right by Truman's Secretary of State, Dean Acheson, as 'primitives', political and economic neanderthals rooted in an earlier and cruder age.[12]

In launching their attack, Taft and his allies rejected the eastern establishment wing of Republicanism which was part of the bipartisan multinational bloc. It was this group that turned to Eisenhower to save the party from the 'reactionaries' and win the 1952 election. Eisenhower's function was to hold the line, restoring consensus on foreign and defence policy.[13] Conservative on domestic issues and opposed to the further growth of the big state, Eisenhower was firmly committed to collective security, NATO and the priority of Europe in American foreign policy. It was on this issue that he chose to emphasize his differences with Taft, condemning him as an isolationist who would withdraw into a fortress America.[14] Eisenhower won the nomination and ran on an ambiguous foreign policy platform that condemned containment and called for rollback while endorsing NATO and American membership of the UN. This was the product of a compromise with the right, embittered by the failure of Taft, 'Mr Republican', and was an early indication of Eisenhower's determination to work with all sides of the party. He refused, however, to endorse massive retaliation, a doctrine which he associated with fortress America concepts, and never warmed to liberation as a campaign theme. In the end Eisenhower's foreign policy commitments were reduced to an implied pledge to end the Korean War, without specifying what methods he intended to employ.[15] It is ironic that, once elected, Eisenhower was to adapt some of Taft's ideas in formulating a policy for his administration.

In shaping a 'New Look' for American foreign and defence policy, Eisenhower was acutely conscious of the relationship between means and ends, an approach encouraged by his military training as well as his fiscal conservatism.[16] In this respect he shared Taft's concern that NSC-68 was likely to destroy the structures and values it was meant to defend. In domestic policy, Eisenhower was an admirer of Hoover, believing that big government had gone too far under Roosevelt and Truman. He advocated voluntary cooperation amongst all the elements in the political economy rather than state action as the answer to the problems of industrial America, embracing what he called the middle way between statism and socialism. In practice this meant the creation of a corporate commonwealth which retained key elements of New Deal welfare capitalism such as social security, thus sustaining a process begun under Roosevelt that substituted consumption for politics.[17] Eisenhower realized, however, that a harmonious, orderly and smoothly functioning corporate commonwealth at home could not be maintained without a functioning capitalist order abroad based on an Open Door which allowed the United States and its allies free access to markets and sources of raw materials. As he emphasized in his first inaugural address, self-interest as well as idealism linked the United States to the wider world: 'No free people can for long cling to any privilege or enjoy any safety in economic solitude.... We need markets in the world for the surpluses of our farms and our factories. Equally, we need for these same farms and factories vital materials and products of distant lands.'[18] It was on this point that he profoundly disagreed with Taft, Hoover and others on the Republican right whom he condemned as isolationists.

Eisenhower did not share the view of the drafters of NSC-68 that large armaments expenditures would not damage the economy or threaten traditional institutions and values. He was convinced that 'unrestrained spending could alter the very nature of American society, either through the debilitating effects of inflation or through regimentation in the form of economic controls'.[19] Although he was sometimes accused of fearing inflation more than communists, Eisenhower was making more than an economic point. He regarded core American values as dependent on the free enterprise system, a system that could not survive indefinitely the dramatic and costly military build-up initiated by NSC-68. As he remarked to the National Security Council on 7 October 1953: 'We could lick the whole world ... if we were willing to adopt the system of Adolph Hitler ... [but] after all we were engaged in defending a way of life as well as territory, a population, our dollar.'[20] Nor would the American people ultimately bear the burden of world power if this involved reduced living standards or a series of protracted and bloody limited wars on the Korean model. According to Eisenhower: 'You could get the American people to make ... sacrifices voluntarily for a year or for two or three years but no eloquence would sell this proposition to the American people for the indefinite future.'[21] In protecting American hegemony over the capitalist world system, therefore, he sought a programme that would guarantee long-term security 'without bankrupting the nation', a middle way 'between the Fortress America isolationism of Taft and the Keynesian internationalism of Truman'.[22]

The New Look: 'More Bang for a Buck'

In the early summer of 1953 the administration began an intensive review of US foreign and defence policy known as Operation Solarium. Three task forces were established to investigate various options for dealing with the communist bloc. In the background was the knowledge that the United States enjoyed strategic superiority over the Russians as a result of NSC-68, which had accelerated the American atomic bomb programme and improved the capability of the Strategic Air Command: 'By the end of 1953, SAC contained 10 heavy and 25 medium bomb and reconnaissance wings, nearly 23 of which were considered combat ready, along with 28 refueling squadrons, totalling, in all, over 1,500 aircraft, including 1,000 nuclear capable bombers.'[23] It was re-equipping with the B-47, a medium jet bomber, and was preparing to replace the vulnerable B-36 with the long-range B-52, a heavy jet bomber. The USAF also possessed tactical atomic weapons for the first time, as did the carrier aircraft of the US Navy. In October 1952, just before the presidential elections, a hydrogen device was successfully tested.[24] When Eisenhower took office, therefore, the United States was moving into an era of atomic plenty, a situation that contained frightening possibilities. As Trachtenberg emphasizes, 'even as late as 1953 or 1954, one could actually imagine fighting and, in some meaningful sense, winning an air-atomic war. It would probably be a long war, and the devastation would be terrible, but the country would survive as a functioning society'.[25] This superiority, however, was a wasting asset, since the Russians would soon catch up. In particular, the inevitable Soviet development of hydrogen weapons would make a global war unwinnable: 'The combination of increased yields and fallout meant that the new hydrogen bomb was truly an area weapon. The United States could scarcely survive an attack with even a relatively small number of these bombs.'[26]

In this situation one possiblity was preventive war to cripple the Soviet Union before the Russians had the capacity to launch a knock-out blow. Although such a course was not considered by Operation Solarium, it enjoyed the tacit support of Admiral Radford, the Chairman of the Joint Chiefs of Staff, and some of his Air Force colleagues.[27] As he warned the National Security Council on 24 November 1954, once a nuclear balance was achieved:

> the relative power position of the US would have so changed that the US could no longer count on the Russians being afraid of starting general war. Moreover, the Joint Chiefs had pointed out that they could no longer guarantee a successful outcome for the US in such a war ... assuming that the objectives of Soviet Communism were unchanged, the Joint Chiefs of Staff believed that some time or other the Soviet Union would elect to force the issue ... if we continue to pursue a policy of simply reacting to Communist initiatives instead of forestalling Communist action, we cannot hope for anything but a showdown with Soviet Communism by 1959 or 1960.[28]

The implications of these remarks were obvious.

Eisenhower himself sometimes toyed with the option of preventive war. As he informed Dulles in August 1953, it had to be assumed that the Russians were prepared to use weapons of mass destruction. The United States thus faced the prospect of an indefinite nuclear arms race, designed to maintain a position in which:

> we would be constantly ready, on an instantaneous basis, to inflict greater loss upon the enemy than he could reasonably hope to inflict on us. This would be a deterrent – but if the contest to maintain this relative position should have to continue indefinitely, the cost would either drive us to war – or into some form of dictatorial government. In such circumstances, we would be forced to consider whether or not our duty to future generations did not require us to *initiate* war at the most propitious time that we could designate.[29]

As late as 1960, disappointed by the failure of the Paris summit and tired of 'Khrushchev and his threats', Eisenhower 'strongly intimated that he wished there was no moral restriction that prevented him from one night pushing the proper button and sending all of our atomic bombs in the direction of the Communist bloc'.[30] Such outbursts, however, were 'merely isolated expressions of frustration. It was too late for anything like this to be seriously considered as a real policy option'.[31] Truman had expressed similar sentiments during the Korean War without ever seriously intending to put them into practice.[32]

The nearest that Operation Solarium came to discussing preventive war was with Task Force C, which was instructed to frame a programme 'to produce a climate of victory' in the confrontation with the Soviet Union. Its report called for the rollback of communist power by a 'forward and aggressive political strategy in all fields and by all means: military, economic, diplomatic, covert and propaganda'. This would involve expenditures of up to $60 billion per annum in the short term but would result in long term savings because of the progressive elimination of Russian power. Although such an aggressive policy would increase the risk of global war, it was justified by the nature of the communist system: 'The US cannot continue to live with the Soviet threat. So long as the Soviet Union exists, it will not fall apart, but must and can be shaken apart.' The first stages of the programme had to be completed before the Russians were 'capable of dealing a destructive blow to the United States (five years)'.[33] The other teams were less aggressive. Task Force A investigated the NSC-68 approach, containing the Soviet Union by building positions of strength and exploiting its vulnerabilities by 'various covert and overt means'.[34] Its report offered no prospect of early reductions in the military budget. Task Force B was asked to consider a programme which drew firm lines around the perimeter of the Soviet bloc, utilizing the 'warning of general war as a primary sanction against further ... aggression'. According to its report, such a course would force the Soviet Union onto the defensive and reduce the economic costs of the cold war to the United States and its allies.[35]

The Eisenhower administration constructed a policy which incorporated elements of all three options. A central component of the New Look was the threat of massive retaliation proposed by Task Force B. Although John Foster Dulles had advocated this approach in *Life* magazine as early as May 1952, Eisenhower had refused to incorporate it into the Republican Party platform. According to Eisenhower, an emphasis on air/atomic striking power was too close to the Fortress America ideas of Taft.[36] It became central to his post-election policy, however, because it offered the only real means of reducing the costs of containment, with all their dangers to the American system, and of gaining 'more bang for a buck'. According to NSC-162/2, the October 1953 National Security Council memorandum that emerged from discussion of the task force reports, the United States had to

> develop and maintain, at the lowest feasible cost, requisite military and nonmilitary strength to deter and, if necessary, to counter Soviet military aggression against the United States or other areas vital to its security. The risk of Soviet aggression will be minimized by maintaining a strong security posture, with emphasis on adequate offensive retaliatory strength.... This must be based on massive atomic capability, including necessary bases.... In the event of hostilities, the United States will consider nuclear weapons to be as available for use as other munitions.[37]

In his State of the Union message three months later, Eisenhower announced that US policy was to deter aggression by maintaining 'a massive capability to strike back'. This policy favoured the air force and the navy over the army, allowing reductions in the military budget.[38] There was an element of pre-emption in massive retaliation intended to put the communist bloc on the defensive by encouraging uncertainty about what type of Soviet action might

17

trigger an American decision for global war, a shift from symmetrical to asymmetrical containment.[39]

In embracing atomic striking power, however, NSC-162/2 did not reject collective security and NATO, the focus of Eisenhower's disagreement with the Republican right in 1952. Alliances were considered vital both as a means of sharing the economic burdens of the cold war and as a way of providing bases for American medium-range bombers around the periphery of the Soviet Union. Moreover, as under Truman, the main priority remained the promotion of German rearmament and the integration of West Germany into the scheme of European defence. Although US troops in Europe were to be reduced as part of the cost-cutting New Look, it was recognized that precipitate action would endanger NATO. The European allies would lose heart if they suspected that the United States was withdrawing into a Fortress America defended by the bomb, and might drift into neutralism. The administration solved this problem by nuclearization, the forward basing of tactical atomic weapons which substituted technology for expensive military manpower: another example of seeking 'more bang for a buck'.[40]

If air striking power, alliances and tactical atomic weapons offered a means of holding the line against communist expansion, NSC-162/2 also incorporated a limited element of rollback, though a pale shadow of the Republican campaign platform and the kind of total cold war advocated by Task Force C. According to NSC-162/2, the United States 'should take feasible political, economic, propaganda and covert measures designed to create and exploit troublesome problems for the USSR, impair Soviet relations with Communist China, complicate control of the satellites, and retard the growth of the military and economic potential of the Soviet bloc'.[41]

The psychological warfare efforts of the previous administration were stepped up under C.D. Jackson, a former executive of Time Inc., and the CIA was given a higher profile under Allen Dulles, the brother of Eisenhower's Secretary of State. These developments reflected the President's strong personal belief in the efficacy of covert warfare stretching back to his time as Supreme Allied Commander in Europe during the Second World War. During his two terms the CIA was to play a key role in containing revolution in the third world, ensuring that countries like Iran, Guatemala and South Vietnam remained locked into a world economic system dominated by the United States and its allies.[42] It was less active in Eastern Europe, however, abandoning the kind of para-military operations carried out under Truman in the Ukraine and Albania.[43] In this respect the New Look never measured up to the policy of boldness advocated by Dulles in his *Life* magazine article of May 1952. As the Soviet leader Nikita Krushchev later remarked: 'Dulles knew how far he could push us, and he never pushed us too far.'[44]

Since preventive war was ruled out, NSC-162/2 accepted that the Soviet Union would continue to develop its atomic capabilities. The goal of security

18

policy therefore had to be 'to create, prior to the achievement of mutual atomic plenty, conditions under which the United States and the free world coalition are prepared to meet the Soviet-Communist threat with resolution'.[45] This 'in effect, acknowledged the sanctity of the Soviet sphere of influence in Central and Eastern Europe'.[46] Dulles himself privately recognized that Washington had accepted a status quo based on the Yalta agreements, whatever his public rhetoric to please the Republican right. As Divine remarks, his 'moralistic and often ponderous public statements gave him the reputation, which he cherished, of being a dedicated crusader against the Soviets [but] behind the scenes he proved to have a lucid understanding of the realities of world politics and a surprising gift for the give-and-take of diplomacy'.[47] At an NSC meeting in November 1954, Dulles rounded angrily on those who still advocated rollback and even preventive war. Accused by Admiral Radford of excessive caution, he asked the chairman of the JCS to explain how

we were to prevent the Soviet Union from achieving ... a nuclear balance of power without going to war with the USSR? Certainly no actions on the periphery of the Soviet Union would stop the growth of the atomic capabilities of the Soviet Union ... the views of the Joint Chiefs involved a difference with his own ... [the JCS] favored the US taking bigger risks for bigger goals. His guess was ... that what the military was really advocating was that we should tell the Soviets that they must restore freedom to Czechoslovakia by a certain date 'or else'.[48]

Eisenhower shared Dulles' caution. As early as September 1953, shortly after the Russians had detonated their first hydrogen device, he remarked that this new development had been much on his mind: 'Even before that, he had doubts ... about how much we should poke at the animal through the bars of the cage.'[49] According to the President, the advent of atomic weapons had changed the nature of war. It no longer presented the options of victory or defeat but only alternatives 'in degrees of destruction'.[50] As he informed the leader of South Korea, Syngman Rhee, a bellicose advocate of rollback, in 1954: 'Let me tell you that if war comes, it will be horrible.... Atomic war will destroy civilization.... There will be millions of people dead ... if the Kremlin and Washington ever lock up in a war, the results are too horrible to contemplate. I can't even imagine them.'[51] The logic of the situation was clear. If preventive war was ruled out, and rollback was too dangerous, there was little left but peaceful co-existence, a startling conclusion for an administration that had capitalized on the frustrations of containment under Truman and Acheson in the 1952 election campaign.

Managing the Cold War: Eisenhower and Detente

In March 1953, shortly after Eisenhower took office, Joseph Stalin died and his successors proclaimed a policy of peaceful co-existence. According to the new head of the Soviet Communist Party, Georgi Malenkov, there were no disputes between East and West that could not be settled by peaceful means.[52] Russian diplomacy had enjoyed few successes during Stalin's last years. The United States had responded to the war in Korea by increasing its nuclear and conventional forces. It had also used the opportunity to promote the rearmament of West Germany and a peace treaty with Japan, thereby building positions of strength around the Soviet perimeter. Detente was probably designed to slow down this process and to relieve international tensions while the new communist leadership established itself.[53] There was also a clear desire to seek a more stable relationship with the United States as it moved into a period of nuclear plenty. The Russians were as aware as the Americans of the possibility of preventive war, and the rhetoric of massive retaliation can have done little to reassure them. Moreover, they probably knew about the transfer of complete nuclear weapons from the Atomic Energy Commission to the military initiated by Eisenhower in June 1953, a process designed to reduce the risks of a knock-out blow to the US stockpile and to improve the ability of the Strategic Air Command to retaliate against Moscow.[54] As the President himself admitted, the Russian leaders must have been 'scared as hell' of what the United States might do.[55]

Although deeply suspicious of Soviet motives, Eisenhower realized that the United States would have to respond in a positive way to these new developments. For psychological warfare purposes alone Washington could not be perceived as too harsh and inflexible. Moreover, as the President himself remarked, people were becoming tired of the stale rhetoric of the cold war. They had to be offered something more positive than mere confrontation.[56] From the beginning, therefore, negotiations played an important role in the New Look, which recognized that fear of massive retaliation might even make the Russians seek genuine agreements with the West. As early as 16 April 1953, Eisenhower responded to Russian proposals for detente in a major speech before the American Society of Newspaper Editors which emphasized the costs of the cold war. According to the President, every weapon made diverted funds from more productive purposes. The arms race was 'not a way of life ... in any true sense. Under the cloud of threatening war it is humanity hanging from a cross of iron'. He called upon the Russians to join the United States in nuclear disarmament and to devote part of the money saved to a fund for world development. As a first step Moscow should sign an Austrian peace treaty, conclude a Korean armistice, agree to German reunification and restore freedom to Eastern Europe.[57]

On one level this was simply a propaganda move designed to capture the psychological initiative. Eisenhower realized there was little likelihood of the Russians agreeing to terms that involved total capitulation to the United States. Moreover, neither he nor Dulles were prepared for serious negotiations with Moscow in advance of French ratification of the European Defence Community (EDC), a structure devised under Truman as a means of promoting West German rearmament, and they staved off pressure from the British prime minister Winston Churchill for an early summit conference. It was feared in Washington that the Russians would use a summit to block this process, promoting their own scheme for a united but neutral Germany. The Americans rejected the idea of neutralization and insisted that a reunited Germany had to be free to join NATO, an outcome wholly unacceptable to the Russians.[58] While the American position involved an acceptance of partition, Eisenhower hoped that in the longer term West German political, economic and social progress would prove an irresistible attraction to the population of the communist East.[59] On another level, however, the speech set the tone for Eisenhower's presidency by emphasizing the need for international cooperation to control the nuclear arms race.

In July 1953, Eisenhower remarked to the newly-appointed head of the Atomic Energy Commission, Lewis Strauss: 'Lewis, let us be certain about *this*; my chief concern and your first assignment is to find some new approach to the *dis*arming of atomic energy ... the world simply must not go on living in the fear of the terrible consequence of nuclear war.'[60] With this remark, Eisenhower touched on the central paradox of his national security policy. Nuclear weapons were vital to the New Look, but as Russia moved towards nuclear parity the United States would find itself involved in an open-ended arms race to maintain the deterrent value of massive retaliation: a development which would create as many problems as it solved. Eisenhower noted as early as August 1953 that more and more resources would be required if the United States was to remain capable of inflicting greater losses on the enemy 'than he could reasonably hope to inflict on us'. The ultimate result might be to drive the country into war 'or into some form of dictatorial government'.[61]

Although the cost of nuclear developments could be shared with allies like the British, something that Eisenhower was anxious to encourage by revising the restrictive atomic legislation of the Truman period, an open-ended nuclear arms race would thus endanger the very existence of the American domestic system.[62] At the end of the road loomed the garrison state or war. The second alternative was even worse than the first, for with the advent of the hydrogen bomb there could be no winners. A Russian attack on the United States would bring total economic collapse. Up to 65% of the population would require medical treatment which in most cases would be unavailable. The United States could do three times as much damage to the Soviet Union, destroying it as a functioning society, but this hardly constituted victory in the traditional sense.[63] In other words, the New Look was ultimately no more capable of reconciling means and ends than NSC-68. Paradoxically, its very emphasis on nuclear retaliation demanded arms control and detente. Having developed new kinds of weapons, the United States found that they imposed their own political imperatives which overshadowed the original purposes they were meant to serve. The only way out of the nuclear dilemma was by negotiation. However much they differed, the two superpowers had one common interest: survival.

During his first term Eisenhower launched two initiatives on arms control which developed the theme of his address to the newspaper editors. On 8 December 1953, in a speech to the United Nations, he proposed that the Soviet Union join the United States in promoting the peaceful uses of atomic energy. Each should turn over a proportion of its stockpile to a UN International Energy Agency which would use the fissionable material like a global Tennessee Valley Authority to provide 'abundant electrical energy to the power-starved areas of the world'. Two years later at Geneva, the first summit conference since Potsdam a decade earlier, he launched his famous 'Open Skies' plan, designed to promote arms limitation by solving the difficult issue of inspection. According to Eisenhower, the two superpowers could guarantee themselves against cheating by mutual air reconnaissance, a kind of spying by international agreement.[64] Neither plan proved acceptable to the Russians, for in both cases the United States would have gained the main advantages. Nevertheless they were signals that the United States believed arms control was an important issue and regarded the Soviet Union as a legitimate negotiating partner in the new hydrogen age. Nikita Khrushchev, who was emerging on top from the power struggle that followed Stalin's death, recognized this essential point. As he later recalled, the Soviet delegation returned from Geneva in 1955 'knowing that we hadn't achieved any concrete results' but 'realizing now that our enemies probably feared us as much as we feared them.... They realized that they would have to build their relations with us on new assumptions and new expectations if they really wanted peace'.[65]

The new 'Spirit of Geneva' suffered a setback in October 1956 when Soviet tanks crushed the Hungarian rebellion. Behind the public outrage, however, US policy accepted the status quo. There was no duel at the brink over Hungary. During his second term Eisenhower continued to seek an arms agreement, defining this as the most important objective of his presidency. After 1956 US efforts, recognizing public concern at the impact of unrestricted testing on health and the environment, focused on a comprehensive nuclear test ban treaty as the first step towards some wider arrangement.[66] Eisenhower's approach to the question, however, was full of contradictions which stemmed from a view of the Russians unchanged since the outbreak of the cold war. If he wanted to control the arms race, he also wanted to stay ahead of the Soviet Union. The Russians could not be allowed to gain any technological or quantitative advantage under the camouflage of a test ban. Since it was the nature of communists to cheat and lie, the United States always had to be vigilant. As he informed Winston Churchill in December 1953, Russia was 'a woman of the streets and whether her dress was new, or just the old one patched, there was the same whore underneath'.[67] This led the President to take a tough line on inspection to an extent that sometimes proved counter-productive, providing a point of pressure for hardliners such as the scientist Edward Teller who doubted the wisdom of any arrangement with Moscow. As Soapes remarks, Eisenhower was 'prepared to take only limited risks to achieve his goal, and low-risk strategies usually net limited rewards'.[68] Moreover, in the absence of an agreement on inspection, Eisenhower continued to authorize U-2 spy plane flights over the Soviet Union, a unilateral version of 'Open Skies' initiated in 1956.[69] While this programme was meant to guarantee US security, it ultimately conflicted with Eisenhower's wider aims when Francis Gary Powers was shot down over the Ukraine in May 1960. The repercussions of this affair helped undermine the prospects of a comprehensive test ban treaty and led to the collapse of the Paris summit.[70]

The failure of the test-ban negotiations was only one of the frustrations of peaceful co-existence during Eisenhower's second term. Khrushchev used the propaganda coup of Sputnik in 1957 and the emerging nuclear stalemate to pursue a more adventurous Soviet policy than in the years immediately after Stalin's death, when an American preventive strike had seemed a real possibility. In particular he attempted to reopen the German question by applying diplomatic pressure over Berlin in 1958. In dealing with the international and domestic repercussions of these developments, Eisenhower tried to avoid a sense of crisis. He adopted a moderate approach over Berlin which avoided anything approaching an ultimatum and which contrasted strongly with the sense of national emergency deliberately created by his successor.[71] At home he was impatient with domestic critics who claimed that the Russians were ahead in the cold war and who called for huge new investments in science, education and the aerospace industry to overcome the supposed missile gap demonstrated by Soviet successes in space. As his science adviser James Killian later recalled, demands from the Democrats for increased military spending seemed to Eisenhower more like a plea for state subsidies to the aerospace industry than a national security programme.[72]

His Farewell Address returned to the theme of his first major speech in April 1953, emphasizing the dangers to the American way of life posed by costly military budgets. It was an implicit rebuke to his successor John F. Kennedy, who was clearly committed to return to military Keynesianism as a means of containing the Russians and managing the economy.[73] Although widely admired at a later stage for its warning about the growth of the military/industrial complex, the speech failed to admit that Eisenhower himself had been unable to balance national security with arms control, means with ends, or financial conservatism with the demands of the cold war. This would have demanded a redefinition of US interests, a step that his administration was never prepared to take. Eisenhower's belief in the Open Door and the need to prevent communist expansion everywhere, even at the risk of over-extending American power, meant that a price had to be paid. In his second term, military spending continued to average 9.5% of GNP, a fall of around only 3% from the peak years of NSC-68, despite the fact that the United States was no longer involved in the Korean War.[74] These figures hardly suggest that under Ike the defence industry went hungry; in fact, despite his exaggerated fears about the impact of the arms race on the American system, the United States remained in a state of permanent semi-mobilisation. Ultimately Eisenhower was unable to reconcile arms control with the desire to stay ahead of the Russians. In this respect the New Look had merely held the line, a characteristic of Eisenhower policies in so many fields.

Cracking the Monolith: Massive Retaliation in the Far East

If peaceful co-existence was the basis of the US relationship with the Soviet Union, the situation was very different with regard to the People's Republic of China. It was in the Far East that the major crises of the Eisenhower period occurred, and there too that the United States came closest to the brink of nuclear war. A variety of reasons dictated a harsh policy towards China. When Eisenhower took office, the United States had already been fighting the Chinese in Korea for over two years, and for many Beijing was a much more tangible and immediate enemy than Moscow. The right-wing of the Republican Party blamed the Democrats for the fall of China to communism and called for moves to end the Korean War by a direct assault on the mainland using American air power and the troops of the discredited Guomindang regime on Taiwan (Formosa).[75] For Eisenhower and Dulles a tough line on China was the price of maintaining party unity and containing criticism from the right about peaceful co-existence with Russia: 'Substantive agreements with China ... were politically unfeasible ... to have pursued this course during the McCarthy period was very nearly impossible.'[76]

China policy, however, was more than a tool of party integration. It also served important global purposes. If the New Look was to be taken seriously, a vital element in negotiating with the Russians, the United States had to demonstrate its readiness to employ nuclear weapons where its interests were threatened.[77] China was the safest place to make such a demonstration since, unlike the Soviet Union, it lacked the capacity to retaliate. Nuclear pressure would not only humiliate and discredit hardline communists in Beijing, perhaps securing their ultimate overthrow, but might also encourage a Sino-Soviet split. The Russians would never risk war with the United States for the sake of China, and this could only complicate a relationship that the Americans knew was already strained, however much they talked in public about a communist monolith. Paradoxically, the more the Chinese were forced to turn to Russia, the greater the chances of a Sino-Soviet quarrel. Co-existence in Europe and confrontation in Asia were thus two aspects of the same policy, a policy designed to drive a wedge into the communist bloc and make the world a safer place for the United States and its allies.[78]

Eisenhower's China policy took two forms. The first was to build positions of strength around the periphery of China utilizing Asian manpower backed by US economic assistance. Local armies would deal with local threats. If China intervened, as in Korea, the United States would reply with tactical atomic weapons. Eisenhower was prepared to use tactical bombs against targets in both Manchuria and North Korea in the spring of 1953 to break the deadlock at the armistice talks and end the war. Although the role of this threat in securing a truce that July has been much exaggerated, it was clear that under Eisenhower there would be no more limited wars in Asia. The Republic of Korea (ROK), which the United States had intervened to protect in 1950, became a model for the rest of Asia. After the armistice the ROK army was built up to twenty divisions, sufficient to maintain internal security and contain the threat from the North. If China resumed the war at any stage, however, tactical atomic weapons would be used immediately against both North Korea and Manchuria, a threat implicit in the warning of greater sanctions which accompanied the armistice.[79] As Eisenhower explained to Churchill at the Bermuda conference of December 1953, if 'war came or if there were to be a serious breach of the armistice in Korea, the people of the United States would never understand it if the weapon were not used'.[80] This message was pushed home to Beijing in September 1953 by Operation Big Stick, a mass flight by the heavy B-36 bombers of the Strategic Air Command to Japan. In the next few years the Americans reduced the number of troops based in South Korea but underlined their continued commitment to the ROK by replacing them with forward based tactical atomic weapons.[81] Korea was important, not just as a symbol of US credibility, but also because of its strategic and economic significance to Japan, the centre of US influence in the Pacific. In this respect Eisenhower followed a pattern established under Truman that based Far Eastern policy on the need to guarantee Japan the economic resources it required for a functioning capitalist economy and the sense of military security necessary to prevent a disastrous drift into neutralism.[82]

If this consideration shaped US policy in North-East Asia, it was also fundamental to developments in Indochina, where the ROK provided a model for the creation of an anti-communist bastion in another divided Asian nation: Vietnam. Since early 1950, Washington had backed the French war effort in Indochina against the communist Vietminh, defining the resources of the area, including rice, as vital to a regional economy centred on Japan.[83] In 1954, however, during the crisis that surrounded the siege of Dien Bien Phu, Eisenhower had to decide whether or not to go beyond economic aid and intervene directly on the side of the French, perhaps employing tactical atomic weapons: a course favoured by some of his advisors, including the chairman of the Joint Chiefs, Admiral Radford. For Radford it was important to secure some kind of cold war victory while a window of opportunity, based on American nuclear superiority, existed. If the ultimate result was to trigger global war with Russia, that war was best fought while Soviet ability to retaliate was limited.[84] Eisenhower, however, refused to go to the brink for French colonialism, although plans were made for atomic strikes on targets in Hainan and south China if Chinese volunteers openly intervened in Indochina as they had in Korea. Instead, at the Geneva conference of 1954, Washington accepted a Korean solution: a ceasefire agreement that created an independent Laos and Cambodia, while leaving Vietnam divided along the 17th parallel, pending elections. The United States refused to sign the Geneva Accords, although Dulles promised not to undermine them by the 'threat or use of force'. From the beginning, however, Washington tried to draw the line against further communist expansion, constructing the South East Asia Treaty Organization (SEATO), ousting the French from South Vietnam and creating there an anti-communist state modelled on the ROK. According to the President, South Vietnam had to be preserved to prevent a falling domino effect that would deliver all of South-East Asia to the communists.[85]

While building anti-communist bastions on the periphery of China, the United States continued to deny the legitimacy of the regime in Beijing. Like its predecessor, the Eisenhower administration kept the communists out of the United Nations and treated the Guomindang on Taiwan as the real government of China. The economic sanctions imposed during the Korean War were maintained and American citizens were refused permission to travel to the mainland. Although it was not allowed to intervene in Hungary, the CIA was encouraged to arm and train Tibetan guerrillas and to wage para-military warfare on the Chinese mainland.[86] As the NSC emphasized in 1953, the broad aim was to 'oblige the USSR to carry the burden of assisting Communist China' and to impede 'general international acceptance of the Chinese Communist regime'.[87] Privately, some American officials were critical of the Guomindang leader, Jiang Jishi (Chiang Kai-shek), and his ambition to liberate China. As Vice-President Nixon informed a British official in November 1953, Jiang and the men around him were discredited. The Generalissimo was 'a liability and not an asset'.[88] Eisenhower was irritated by Jiang's admirers in the Republican party, led by Senator William Knowland of California, who was nicknamed the Senator from Formosa. As Ike caustically remarked, in Knowland's case there was no ultimate answer to the question: how stupid can you get?[89] At the same time, however, Taiwan could not be abandoned. It was useful to pay lip service to the myth of the Guomindang, not only to preserve party unity but also to maintain pressure on Beijing. As long as the US backed the regime on Taiwan, the Chinese communists faced a possible military threat on their flank that might distract them from adventures elsewhere. Moreover, the very existence of Jiang was a reminder of the penalties for supporting Moscow in the cold war. While many aspects of this policy, such as the denial of the UN seat, might seem like mere pinpricks, they were important to a China determined to escape the legacy of the nineteenth century and to secure equal treatment within the international system. In this sense the message from Washington was clear. China would remain a pariah as long as the alliance with Russia lasted.

The policy of maintaining pressure on China lay behind the nuclear threats issued by Washington during the offshore islands crisis of 1954/55.[90] Jinmin (Quemoy) and Mazu (Matsu), just off the Chinese coast, were regarded by Jiang as springboards for the liberation of the mainland. They supported the Guomindang naval blockade of Fuzhou (Foochow) and Xiamen (Amoy) and were also used to launch raids on the mainland. On 3 September 1954 the communists began shelling the islands in what was widely regarded as the prelude to an amphibious assault. Beijing was probably responding to the creation of the SEATO pact and rumours that Washington planned a military alliance with Taiwan, perhaps linked to a wider North-East Asian security system including Japan and the ROK. The islands were the only available point of pressure to demonstrate Chinese displeasure and perhaps to force Washington into negotiations with Beijing.[91] Eisenhower was reluctant to become involved in a war over outposts he considered of little military importance. On the other hand he was unwilling to allow Beijing a prestige victory, and accepted Dulles' argument that if the islands fell morale on Taiwan would collapse. Such an outcome would create a psychological domino effect throughout the Far East, undermining faith in American power and making communism appear the wave of the future.

At first Eisenhower attempted to deter an attack by deliberate ambiguity, emphasizing American commitments to the security of Taiwan through the Formosa Resolution of January 1955 and the mutual defence treaty ratified the following month, while refusing to define precisely what Washington would do in the event of an assault limited to the offshore islands. Privately, the President tried to persuade Jiang to evacuate his threatened garrisons, and manouvered him into abandoning the Dachen (Tachen) group, where the communists landed in January 1955. On 15 March, however, with rumours circulating of an imminent Chinese assault timed to coincide with the opening of the Bandung conference of non-aligned nations in April 1955, Dulles openly threatened American employment of tactical nuclear weapons. At a press conference the following day, Eisenhower remarked that in combat there was no reason 'why they shouldn't be used just exactly as you would use a bullet or anything else'.[92]

Eisenhower later recalled that his aim had been to deter Beijing.[93] In issuing his nuclear threat, the president was gambling that the Chinese would not risk war without Soviet backing and that the Russians would withold their support. As he explained to the NATO commander, General Alfred Gruenther, in February 1955:

> I do not believe that Russia wants war at this time – in fact, I do not believe that if we became engaged in a rather bitter fight along the coast of China, Russia would want to intervene.... I am convinced that Russia does not want, at this moment, to experiment with means of defense against the bombing that we *could* conduct against her mainland.... I assume that Russia's treaty with Red China comprehends a true military alliance, which she would either have to repudiate or take the plunge. As a consequence of this kind of thinking, she would probably be in a real dilemma if we got into a real shooting war with China.[94]

Eisenhower's judgement was supported by reports that emphasized Soviet reluctance to become involved in a major war with the United States over the offshore islands. The US joint intelligence staff 'agreed that the Soviet leaders, aware of their country's small nuclear stockpiles and inadequate delivery capabilities, would not risk Russia's survival for China in war against the United States'.[95] In fact, the prospect might even sharpen Moscow's desire for detente. Indirect evidence that Russia had exercised restraint during the crisis was provided in June 1955 when a Soviet official informed the US ambassador that while the Russians were sharing scientific and technical information with China 'they had not given [the] Chinese either [the] bomb ... or facilities for its manufacture'.[96]

In retrospect some historians have described Eisenhower's handling of the crisis as a masterpiece that used 'a measured nuclear threat to warn the Chinese without insulting them or provoking them into an attack. The beauty of Eisenhower's policy is that to this day no one can be sure whether or not he would have responded militarily to an invasion of the offshore islands, and whether he would have used nuclear weapons'.[97] This view underestimates the alarm caused to the European allies, led by Britain, who were never convinced of the necessity of holding the outposts. If the Sino-Soviet alliance was weakened, the 'special relationship' with Britain was also strained.[98] It also fails to take into account the impact at home, where many doubted that the stakes involved justified the employment of atomic weapons. Lastly, it overestimates Eisenhower's ability to control the situation. At the height of the crisis, the United States tried to persuade Jiang to evacuate Jinmin and Mazu in return for a blockade of the mainland. Jiang distrusted the Americans and refused. It is difficult to understand how Eisenhower could have believed that this scheme offered a peaceful solution, since the Chinese would certainly have retaliated against US warships imposing the blockade. Perhaps Jiang was correct in suspecting that the Americans had no intention of carrying out the plan

28

after the offshore islands had been evacuated. He had been the victim of a similar trick in January when he abandoned the Dachens (Tachens) in return for an American promise to guarantee Jinmin and Mazu, only to discover after the event that the guarantee was no longer on offer.[99]

Washington could not claim to have deflated Chinese prestige during the crisis, a major aim of US policy. At the Bandung conference Zhou Enlai seized the diplomatic initiative, not by announcing an invasion but by emphasizing China's peaceful intentions, an approach that impressed third world delegates alarmed by US nuclear threats. According to Zhou, the Chinese were willing 'to discuss the question of relaxing tension in the Far East and especially the question of relaxing tension in the Taiwan area'.[100] Although the crisis was subsequently defused by diplomatic contacts, US negotiations with China quickly broke down. Washington insisted that Beijing renounce the use of force against Taiwan, a demand rejected by the communists as outside interference in Chinese domestic affairs. Such a concession would have confirmed the independence of Taiwan and the emergence of two Chinas, an outcome wholly unacceptable to a regime dedicated to re-establishing Chinese territorial integrity. The result was the second offshore islands crisis on 1958 in which Washington again threatened to go to the nuclear brink. As in the first confrontation, Soviet support for Beijing was meagre, and the Chinese eventually allowed the crisis to fade away.[101] In contrast to their policy towards the Soviet Union, Eisenhower and Dulles had thus proved unwilling to build bridges to China on anything but the most limited scale. It was to take the Sino-Soviet split and a lost war in Vietnam to move US policy in new directions.

Conclusions

Eisenhower left a mixed legacy to his successors as the United States entered a new decade. In Europe his administration was the first to wrestle with the paradoxes of power in the nuclear age. On one level he recognized that the cold war must continue as long as the Soviet Union existed. On another he understood that it was a process that could no longer be managed by simple confrontation. There had to be a degree of co-existence and even negotiations with the enemy. In seeking agreements, primarily in the field of nuclear armaments, however, he was never able to reconcile the demands of national security, staying ahead of the Russians, with his desire for limitations, a problem that was also to plague his successors. In Asia his legacy was more mixed. He managed to hold the line against China by employing the nuclear threat, and perhaps hastened a Sino-Soviet split by his hard line. On the other hand his policy in the area had unforeseen and unwelcome results. The confrontation with China confirmed the determination of Beijing to secure equal treatment and proved that equal treatment in the modern world sprang from possession of the bomb. The Chinese leaders had only to contrast Eisenhower's obvious reluctance to bait the bear with his greater readiness to confront the dragon. The result was to speed up the Chinese bomb programme and the emergence of China as a nuclear power. As Mao explained to the Central Committee of the Chinese Communist Party in April 1956: 'In the world of today, we cannot be without this thing if we do not want to be bullied by others.'[102]

The confrontation with China was itself part of a policy that opposed revolutionary nationalism in Asia as a dangerous threat to the kind of Open Door world demanded by the United States. As McMahon has emphasized, in the Eisenhower years the United States neither liked nor understood third world nationalism, in this respect compounding the errors of its predecessor by interpreting essentially North/South struggles in East/West terms.[103] The moderation that characterized US policy in Europe was never evident in the developing areas, and the results were often tragic. The price paid by the people of Asia for the maintenance of American empire was high. In this respect, moreover, Eisenhower left one ticking time-bomb to his successors: Vietnam. Perhaps more than any other president, Eisenhower could have avoided direct US involvement in Vietnam. He could have accepted the Geneva verdict and blamed French mismanagement for the loss of a war which was at that stage not an American fight. Instead he plunged in, created South Vietnam and staked American prestige on its survival in circumstances that were always more unfavourable than those in South Korea, on which the Republic of Vietnam was modelled. Before he retired his experiment was already beginning to unravel, but by then it was too late to retreat. Under his successors the United States was to be sucked into an open-ended conflict with Vietnamese nationalism that would destabilize the American system Eisenhower wished to preserve and accelerate the demise of an American Century he had pledged to maintain.

NOTES

1. Robert A. Divine, *Eisenhower and the Cold War* (New York and Oxford: 1981); John Lewis Gaddis, *Strategies of Containment* (New York and Oxford: 1982); Stephen Ambrose, *Eisenhower the President* (London: 1984).
2. Richard H. Immerman, ed., *John Foster Dulles and the Diplomacy of the Cold War* (Princeton: 1990).
3. Walter LaFeber, *The American Age: United States Foreign Policy at Home and Abroad Since 1750* (New York and London: 1989), pp. 543-45; Ambrose, pp. 618-27.
4. Gaddis, *Strategies of Containment*, pp. 98-106; Callum A. MacDonald, *Korea: The War Before Vietnam* (London: 1986), pp. 22-25.
5. NSC-68, 'United States Objectives and Programs for National Security', 14 April 1950, US Department of State, *Foreign Relations of the United States, 1950* (Washington, D.C.: 1977), vol. 1, p. 311. (Hereafter *FR*, followed by year, volume number and page references.)

6. MacDonald, *Korea*, pp. 79-80; Ronald Radosh, *Prophets on the Right: Profiles of Conservative Critics of American Globalism* (New York: 1974), pp. 176-95.
7. Robert A. Divine, *Foreign Policy and US Presidential Elections*, vol. 1 (New York: 1974), pp. 8-11.
8. Gaddis, *Strategies of Containment*, p. 120.
9. MacDonald, *Korea*, pp. 79-80.
10. MacDonald, *Korea*, pp. 79-80.
11. Bruce Cumings, *The Origins of the Korean War, vol. 2: The Roaring of the Cataract* (Princeton: 1990), pp. 79-120.
12. Cumings, pp. 79-120.
13. Richard A. Malenson, 'The Foundations of Eisenhower's Foreign Policy: Continuity, Community and Consensus', in Richard A. Malenson and David Mayers, eds., *Reevaluating Eisenhower: American Foreign Policy in the 1950s* (Urbana and Chicago: 1987), pp. 40-41.
14. Malenson, p. 43.
15. Divine, *Foreign Policy and Presidential Elections*, pp. 33-37, 50-76.
16. Gaddis, *Strategies of Containment*, pp. 134-36.
17. Robert Griffith, 'Dwight D. Eisenhower and the Corporate Commonwealth', *American Historical Review*, 87 (1982), 87-122.
18. Peter Lyon, *Eisenhower: Portrait of the Hero* (Boston and Toronto: 1974), p. 498.
19. Gaddis, *Strategies of Containment*, p. 134.
20. 'Memorandum of Discussion at the 165th Meeting of the National Security Council', 7 October 1953, *FR, 1952-1954*, vol. 2, pp. 519-21.
21. *FR, 1952-1954*, vol. 2, p. 521.
22. Malenson, p. 49.
23. David Alan Rosenberg, 'The Origins of Overkill: Nuclear Weapons and American Strategy, 1945-1960', *International Security*, 7 (Spring, 1983), 29.
24. MacDonald, *Korea*, pp. 247-48.
25. Marc Trachtenberg, *History and Strategy* (Princeton: 1991), p. 133.
26. Trachtenberg, pp. 133-34.
27. Trachtenberg, p. 143.
28. NSC, 225th Meeting, 24 November 1954, *FR, 1952-1954*, vol. 2, p. 791.
29. 'Memorandum by the President for the Secretary of State', 8 September 1953, *FR, 1952-1954*, vol. 2, p. 461.
30. Trachtenberg, pp. 145-46.
31. Trachtenberg, pp. 145-46.
32. Barton Bernstein, 'New Light on the Korean War', *International History Review*, 3 (1981), 271-72.
33. 'Summaries Prepared by the NSC Staff of Project Solarium, Presentations and Written Reports', Undated, *FR, 1952-1954*, vol. 2, pp. 416-34. A fourth alternative, D, for preventive war was dropped just before the review began. See Richard H. Immerman, 'Confessions of an Eisenhower Revisionist: An Agonizing Reappraisal', *Diplomatic History*, 14 (1990), 337.
34. *FR, 1952-1954*, vol. 2, pp. 399-412.
35. *FR, 1952-1954*, vol. 2, pp. 412-16.
36. MacDonald, *Korea*, pp. 156-57.
37. 'NSC 162/2', 30 October 1953, *FR, 1952-1954*, vol. 2, pp. 590-97.
38. Samuel F. Wells, 'The Origins of Massive Retaliation', *Political Science Quarterly*, 96 (1981-82), 33-42.

39. Trachtenberg, pp. 146-52.
40. Trachtenberg, pp. 163-68.
41. *FR, 1952-1954*, vol. 2, pp. 590-97.
42. Blanche Wiesen Cook, 'First Comes the Lie: C.D. Jackson and Psychological Warfare', *Radical History Review*, 31 (1984), 42-71; John Ranelagh, *The Agency: The Rise and Decline of the CIA* (London: 1987), pp. 229-376; Rhodri Jeffreys-Jones, *The CIA and American Democracy* (New Haven and London: 1989). pp. 81-117.
43. Nicholas Bethell, *The Great Betrayal* (London: 1984); Harry Rositzke, *The CIA's Secret Operations* (New York: 1977).
44. Edward Crankshaw, ed., *Krushchev Remembers* (London: 1971), p. 361.
45. *FR, 1952-1954*, vol. 2, pp. 590-97.
46. David Mayers, 'Eisenhower's Containment Policy and the Major Communist Powers', *International History Review*, 5 (1983), 59.
47. Divine, *Eisenhower and the Cold War*, p. 22.
48. NSC, 225th Meeting, 24 November 1954, *FR, 1952-1954*, vol. 2, pp. 788-95.
49. Cutler to Eisenhower, 6 September 1953, *FR, 1952-1954*, vol. 2, p. 457.
50. Divine, *Eisenhower and the Cold War*, p. 116.
51. Gaddis, *Strategies of Containment*, pp. 173-74.
52. MacDonald, *Korea*, p. 182.
53. Mayers, 62-63.
54. Rosenberg, 27.
55. Trachtenberg, p. 150.
56. Ambrose, *Eisenhower*, pp. 1-96.
57. Ambrose, *Eisenhower*, pp. 1-96.
58. Anne Marie Burley, 'Restoration and Reunification Eisenhower's German Policy', in Malenson and Mayers, eds., pp. 230-39.
59. Trachtenberg, p. 175.
60. Divine, *Eisenhower and the Cold War*, p. 111.
61. 'Memorandum by the President to the Secretary of State', 8 September 1953, *FR, 1952-1954*, vol. 2, pp. 460-63.
62. On nuclear burden sharing see Timothy J. Botti, *The Long Wait: Forging the Anglo-American Nuclear Alliance* (New York, Westport and London: 1987).
63. Robert H. Ferrell, ed., *The Eisenhower Diaries* (New York and London: 1981), pp. 311-12.
64. Divine, *Eisenhower and the Cold War*, pp. 112-22.
65. Nikita Khrushchev, *Krushchev Remembers*, trans. Strobe Talbott (New York: 1971), p. 363.
66. Divine, *Eisenhower and the Cold War*, pp. 124-25. For a full account of the test ban negotiations see Robert A. Divine, *Blowing on the Wind: The Nuclear Test Ban Debate, 1954-1960* (New York: 1978).
67. John Colville, *The Fringes of Power: Downing Street Diaries, 1939-1955* (London: 1985), p. 682.
68. Thomas F. Soapes, 'A Cold Warrior Seeks Peace: Eisenhower's Strategy for Nuclear Disarmament', *Diplomatic History*, 4 (1980), 69. See also Robert A. Strong, 'Eisenhower and Arms Control', in Malenson and Mayers, eds., pp. 241-66.
69. Ranelagh, pp. 310-22.
70. Jeffreys-Jones, pp. 112-13.
71. Trachtenberg, passim. On the impact of Sputnik see Dale Carter, *The Final Frontier* (London and New York: 1988), pp. 120-152.

72. James R. Killian, Jr., *Sputnik, Scientists and Eisenhower* (Cambridge, Mass. and London: 1982), pp. 237-38.
73. Strong, pp. 260-63.
74. Figures in Gaddis, *Strategies of Containment*, p. 359.
75. MacDonald, *Korea*, pp. 154-55.
76. Mayers, 81.
77. H.W. Brands Jr., 'Testing Massive Retaliation: Credibility and Crisis Management in the Taiwan Straits', *International Security*, 12, 4 (Spring, 1988), 148-51.
78. Mayers, 63 - 68; John Lewis Gaddis, *The Long Peace: Inquiries into the History of the Cold War* (New York and Oxford: 1987), pp. 174-94.
79. Callum MacDonald, *Britain and the Korean War* (Oxford: 1990), pp. 92-93; Rosemary Foot, 'Nuclear Coercion and the Ending of the Korean War', *International Security*, 13, 3 (Winter, 1988-89), 92-112; Roger Dingman, 'Atomic Diplomacy During the Korean War', *International Security*, 13, 3 (Winter, 1988-89), 50-91.
80. Foreign Office minute, 5 December 1953, FK1241/6 FO371/105574, Public Record Office, London. (Hereafter PRO.)
81. Peter Hayes, Lyuba Zarsky and Walden Bello, *American Lake: Nuclear Peril in the Pacific* (London: 1987), pp. 52-53, 72.
82. Cumings, pp. 35-117.
83. Cumings, pp. 35-117.
84. Trachtenberg, pp. 143-44; Richard H. Immerman, 'Between the Unattainable and the Unacceptable: Eisenhower and Dienbienphu', in Malenson and Mayers, eds., pp. 130-33.
85. Stanley Karnow, *Vietnam: A History* (London: 1984), pp. 198-204, 213-24.
86. Ranelagh, pp. 335-36; Victor Marchetti and John D. Marks, *The CIA and the Cult of Intelligence* (New York: 1980), pp. 101-3.
87. NSC 162/2, 30 October 1953, *FR, 1952-1954*, vol. 2, pp. 460-63.
88. Memorandum by Malcolm MacDonald, 26 November 1953, FC10345 FO371/105221, PRO.
89. Ferrell, ed., p. 291.
90. For a full account of the crisis see J.H. Kalicki, *The Pattern of Sino-American Crises* (Cambridge: 1975), pp. 120-58.
91. Kalicki, pp. 127-33.
92. Divine, *Eisenhower and the Cold War*, pp. 65-66.
93. Dwight D. Eisenhower, *Memoirs, Vol. 1: Mandate For Change, 1953-1956* (New York: 1963), pp. 476-77.
94. Eisenhower to Gruenther, 1 February 1955, *FR, 1955 - 1957*, vol. 2, pp. 189-93.
95. Mayers, 73.
96. Bohlen to Department of State, 6 June 1955, *FR, 1955 - 1957*, vol. 2, pp. 587-88.
97. Divine, *Eisenhower and the Cold War*, pp. 65-66.
98. Michael Dockrill, 'Britain and the Offshore Islands Crisis, 1954-1955', in Michael Dockrill and John W. Young, eds., *British Foreign Policy, 1945-1956* (London: 1989), pp. 173-96.
99. Gordon H. Chang, 'To the Nuclear Brink: Eisenhower, Dulles and the Quemoy Crisis', *International Security*, 12, 4 (Spring, 1988), 96-122.
100. Mayers, 77.
101. Kalicki, pp. 168-208; Dwight D. Eisenhower, *Memoirs, Vol 2: Waging Peace, 1956-61* (London: 1966), pp. 292-304.

102. 'Mao Zedong and China's Atomic Bombs', *Beijing Review*, September 5th-11th 1988, 25-26. See also John Wilson Lewis and Xue Litai, *China Builds the Bomb* (Stanford: 1988), pp. 21-35.
103. Robert J. McMahon, 'Eisenhower and Third World Nationalism: A Critique of the Revisionists', *Political Science Quarterly*, 101 (1986-1987), 453-73.

Evasive Action: War, Peace and Security in the Fifties

Dale Carter

In late November 1950 Chinese troops, having crossed the Yalu River under cover, entered the fighting in strength against General Douglas MacArthur's UN forces in Korea. The United Nations Command, MacArthur later recalled in his memoirs, 'faced an entirely new war'. It was, he feared, a war that could yet end in disastrous defeat unless further, and perhaps drastic, measures were taken. For all its destructiveness, visibility, and expense, however, MacArthur's 'new war' was but the trailing edge of a long established form of conflict, one whose primacy had been seriously if not irrevocably undermined over five years earlier when the collapse of the Third Reich and the detonation of atomic bombs over Hiroshima and Nagasaki brought the Second World War to a close. The conflicts MacArthur was familiar with would not, of course, disappear. In the forty years since the end of hostilities in Europe and the Pacific, similar battles were to result in the deaths of perhaps another twenty-five million people. They would nevertheless be displaced and largely restricted to the margins of their previous domain. In this sense, MacArthur's was less a new war than an old, and increasingly obsolescent, war in a new place.[1]

But, as Lieutenant Hearn's observations on 'the osmosis of war' in Norman Mailer's *The Naked and the Dead* (1948) imply, this displacement had more than just geographical dimensions. In Thomas Pynchon's epic fiction, *Gravity's Rainbow* (1973), the Second World War, its powers now exhausted, is not so much exported as *absorbed*; rather than being posted overseas, its agents are demobbed. As he wanders through the scattered wreckage of Berlin in the wake of the German surrender, Pynchon's Tyrone Slothrop senses that the chaos and slaughter of the war have engendered an enormous 'inverse mapping'. Everything, not just the bombed-out buildings that litter the streets, has been 'turned inside out'. For Pynchon, the Allied soldiers who patrol the city and guard the housing compounds surrounding the Potsdam conference site are strictly temporary features: representatives of an institution now rendered both unnecessary and counter-productive. It is the exhausted civilian inhabitants of Hitler's former capital that foreshadow the shape of wars to

35

come. From now on, Slothrop discovers, 'the civilians are outside ... the uniforms inside'.[2]

If long-established military forms of conflict had been superseded, whether by transportation or absorption, the civilian struggles that followed bore little apparent resemblance to those of the pre-war era. No Great Depression, for example, returned to the surface of life. Ten years after wartime populations from Berlin to Bel Air had taken on new occupations, indeed, both soldiers and soup-kitchens had largely vanished. Where they had gone and the nature of the struggles that replaced them are again dimly foreshadowed in the ruins of Pynchon's Berlin, where survivors no longer march to the 'straight-ruled' dictates of military command but respond to 'laws of least discomfort'. They are prefigured, too, at the conclusion of *The Naked and the Dead*, where Major Dalleson, wondering how he can hold recruits' attention in basic training now that the Pacific campaign is over, decides to display map-reading techniques using as his imaginary terrain a 'full-size color photograph of Betty Grable in a bathing suit'.[3] The new configurations are most explicitly articulated, however, in one of Thomas Pynchon's earlier fictions. Heading downtown on a New York subway train in Pynchon's mid-Fifties based first novel, *V.* (1963), Benny Profane wonders what has become of the Depression America he had been born into before the war. 'All around him were people in new suits, millions of inanimate objects being produced brand-new every week, new cars in the streets, houses going up by the thousands all over the suburbs he had left months ago. Where was the depression?'[4] The answer gives further access to the post-war structure of conflict. Like the war it preceded, the Depression had not so much been abolished as absorbed into a dense network of promises, products, and prosperity. The carriage which drew away from the wreckage of 'Pain City' at the beginning of *Gravity's Rainbow*, evacuating not merely a few passengers but an entire generation to the further reaches of 'Happyville', was an exercise in basic training. America was being drawn into a new struggle, one that would rage across the outskirts of the sumptuous and characterize the 1950s as much as slump and shell-shock had the previous two decades.

An exchange between Roger Mexico and Jessica Swanlake near the beginning of Pynchon's epic – 'don't you know there's a war on, moron? yes but ... where *is* the war?' – anticipated the grounds of that struggle. Fought out along the evacuation routes leading from warfare to peacetime, from Pynchon's Pain City towards Happyville, the war beyond the war took on novel and often incongruous forms, flared up anywhere, and was anticipated everywhere: from the gleaming surfaces of Profane's New York to the shade of the suburbs beyond. While armed conflict (as in Korea) defined its outer reaches, there were no longer front lines, rear areas, or safe havens in this struggle, nor clear distinctions between armed forces and non-combatants, tours of duty and furloughs, blitzes and all-clears.[5] Instead, this new war escalated imperceptibly between the abiding yet secluded threats of atomic annihilation and material deprivation and the incessant yet disposable promise of automatic life. Across these indistinct regions of undeclared combat covering the vast open spaces and narrow trenches that separated the MacArthurs from the Profanes – between domesticated ease and colonial tensions, open plan suburbs and armoured subways, shopping centres and insane asylums, upholstered lounges and padded cells – Fifties America was reproduced and consumed as a precarious interface of inflicted exterior power and imagined interior collapse, of sanctioned enforcement and feared retribution.

If the battlefield had changed, so too had the troops. During the 1950s the frontlines that had replaced the previous decade's breadlines were in turn overrun by new legions: the massed ranks of soldier-worker-consumers whose activities came not simply to inflect the writings of Mailer, Pynchon, and others but to dominate the thinking of the nation's official advisors, from politicians and planners to sociologists and salesmen. In *The Public Burning*, Robert Coover's 1977 fiction on the 1953 execution of Julius and Ethel Rosenberg, New York City's 'Friday-morning commuters' are the very image of post-war capitalism's new private army: one moment 'beset with nightmare visions of Soviet tanks in Berlin, dead brothers lying scattered across the cold wastes of Korea, spreading pornography and creeping socialism, Phantomized black and yellow people rising up in Asia and Africa', the next 'dreaming peacefully of baseball, business, and burning hayricks' under the joint command structure of Frankie Laine, Uncle Sam, and Nelson Eddy. Shuttling across the same streets that Benny Profane would traverse two years later, meandering, like Pynchon's human yo-yo, inside 'the aisles of a bright, gigantic supermarket, [their] only function to want', Coover's commuters move characteristically at the intersection of induced anxiety and desire.[6]

If the forces had changed, so finally had their tactics. As the post-war fictions of Mailer and Pynchon imply, it was no longer the writings of Clausewitz but those of Wilhelm Reich and Hannah Arendt that described the new rules of engagement. Where there were no clearly defined enemies and allies, only suspects and collaborators, established methods needed revision. Where there were neither glorious victories nor devastating defeats, only conditions of immanent tension and perpetual competition, survival techniques necessarily altered. Where violation and sacrifice were endemic, neutrality meaningless, and engagements obligatory but inconclusive, new movements took shape. During the 1950s, blitzkrieg, begging and bug-out were no longer sufficient or necessary. In their place came evasive action.

Just as the displacement of war was more than geographical, so what David Riesman in *The Lonely Crowd* (1950) regarded as the definitive movement of the post-war era – from 'inner-' to 'other-directedness' – was more than psychological. During the 1950s the predominant movement, *the* other direction, was outwards. Between 1950 and 1960 suburban America grew forty times as fast as the nation's central city areas. The cores of many cities, including New York, San Francisco, and Chicago, experienced not simply relative but absolute population loss. While suburbanization was hardly a new phenomenon, by the end of the decade post-war economic and demographic growth, Federal tax incentives and mortgage assistance, new mass production house building techniques, increases in real wage levels, continued growth in automobile ownership, cheap energy, and a road building programme that culminated in passage of the 1956 Interstate Highway Act, had combined to make the evacuation of the inner city one of the central myths of American life.[7]

The evacuation's official objective, to which the imaginative and material products of labour and desire, accumulation and indulgence, alienation and repression were devoted in ever-growing quantities, was the intersection of liberty and security: the decade's central Cold War fetish. The drive began less at home than with a new home. In the late 1940s, the *New York Times* reported, the establishment of the nation's largest single-builder housing development at Levittown, Long Island, had helped turn 'the detached single-family house from a distant dream to a real possibility for thousands of middle class American families'. The construction of over fifteen million new homes between 1950 and 1960 turned the drive into a stampede. Every day some three thousand acres of greenery were bulldozed to make way for the largest single capital investment programme in American history. Within six years of its first settlement, the original Levittown had seventy thousand residents. But the settlers could never quite settle. Though prospective purchasers had queued to get in, some of them for days, such was the need to have *arrived*, deliverance called for more than patience and a Veterans Administration mortgage. The incessant conversion of evacuees into suburbanites – during the decade their numbers swelled by nineteen million – kept the safe haven contested ground. The myth moved too. For the agents and symbols of what a July 1950 *Time* cover story on William Levitt called 'a new way of life', there could be 'no plateau'. They faced, in the words of William H. Whyte, 'only the rungs of a ladder'.[8]

A line from the screen version of William Inge's 1955 play *Bus Stop* (Joshua Logan, 1956) offered a step up. 'For a wedding present', Don Murray tells Marilyn Monroe, 'I'm getting you a deep freeze or an electric washer or any other major appliance you want.' Romantic love clearly remained a popular necessity: the marriage of film actress Grace Kelly to Prince Rainier III of Monaco in April 1956 attracted eighteen hundred reporters and photographers. For millions of Americans, however, personal magic was increasingly challenged by consumer appeal: what Max Lerner in *America as a Civilization* (1958) described as 'the sheer delight in a gadget-cluttered environment, with new devices and new models constantly replacing earlier ones'. William Levitt's decision to include fitted televisions, washing machines, refrigerators, and stoves in the purchase price of his homes only anticipated a broader offensive. Between 1950 and 1960 the number of televisions in America increased by 45 million, of telephones by 31 million, and of registered automobiles by 21 million. During the same period the value of all goods and services purchased jumped from $195 billion to $327.8 billion, of which a rising proportion was being spent on furniture and household equipment. As the national swimming pool population grew from 42,000 to 240,000, so sales of lawn and porch furniture almost tripled. The decade saw plastic flamingoes, ducks and gnomes massing in numbers. The introduction of the TV dinner in 1954 was only part of what *House and Garden* magazine celebrated that year as 'The Pushbutton Way to Leisure'. The rest included electric dishwashers, blenders, and lawn trimmers, automatic coffee percolators, and portable barbecues. In 1955 Americans comprised 6% of the world's population but tuned into 30% of its radios and televisions, answered 60% of its telephones, and drove 75% of its automobiles. When Don Murray had finished plumbing in Marilyn Monroe the following year, they joined the 89% of American households with washing machines (96% boasted refrigerators). During the 1950s the claim of Hazel Motes in Flannery O'Connor's *Wise Blood* (1952) – 'nobody with a good car needs to be justified' – articulated increasingly common lore for a culture virtually defined through its mobility dreams. By the end of the decade there were more cars in Los Angeles county than in the whole of South America or Asia.[9]

But successful evacuation required more than just geographical movement and social elevation. It also demanded a variety of physical and psychological reinforcements. There was, on the one hand, a growing investment of personality in commodities, particularly automobiles: Cadillac – flashy; Pontiac – stable and conventional; Mercury – assertive and modern, according to one study carried out in Chicago. On the other hand, there was a comparable investment of commodities in personality: a reproduction, that is, of the 'Bodies by Fisher' concept well beyond the freeways. Marshall McLuhan's probe into 'the folklore of industrial man', *The Mechanical Bride* (1951), includes essays entitled 'Love-Goddess Assembly Line' and 'Corset Success Curve'. Three years later, in Thomas Pynchon's *V.*, Benny Profane watches Rachel Owlglass chatting to her sports car in 'm.g. words' and 'fondl[ing] the gearshift'. Though Profane accuses her of being 'an accessory ... a part ... like a radio, heater, windshield-wiper blade', he still wonders whether female resistance to male advances could be measured in ohms, and even looks forward to the production of 'an all-electric woman' made of interchangeable parts and supplied with a maintenance manual.[10] Marilyn Monroe, a major dream figure in American life for much of the decade, was described as 'a curious plastic amalgam' whose features included a 'famous wiggle ... wound into her by Mattel'. Grace

Kelly's cooler appearance in *High Society* (Charles Walters, 1956) only made her Bing Crosby's 'Miss Frigidaire'. Since successful bridegrooms had to be mechanical too, however, she was hardly alone. 'The Tough as Narcissus', 'Bogart Hero', and 'I'm Tough' – all pieces from McLuhan's first volume – define the well-tuned man as a combination of strength and precision, efficiency and reliability: qualities that made William Holden the most consistently employed and one of the most popular of the era's Hollywood leads. Expressions of industry obviously differed. The year Holden starred as a successful design engineer in *Executive Suite* (Robert Wise, 1954), some 11 million weekend carpenters armed with 25 million power tools were drilling, sawing, and sanding their way through 180 square miles of plywood. Do-it-yourself had become a major new testing ground for male competence. The year Monroe made *Bus Stop*, American women were spending some $2.5 billion on cosmetics and toiletries, clothing and fashion aids, and commercial beauty or slimming parlours. Dressed up or messed up, however, artifice buttressed the Fifties as much as illusion infected the Thirties.[11]

But Samuel Levitt's split-levels and Rachel Owlglass's MG, Major Dalleson's Betty Grable picture and Marilyn Monroe's new kitchen were still only pieces of the action. Coover's recognition in *The Public Burning* is that the evacuation proceeds at the collective intersection of dream *and* nightmare, anticipation *and* memory, satisfaction *and* anxiety. The housing lobby were quick to spell it out. Citing an example of its ostensibly libertarian coding – 'Escape to Scarborough Manor. Escape from cities too big, too polluted, too crowded, too strident, to call home' – Kenneth T. Jackson concludes that 'as early as the 1950s, suburban real-estate advertisements were harping on the themes of race, crime, drugs, congestion, and filth'. The rapid settlement of the nation's Scarborough Manors indicated that evacuees not only spoke the language but understood its implications. If the liberty and security suburbia embodied required vigilance, then the evacuation sanctioned and demanded repression. The most obvious form this took was over the question of race. Suburban residents – overwhelmingly white – turned first to restrictive covenants and zoning laws to control access to their territory. Where such methods proved ineffective or were judged illegal, home owners used force. Five years after the opening of Levittown, Pennsylvania in 1952, the first black residents were greeted by verbal abuse, burning crosses, confederate flags, and a loudspeaker system broadcasting 'Old Man River'. Their experience was hardly unique. By the end of the decade, none of the 82,000 people living in Levittown, Long Island, were black.[12]

However, since what was left behind or held at bay constituted a nightmare myth equal to that fuelled by popular mobility, the repressed always threatened to return. During the 1950s, fears of disaster, invasion or subversion, multiplied at the same time as dreams of liberation – indeed sometimes within the very instruments of liberation. One of the young suburbanites interviewed by

Benita Eisler for her *Private Lives: Men and Women of the Fifties* (1986) recalled that her mother 'was really scared of the depression. Dropping back into poverty was always real for us, because it was my mother's deepest fear'. (The contexts included the vital role played by credit in fuelling post-war economic growth: in 1960, following a decade in which total consumer debt had risen three times as fast as total personal income, one insurance company reported that the average American family was about three months away from bankruptcy.) The recollection of another – 'In Tulsa, Oklahoma, in 1953, if you couldn't get behind the wheel you were dead, socially' – gave deprivation anxieties rather more concrete expression. But the reverse was also true. Inside every new automobile, around every other corner, disaster idled. Eisler reports that parental 'fantasies seemed filled with car collisions, smashed bones, concussions, flash fires; summer outings that ended in death by drowning or diving into too-shallow water; blindings and poisonings'.[13] Mid-decade insurance statistics revealed that 600,000 Americans a year were cutting fingers in saws, receiving shocks from electrical equipment, or getting burned as a result of inflammable paint spraying accidents. By 1960, hundreds of thousands of those who had got behind the wheel during the decade were dead, literally. The elimination of others was no accident. Since the myth could not accommodate internal subversion, social problems – the alcoholic mother, the violent father – had to be endured stoically as private failures. The cults of relaxation and tranquillizers (such as Miltown) established themselves simultaneously as essentials of American life; with or without publicity, alcoholism thrived.[14]

Even as suburbia kept violence, crime, ethnic minorities and the spectre of disorder at bay with a combination of zoning regulations and lawnmowers, its fears continued to resurface. The happy couple in the 1956 Chevrolet advertisement recommending two cars for every family could claim that 'Going Our Separate Ways We've Never Been So Close'. The satirical comedian Mort Sahl may have joked in 1958 that there were so many gadgets in his house – wristwatches, binoculars, stereo systems – he never had to talk to anyone. But in the movies suburban suffering was endemic. In *Running Time: Films of the Cold War* (1982), Nora Sayre concludes that from Fred Zinneman's *The Men* (1950) to Nunnally Johnson's 1956 screen version of Sloan Wilson's 1955 best-seller *The Man in the Gray Flannel Suit*, 'emotional deprivation was the ground note of the period'. The key phrases were: 'What's the matter with us?' and 'Why don't we talk any more?' A progressive inanimation resonated across the culture. Isaac Asimov's *I, Robot* had been published in 1950. The next year McLuhan observed in *The Mechanical Bride* that 'those who are confused or overwhelmed by a machine world are encouraged to become psychologically hard, brittle and smoothly metallic'. They stood 'in danger of being frozen into ... helpless robot[s]' – or, perhaps, Barbie Dolls (first marketed in 1959). Soon after its launch in 1955, the *Village Voice* started carrying Jules Feiffer's cartoons of men and women whose half-digested Freudianisms entangle them in a disabling combination of smugness and isolation, leaving them unable to communicate. Feiffer's first published collection, entitled *Sick Sick Sick: A Guide to Non-Confident Living* (1959), updated the stoical whimsy of James Thurber's pre-war characters. The term *togetherness* had been coined in a May 1954 *McCall's* magazine editorial celebrating family life and the cooperative marriage. Two years later Grace Metalious' *Peyton Place* began the climb that in 1958 would take it past Erskine Caldwell's *God's Little Acre* (1933) at the top of the all-time best-selling novels list. In 1957 Betty Friedan started gathering the materials that in *The Feminine Mystique* (1963) exposed the *McCall's* world as a structure of disabling anonymity. By 1960 Thomas Pynchon's 'Togetherness' was parodying nuclear family life by concentrating on handling techniques for the Bomarc guided missile.[15]

Though *Peyton Place* outsold its fictional competitors and quickly spawned a popular television series, it was Sloan Wilson's autobiographical novel of the American Everyman, *The Man in the Gray Flannel Suit* (1955), that more closely articulated the evasive actions of post-war white American life. A dramatized version of the materials collected in sociological studies like C. Wright Mills's *White Collar* (1951), William H. Whyte's *The Organization Man* (1956), Vance Packard's *The Status Seekers* (1959), and Riesman's *The Lonely Crowd* (1950), Wilson's novel records Tom and Betty Rath's movement across bourgeois America as a nervous manoeuvring within an accessible but restrictive environment. Perched half-way up Whyte's ladder between the conflicting demands of career advancement and family life, personal fulfilment and social responsibility, Tom's commuter necessity is generated within a complex of fears and desires, memories and anticipations. He wants, in Wilson's words, 'to create an island of order in a sea of chaos'. Life as a drainage and reclamation activity is, however, continuously threatened by its own eddies. Though the island has to be 'made of money, ... the root of all order', the roots of money itself feed Tom's subsurface fears. He is haunted by the spectre of being overwhelmed by the demands of a new, well-paid, but exhausting post; of being cast adrift and sunk, having quit in disillusion. Though office work and Greentree Avenue are agencies and expressions of social elevation, they are experienced as enclosing spheres of phoniness, tension, and the inanimate. Tom's dream of salvation is therefore driven forward against nightmare premonitions of disaster ('something hanging over us') in words reminiscent of the narrator's in James Thurber's equally evasive *A Room to Hide In*: 'you have to believe everything will turn out all right, even if it doesn't. You can't go on worrying all the time; it has to stop someday. You can't really believe the world is insane; and you have to believe everything's going to turn out all right.'[16]

Anticipation and nostalgia are equally compromised as sources of freedom.

Betty Rath's past, a dream of pre-war courtship, only gilds memories of childhood isolation; her future, the conviction that 'everything's going to turn out all right', is tempered by the fear that motherhood can mean only duty, enforced responsibility and superficial cheer. Tom's past, a dream of wartime sexual indulgence, threatens to become a 'chamber of horrors' once exposed to the present and Betty; his future, a belief in marital perfection, is shadowed by the spectre of personal submission to the needs of his employer. Their interim arrangements largely rearrange existing terms of punishment and indulgence: they speak of 'no more television', 'no more homogenized milk', and resolve to 'start doing the things we believe in'. Ultimate deliverance is strictly circumscribed or routinely fantastic: 'an entirely different sort of life', 'a trip somewhere', the murder of a superior at work. The novel's solution is, therefore, necessarily fortuitous: Tom inherits twenty acres of prime building land, makes a successful re-zoning application, and looks forward, in the words of an eager property developer, to 'a possible take of $800,000 before taxes, if ... handled right'. The Raths' evacuation, though less dependent on the intervention of Thurber's pre-war good wizards than on Horatio Alger's Victorian good fortune, is strictly twentieth century. As more Greentree Avenues spring up on the site, so they find at least temporary sanctuary by drafting additional recruits for the struggle they have struggled to evade. As Tom concludes towards the end of the novel: 'God's in his heaven, all's right with the world.'[17]

Tom Rath's abstract identification of religious and secular securities was repeated across the social structure. The early 1950s in particular witnessed a significant religious revival. During the 1950s total church membership rose from 86.8 million to 114 million, while prayers preceded everything from President Eisenhower's cabinet meetings to Texan bathing beauty contests. When the Revised Standard Version of The Bible was published in 1952, it jumped to the top of the best-seller list, with two million copies purchased that year. In 1953 President Eisenhower's inaugural parade was led by 'God's Float', and the Bible was replaced at the top of the best-sellers list by Lloyd Douglas's religious fiction, *The Robe*. Five of the top six non-fiction best-sellers that year had religious themes (these included *Pray Your Weight Away* and *The Power of Prayer on Plants*). During 1954 Congress amended the pledge of allegiance to include the phrase 'under God' after 'one nation'. Meanwhile, the Ideal Toy Company put a doll on the market whose flexible knees allowed it to assume a praying position. In 1955 'In God We Trust' was added to all American currency. From 1956 onwards certain denominations of that currency could be devoted to the 'Dial-A-Prayer' facility recently introduced in New York City. By 1958, two dollars were being spent on new church buildings for every dollar invested in the construction of public hospitals.[18]

The religious revival was intimately connected with the rise of a new generation of popular religious figures on the national stage. In 1949 a young Baptist evangelist from North Carolina named Billy Graham had begun attracting massive crowds and numerous converts during a three week Christian revival crusade in Los Angeles. Graham recognized that the products of the affluent society provided little of spiritual value in themselves. He was nonetheless quick to adopt the latter's methods. In 1951 Graham, by now a national celebrity, converted himself into the Billy Graham Evangelist Association. Three years later he made his first appearance on the cover of *Time* magazine. By 1955 Graham's Minnesota headquarters was administering a multi-million dollar annual budget, the product partly of sales of his highly popular volumes *Peace With God* (1953) and *The Secret of Happiness* (1955). Graham's radio show, *The Hour of Decision*, was meanwhile being broadcast over a thousand stations to twenty million regular listeners. Backed by the Hearst and Luce press empires, *Reader's Digest*, and other conservative publications, Graham also made use of his own regular television show to market Christianity like any other new commodity. God, he insisted, was 'the greatest product in the world', with salvation his main selling feature. By 1957 Graham's organization was interviewing commuters in New York City to evaluate the impact of its subway advertising on a new market.[19]

Whereas Graham appealed to lower class Americans, primarily from small town fundamentalist backgrounds, the Reverend Norman Vincent Peale concentrated on the urban middle class. The first of his many books, *The Power of Positive Thinking* (1952), taught what he called 'applied Christianity' and topped the best-seller list until 1955. Like Billy Graham, Peale had his television and radio shows, as well as a regular column in *Look* magazine. Like Graham, he made the fantasy of personal salvation a profitable business. His Marble Collegiate church in New York City incorporated a salesroom offering not only copies of his books but also records, greetings and Christmas cards, sermons, and other commodities. Like Graham, too, he was highly popular. Peale's broadcasts combined pre-New Deal conservatism, the cult of success through personal effort, and the necessity of adjustment through a series of examples: wealthy businessmen, top sportsmen, military leaders. The general public clearly needed this form of social reassurance, a blend of Horatio Alger rags-to-riches stories and Dale Carnegie self-help theories. So too did corporate America. US Steel subsidised subscriptions to his magazine, *Guideposts* (total circulation: 800,000) for their workforce. In 1954 Peale was named one of the nation's Twelve Best Salesmen by the US Chamber of Commerce. When recession struck during the autumn of 1957, Boston businessmen launched their own 'power of positive selling' campaign.[20]

While Graham and Peale worked the Protestant denominations, Bishop Fulton J. Sheen held his own masses through his radio show *The Catholic Hour*. His television series *Life is Worth Living* ran from 1952 to 1957, reached ten to twenty million viewers, and within a year of its first screening had surpassed Milton Berle at the top of the Nielsen ratings. Sheen received over eight thousand letters per week at one point, and naturally his popularity drew in the advertisers. He also provided encouragement for another of the television preachers who would later enjoy comparable fame. Following the advice given in Sheen's popular guidebook, *God's Formula for Success and Prosperity* (1955), Oklahoma preacher Oral Roberts converted popular belief in faith healing into a private jet, a 280-acre ranch (complete with its own landing strip), and annual revenues of over fifty million dollars. (Not surprisingly, both Bishop Sheen and Oral Roberts became two of the main targets in the great American satirist Lenny Bruce's investigation of organized religion in the second half of the decade.)

Billy Graham, Norman Vincent Peale and Fulton Sheen had something else in common besides their popularity. Though he did preach a colour-blind faith to integrated audiences, Graham remained silent on most social issues. On communism, however, he spoke out: the Soviet Union, he taught, embodied 'a great sinister anti-Christian movement masterminded by Satan' which had 'declared war upon the Christian God'. If Graham disliked trades unions, strikes, and the welfare state, Norman Vincent Peale was positively hostile to all forms of progressivism: anti-unions, anti-income tax, anti-social security, anti-minimum wages. In 1948 he supported the reactionary General Douglas MacArthur for president and denounced the late president Franklin Roosevelt as a dictator. Fulton Sheen's political opinions ranged from support for Franco to opposition to any form of liberalism in education. A veteran Catholic anti-communist of twenty years standing, Sheen saw subversion everywhere and regarded peaceful coexistence as a prelude to Soviet domination. While salvation for these men was obviously an individual business, when not engaged in his official duties Sheen also developed a small industry saving the souls of famous ex-communists. It was Sheen who converted both 'Red spy queen' Elizabeth Bentley and former Communist Party member and *Daily Worker* editor Louis Budenz to Catholicism.

Such political activism carried little risk. According to public opinion polls, atheists ranked only second to communists in terms of popular disapproval and four out of five Americans questioned said they would never vote for an atheist presidential candidate. Indeed, anti-communism may have *increased* the popularity of Peale, Graham and their allies. Whatever it was that explained their success, it was probably not the American public's deeply-held religious beliefs. The same opinion polls which demonstrated popular reluctance to vote an atheist into the White House also 'revealed that most Americans were hard pressed to ... distinguish between Protestantism and Catholicism, to explain or even identify the Christian trinity, [or] to distinguish the Old Testament from the New'. A Gallup poll carried out in 1951, at a time when sales of Bibles were increasing rapidly, revealed that a majority of Americans were unable to name any of the gospels. By 1958, a Gallup poll showed that 96% of the population believed in 'God'. But two years later *Elmer Gantry* (Richard Brooks, 1960), which gave a critical portrait of small town evangelical religion during the 1920s, was not only playing to packed houses but winning three academy awards. As Will Herberg put it in his *Protestant – Catholic – Jew* (1955), Americans possessed what he called 'faith in faith' and celebrated a sort of 'religiousness without religion'.[21]

The film industry was quick to turn this sort of faith into hard cash. Making use of publicity phrases like 'sensational sinning', many Biblical epics had little to do with The Bible but paid considerable attention to the presentation of action and eroticism. Mobs, stampedes, crazed lions, and satanic tortures were the very essence of Hollywood; sensuality had to be witnessed in close-up and technicolour before it could be punished. Actors, techniques and scripts were deployed accordingly. In 1953, Henry Koster's screen adaptation of *The Robe* combined Cinemascope and big stars (Richard Burton, Victor Mature, and Jean Simmons), and featured centurions discovering the spot where, as one of them puts it, Jesus 'holes up at night'. *The Robe* secured three Academy Award nominations as well as box office success. In 1951 the most commonly used phrase in Mervyn Leroi's *Quo Vadis* had been 'relax'. By 1956, Anne Baxter was playing the pin-up in Cecil B. De Mille's *The Ten Commandments*, teasing Charlton Heston with such phrases as 'Oh Moses, Moses, you stubborn, splendid, adorable fool'. *Time* magazine described the film as 'three and a half hours of sex and sand'. Inside the theatre, movie critic Murray Kempton saw De Mille 'serving up flesh in pots'. Outside, meanwhile, children queued for souvenir pencils inscribed with phrases such as 'thou shalt not commit adultery'.[22]

While the Legion of Decency preferred to direct its attentions towards the celluloid version of Tennessee Williams' *Baby Doll* (Elia Kazan, 1956), the message inscribed on the pencils was, for a 1950s audience, burdened with tension. To a nation in which, according to Alfred Kinsey's *Report on Sexual Behaviour in the Human Male* (1948), some fifty per cent of married men had been unfaithful to their wives, such commandments were of course privately embarrassing. But in the struggle for security that succeeded World War Two, loss of faith or questionable morality threatened not simply personal distress but national disaster. Hollywood again provided an index. Between 1947 and 1954, the film industry produced around fifty anti-communist features collectively articulating a mythology of unAmerican characteristics and practices. Thus communist fifth columnists associated with 'bad blondes' and 'loose women', and (in *The Red Menace* (R.G. Springsteen, 1949)) used sex as an instrument of subversion. Alternately, they were effeminate or even sexually deviant. In *My Son John* (Leo McCarey, 1952), a mother concludes that her son is a party member on the basis of his commitment to academic study (he has 'more degrees than a thermometer') in preference to football or military service. The perils of Godlessness were similarly encoded. In *My Son John*, only organized religion seems proof against the communist threat: the American Legion father brings his son to his knees with a swift blow from the family Bible, while subversives recoil in terror at the sign of the cross. Similar tensions are presented in *The Iron Curtain* (William Wellman, 1949).

The film industry had not suddenly become another outlet for Bishop Fulton Sheen's opinions, even though as early as 1947 Eric Johnston (head of the Motion Picture Association and the Association of Motion Picture Producers) had announced that 'the rifle the film industry had shouldered in World War Two could not be put down; it had to keep marching to the drums of another martial conflict – the Cold War with international communism'. Rather, under financial threat from the rising challenge of television and recent court rulings, internally divided and riven by industrial strife, and in any event a vulnerable target for conservative pressure groups, Hollywood had responded to the threat of highly-publicized House UnAmerican Activities Committee investigations in 1947 and 1951 by making amends in public. Part penance, part appeasement and part insurance, the cycle of anti-communist films that resulted were designed less to make money or propagate ideologies than simply to contain damage; widely screened as second features, however, they extended the terms in which security was defined.[23]

Moreover, the fact that personal morality or religious faith might constitute new fields of battle or novel weapons in the struggle for security was only symptomatic of a much broader development in evidence across the entire culture. At the diplomatic level, that development involved a gradual extension of explicit and implicit definitions of warfare. In the early post-war years, public thinking about the deepening tensions between Washington and Moscow had been heavily influenced by what Ernest May calls the 'lessons of the past'. Thus the Soviet Union had replaced Nazi Germany in the thinking of policy-makers, while the pre-war failure of appeasement had encouraged and legitimized the subsequent strategy of containment. Even as such equations continued to influence public policy, however, by 1950 they were being augmented. The key State/Defense Department planning document NSC-68 (approved by President Truman on 30 September that year) maintained, for example, that the Cold War, like World War Two, was 'in fact a real war in which the survival of the free world [was] at stake'. Yet while agreeing with such premises, influential drafting committee advisor Robert Lovett added that, in the struggle with the Soviet Union, 'death comes more slowly and in a different fashion'. Truman himself acknowledged an associated shift the same year when he began extending the documentary classification system first introduced during World War Two to *non-military* agencies. Redefining such distinctions, a special report from the US Defense Advisory Commission was insisting by

1955 that 'the battlefield of modern warfare is all-inclusive. Today there are no distant front lines, remote no man's lands, far off rear areas. The home front is but an extension of the fighting front'. Such ideas were not completely novel. From the latter perspective, as Daniel Yergin has shown, the broadening of long-established military definitions of 'defence' into the strategic concept of 'national security' had prompted policy-makers to think expansively even before the collapse of the Axis powers. As 'the range of threats [became] limitless', Yergin writes, the doctrine of national security demanded that 'the nation ... be on permanent alert'. Between the late 1940s and early 1950s, however, a series of international and domestic developments – ranging from the Chinese Revolution to the Korean War, from the first Soviet atomic bomb test to the arrest of alleged 'atom spies' Julius and Ethel Rosenberg, from the trial of Alger Hiss to the rise of Senator McCarthy – extended the concept of total security into something of a fetish both at home and abroad.[24]

The mechanisms of extension were complex. It is, on the one hand, evident that the post-war red scare was actively promoted (for a variety of sometimes conflicting reasons) by a range of established interests within the power structure. Thus, the demonic vision of Moscow then taking shape in the minds of American policy-makers was effectively popularized during the early years of the Cold War through the concept of 'red fascism'. More specifically, the Truman Doctrine speech of March 1947 was, as Senator Arthur Vandenberg advised the president at the time, carefully calculated to 'scare hell out of the country'. Senator Joseph McCarthy's influence likewise owed more to the efforts of political elites than to the impact of populist rhetoric: the significance of the accusations and headlines derived less from his 'one man riot' than from an assault by conservative establishment interests such as the US Chamber of Commerce (unwittingly abetted by President Truman) on the labour movement and elements of the New Deal system.[25] On the other hand, elite politics alone scarcely accounted in full for the red scare's impact. What Athan Theoharis described as *Seeds of Repression* – whether Truman's foreign policy warnings or McCarthy's domestic accusations – could not thrive in stony ground. In abstract terms, as Jacques Ellul put it in his *Propaganda* (1962), 'for propaganda to succeed, it must correspond to a need for propaganda on the individual's part'. More concretely, while the so-called 'status anxiety' interpretation cannot grasp all of the more significant dimensions of the red scare, it may draw attention to the roots of some of the needs Ellul refers to. When Samuel Stouffer carried out a series of public opinion surveys during the summer of 1954, less than one per cent of those he questioned may have mentioned communism or civil liberties when asked to identify their main worries in life. Worries there nevertheless were: primarily about personal, financial and medical problems, ranging from mortgages, loan repayments, and hospital bills to over-demanding children and college expenses.[26]

While the mechanisms by which security concerns were reproduced across the nation may appear divergent to the point of incompatibility, a sense of their actual symbiosis may be crucial to an understanding of the red scare's heterogeneous, nightmarishly absurd, nature. If the communists were at once the problem and not the problem, then the threat they posed could be treated accordingly. Thus while over sixty per cent of those questioned in a Gallup poll only two months after the outbreak of the Korean War felt that the nation was 'already in World War III', that same summer Dearborn, Michigan felt able to crown a Miss Loyalty in a beauty pageant. Similarly, only a few months before the Rosenbergs were executed in June 1953, comedians Bud Abbott and Lou Costello could write to the recently-inaugurated President Eisenhower offering anti-communist jokes for the Voice of America. US troops continued waging war in Korea against Chinese communists whose intervention in the fighting had led the *New York Times* to inform its readers that 'DANGER OF ATOM BOMB ATTACK IS GREATEST IN PERIOD UP TO THIS FALL'; 'father of the atom bomb' Robert Oppenheimer was meanwhile reporting that a high ranking US Defense Command officer had informed him 'that it was not our policy to attempt to protect this country, for that is so big a job that it would interfere with our retaliatory capabilities'. (Six years later, still virtually unprotected, Americans would read in *Life* magazine of a couple who spent a two week honeymoon in a bomb shelter, complete with radio and telephone.)[27]

However diverse its manifestations and however disparate the mechanisms by which it was reproduced, the red scare's latent tendency towards Orwellian paralysis was clear — even if some of the consequences appeared more absurd than dictatorial. Across Indiana, loyalty oaths were required of professional wrestlers; the same applied to New York State lavatory attendants; in one New York town, such oaths were a precondition for obtaining fishing licenses for municipal reservoirs; in Pasadena, California, a three-year-old child was asked to sign a loyalty oath before acting as a model for an art class at a publicly-subsidized college (since the child was unable to write, she was unable to work). Samuel Stouffer's 1954 sampling of popular grounds for suspicion of neighbours and colleagues — 'he was always talking about world peace', 'I saw a map of Russia on a wall in his home', 'I just knew, although I don't know how I knew' — provided further evidence which, while atypical, was by no means unique. Within six years of its first calls for a purge of government agencies, the US Chamber of Commerce was demanding a purge of the loyalty boards previously established to carry out the purge. As Arthur Miller later remarked, 'once you develop a siege mentality, anything is believable'.

If for some anything could be believed, for others it might be proven. I.F. Stone may have argued in 1955 that 'when a man is up on loyalty or security charges ... the tribunal is not dealing with an act but ... is engaged in an exercise in clairvoyance', yet as early as April 1951 an American foundation had 'offered $100,000 to support research into the creation of a device for detecting traitors'. In these circumstances, popular reaction was understandable. On 4 July that year a reporter from the Madison, Wisconsin, *Capital Times* invited people on the state capital's streets to sign a petition containing the preamble to the Declaration of Independence and portions of the Bill of Rights: of 112 invited, 111 refused, many complaining of the petition's communist overtones. Other evidence suggested that, for certain occupations, such reactions were not only understandable but essential. Four years later, a report on the US Army's internal security programme concluded that, based on the Army's own screening procedures, 'the ideal draftee [was] an only child of spontaneous generation who, despite a hermit childhood, [had] miraculously acquired the ability to read and write English but [had] never made use of these skills'.[28]

If withdrawal into the private appeared to offer one strategy for survival, then, in the popular imagination in particular, commitment to the public furnished another. As acted out by long-serving FBI Director J. Edgar Hoover, such commitment again articulated not only the intractable logic of, but also perhaps the irrepressible anxieties within, the decade's security drives. For Hoover, there was only one objective, pursued with what Frank Donner has described as an indefatigable and monomaniacal intensity. From his first publication of the decade ('50,000 Communists' in *US News and World Report* on 12 May 1950) to his last ('Communist Party, USA' in *Ave Maria* on 30 April 1960), via scores of other articles and the best-selling *Masters of Deceit* (1958), the communist (or, as he pronounced it, 'commonist') menace that lurked in labour unions, the civil rights movement, colleges and schools was identified: 'a freak [that] has grown into a powerful monster endangering us all'; a 'traitorous force ... constantly gnawing away at the very foundation of American society'.[29] His professional career marked, in the words of one biographer, by a 'search for total order and perfect security', and his private life increasingly shaped by his neurotically rigid struggle against any and all forms of unpredictability, Hoover in public remained the selflessly committed pillar of rectitude and guardian of national security. Dependent on the spectre of a Communist Party whose very attenuation he translated into proof of growing danger (not to mention an argument for growing FBI budgets), Hoover also became a major totem of American life: bedecked with awards and deluged by letters from admirers seeking advice on everything from public education to bingo.[30]

Although such public commitment was less typical than withdrawal into the private, and while Hoover's one-man maxims of fidelity, bravery and integrity proved harder to satisfy than the chorus of inducements to 'relax' that flooded American culture during the 1950s, the Director's popularity was nevertheless understandable. For, perhaps more than anyone else, Hoover identified in communism and its agents the decade's ultimate escape hatch: not simply the complete enemy necessary to legitimate demands for total security, but a safety valve general enough to relieve the decade's broader pressures. Increasingly attuned to Max Lerner's 'gadget-cluttered environment', for example, Americans might find in the popular image of robotic, programmed communists a lightning-rod for domestic inanimation. Attracted in ever-larger numbers to television and psychiatry, they might see in alleged communist 'brainwashing' in Korea a fate worse than *The Milton Berle Show* or Miltown. Employed within and administered by vast organizations to an ever-greater degree, they might derive from the communists' own alleged facelessness some compensation for feelings of loss of identity. Wherever there were tensions – whether at work, at home or across American society – there were the communists to shoulder the blame: instruments of authoritarianism, agents of sexual disorder, promoters of family breakdown, exploiters of racial enmity. In this sense, when Arthur Miller wrote in his memoirs about 'the guilt ... of holding illicit, suppressed feelings of alienation and hostility toward standard, daylight society', a guilt which necessitates a 'projection of one's own vileness onto others in order to wipe it out', his words applied well beyond the text of *The Crucible* (1953) or the practices of the House UnAmerican Activities Committee.[31]

It was not, of course, simply guilt that such manoeuvres wiped out. As David Caute's *The Great Fear*, Victor Navasky's *Naming Names*, Cedric Belfrage's *The American Inquisition* and other works make plain, so too were friendships, careers, families and lives: hardly materials from which Bud Abbott and Lou Costello could have derived comedy material. But such were the predatory demands of those who required and demanded security. Not surprisingly, while collateral damage was extensive, the ostensible targets of such drives were less immune than imaginary. Attorney General Brownell admitted in February 1954 that since coming to power the Eisenhower administration had fired some 2,200 'security risks'. Only a handful of these cases related to disloyalty, however, and in none were communists involved. As syndicated newspaper columnists Joseph and Stewart Alsop observed, after a year in office the administration's score stood at 'communists smoked out, nil; suspected dangerous thinkers abolished, four'.[32]

As much and as little was achieved elsewhere. Thus the drive for suburban security continued even as evidence accumulated, both of its necessity and its ultimate futility. In October 1949, after the detonation of the Soviet Union's first atomic bomb was announced, the *New York Journal-American* published a half-column picture showing Manhattan engulfed in 'waves of havoc and death'. In June 1950, following the outbreak of the Korean War, an advertisement in the *New York Times* warned readers that 'the war is on, the chips are down ... every man's house will be a target area before this ends'. Two years later, Democratic presidential candidate Adlai Stevenson quoted CIA Director

Walter Bedell Smith to the effect that 'we cannot let our guard drop even for a moment. The only assumption is that no place is safe'. In March 1954 the assumption was supported when, at a presidential news conference, Atomic Energy Commission Chairman Lewis Strauss informed reporters that, with the development of the hydrogen bomb, a single such weapon could 'take out' the entire New York City metropolitan area in one go. Under these circumstances, to return to the language of Pynchon's *Gravity's Rainbow*, the evacuation to Happyville appeared futile: Pain City would always be there. Yet, much like the quest for subversion, the movement proceeded apace. Norman Mailer's subsequent observation – 'obviously we were afraid of something more than the communists' – provided a clue to a process whose motives were often obscure. During the 1950s, from pulpit to paperback, from Broadway to bomb shelter, from cinema to Congress, evasive action remained the norm.[33]

Notes

1. Douglas MacArthur, *Reminiscences* (1964; New York: Fawcett, 1965), p. 426; Fred Halliday, *The Making of the Second Cold War* (London: Verso, 1983), p. 81. On the increasing obsolescence of armed conflict in the industrial world, though emphasizing the impact of conventional, not atomic weapons, see John Mueller, *Retreat From Doomsday* (New York: Basic Books, 1989).
2. Norman Mailer, *The Naked and the Dead* (Boston: 1948; London: Panther, 1964), pp. 274-6; Thomas Pynchon, *Gravity's Rainbow* (New York: Viking, 1973), pp. 372-3.
3. Pynchon, *Gravity's Rainbow*, pp. 372-3; Mailer, *Naked and the Dead*, p. 606.
4. Thomas Pynchon, *V.* (London: Jonathan Cape, 1963), p. 148.
5. Pynchon, *Gravity's Rainbow*, p. 54.
6. Robert Coover, *The Public Burning* (1977; Harmondsworth: Penguin, 1978), pp. 136-9; Pynchon, *V.*, p. 37.
7. Vance Packard, *The Status Seekers* (New York: 1959; Harmondsworth: Penguin, 1962), p. 81; Richard Polenberg, *One Nation Divisible: Class, Race and Ethnicity in the United States Since 1938* (Harmondsworth: Penguin, 1980), pp. 127-34; Charles C. Alexander, *Holding the Line: The Eisenhower Era, 1952-1961* (Bloomington: Indiana University Press, 1975), p. 125; Thomas Stanback, Jr. and Richard Knight, *Suburbanization and the City* (New York: Allanheld, Osmun and Co., 1976), pp. 24-52; David Goldfield and Blaine Brownell, *Urban America: From Downtown to Notown* (Boston: Houghton Mifflin, 1979), pp. 320, 343-53; Theodore White, *The Making of the President, 1960* (1961; London: Jonathan Cape, 1964), 216; Douglas Miller and Marion Nowak, *The Fifties: The Way We Really Were* (New York: Doubleday, 1977), p. 7.
8. Kenneth T. Jackson, *Crabgrass Frontier* (New York: Oxford University Press, 1985), pp. 235-7; J. Ronald Oakley, *God's Country: America in the Fifties* (New York: Dembner Books, 1986), pp. 113-4; William H. Whyte, *The Organization Man* (New York, 1956; Harmondsworth: Penguin, 1960), p. 282; Miller and Nowak, pp. 133-4; White, pp. 217, 219.

9. Bureau of the Census, *Statistical Abstract of the United States: 1951* (Washington: US Government Printing Office, 1951), pp. 259, 261, 453; Miller and Nowak, p. 133; Alexander, p. 104; *Statistical Abstract: 1961*, pp. 300, 508; *Statistical Abstract: 1963*, pp. 325, 570; Max Lerner, *America as a Civilization: Life and Thought in the US Today* (London: Jonathan Cape, 1958), p. 251; Jackson, p. 236; Oakley, pp. 228-31, 236, 300-301.

10. Peter Lewis, *The Fifties: Portrait of a Period* (1978; London: Herbert Press, 1989), p. 21; Marshall McLuhan, *The Mechanical Bride* (1951; Boston: Beacon Press, 1967), pp. 93-101, 152-4; Pynchon, *V.*, pp. 27, 383, 385.

11. Benita Eisler, *Private Lives: Men and Women of the Fifties* (New York: Franklin Watts, 1986), pp. 53-4, 125, 42-3; McLuhan, pp. 129-31, 141-7; Oakley, p. 301.

12. Jackson, pp. 106, 115, 241, 285.

13. Vance Packard, *The Waste Makers* (1960; London: Longman, 1961), pp. 148, 154; Eisler, pp. 32-3, 105.

14. Eric Goldman, *The Crucial Decade – And After* (New York: Vintage, 1960), p. 263; Oakley, p. 313; Jackson, pp. 106, 115, 241; Eisler, pp. 169-70.

15. Nora Sayre, *Running Time: Films of the Cold War* (New York: Dial Press, 1982), pp. 122-6; Lewis, pp. 18, 62-3; McLuhan, pp. 97, 141; Betty Friedan, *The Feminine Mystique* (1963; Harmondsworth: Penguin, 1976), p. 42; Thomas Pynchon, 'Togetherness', *Aerospace Safety* (December, 1960), pp. 6-8.

16. Sloan Wilson, *The Man in the Gray Flannel Suit* (1955; Markham, Ontario: Paperjacks, 1985), pp. 11, 13, 131, 151-2, 164, 177, 221-3; Eric Mottram, *Blood on the Nash Ambassador* (London: Hutchinson Radius, 1989), p. 131.

17. Wilson, pp. 96-7, 135, 151-4, 172, 200, 220, 237, 279, 331-2, 358, 367; Mottram, p. 131.

18. Paul Carter, *Another Part of the Fifties* (New York: Columbia University Press, 1983), p. 116; Oakley, pp. 319-20, 324; Goldman, p. 305.

19. Oakley, pp. 321-2.

20. Oakley, pp. 323-4; Carter, *Another Part*, p. 36.

21. Oakley, pp. 322-5; Will Herberg, *Protestant–Catholic–Jew*, rev. ed. (Garden City, New York: Anchor Doubleday, 1960), pp. 90, 260; David Zane Mairowitz, *The Radical Soap Opera* (Harmondsworth: Penguin, 1973), pp. 134-38.

22. Oakley, pp. 320, 325-6.

23. Richard Maltby, *Harmless Entertainment: Hollywood and the Ideology of Consensus* (Metuchen, N.J.: Scarecrow Press, 1983), pp. 63-70, 118-30; Larry Ceplair and Steven Englund, *The Inquisition in Hollywood: Politics in the Film Community, 1930-1960* (Garden City, New York: Anchor Doubleday, 1980), pp. 248-98, 325-45; Les K. Adler, 'The Politics of Culture: Hollywood and the Cold War', in Robert Griffith and Athan Theoharis (eds), *The Specter: Original Essays on the Cold War and the Origins of McCarthyism* (New York: New Viewpoints, 1974), pp. 240-58; Sayre, pp. 79-85, 94; Oakley, p. 304.

24. Ernest May, *Lessons of the Past* (New York: Oxford University Press, 1973); Samuel Wells, 'Sounding the Tocsin: NSC-68 and the Soviet Threat', *International Security*, 4, 2 (Fall, 1979), 129, 135; Frank Donner, *The Age of Surveillance* (New York: Viking, 1980), p. 26: Daniel Yergin, *Shattered Peace: The Origins of the Cold War and the National Security State* (1977; Harmondsworth: Penguin, 1980), pp. 194-201; James Gilbert, *Another Chance: Postwar America, 1945-1968* (Philadelphia: Temple University Press, 1981), p. 96.

25. Michael Rogin, *The Intellectuals and McCarthy: The Radical Specter* (Cambridge, Mass.: MIT Press, 1967); Les K. Adler and Thomas G. Paterson, 'Red Fascism: The Merger of Nazi Germany and Soviet Russia in the American Image of Totalitarianism, 1930s-1950s', *American Historical Review*, 75, 4 (April, 1970), 1046-1064; David Caute, *The Great Fear: The Anti-Communist Purge Under Truman and Eisenhower* (1978; New York: Simon and Schuster, 1979), pp. 30, 349-50; Yergin, pp. 282-3; Peter Irons, 'American Business and the Origins of McCarthyism', in Griffith and Theoharis (eds), pp. 72-89; I.F. Stone, *The Truman Era* (1953; New York: Vintage, 1973), pp. 80-86. Truman's complicity in the rise of McCarthyism is emphasized in Richard Freeland, *The Truman Doctrine and the Origins of McCarthyism* (New York: Knopf, 1972); and Athan Theoharis, 'The Rhetoric of Politics: Foreign Policy, Internal Security, and Domestic Politics in the Truman Era, 1945-1950', in Barton Bernstein (ed), *Politics and Policies of the Truman Administration* (Chicago: Quadrangle, 1970).

26. Athan Theoharis, *Seeds of Repression: Harry S. Truman and the Origins of McCarthyism* (Chicago: Quadrangle, 1971); Jacques Ellul, *Propaganda: The Formation of Men's Attitudes*, trans. Konrad Keller and Jean Lerner (1968; New York: Vintage, 1973), p. 121; Daniel Bell (ed), *The Radical Right* (New York: Doubleday Anchor, 1964); Richard Hofstadter, *The Paranoid Style in American Politics* (New York: Vintage, 1965); Samuel Stouffer, *Communism, Conformism and Civil Liberties: A Cross-Section of the Nation Speaks its Mind* (1955; New York: John Wiley and Sons, 1966), pp. 59-60, 68.

27. Wells, 141; Miller and Nowak, p. 433; Dale Carter, *The Final Frontier: The Rise and Fall of the American Rocket State* (London and New York: Verso, 1988), p. 104; I.F. Stone, *The Haunted Fifties* (London: Merlin Press, 1964), p. 80; Oakley, p. 368.

28. Oakley, p. 73; Stouffer, pp. 156-76; Stone, *Truman Era*, p. 84; Lewis, p. 85; Stone, *Haunted Fifties*, pp. 72-3, 86; Earl Latham (ed), *The Meaning of McCarthyism* (Lexington, Mass.: D.C. Heath, 1965), p. vii; Thomas Reeves, *The Life and Times of Joe McCarthy* (London: Blond and Briggs, 1982), p. 379; Caute, p. 342.

29. Donner, pp. 94, 469; Richard Gid Powers, *Secrecy and Power: The Life of J. Edgar Hoover* (London: Hutchinson, 1987), p. 345; Theoharis, *Seeds of Repression*, p. 259. As a number of writers have pointed out, while much was published under Hoover's name, a good deal of it was ghostwritten. The Director's most significant involvement in *Masters of Deceit* was to pocket the lion's share of the publishing royalties for himself and his backers, as well as the $75,000 Warner Brothers paid for the film rights. See Donner, pp. 94-95; Powers, p. 344.

30. Powers, pp. 313-15; Donner, p. 80. Also worth looking at is the fictional vision of Hoover presented by Robert Coover in *The Public Burning*, p. 25. Authorities differ over the actual size of the Communist Party of the USA during the 1950s. As a rough guide, however, its size decreased from approximately 70,000 members in 1947 to only 10,000 in 1957. Under severe pressure from Federal prosecutions, Congressional hearings, deportations, denaturalization procedures and internal informants, the party's membership rolls consisted increasingly of FBI agents. Dependent upon a credible communist threat for Congressional funding and bureaucratic influence, Hoover argued that the decrease in membership was really a sign of the party's growing secrecy and thus influence. As the communists moved ever further underground or penetrated key industries, he insisted, so more FBI agents than ever were called for. See Donner, pp. 106, 469-70; Victor Navasky, *Naming Names* (New York: Viking Press, 1980), pp. 24-26; Powers, pp. 344-5; Caute, pp. 112-16.

31. Lerner, p. 251; Carter, *Final Frontier*, pp. 99, 110-111; Arthur Miller, *Timebends: A Life* (London: Methuen, 1988), p. 337.
32. Reeves, p. 545.
33. Carter, *Final Frontier*, pp. 103-4; Coover, p. 32; Carter, *Another Part*, p. 13; Robert Divine, *Eisenhower and the Cold War* (New York: Oxford University Press, 1981), p. 115; Norman Mailer, *The Presidential Papers* (1963; Harmondsworth: Penguin, 1976), p. 175.

Bridge Over Troubled Water: Nostalgia for the Fifties in Movies of the Seventies and Eighties

Elsebeth Hurup

> The past is a foreign country:
> they do things differently there.
> L.B. Hartley, *The Go-Between*

In October 1972 a *Newsweek* cover story entitled 'Yearning for the Fifties: The Good Old Days' announced that 'In the grand sweep of American history, the 1950s were one of the blandest decades ever. But now a revival of those very same quiet years is swirling across the U.S. like a runaway Hula-Hoop'.[1] The evidence: fifties rock'n'roll music, fashion, parties, and musicals, which were drawing large crowds across the nation.

Beginning with Peter Bogdanovitch's *The Last Picture Show* in 1971, followed by George Lucas' *American Graffiti* in 1973, this preoccupation with the fifties manifested itself particularly in the movie business. And although the general fifties craze since then has given way to similar sixties and seventies fads, most conspicuously in fashion and music, the fifties as the historical or nostalgic setting for movies continue to hold fascination for film-makers and audiences alike.[2] The ever-growing list includes such well-known titles as *Next Stop, Greenwich Village* (1976), *The Buddy Holly Story, American Hot Wax, Grease, National Lampoon's Animal House* (all 1978), *Coal Miner's Daughter* (1980), *The Right Stuff* (1983), *Back to the Future* (1985), *Peggy Sue Got Married* (1986), *La Bamba, Dirty Dancing* (both 1987), and *Dead Poets Society* (1989).

Inasmuch as nostalgia on a personal level has a tendency to be a generational phenomenon – that upon reaching middle age people are wont to look back on their youth with nostalgic sentiment – on the collective level the persistent absorption with the fifties as the locus for nostalgia, to the comparative disregard of the sixties, is striking, though hardly surprising. With these movies we are looking back across a great divide in modern American history. The trend began at a time when America was still deeply affected by controversy and wounds were still wide open after the turmoil of the sixties. The movies gave expression to a widespread sense of mourning and longing for lost innocence, security and happiness. Not coincidentally, the bulk of the movies which over the years have dealt with the fifties have focused on teen-agers and issues related to growing up.[3]

In the following, three of these movies – *American Graffiti* (1973), *Grease* (1978), and *Peggy Sue Got Married* (1986) – will be discussed. They are all set in the world of high schoolers in Small Town, America, and were suc-cesses at the box-office as well as generally favored by the critics. The discus-sion will seek to shed light on three clusters of questions. The first concerns the 'purely' nostalgic elements in the movies. As will be demonstrated below, nostalgia is something more than mere escapism, but on one level it does func-tion as an escape from present conditions viewed as unsatisfactory or unhappy. It is therefore important to identify the elements which serve to give (at least temporary) relief from these worries, and to ascertain to what extent they are integral to the movies as a whole. Secondly, for the nostalgic 'exercise' to succeed there must be a dialogue between the past portrayed and the present. In other words, there must be some link to the present, a bridge, as it were, across which the nostalgic time-traveller can move back and forth. The task then is to determine how this bridge or link to the present is established. Finally, what might be the explanation for the considerable nostalgic sentiment expressed in movies in the seventies and eighties in general? What does the fact that fifties nostalgia in particular has proved so durable mean, and, by way of comparison, why have the sixties so far been largely ignored as a locus for nostalgia?

The Phenomenon of Nostalgia: Some Basic Points

Having outlined the changing definitions of the word, first coined as a medical term in the late seventeenth century, Fred Davis in his *Yearning for Yesterday: A Sociology of Nostalgia* (1979) proceeds to identify a number of aspects and functions of modern-day nostalgia.[4] His basic argument is that nostalgia is one of the means by which man seeks to deflect emotions that may pose a threat of discontinuity. In other words, in times when our sense of identity is threatened, nostalgia establishes links to our past in order to help us through a complicated present and thus carry us onward to the future: 'It leads us to search among remembrances of persons and places of our past in an effort to bestow meaning upon persons and places of our present (and to some degree our future).[5]

However, more than mere remembrance is involved. The 'special' past of nostalgia is one that is imbued with positive qualities, as if seen through a filter which blurs what is painful and negative. Furthermore, the nostalgic past has to be a 'lived' past, that is, personally experienced. Thus, as Davis is careful to point out, because man is a reflexive being, a certain attention to some form of objective truthfulness will usually accompany him on his travels back in time. Yet 'whether what nostalgia claims for the past and present is "really the case"' is irrelevant. Nostalgia 'uses the past − falsely, accurately, or ... in specially reconstructed ways', and 'tells us more about present moods than about past realities'.[6]

Nostalgia is likely to set in during transitional phases in a person's life-cycle. Thus the transition from adolescence to adulthood − leaving home for college or to get married or simply to start working, for example − is fertile ground for nostalgic reverie, since that transition in particular may be experienced as a free fall into the unknown. Interestingly, this very point in the life-cycle, although any point earlier or later in life can be made the object of nostalgia, seems to be the one that most people revert to when they muse about their past, probably because it is so strongly configurated.

Davis stresses that the cause of nostalgia always resides in the present; that the past has to be viewed as irrevocably gone and that the function of nostalgia is to ensure a sense of continuity of identity by focusing on some positive aspects of one's past, while muting the negative. In addition, nostalgia serves to erect benchmarks by which the individual can measure how far he or she has come in terms of personal development.

There seem to be no major differences between what might be termed personal nostalgia and collective nostalgia. Basically the causes and functions of collective nostalgia correspond to those on the personal level: periods experienced as anxiety-ridden, due to major 'historical' events or transitions such as war or rapid cultural change accompanied by a perceived erosion of basic values, may trigger a nostalgic reaction that serves to bridge the gap between then and now and in this way to ease the transition so as to help assimilate the changes.

Davis differentiates between three orders or levels of nostalgic experience. The first order he terms *Simple Nostalgia*: an emotionally conditioned statement that focuses on the good past/bad present contrast: 'Things were better *then* than *now*.' The second order, *Reflexive Nostalgia*, deals with the empirically oriented question, 'Was this the way it was?'. The third order, *Interpreted Nostalgia*, is also concerned with questions, in this instance analytically oriented ones such as 'When and why am I nostalgic?'. To summarize: first order nostalgia is an emotional statement, second and third order nostalgia are questions asked in response to that statement, seeking to verify and interpret it. Depending on the situation all three stages in the nostalgic experience may be encountered by the individual, though the third order probably less frequently than the first two.

The following analysis is based on this trisection and hopefully will lead to a more nuanced understanding of the form, function and cultural significance of Hollywood's preoccupation with the fifties. The nostalgic bent of Hollywood over the past twenty years has often been the target of critics who claim that it is either the result of unwillingness to deal with important, up-to-date issues or evidence of distinct conservative ideologies, possibly both. To the extent that all forms of entertainment are intended to provide a temporary diversion of attention from the more mundane matters in life, the movies are indeed escapist, which is precisely why people go to them. However, rather than being mere escapist entertainment for the masses, as fulfillment of their wish to return to simpler times, the movies in this analysis are very much rooted in the here and now, even if they do use the warm glow of a rosy past to state their case.

Simple Nostalgia: The Good Past

The clusters of questions stated in the introduction are closely related to Davis' trisection. The 'purely' nostalgic elements are those 'designed' to prompt an emotional identification and recognition in the audience that may take them on a tour of their own past.[7]

If nostalgia focuses on positive aspects of the past, what is presented as 'good' in the three movies? Since they focus on high schoolers, it may be somewhat difficult to distinguish between 'period' elements and 'age' elements, that is the life and experiences of the teenager as we have known him or her since the mid-fifties. Costumes and hairstyles, and the appearance of buildings and cars, are of course easily identifiable, but once these period details have been established they tend to recede into the general backdrop and play only a marginal part in the films.

In many ways, it is easier to point to the aspects of the period that are *not* there (cf. nostalgia's capacity for muting the negative). Conspicuously absent are political and social issues inextricably linked with the fifties such as the Cold War, the nuclear bomb, and the burgeoning civil rights movement. As Marjorie Rosen states it:

... for me, growing up in the fifties ... meant air-raid drills, crouching in the school basement, two by two, hands protecting our heads; it meant the terror of Sputnik and sleepless nights because my family hadn't built an underground shelter ... the fifties were a reactionary and fiercely frightening decade. They were the political Dark Ages.[8]

On the other hand, according to Benita Eisler in *Private Lives: Men and Women of the Fifties*, these issues were hardly discussed among the young, so to the extent that none of the characters deal with them, the films can be seen to be in keeping with their subject.[9] That of course does not mean that the portrayal is realistic: these things may not have been discussed, but they did have an impact on people's lives. The same applies to the lack of intergenerational conflict. No matter how well-behaved and well-adjusted fifties youth may have seemed and definitely were in comparison to the following decades (juvenile delinquency notwithstanding), parents loomed large and were bound to present problems and obstacles in their lives.[10] Not so in *Grease*: parents simply do not appear. When they do in the other films they are mere props, as in *American Graffiti* (the airport scene), or caring and understanding as in *Peggy Sue Got Married*.

The focal point then, rather than the fifties as such, is youth itself: the energy, exuberance and great expectations which are the birthright of the young. This is a world closed in on itself, saturated in music, painted in brilliant colors and highlighted by perpetual sunlight or enveloped in the magic of seemingly endless summer nights. Each of the three films takes place just prior to the characters' transition into adulthood, and as Davis points out, this serves 'as the prototypical frame for nostalgia for the remainder of life. It is almost as if the depth and the drama of the transition were such as to institutionalize adolescence in the personality as a more or less permanent and infinitely recoverable subject for nostalgic exercise'.[11]

Thus it is not the simple nostalgia that focuses on the fifties as such in the films. The nostalgic elements – the zest and vitality of youth and the sweet pains of growing up, set against a backdrop of sunshine and music – could be located in any decade. What does place them in the fifties are the comments they make on the relationship between nostalgic experience and present reality. Unlike the popular TV-series *Happy Days* (1974-1984), which in its basic premise (as indicated in the title) offers undiluted nostalgia for a bygone era, the three films all come out in favor of the present.[12] That is not to say that there is not an element of wistful longing for the fifties *per se*, but that longing plays a less than prominent role in view of the general rejection of fifties values that underlies each of the three films.

The Dialogue Between Past and Present I: *American Graffiti*

American Graffiti is the story of four high school friends in Modesto, California, one night in 1962. Two of them, Steve and Curt, are to leave the next morning for a college in the East. This is their last night of cruising, hanging out at the drive-in, necking in their cars and other typical teenage activities. Each of the principal male characters represents one facet of what has been handed down as the post-*Rock Around the Clock*, pre-hippie teen: John Milner, the greaser (Paul Le Mat); Toad, the awkward, bespectacled nerd (Charlie Martin Smith); Steve, the clean-cut all-American boy (Ron Howard); Curt, the individualist intellectual (Richard Dreyfuss). In minor roles, two other types are considered: Joe, the leader of the town's juvenile delinquents, the Pharaohs (Bo Hopkins), and the out-of-town challenger to John Milner, Bob Falfa, macho incarnated (Harrison Ford). The main theme, what to do with one's life after adolescence, is centered on the juxtaposition of John Milner, who at twenty-one is already living in the past, and Curt Henderson, who, although reluctant to leave his hometown and with it everything he has known his whole life, eventually embraces the future.

The contrast between John and Curt is suggested in the very first sequence, when Steve is trying to shame Curt out of his misgivings about leaving the next day: 'You want to wind up like John? You just can't stay seventeen forever.' It is further established in the following scene when John and Curt are discussing the prospects of picking up girls, with John lamenting that 'the pickings are really getting slim. The whole strip is shrinking. I remember five years ago ... it was really something'. The point is finally driven home in John's angry outburst at Curt's wanting to go to the freshman dance at their old high school – for old times' sake: 'Go ahead, Curtsy-baby. You go over there and remember all the good times you won't be having. I ain't going off to no fancy college. I'm staying right here, having fun as usual.' The point is that John is not really having fun. With his hair slicked back, his sullen expression and a pack of cigarettes rolled up in the sleeve of his tee-shirt, John is the self-styled James Dean of the group who is already nostalgic for the fifties and who resents the popularity of the Beach Boys: 'I don't like that surfer shit. Rock'n'roll's been going down hill ever since Buddy Holly died.' John is stuck in time, an anachronism, and he is aware that the world is moving past him. Kids his age have left or are about to leave; younger guys threaten his position as the number one car racer in the valley; and on this particular night he winds up cruising with the under-aged Carol (Mackenzie Phillips), whom he just cannot get rid of.

Fittingly, John's car is a relic from the past, a 1932 Deuce Coupe. Curt, on the other hand drives a 2CV, a French car in the mother country of the automobile. This fact immediately establishes Curt as the individualist who has a wider perception of the world. Caught between wanting to leave and staying on, he spends the night chasing a blonde in a white Thunderbird, who becomes 'the dazzling beauty' he has been searching for all his life. Curt is the only one of the group who seems to be in contact with a variety of people. His teacher, Mr. Wolfe, who studied for only one semester at a college in Vermont before returning to Modesto (he is 'not the competitive type'), urges him to leave. Two members of the Moose Lodge, which has awarded him a $2,000 scholarship, hope that he will become a Moose someday. His ex-girlfriend,

61

teases him about his ambition to shake hands with President Kennedy, calls him wishy-washy. The Pharaohs, who force him to partake in a couple of not-so-innocent pranks, subsequently invite him to become a member. And there is Wolfman Jack (played by himself), the mystical pop-guru, the teenager's best friend, whose whereabouts are the subject of much discussion.

All these people represent values and life-styles that Curt ultimately has to reject. Mr. Wolfe is enlivening a boring existence with the cheap thrill of an affair with one of his students. Curt's ex-girlfriend is hoping for a renewal of their relationship; membership of the Moose Lodge appeals to him about as much as that of the Pharaohs; and Wolfman Jack turns out to be just a rather ordinary man, eating half-melted popsickles, while broadcasting pre-recorded messages from a ramshackle station on the outskirts of town.[13]

The identity of the blonde is never fully established. Some say that she is a prostitute, others that she is a married woman; but Curt stays true to his vision and refuses to believe that she is anything less than the perfect incarnation of his hopes and dreams. It is because of her that he goes to see Wolfman Jack, hoping that he will broadcast a message to her. While the others are out on Paradise Road, watching a drag race between Milner and Falfa, Curt is waiting, hoping to receive a call from her. She does call, but hangs up when he asks for her name, yet the next morning she seems to be pointing him in the right direction: looking out the window from the plane, he spots the white Thunderbird on Paradise Road, heading out of town.

Steve and his girlfriend, Curt's sister Laurie (Cindy Williams), spend the night trying to establish the rules for their continued relationship while he is away at college. Steve has his future mapped out. We are never told what it is he wants out of life, only that 'it's just not in this town'. There is no doubt in his mind that he and Laurie eventually will marry – but then again, it wouldn't hurt to date other people. Laurie is hurt, although she tries to conceal it and in the course of the night she seeks to come to terms with the new situation. This leads to a number of confrontations with Steve, who not only mistakenly believes that everything has been worked out, but who also wants Laurie to have sex with him – as a token to remember him by. For Laurie, however, sex belongs to the marital bedroom and whatever the world outside Modesto may have to offer, she is not interested. Not that she is passive or averse to taking the initiative to get what she wants: *she* led *him* through the initial steps in their courtship, as he was too shy. But there are definite limits to how far she will go – in terms of sex as well as the future. Upset by Steve's advances in the car, Laurie throws him out and takes off. Later she goes cruising with Bob Falfa, a fling with rebellion that ends in the wreckage at dawn on Paradise Road and convinces Steve that he had better stay on, at least for another year.

Basically Steve is as firmly lodged in the fifties sensibility of middle-class security as Laurie. His own little rebellion – telling off a teacher at the dance

– is conducted from a point of safety: there can be no repercussions since he has already graduated. In the end, Steve opts for solid citizenship; ironically his future profession, that of insurance agent, reflects the basic premise of the lifestyle he chooses: security and the prevention of serious economic damage in case of accidents.

If Steve is already middle-aged, Toad is barely out of puberty. Clumsy and not particularly handsome, he is the archetypical insecure nerd whose attempts at acting cool and manly (emulating John) always fall flat and fail to impress anyone. He is the lowest in the teen hierarchy as he does not have his own car, so when Steve hands him the keys to his car, to be his for the duration of the fall semester, he is ecstatic: 'Tonight everything is gonna be different.' Miraculously his dreams do come true as he manages to pick up the Sandra Dee look-alike, Debbie (Candy Clark). At the outset, we are encouraged to believe that she is the typical dumb blonde, but gradually she reveals herself as a healthy mixture of sweet and tough: completely capable of standing up for herself, she is into motorbikes and booze and does not seem to be scared of anything. Throughout the night, Toad's attempts at impressing Debbie are repeatedly thwarted, yet when finally he gives up and allows himself to be just an ordinary guy, she comforts him and suggests that he give her a call the next day. She does not mind that he does not own a car. On the contrary she is happy to learn that he has a Vespa: it is less than the cool ideal of a motor-bike, but still it is close enough. It will do.

Supposedly, then, Toad has learned something about reality: that he does not have to pretend or tell lies to make an impression on people. Yet he is enthusiastic when his hero John Milner wins the drag-race and he refuses to accept John's realistic appraisal of the situation: that Falfa would have won had his car not gone off the road. John knows that his days as champion are numbered, but Toad assures him 'you'll always be number one, John. You're the greatest'. John lets himself be persuaded by Toad's admiration and even includes him in his self-deception: 'OK, Toad! We'll take 'em all.' Both of them are reluctant to face reality and neither is equipped to make the transition into an awareness of a larger world in the sixties. As the closing titles tell us, John, like James Dean nine years earlier, is killed in a car accident, while Toad is reported missing in Vietnam in 1965.

Unbeknown to the characters but appreciated and understood by the audience, this is not only their final night as adolescents, when the world is enveloped in darkness and the enchantment of the neon signs, street lamps and tail lights of cars endlessly floating up and down Main Street is the stuff that dreams are made of. It is also one of the final nights of an era that only ten years later seems like ancient history. *American Graffiti* portrays the teen world of the fifties as one of private lives led in cars, shielded and cut off from society by a metal frame and wall-to-wall music. Fittingly, the wreckage at dawn on Paradise Road foreshadows the violence of the era about to begin.

It also indicates that in order to deal with the sixties one has to get out of the car and engage with the world in broad daylight. This is what Curt does. As his plane climbs upward, the radio signal can no longer reach his portable radio and he turns it off. The protective wall of sound gives way to a broader perspective on the world and the object for his quest the night before – the blonde in the white T-Bird – quickly becomes a mere speck in the distance. The fifties, with their emphasis on complacency, predictability and constraints, cannot live.

One aspect of *American Graffiti* that has been obscured over the years is the fact that most of the actors at the time were unknown. In the early 1990s the cast reads like a *Who's Who* of the entertainment industry of the seventies and eighties, but in 1973 only Ron Howard was well-known, literally having grown up on TV in *The Andy Griffiths Show* (1960-68). This fact served to emphasize the universality and ordinariness of the events depicted, just as the episodic structure and the music (none of which was specially made for the film) underscored the impression of a documentary: 'a slice of life' as it was in 1962. But by highlighting the conflict between the impulses, on the one hand, to move ahead and, on the other, to stop the flow of time and preserve things the way they are at any given moment, *American Graffiti* uses the nostalgia inherent in the setting and the situations to demonstrate that we have indeed moved forward and that in the process we have gained more than we have lost.

The Dialogue Between Past and Present II: *Grease*

The rites of passage theme of *American Graffiti* may be extended to include the rites of passage that America underwent between the end of the story and the release of the movie. Quite apart from the changes experienced on the personal and societal levels, the film industry itself has experienced its own rites of passage. The two most uniquely American genres, the Western and the Hollywood musical, have been in decline since the fifties. The old formulas are now exactly that: old and outdated. At the point of extinction, the two genres are occasionally revived, but often in a tongue-in-cheek fashion: we know that you know, but let's try and have some fun anyway.

Grease (Randal Kleiser, 1978) is a perfect example. It seemingly depicts the innocent, happy-go-lucky teenage world of the late fifties. However, on closer inspection, the apparent innocence evaporates as so much hot air. This is satire, heavy-handed and direct, in 'brash, comic-book style'.[14]

Sandy (Olivia Newton-John) and Danny (John Travolta) have had a summer romance; she is supposed to return to her native Australia at summer's end, but due to a change of plans she enrolls at Rydell High, where she meets Danny again. This Danny is not quite the sweet, gentlemanly one she met at the beach. On the contrary, he is the school's coolest greaser, member of the leatherclad Thunderbirds and with a reputation as a ladies' man. An improbable combination in this new context, the two of them enter a stormy relationship, set against that of the more compatible couple of Kenickie (Jeff Conaway) and Rizzo (Stockard Channing).

Danny momentarily loses his cool when he is first re-united with Sandy, but under the interested scrutiny of the Thunderbirds and their female counterparts, the Pink Ladies, led by Rizzo, he quickly regains his composure and feigns indifference to her. Later, he tries to explain: 'It wasn't me, you gotta know that, I mean ... it was me of course, but it wasn't me.' What Danny has such a hard time explaining is the fact that Sandy is a new experience to him. Innocent and pure, she is romance personified. After an argument at the drive-in, Danny dejectedly gives voice to his feelings:

> Someday, when high school is done
> Somehow, some way, our two worlds will be one
> In heaven, forever, and ever we will be.

This, the very ideal of romantic love, is juxtaposed to images of the settled, middle-class life as well as a pun on the sexual consummation of a relationship through the ads for refreshments playing in the background: cartoons of families going to the movies and a sausage flipping up and down before finally jumping into a roll, in the process turning into a hot-dog.[15] Actually, this softer side to Danny is already hinted at in the first exchange between him and his buddies: 'I did meet this one chick, she was sort of cool.' 'You mean she put out?' 'Oh, come on Sonny, is that all you ever think about?'

Even so, Sandy is as much a sexual obsession as a romantic one, illustrating the impossible double bind for the fifties male: looking up to the girl on the pedestal while desiring the willing woman in the gutter. The conflict is conveniently resolved when Sandy changes her image to that of the virgin whore; a solution that, from a fifties as well as a 1978 point of view, is completely unacceptable.

Thus the theme of romantic love, so prevalent in the idealized fifties world of courtship and matrimony, as Betty Friedan's *The Feminine Mystique* made clear later, and essential in Hollywood musicals, comes under heavy attack throughout the movie. The treatment of the Sandy-Danny relationship is a send-up and a mocking of the values that complicate their romance. The parody is indicated from the very start, first in the overblown presentation of their summer together, complete with crashing waves, spectacular sun-sets and promises of eternal love to the tune of 'Love Is a Many Splendored Thing', a big hit in the fifties. Next, in the cartoons that serve as title cards, Sandy is seen as straight out of Walt Disney's *Cinderella*. In fact, Sandy is Cinderella reincarnated, but with a twist. When Sandy and Danny are finally united, the camera focuses on her red high-heeled slipper, an obvious reference to Cinderella's glass slipper. But Sandy in her totality could not be further removed from the fairy-tale: she has been transformed from the sweet, virtuous girl next door into a sex-pot, albeit a rather streamlined and antiseptic one, rather resembling a Barbie doll. Not only that: her prince has secretly been working on a transformation in the opposite direction. However, more than a change of clothes and hairstyle is needed to move into modern times, and Sandy and Danny remain relics of a time gone by, stuck in anachronistic modes of behavior that will not see them through what is to come in the sixties and seventies.

Kenickie, on the other hand, is more realistic than Danny. He harbors no romantic notions about virginal innocence, and his attempts at chivalry toward Rizzo are tongue-in-cheek: grinning, he offers her a ride in his battered car, 'your chariot, my lady'. His 'plan to stay home a lot?' to Rizzo's refusal to help pay for a treat at the malt-shop – 'my Dutch-treat days are over' – places their relationship in the 'equalized' seventies rather than in the fifties. Rizzo has no illusions about men and romance, either. When Sandy first describes Danny as 'sort of special', Rizzo dismisses the idea: 'there's no such thing.' She has a hard time believing Sandy's fairy tale: 'true love and he didn't lay a hand on you? Sounds like a real creep to me.' Later she says of Danny: 'unless you have wheels and a motor he won't know you're alive.' Her song 'There are worse things I could do' criticizes the fifties double standard of the virtuous woman who uses all the tricks of her trade to lure a man into her net:

I could flirt with all the guys
Smile at them and bat my eyes
Press against them when we dance
Make them think they stand a chance,

whereupon she refuses to put out until the wedding-night. In the fifties world, sex is 'dirty' and not supposed to be enjoyed by the unmarried woman. But Rizzo likes sex. When Kenickie's condom breaks – he bought it in the seventh grade – she only hesitates for a moment, exclaims 'oh, what the hell!' and throws all caution to the wind. For her, waiting for Mr. Right amounts to throwing her life away *On a dream that won't come true.* Furthermore, she refuses to use the stereotypical female ploy of getting what she wants by crying: 'But to cry in front of you/ That's the worst thing I could do.' When she thinks that she may be pregnant she does not expect Kenickie to bail her out by marrying her; on the contrary, she rejects his offer of help. Rizzo is the new woman, the self-reliant 'I can take care of myself – and anyone else who comes along' realist, pragmatic and unsentimental. When finally Rizzo and Kenickie are reunited and he offers to 'make an honest woman' of her, she only consents after he has repeated the offer, and then she is rather down-to-earth about it: 'Well, it ain't moonlight and roses.' The juxtaposition of Sandy and Rizzo clearly demonstrates the intersection of the old fifties ideal of womanhood – in its glaring contradictions – with the reality of the emerging woman of the seventies.

The male icon of the fifties, the greaser in black leather and d.a. haircut, has two incarnations in *Grease*: the fifties stereotype and the watered-down seventies version. The greaser in the fifties was seen as a menacing type, if not necessarily a criminal then at least a borderline case. No 'nice' girl would come anywhere near this type. And yet we are asked to believe that Sandy stays in love with Danny after she has met him again and that she even transforms herself into the corresponding image of the 'bad' girl in order to make the relationship work. But just below the surface both Danny and Kenickie are good citizens who have the potential eventually to make the crossover from adolescent 'grease-hood' to 'mature' adulthood. Kenickie informs his incredulous buddies that during the summer he has been working, 'saving up to get me some wheels'. At the end of the movie, this is matched by Danny: 'While you coons were out stealing hub caps I lettered in track.' So in effect what we are presented with here is a 'de-menaced' greaser set against the 'bad' type, personified by the members (and particularly the leader) of the Scorpions, the rivals of the Thunderbirds. This distinction is also made in *American Graffiti* in the presentation of John Milner and Joe, the leader of the Pharaohs.

The past and the present are more obviously intertwined in *Grease* than in *American Graffiti*. Most of the music, although based on rock'n'roll formulas of the fifties (and there are a few authentic fifties tunes as well), has a decidedly seventies ring. The new improved status of women in the seventies is reflected in the fact that not only is the principal a woman, but what is more, the *auto shop teacher* is too – and married, to boot. The casting is a scoop: two of the hottest stars of the seventies, Olivia Newton-John and John Travolta, surrounded by well-known faces that span forty years of entertainment: Frankie Avalon of the sixties; Edd Byrnes, Sid Caesar and Dody Goodman of the fifties, Eve Arden of the forties and Joan Blondell of the thirties. In *Grease* all generations come together in an all-out celebration of youth, but the irony is hard to miss. In the final scene, while everyone is singing *We'll always stay together*, Sandy and Danny take off in a car, and ride high up into the clouds, already breaking the promise in the song. The togetherness that is part and parcel of the high school experience, expressed for example in pep-rallies prior to football matches, or in indulgence in slightly outrageous behavior that parents do not know about, is limited to just that period; and the end titles – pages of the Rydell High School Yearbook – illustrate the point. The pictures convey the spirit, the friendships, the activities and events, but they are frozen moments of joy that can never be recaptured. While former high school students get on with their lives, their yearbooks gather dust on the shelf: testimonials to the inevitable passage of time.

The Dialogue Between Past and Present III: *Peggy Sue Got Married*

Time travel had sporadically been a Hollywood theme since the 1920s. Most of the time travelers covered several centuries, if not millennia, and experienced severe culture shocks, shared by the audience. Regularly featuring futuristic technology, such films were exercises in far-out imagination.[16] In the 1980s, the genre suddenly blossomed. Most of the movies still had their protagonists travel through considerable time spans, but four of them covered only a few decades, which was new.[17] But then, so many things have changed since the sixties that the culture shock is almost as severe as if the time span had been a hundred years. In *The Final Countdown* (1980), the U.S.S. *Nimitz* enters a time warp and finds itself in the Pacific the day before the Japanese attack on Pearl Harbor. Should we interfere with history as we know it? The question becomes a moot point as the carrier enters yet another time warp and is transported back into present time. In *The Philadelphia Experiment* (1984), a sailor on a World War Two ship falls into a hole in time and winds up in 1984. Two fairly recent movies *Back to the Future* (1985) and *Peggy Sue Got Married* (Francis Coppola, 1986) are even closer to home: their protagonists get a chance to take a look at America anno 1955 and 1960, respectively. They were released at a time when the United States, led by Ronald Reagan (himself a man of the past as well as very much of the present) was trying to reorganize its self-image, to turn the clock back to the happy days before trauma set in, much in the spirit of Scott Fitzgerald's Jay Gatsby and his 'Can't repeat the past? ... Why of course you can! ... I'm going to fix everything just the way it was before'.[18]

Peggy Sue (Kathleen Turner), however, has no desire to fix everything the way it was before; on the contrary. As the movie opens, she is getting ready to go to a 25th high school reunion. The mother of two and owner of a bakery business, she is separated from her husband Charlie (Nicholas Cage), who has left her for a younger woman. At the reunion, she tells a friend that she never dated anybody but Charlie and that they got married too young, ending up blaming each other for all the things they missed in life. If she knew then what she knows now, she would do a lot of things differently. Suddenly taken ill, she faints and wakes up back in 1960, shortly before graduation. With her, we return to the world of *American Graffiti* and *Grease*, but this time the present is superimposed on the past in the movie itself. Peggy Sue, with all the wisdom of middle-age, gets to relive the most crucial period in her personal history: the one immediately preceding her wedding.

This, then, is the ultimate nostalgia trip. But although Peggy Sue does relish the opportunity to relive certain happy moments with her family and friends and to make up for past omissions, such as telling her parents that they are the best parents a girl could ever want or spending a night with a boy she had a crush on in high school, she is not happy with the fifties scene in general. This conflict is continuously highlighted throughout the movie and underscores the distance she, as well as society at large, has travelled between then and now. One telling example is her mother's (Barbara Harris) perplexity, when in the morning Peggy Sue tells her to sit down and have breakfast with the rest of the family: 'You want me to sit?'

Peggy Sue I was the girl next door, well-behaved and popular, and, in accordance with the general standards at the time, definitely planning to marry Charlie. Peggy Sue II, the one who has lived through that marriage and its disintegration, as well as the loosening of standards and codes of society, is feisty and rebellious. She is determined to change her destiny, which leads to clashes with a bewildered Charlie, who does not understand what has gotten into her. Charlie himself dreams of a career as a pop-star, which runs counter to his father's plans for him to take over the family's appliance store. Peggy Sue knows that Charlie's dream will never be realized and she also knows that this fact will create problems for them in the future, so she is rather inclined to break up with him. On the other hand, through the course of her experience, she is also reminded of how genuine Charlie's love for her is, as well as how much music means to him.

After a fight with Charlie, Peggy Sue runs into Michael Fitzsimmons (Kevin J. O'Connor), the school's black-clad intellectual, scorned by his peers as 'that Commie Beatnik'. They take off on his motorbike, smoke pot (brought back from the future – she found it in the pocket of her dress), talk and eventually make love under the stars. A great poet-to-be, Michael has no patience with the regimented small-town life as he knows it: 'I'm gonna check out of this bourgeois motel.' Peggy Sue I would not have known what he is talking about, but Peggy Sue II does. When he asks her if she is going to 'marry Mr. Blue Impala and graze around with all the other sheep' for the rest of her life, she announces: 'No, I already did that. I want to be a dancer.'

When Peggy Sue's friends Maddy (Joan Allen) and Carol (Catherine Hicks) show up to find out what the situation is with Michael and her, Maddy is upset:

> But I always thought that you were gonna marry Charlie? And that Carol would marry Walter and I would marry Arthur and we'd all live on the same street and take our kids to the park together and have barbecues every Sunday. It's gonna spoil everything if you and Charlie break up. That Michael Fitzsimmons doesn't look like the barbecue type.

Maddy's vision of the future is an echo of the final song in *Grease*: 'We'll Always Stay Together.' It is poignant in its precise description of the fifties ideal – and with the hindsight of the eighties hopelessly naive. Compare Benita Eisler's description of the phenomenon:

> When we were young, imagination, like meaningless sex, was a risky exercise. Indulging in either could deflect a young woman from her primary purpose of finding a

marriageable young man. Most of my friends were in no danger of getting sidetracked. With Mr. Right's résumé in hand, they had their lives squared away. From their conversations topographical maps, like the U.S. Army serial photographs, took shape. The future unfolded to the farthest horizons. They knew every rise and meander of the terrain – towel monograms and silver patterns, houses, cars, numbers of children and kinds of communities they would live in – forever.... The blueprint was their parents' way of life. The future was the past.[19]

Peggy Sue, in an attempt to get a scientific explanation of what has happened to her, seeks out Richard Norvik (Barry Miller), the school's prototypical egg-head, who is just as much an outsider as Michael Fitzsimmons. She convinces him that she really is a time-traveler and Richard is at once puzzled and excited about the future technological innovations that she describes for him. He suggests they enter into a partnership – they could make millions on Peggy Sue's knowledge of the future – and eventually he proposes to her, as a way of changing her destiny.

But neither of the alternatives to Charlie – Michael or Richard – is a viable option, although she knows that each of them will be successful in the future, Michael as a poet, Richard as scientist and inventor, whereas Charlie's dream of stardom will be reduced to that of rather ridiculous commercials for his appliances store on the local TV-channel. Marriage is simply out of the question: 'Peggy Sue got married. Case closed. I don't want to marry anybody.' Realizing that she has to get away from Charlie in order not to repeat her mistake, she goes out into the country to visit her grandparents. In the warm glow of days gone by, visually conveyed in the almost smoldering colors of a huge tree outside the grandparents' cottage, seen against the setting sun, and later in the flames in the fireplace, Peggy Sue reveals her secret. Grandma immediately grasps what Peggy Sue's experience is all about – 'Right now you're just browsing through time' – and advises her to choose the things she will be proud of, 'the things that last'. Peggy Sue is not in doubt: she is proud of her children. Even if life has not turned out to be what she expected, they have made it all worth while. Thus, through the nostalgic trip to her past, Peggy Sue gains the strength to deal with her present, that is, to wake up from the coma that serves as the explanation for her experience. A sense of continuity has been re-established, the gap between the past and the present has been bridged. Not only that, Peggy Sue has gotten a sense of direction for the future as well. Toward the end of her visit to her grandparents she mentions to her grandfather that when he and grandma are gone, the family will be gone, too: she never sees her cousins anymore. Grandpa's response is that 'it's your grandma's strudel that has kept the family together'. After she wakes up, Charlie asks for a second chance. He has broken up with his young girlfriend: 'I got tired of translating everything to her. She thought the Big Bopper was a hamburger.' Peggy Sue needs time to think it over but she does invite Charlie over for dinner with the children: 'I'll make a strudel.' Her frustration over the fact that she was unable to alter her destiny in the past gives way to the realization that she is not powerless in terms of shaping her future and she will do so by using what she learned on her trip back to her youth.

Reflexive Nostalgia: Conclusion

In the main, Davis' term Reflexive Nostalgia covers the set of empirically oriented questions pertaining to the validity of the nostalgic image of the past. Thus what Davis calls the 'voice of a Truth Squad' is introduced, 'wanting to question, deflate, correct and remind'.[20] In *Peggy Sue Got Married* that voice is fundamental to the story, as Peggy Sue by way of time-travel is given the opportunity literally to relive the past. In *American Graffiti* the questioning is more indirect, contained as it is in the juxtaposition of John Milner and Curt. This juxtaposition in combination with the audience's knowledge of impending change serves to emphasize the rejection of the codes of behavior and values of the fifties that is the underlying message of the film. The same applies to *Grease* in its send-up of the Danny – Sandy relationship set against that of Rizzo and Kenickie, who display more mature (read: post-fifties) attitudes toward relationships. In this way the nostalgic presentation is tempered as we realize that we would feel just as out of place in the fifties as Curt, Rizzo and Peggy Sue do. The present may be problematic and fraught with insecurity and uncertainty, but the solution is not to return to the fifties. It is a nice place to visit, but we would not want to live there.

Interpreted Nostalgia: Why the Fifties?

In the *Newsweek* story from 1972 mentioned in the introduction, one of the explanations for the fifties revival offered was that 'to fans of the current revival, the point of it all is that the '50s seem to be more fun than anything going on now – or probably then'.[21] A Boston disc jockey, however, did not take it very seriously: 'It's just like the early '60s.... That was when there was the first oldies craze, because there was a big lull in music and the population was waiting for something to happen. Finally the Beatles came along in '64. We are in the same lull now, and the '50s are filling in.'[22]

Jeff Greenfield, author of *Where Have You Gone, Joe DiMaggio?*, an account of the fifties, offered this explanation: 'The generation that grew up in the '50s is now equipped to revive itself. We are now old enough to be TV producers and film distributors. In ten years, people will be reminiscing about the '60s. It's not surprising that the '50s are back now. All it means is that a new generation is feeling its age.'[23]

However, twenty years later, we are still waiting for Jeff Greenfield's prediction of a sixties revival to come true, at least on a scale comparable to the fascination with the fifties. There have been sporadic glimpses, of which the TV-series *The Wonder Years* and *Crime Story* are the most obvious examples. Even so, both belong more to the fifties category than to the sixties. *The Wonder Years* only occasionally takes the events of the sixties into account, as our hero grapples with the more pressing, universal issues of adolescence. *Crime Story* is set in the early sixties and the basic plotline of a crime unit investigating a mobster hark back to the 1959-1963 series, *The Untouchables*, which in turn was loosely based on actual events in the 1930s. As regards theatrical movies, the bulk have concentrated on the Vietnam War, hardly nostalgic material. Even a seemingly clear-cut nostalgia piece like Oliver Stone's *The Doors* (1991) paints a somber and tragic picture of the self-destruction through drugs and alcohol of the unofficial poet laureate of the sixties, Jim Morrison.

By way of contrast, America's infatuation with the fifties is as pronounced as ever. Two new shows, currently popular on network TV are CBS's *Brooklyn Bridge*, an affectionate look back at growing up in Brooklyn in the mid-fifties; and NBC's *I'll Fly Away*, which is reminiscent of Harper Lee's novel *To Kill a Mockingbird* and portrays life in a Southern town in the late fifties. Some of the latest movies, set in the fifties, include *Guilty by Suspicion* and *Havana* (1991), *The Man in the Moon*, *The Mambo Kings*, and *School Ties* (1992).

The explanation for this seemingly never-ending preoccupation with the fifties is, not surprisingly, to be found in the events and transformations which through the sixties and the seventies continually threatened to erode the optimism and confidence that for so long have been characteristics of the American self-image. By the early seventies, Americans had witnessed what Fred Davis calls

> perhaps the most wide-ranging, sustained and profound assault on native belief concerning the 'natural' and 'proper' that has perhaps ever been visited on a people over so short a span of time.... the notion that blacks are as good as whites ... that woman is man's equal ... that to be homosexual is neither criminal or sick ... the hippie's celebration of hallucinogenic drugs; the Flower children's scornful disdain of the Protestant work ethic; the *Playboy* 'philosophy' of a 'screw is just a screw'; the apparent licence ... to disrespect and denigrate authority ... and so forth.[24]

In this context, the fifties is certainly the last peaceful period in recent history. While in the main I agree with Fred Davis' basic premise that the cause of the nostalgic reaction resides in the present and that to emphasize a previous period's superior qualities as the incentive is to confuse cause and effect, it nevertheless seems plausible to make an exception with regard to the fifties. Author Irving Shulman has put it this way:

We're most nostalgic, it seems, about the fifties – for some very good reasons. That was a time when wars were settled, there was a father in the White House, and countries were relatively at peace. We were busy making large families, and children were still considered a blessing. Prosperity was at hand and in the land. People were well mannered, crime was controlled, streets and neighborhoods safe, and the motor vehicle still seemed to be a safe animal to have around. Those days are light years away.[25]

The fifties may be considered the adolescence of modern America. It was a decade of optimism, confidence, peace and prosperity, a time when every-thing seemed possible and there was no limit to expectations for the future. At the same time, of course there were doubts, there were problems, but in retro-spect, given our knowledge of what came after, these problems and doubts take on the same qualities that a mature adult perceives his or her trials and tribulations of adolescence: they were very real at the time, but seem simple and manageable in comparison to those that demand attention later in life. Through the collective search for identity and the effort to regain a sense of continuity and stability in the midst of chaos, the fifties have become a cultural icon, our perception being filtered through the stylizing lens of Hollywood. As more than two thirds of the movies that so far have dealt with the fifties have focused on adolescence or early adulthood, with all that involves in terms of innocence and great expectations for the future, the connection between the fifties and youth on the mythical level has also been firmly established. Just as the individual's youth, with time, takes on mythical qualities, so too have the fifties in the collective consciousness. As Daniel Patrick Moynihan, Assistant Secretary of Labor in the Kennedy administration, said shortly after Kennedy's assassination, in response to Mary McGrory's 'We'll never laugh again': 'We'll laugh again. It's just that we will never be young again.'[26]

Notes

1. *Newsweek,* 16 Oct 1972, p. 78 (International edition, p. 54).
2. The boundaries of the fifties are somewhat loose as I include the early sixties under this heading. Much is to be said for the notion that the fifties ended with the assassination of President Kennedy in 1963, although it can be just as convincingly argued that they ended with his inauguration in 1961. The former is based on the impact the assassina-tion had on the American people. Kennedy's death ushered in a period of profound dis-location in American society at large and has thus become a symbol of the recurring crises that came to mark the nation in the subsequent decades. The latter takes as its point of departure the assumption that with the youngest elected president in history taking over from one of the oldest, America was now stepping into a new and invigor-ating phase of history. Since the demarcation line has to be drawn somewhere, for the purposes of this study I have found November 1963 to be the most suitable boundary.
3. Films set in the fifties, produced since 1971, listed thematically (probably not exhaustive):

Young in the Fifties: *The Last Picture Show* (1971); *American Graffiti* (1973); *Badlands* (1973); *The Lords of Flatbush* (1974); *Our Time* (1974); *Return to Macon County* (1975); *Next Stop, Greenwich Village* (1976); *Ode to Billy Joe* (1976); *Sparkle* (1976); *Fraternity Row* (1977); *September 30, 1955* (1978); *Grease* (1978); *National Lampoon's Animal House* (1978); *The One and Only* (1978); *The Wanderers* (1979); *The Great Santini* (1979); *Rock 'n' Roll High School* (1979); *Heart Beat* (1980); *Those Lips, Those Eyes* (1980); *Porky's* (1981); *Come back to the Five and Dime, Jimmy Dean, Jimmy Dean* (1982); *Diner* (1982); *Grease 2* (1982); *Porky's II: The Next Day* (1983); *Sam's Son* (1984); *Porky's Revenge* (1985); *Back to the Future* (1985); *Mischief* (1985); *Peggy Sue Got Married* (1986); *Stand By Me* (1986); *Desert Bloom* (1986); *Dirty Dancing* (1987); *Hairspray* (1988); *A Night in the Life of Jimmy Reardon* (1988); *Aloha Summer* (1988); *Everybody's All American* (1988); *Dead Poets Society* (1989); *Heart of Dixie* (1989); *The Man in the Moon* (1992); *The Mambo Kings* (1992); *School Ties* (1992).

Rock'n'roll: *Let the Good Times Roll* (1973); *The Buddy Holly Story* (1978); *American Hot Wax* – disc jockey Alan Freed (1978); *The Idolmaker* – rock producer Bob Marcucci (1980); *This Is Elvis* (1981); *La Bamba* – Ritchie Valens (1987); *Great Balls of Fire!* – Jerry Lee Lewis (1989).

Witch Hunters: *The Way We Were* (1973); *The Front* (1976); *Daniel* (1983); *The House on Carroll Street* (1988); *Guilty by Suspicion* (1991).

Assorted movies Involving the Fifties: *M*A*S*H* (1970); *Lenny* (1974); *Macon County Line* (1974); *W.W. and the Dixie Dancekings* (1975); *One Flew Over the Cuckoo's Nest* (1975); *F.I.S.T.* (1978); *The Brink's Job* (1978); *Escape From Alcatraz* (1979); *Cuba* (1979); *Coal Miner's Daughter* – Loretta Lynn (1980); *Raging Bull* – Jake La Motta (1980); *The Right Stuff* (1983); *Sweet Dreams* – Patsy Cline (1985); *Blaze* – Louisiana governor Earl Long (1989); *Driving Miss Daisy* (1989); *Parents* (1989); *Havana* (1991).

4. The term is coined from the Greek *nostos*, to return home, and *algia*, a painful condition, i.e. homesickness.

5. Fred Davis, *Yearning for Yesterday: A Sociology of Nostalgia* (New York: 1979), p. vii.

6. Davis, pp. 15 and 10-11.

7. Collective nostalgia operates on various levels when it comes to age-groups in the audience, depending on how far removed the latter are from the period and its representatives, the characters in the movies. In the current instance the key figure is the fifties teenager. Those viewers who in 1973 were old enough to remember their own adolescence in the fifties were likely to experience a kind of 'first-hand' nostalgia. The nostalgia experienced by those who came of age in the sixties may have been triggered more by the condition of youth. Later still, teens of the late seventies/early eighties may have 'remembered' their parents' youth – a sort of second-hand nostalgia – while at the same time identifying with the characters and situations 'first-hand', regardless of time-period.

8. Marjorie Rosen, 'Grease', *American Film*, 3, 4 (1978), 10.

9. Benita Eisler, *Private Lives: Men and Women of the Fifties* (New York: 1986), p. 8.

10. Consider the title of Paul O'Neil's 30 November 1959 *Life* magazine article on the Beats: 'The Only Rebellion Around'.

11. Davis, p. 59.

12. The series was so wholesome and bland that according to Harry Castleman and Walter Podrazik it could really be from the fifties. (*Harry and Wally's Favorite TV Shows* (New York: 1989), p. 213.) According to Garry Marshall, the Executive Producer of the show, this was exactly the point: 'I couldn't figure out how I could do a realistic comedy about young people today and avoid drugs and avoid the sexual revolution,

because I knew they wouldn't put that on television. So I said, What's the use? It's not real, people are gonna watch it and say: "Baloney, that isn't life." Then it crossed my mind – how can I beat this? I can do it if I push it back in time – to the 'Fifties. If I'm not doing drugs, and I'm not doing the sex things, then the audience will buy it and they'll say: "That's right, it's not today. But that's the way it was."' Quoted in Donna McCrohan, *Prime Time, Our Time: America's Life and Times Through the Prism of Television* (Rocklin, Calif.: Prima Publishing and Communications, 1990), p. 252.

13. Actually the real Wolfman Jack, who plays himself in the movie, broadcast from just across the border, in Tijuana, Mexico. The signal from his station was so powerful that it was illegal by FCC regulations, no doubt an additional reason for his popularity among teenagers.

14 James Monaco, *American Film Now* (New York: 1979), p. 284. See also Deborah Thomas's article on *Grease* in 'American Cinema in the '70s', *Movie* [London], 27/28 (1980-81), p. 94: 'despite its ostensible 'fifties setting, *Grease* is less a nostalgia movie than an unsentimental critique of the 'fifties state of mind. It is a 'fifties movie embedded in a 'seventies sensibility, and herein lies much of its not-inconsiderable distinction.'

15. The suggestive cartoon of the sausage jumping into the bun was a mere coincidence. The film company had borrowed a number of old commercials for movie theaters and this one happened to be shown during the rehearsal of the song.

16. The most notable of these movies were *The Planet of the Apes* series (1968-1973), about a group of astronauts who get caught in a time warp and land on a planet run by apes. The planet turns out to be the Earth in the very distant future. The 1970s also saw the adaptation of Kurt Vonnegut's novel *Slaughterhouse Five* (1972); Woody Allen's spoof on the genre, *Sleeper* (1973); and *Time After Time* (1979), the story of H.G. Wells following Jack the Ripper from Victorian England to contemporary America in his time machine.

17. In *Somewhere in Time* (1980) a young playwright falls in love with a woman in an old picture and wills himself back to 1912 to meet her; in *The Terminator* (1984) Arnold Schwartzenegger is a robot sent back to the past (that is, the present) in order to change the future; and in *Bill & Ted's Excellent Adventure* (1989) two high schoolers about to flunk a history course are given the opportunity to go traveling through time and meet historical figures such as Napoleon, Joan of Arc and Abraham Lincoln.

18. F. Scott Fitzgerald, *The Great Gatsby* (New York: 1925), p. 73.

19. Eisler, p. 150.

20. Davis, p. 21.

21. *Newsweek*, 16 October 1972, p. 78 (International edition, p. 54).

22. *Newsweek*, 16 October 1972, p. 82 (International edition, p. 58).

23. *Newsweek*, 16 October 1972, p. 82 (International edition, p. 58).

24. Davis, pp. 105-106.

25. Marilyn Tucker, 'The Return of Shulman's Characters', *San Francisco Examiner and Sunday Chronicle*, April 22, 1973, *This World* section, p. 35. Quoted in Davis, p. 20.

26. Quoted in Arthur M. Schlesinger, Jr., *A Thousand Days: John F. Kennedy in the White House* (Boston: 1965), p. 937.

Dusk and Dawn: Black Protest in the Fifties and Forties

Peter Ling

In many general accounts of the 1950s, three events – the US Supreme Court's *Brown* decision of 1954, the Montgomery bus boycott of 1955-56, and the Little Rock crisis of 1957 – are enough to place race relations alongside the Red Scare as a vital counterpoint to the alleged comfort, conformity and complacency of the age of Ike.[1] In each case, the significance of the events themselves is heightened by the knowledge that they constitute vital milestones along the road to the disquiet, dissent, and drama of the 1960s. The Warren court's rejection of the separate but equal doctrine gave added moral legitimacy to and a constitutional basis for the protests of the 1960s. The bus boycott indicated the potential of non-violent mass action as a protest strategy and of Martin Luther King, Jnr. as an eloquent advocate of black rights. For its part, the Little Rock schools crisis confirmed both the hardening of white southern attitudes after *Brown* and the necessity of compelling the federal government to intervene to secure black rights. Thus, these events of the 1950s seem to suggest a gathering of momentum. Knowing how and when the civil rights movement ended, we can feel confident and positive, or so it seems, about its origins.

Yet, as Eric Foner acknowledges at the end of his recent magisterial account of the first Reconstruction: 'hindsight can be a treacherous ally. Enabling us to trace the hidden pattern of past events, it beguiles us with the mirage of inevitability, the assumption that different outcomes lay beyond the limits of the possible.'[2] Certainly, it is a rare historian of the 1950s who can write without the sirens of the 1960s singing in his or her ears, and so, the ability to keep different outcomes in mind is to be applauded. But another related hazard of historical interpretation is that each generation brings to the task of interpretation its own concerns, so that the significance of past events is re-cast by the powerful enchantment of contemporary issues. In this instance the impulse for the most recent interpreters of the civil rights movement has been to relate the movement's course and character to the persistence of black economic deprivation as a national phenomenon more than a generation after the civil rights 'revolution'.[3]

From this perspective, legal (as opposed to actual) desegregation almost seems too small a gain, because it has left too much racial discrimination intact. The milestones of the movement in the 1950s may have represented gains in the battle for respect, whether for a child in the school-room or for an adult riding the bus, but they rarely represented tangible material improvements to the economic well-being of the black community. Indeed, during the 1950s, the economic position of black American males faltered.[4] Accordingly, alongside the 'Whig' progressive view of the movement which dominates the celebrations of Martin Luther King Day, there are now less laudatory interpretations. Common to this view is a hostility to American liberalism as a bankrupt tradition whose advocates misled African-Americans with false promises. This essay examines two such critical perspectives on the development of the movement: the first from radical labour historians, and the second from a black nationalist perspective. Both seek to portray the 1950s as an era of strategic misjudgement in the struggle for black rights.

The Lost Opportunity

The task of breaking the familiar positive conceptualization of the civil rights story of the 1950s can begin with a reappraisal of developments in US race relations during the preceding decade. The 1940s are no longer the 'forgotten years' of the Negro revolution.[5] Indeed, they are the crucial focus for those who argue that an organized labour-civil rights protest coalition was forged in this decade which offered opportunities for racial progress greater in some respects than that secured by the movement of the 1960s.[6] To evaluate this claim, one has to consider the viability of the movement in the 1940s, that offspring of the Popular Front of the late 1930s whose organizations both in the labour movement and among civil rights groups were broken by the repression of the Red Scare.

No one denies that the political influence of black Americans and their position within organized labour improved to some extent during the Roosevelt years, and few would disagree that the foundation for this change was demographic: a migration from the South to the northern industrial centres.[7] Indeed, since this migration continued in the post-war years the militancy of these transplanted blacks underlines for students of the 1950s how the Movement began in movement; not simply a movement North, but also an interaction between black northerners, ex-southerners in the North and those still living in the South.[8]

By emphasizing the unprecedented role of the southern black clergy (King's Southern Christian Leadership Conference) and of students (the Student Nonviolent Coordinating Committee), and the adoption of non-violent direct action as a strategy against southern Jim Crow, early accounts of the civil rights movement stressed the 'break', both institutional and intellectual, between the generation of 1940 and that of 1960.[9] More recently, however, it has become common practice to point to the continued presence of certain significant figures from the protest campaigns of the 1940s. As editor of *The Crisis* in the war decade, Roy Wilkins was already well placed to succeed Walter White as head of the National Association for the Advancement of Colored People (NAACP). The Student Nonviolent Coordinating Committee's early mentor, Ella Baker, was similarly active in the Association's New York office in the 1940s, while the future co-ordinator of Citizenship Schools for the Southern Christian Leadership Conference, Septima Clark, was a leading light in the NAACP's South Carolina chapter.[10] Two leading instigators of the Montgomery bus boycott, Rosa Parks and E.D. Nixon, were both to be found hard at work coping with a wartime increase in NAACP membership in Montgomery from four hundred to two thousand.[11] To those who detect continuity as much as change, figures such as Bayard Rustin and James Farmer are particularly emblematic; both helped to found the non-violent and interracial Congress of Racial Equality in Chicago in the 1940s.[12] Among other 'young Turks' of the 1940s whose careers reached their climax in the 1960s was the most important black politician of his generation, Adam Clayton Powell, Jnr. He was already using the social activism of his church to become Harlem's Congressman in the 1940s.[13] While scarcely young in 1940, A. Philip Randolph of the Brotherhood of Sleeping Car Porters emerged as the major black protest leader during the war years to become the most eminent black labour leader ever. He is arguably a telling example of how much deeper the movement's roots were than a narrow focus on King and the students' sit-ins would suggest.[14] Individually or cumulatively such names suggest that the emergence of the civil rights movement did not await the rise of a new generation. Moreover, the type of protest undertaken by such people in the 1940s has been examined to ascertain how far the movement of the 1950s drew upon their example.

A. Philip Randolph's March on Washington Movement (MOWM) was the most dramatic black protest campaign of the 1940s.[15] Using the threat of a mass march by blacks on the nation's still-segregated capital, Randolph induced President Roosevelt to issue Executive Order 8802 in 1941 establishing a Fair Employment Practices Committee (FEPC) to monitor a policy of no racial discrimination in the expanding defence industries.[16] Randolph had been one of the black leaders who pressed Roosevelt on the issue of African-American recruitment into the armed forces in the run-up to the 1940 election. Frustrated by this experience, he apparently reached the same conclusion about FDR's attitude to blacks as would historian Frank Freidel later, namely, that Roosevelt 'was disposed to capitulate when they could muster sufficient force'.[17]

Since the march never actually took place, it is impossible to say whether Randolph actually had one hundred thousand Afro-Americans ready to march. More certain is the fact that his militancy on this question aroused enough popular support to compel the NAACP to endorse the project, since otherwise the cautious senior black protest group would have avoided a scheme involving all-black mass mobilization so markedly different to NAACP legalism. As befits a labour leader, Randolph believed that the defence employment issue had an immediate mass appeal since it represented jobs, wages, and enhanced opportunities. 'Without an issue which is clear, understandable and possible of realization', he wrote in August 1941, 'the masses cannot be rallied'. His 'blacks only' policy has been seen as equally hard-headed and astute. His recent experience with the National Negro Congress made him fear that the most readily available white aid would be from communists who would try to subordinate the movement to the Party's agenda. This attitude clearly limited the potential scope of an alliance between organized labour in the shape of the Congress of Industrial Organizations (CIO) and black civil rights groups, and Randolph has been criticized on these grounds. The racial appeal to blacks to march alone, however, was also intended in Randolph's own words 'to break down the slave psychology and inferiority complex in Negroes which comes and is nourished with Negroes relying on white people for direction and support'.[18] A fascinating literary gloss on Randolph's views is, of course, provided by Ralph Ellison's novel *Invisible Man* (1952) in which race and class ideologies compete for the protagonist's loyalty.

Randolph recognized that while job discrimination was the bread-and-butter issue facing African-Americans in World War Two, segregation in the armed forces was the more emotionally charged cause. When the MOWM dissolved as an organization, Randolph's energies were directed into the National Council for a Permanent FEPC and the Committee against Jim Crow in Military Service and Training. The unsuccessful FEPC campaign peaked in the first year of the Truman administration, but the military desegregation campaign intensified as the Cold War led to proposals for an unprecedented peacetime mobilization.[19] By 1948, Randolph and black Republican Grant Reynolds had organized the League for Non-Violent Civil Disobedience Against Military Segregation, which pressed Truman to desegregate the armed forces or face the embarassment of a widespread refusal to serve by black Americans. Admittedly, Truman's Executive Order 9981, issued on 26 July 1948, reflected principally the victory of liberal forces at the Democratic convention earlier that month as well as Truman's desire to contrast his own active pursuit of equal rights to the inactivity of the Republican-dominated Congress which he had called into special session on 26 July. But the desegregation order was also timed to avert the Randolph campaign, since the new draft was scheduled to begin in August. Assured by the president's staff that desegregation would proceed, Randolph announced the end of the civil disobedience campaign on 18 August.[20]

Randolph's tactics of threatened direct action had again achieved their objective, yet they retained an element of bluff. A vital element in such tactics was national publicity, and in this respect Randolph's New York base was an advantage. Although he was himself a southerner by birth and schooling, Randolph had settled in New York at the time of the Great Migration of the First World War years; and while his Pullman porter followers were necessarily dispersed throughout the nation, the Brotherhood would not have survived without strong organizational bases in the North, notably in Chicago, Detroit and New York.[21] The mass rallies which Randolph organized to mobilize the MOWM were notably well-attended in these cities. Black protest in the 1940s commanded national attention from a northern base. In this respect, the 1950s witness an important shift southwards. This sectional orientation has implications for our assessment of the labour-civil rights coalition. Organized labour's relative strength in the North in the early 1940s prompted an alliance principally on labour's terms and at its instigation.

The subsequent decline of union influence in national politics meant that black protest in the 1950s emerged largely on its own terms and sought allies at its own instigation. The northern character of 1940s protest is confirmed by a consideration of other movements. One of Randolph's associates in the late 1930s 'Jobs-for-Negroes' campaign was the young pastor of Harlem's Abyssinian Baptist church, Adam Clayton Powell, Jr.. Powell organized a bus boycott against the Fifth Avenue Coach Company and New York Omnibus Corporation in March 1941. The month-long boycott kept sixty thousand people off the buses each day at a daily cost to the companies of three thousand dollars. Significantly, the boycott supported a strike by the Transportation Workers Union, which had included in its demands the hiring of black drivers and mechanics. The eventual settlement on 29 April 1941 required the hiring of one hundred black drivers and seventy mechanics and a policy of equal hiring until black employment equalled seventeen per cent, the percentage of blacks resident in Manhattan.[22]

This incident underlines the advantages to blacks of a labour alliance in the 1940s. The mutual benefits of interracial solidarity were recognized by the Congress of Industrial Organizations (CIO), the success of whose tactics in the North led to the launch of the 'Operation Dixie' unionization drive in May 1946. Such northern protest successes and the labour support they enjoyed provide much of the evidence offered by historians who stress the potential of the 1940s movement. However, one has to bear in mind the location of Powell's success: Harlem, the nation's 'Negro mecca' in the North; and the time: spring 1941 – in other words, before Pearl Harbor, and before the war intensified racial tensions.[23] By contrast, when Montgomery blacks launched their more famous bus boycott in 1955, local company officials were able to point to a white union-backed colour bar as a major obstacle preventing the employment of black drivers.[24]

The performance of the wartime FEPC in the South had also revealed the immense difficulties that the post-war CIO recruiting drive would face. The FEPC was more token than substance, as Randolph's critics had complained when he called off the march. It had no powers of enforcement, and Roosevelt's choice as FEPC chairman, Mark Ethridge, a southern moderate, hurried to reassure the powerful southern Democratic bloc. He offered his opinion that 'there is no power in the world – not even in all the mechanized armies of the earth, Allied and Axis – which could now force the Southern white people to the abandonment of the principle of social segregation'. Nor did the agency's attitude improve with Ethridge's departure. Only 227 of the 1,108 complaints dealt with by the FEPC were resolved.[25] Thus, the federal government remained a cautious and reluctant executor of any racial reform policy, since it feared white majority sentiment, especially in the South.

Prominent national labour leaders also had reason to be cautious. Rank-and-file prejudice had not been left behind when the CIO broke away from the endemically racist American Federation of Labor in 1935. Flagship CIO unions like the UAW had experienced racial divisions within their own membership during the war. Before unionization, the black community's leading white ally had been the Ford Motor Company management, and so the UAW's victory in the 1941 Ford strike had marked an important shift in black Detroit's loyalties. The NAACP's Walter White wrote to the labour activist and pacifist A.J. Muste after the Ford strike that 'Thomas Addes [a prominent leftist] ... and other top officials of the UAW-CIO impressed me as being sincere in their efforts to keep all of the promises to the Negro Ford workers. But a large number of the [white] workers come from Mississippi, Arkansas, Tennessee and other states of the deep South. They have brought with them to Detroit many of their prejudices, though some of these have been broken down. A great deal however remains to be done'. White workers at other Detroit plants were equally antagonistic to black advancement, and forced the UAW leadership to uphold its public declarations of black-white solidarity. The Ku Klux Klan actively recruited Detroit auto workers, especially at the Packard plant. At the time of the Packard hate strike in June 1943, when twenty-five thousand white workers walked out in protest at the assignment of blacks to semi-skilled jobs, UAW President R.J.Thomas declared that the UAW 'will fight for equal rights for all workers regardless of color. If the KKK and the rest of the nightshirt boys want to fight the union on this issue, we are ready and willing to take them on'.[26]

Despite such fighting talk, the UAW trod a difficult path in its advocacy of interracialism. The structure of work relations did sometimes enable workers of both races to perceive common grievances and the necessity of solidarity. In this context, blacks might have a class consciousness that motivated their protest actions. Conditions in foundries, for instance, were often harsh. Moreover, the concentration of black employment in these phases of production also gave them a potentially powerful strategic role in labour struggles. In this respect, white workers might learn to acknowledge the value of black support. Occasionally, such respect would extend to a more general union support for black civil rights. In the main, however, workplace solidarity did not retain its vigour outside the factory gates. Non-southern whites resented black competition. The massive influx of war workers into Detroit, for example, produced a contest for housing as well as jobs, as illustrated by the Sojourner Truth riot of 1942. A government intelligence report on the incident saw the clash as stemming from a change in both white and black expectations. 'The second generation Poles were the first to take up the battle cry for segregation and discrimination. Like others of foreign descent in Detroit they were beginning to fear competition of young and status conscious Negroes in jobs. The younger Poles are now inducing anti-Negro attitudes among the older generation and the Negroes are being forced out of Hamtramck.'[27]

The Ku Klux Klan was implicated in the Sojourner Truth controversy and in the so-called 'hate strike' wave. It was shortly after this strike wave that an incident on Belle Island amusement park precipitated the Detroit riot of 1943. During the disturbances, the conduct of Detroit's police and its subsequent endorsement by Mayor Jeffries indicated that he had reneged on his promise to end police brutality against the black community. Jeffries's easy re-election victory in late 1943 consequently indicated the strength of the white backlash, which not even the UAW could overcome.[28] If the new labour history deserves praise for reminding us that black workers saw themselves as workers as well as blacks, the old orthodoxy still has validity in its emphasis on the way white workers saw themselves as whites as well as workers. While the union leadership might see the imperative of solidarity and be able to convince white workers of the expediency of interracial action on the shopfloor, its hegemony beyond the plant gates was too contested to ensure white support for black aspirations in terms of housing and education. The most that can be said was that the issue was contested and that white working class hostility to black civil rights should not be automatically assumed.

If racial tension was aggravated by the civilian migration of white and black southerners northwards, it was similarly intensified by the military mobilization of white and black northerners which led to their sojourn at training camps in the South. Pete Daniel notes how white northern recruits seized upon the race issue as a focus for their discontent at the boredom of life on southern rural bases. Simultaneously, northern black soldiers, unaccustomed to legal segregation, were reported to 'fiercely hate Southern conditions. They talk against discrimination on every occasion and encourage violence as a way out'.[29]

Military service in this respect is a neglected strand of the new labour history, yet the shared experience and the camaraderie it bred among black recruits made southern training camps the equivalent of factories or mines in terms of social relations. Grievances and struggles bred militancy which spread to some extent to the local population. Enlisted blacks were assured the warmest welcome in southern black churches, which were key communal institutions. There was a tradition, similar to that found among immigrants who returned to Europe, whereby local people gave a hearing to those who had 'seen the world'. Moreover, by the deprived economic standards of the plantation South, army pay – as planters pointed out testily – represented a respectable income, and this made the soldiers still more welcome congregants to the local pastor and his flock. Such an altered congregation inspired the preaching of less submissive texts, and, given the itinerant character of many southern black pastorates, the new lessons got around.

One should not exaggerate the transformation, but there is evidence of a shift. Federal observers remarked with surprise from Mississippi that 'the Negro church has become the means here and there for encouraging the Negroes to resist the controls which the landlord has held over them. Ideas about "rights" are being introduced in a few instances to Negro share-croppers through Negro preachers and their educated white and Negro friends'.[30] After the war black veterans, both occasionally in practice and more constantly in the perception of white southerners, became dissenters against the Jim Crow system. Veterans like the young Medgar Evers of Mississippi returned home prepared to fight for the vote. Hundreds of others met in Atlanta, Georgia in December 1945 to pledge themselves to support a campaign for the 'full share of democracy' for which they had fought. The NAACP's legal victory against the all-white primary in *Smith v Alwright* (1944) encouraged black voter registration. Between 1940 and 1947 the proportion of eligible black voters registered in the South rose from two to twelve per cent, mainly in the cities and outside the Deep South. In response, white southerners resorted to lynching and other acts of violence.[31] Among the most notorious incidents was the punching out of the eyes of Sergeant Isaac Woodard by an Aiken, South Carolina policeman, only three hours after Woodard completed his army service. When Walter White recounted this atrocity to President Truman at a White House meeting on 19 September 1946, Truman is alleged to have exclaimed: 'My God! I had no idea that it was as terrible as that! We've got to do something!'[32]

This wave of racial attacks provided a focus for the national campaigning energies of black radicals like Paul Robeson and in particular for the Civil Rights Congress (CRC).[33] The Congress was an amalgamation of the National Negro Congress, the International Labor Defense and the National Federation for Constitutional Liberties in 1946. It was pushed to prominence by William Patterson, best known for his polemical attack on US racism, *We Charge Genocide* (1951), which was presented as a petition to the United Nations indicting the US government. Under Patterson, the CRC focused heavily on cases of judicial repression such as those of Willie McGee, Rosa Lee Ingram, the Trenton Six, and the Martinsville Seven. Like the Communist Party in the famous Scottsboro Case of the 1930s, the CRC always differed from the NAACP in its emphasis on mass protest as well as legal manoeuvre. As the legal appeal process neared exhaustion, the CRC launched a 'program of action to save Willie McGee' which included petitions, lobbying politicians by mail or in person, meeting ministers, pickets, work stoppages, parades and constant publicity. The last was especially evident overseas, where the McGee case in particular caused the US government international embarassment as the Cold War deepened.[34]

Although the NAACP appreciated that international support was an additional source of pressure on the federal government for racial reform, it refused to join the CRC in the struggle to save Willie McGee. Indeed, the publicity the latter thus gained prompted the NAACP to attack its radical rival for black protest funds. At the NAACP annual convention in 1951, Walter White told the audience:

> When next Communists or anyone else come to you for funds to 'save Willie McGee' ask them these questions: Does your organization account to the public through a certified public accountant's audit of all monies raised and expended? What is your record of success or failure in such cases? Is your purpose honestly to save Negroes from injustice or is it to show up and ridicule American judicial processes? Is the master you serve freedom and democracy or some other form of government or ideology?[35]

Hence, just as the Red Scare impelled the labour movement to purge its ranks of communists, it simultaneously intensified the desire of black civil rights leaders to distance themselves from the so-called 'unAmerican' left.[36] It is this purge which is central to the argument that an opportunity for racial advancement was lost at the end of the 1940s and that the 1950s could not recover it. However, even the example of the UAW in Detroit used by Korstad and Lichtenstein to illustrate the vigour of organized labour's commitment to black rights becomes less persuasive in the context of Jeffries' victory over UAW opposition in the Detroit mayoral election of 1943, and of the potent ethnocultural origins of anti-communism in the postwar labour movement, which ousted the left in unions like the UAW.[37]

Another well-known antecedent of the civil rights movement was the Congress of Racial Equality (CORE), because of its emphasis on non-violence and devout integrationism. While the newly formed CORE had cooperated with the MOWM, leading figures like James Farmer still took the view that: 'Trying to break down social and economic barriers of segregation while nurturing mental barriers of segregation is fantastic.... We cannot destroy segregation with the weapon of segregation.' This integrationism indicated a philosophical comity that would later allow Farmer to work prominently for the NAACP, while its emphasis on non-violent direct action led to his fellow Chicago

CORE member Bayard Rustin becoming an important advisor to Randolph and much later, to Martin Luther King. However, CORE was a minor player in the context of the 1940s. At the outset, for instance, CORE struggled to distinguish itself from A.J. Muste's pacifist Fellowship of Reconciliation (FOR) because of overlapping membership and a considerable financial dependence on the older organization. While pacifism was a logical companion to nonviolence, its objectives in war-time were likely to drain energies from the racial agenda of CORE. Bayard Rustin, for instance, was jailed in 1944 as a conscientious objector.[38]

CORE's dreams of launching a national campaign of non-violent action culminated in the so-called Journey of Reconciliation in 1947. This first Freedom Ride throws further doubt on the viability of the blacks-with-organized-labour coalition. In *Morgan v Virginia* (June 1946) the Supreme Court had ruled that it was unconstitutional for the Virginia legislature to require segregation on interstate motor carriers.[39] However, given the difficulty of separating interstate and intrastate travellers, the bus lines made little attempt to desegregate. To CORE activists this non-compliance demonstrated the inadequacy of a legalistic approach, and they resolved to force implementation by non-violent direct action. The FOR provided the financial backing for a group of sixteen men (eight whites and eight blacks) to travel by bus through the upper South: Virginia, North Carolina and Kentucky. The travellers experienced little trouble in Virginia but Bayard Rustin, a black law student named Andrew Johnson, and the white editor of the Workers Defense League (WDL) news bulletin, James Peck, were arrested in Durham, North Carolina. At Cargill, a mill town just outside Chapel Hill, in an area specially targeted for unionization by CIO organizers, Johnson and Rustin were arrested again along with Joe Felmet of the white WDL and Igal Roodenko, a white New Yorker. Released on bail, the men narrowly escaped a pursuing crowd of angry whites. The remaining arrests occurred in Felmet's home town of Asheville, North Carolina, where Peck and black Chicagoan Dennis Banks were sentenced to thirty days on a road gang. CORE leaders hoped that the NAACP would take the cases on appeal to the Supreme Court, but the Association judged the existing court record too thin to support a constitutional appeal.[40]

The Journey is largely remembered as the prototype for the later CORE-sponsored Freedom Ride, and the quiet suppression of the former is contrasted with the outcry that greeted white southern violence in 1961. However, one should also note the leftist-labour background of the white participants. This can be cited as further confirmation, if any were needed, of the character of the civil rights movement of the 1940s. However, as with Clayton Powell's bus boycott of 1941, equally significant is the location. CORE organizers deliberately avoided the Deep South. Their mission was not intended to be provocative, since at this stage CORE was wedded to a redemptive philosophy of non-violence which stressed the re-education of the oppressor. The purpose was indeed reconciliation. Yet even in the Upper South, they met official repression and the threat of vigilante violence. Significantly, the arrests occurred in the mill towns of North Carolina – the focal point of the CIO's unsuccessful Operation Dixie in the summer of 1946.

The importance of unionizing the southern textile industry had increased during the war. Northern mills were closing and southern mills were multiplying. By 1945, there were 250,000 fewer textile workers in the North than in 1940 but 100,000 more below the Mason Dixon line.[41] The textile industry employed more people than any other industry in the South but it was a 'whites only' industry. Indeed, job opportunities were so scant for blacks in textile areas that they were inclined to move away. A 1952 survey found no black weavers, spinners or loom fixers among the 400,000 textile workers in Virginia and the Carolinas.[42] However, the virtual absence of black workers from this key industry did not reduce the explosiveness of the race issue. On the contrary, it magnified its importance, since the economic and social status of the white millworkers (or 'lintheads' as they were called) was so meagre that their psychological share in white supremacy was profoundly significant. Given the depth and rawness of this prejudice, it was easy for the employers to exploit the race issue. As Barbara Griffith explains:

> Viewed from an orthodox segregationist perspective, anyone – especially a fellow Southerner, as many of the Operation Dixie organizers were – who could even *consider* trying to form an integrated union was so flagrantly bucking entrenched custom and reason that a truly extraordinary explanation was called for. How to account for such deviant behavior? The logic was both simple and compelling: Only Communists would seriously try to mix the races in a labor union.[43]

One-third of all southern textile workers lived in North Carolina, and so it became Operation Dixie's major focus. Unfortunately for the CIO, while North Carolina's textile plants were almost 'lily-white', its tobacco and lumber industries employed mainly blacks. Indeed, the CIO's Food, Tobacco, Agricultural and Allied Workers Union (FTA-CIO) was much more successful in its membership drives in the Tarheel state than was the Textile Workers Union of America. The FTA-CIO had unionized the R.J. Reynolds plant in Winston-Salem in 1943, and during Operation Dixie was noted as a radical union which pioneered integrated picket lines. However, this progressiveness could be readily turned against the CIO in the textile industry. William Smith, Operation Dixie's North Carolina director, believed that FTA habitually circulated literature that could be 'deeply harmful' because of its treatment of the race question.[44] Thus, the Journey of Reconciliation drove directly into an already inflamed situation in 1947. Some local people were evidently on the alert for what they deemed to be race-mixing, communistic outside agitators, while others were sufficiently cowed to do nothing to help the CORE riders.

This casts doubt upon Korstad and Lichtenstein's claims about the relative potential of the 1940s and 1950s civil rights movements. By citing the positive experience of the FTA rather than the more crucial defeat of the much larger textile unionization effort, they exaggerate labour's success in the South. Other labour historians have argued for the importance of the marriage between a bi-racial shopfloor insurgency and black communal militancy. In his study of the United Packinghouse Workers of America (UPWA), for instance, Eric Halpern has stressed that the union rebuilt itself after a disastrous 1948 strike on the basis of its large black membership. However, even he concedes that the union's increasing involvement in civil rights campaigning alienated many white workers, particularly in the case of anti-housing discrimination efforts in Chicago. Indeed, once the UPWA moved its Chicago offices from the white ethnic Back-of-the-Yards district to Wabash Avenue in the ghetto, few white members attended meetings. By the 1950s the Chicago branch had been trans-formed from an inter-racial class organization to a black headed and directed institution with dwindling and largely passive white support.[45]

The negative impact of giving priority to black workers' concerns and the susceptibility of white workers to racist appeals both suggest that the radical coalition posited as an alternative to New Deal liberalism was extremely fragile. By comparison, Truman's Democratic Party looked like a much more viable partner to national labour and civil rights leaders. The combination of Truman's endorsement of his Committee on Civil Rights's report *To Secure These Rights* and his Executive Orders constituted an unprecedented presiden-tial commitment to the cause of racial equality. The clear-cut commitment to civil rights legislation in the 1948 Democratic platform was not of Truman's choosing but it still precipitated the Dixiecrat revolt as a sign that elements in the South were ready to say 'Never' on the segregation or 'social' issue. The States' Rights Democratic ticket carried the thirty-eight electoral college votes of Alabama, Louisiana, Mississippi, and South Carolina, plus one from Ten-nessee. The regular Democratic vote southwide fell by a fifth, yet Truman still carried the South's remaining eighty-eight electoral votes.[46]

However costly such defections threatened to be, Truman could afford to make such enemies, whereas his rival on the left, Progressive Henry Wallace, was overwhelmed by them. While black civil rights leaders took Truman's narrow, indeed surprise re-election as confirmation that the black vote did hold the balance of power in presidential contests, had that vote gone to Wallace, the beneficiaries would have been the Republicans. Given the resurgence of corporate management and its Congressional allies in the postwar years, fear of a Republican victory kept the CIO loyal to Truman. The failure of Opera-tion Dixie, alongside so many other setbacks in recent years, stacked the odds in favour of the pragmatists against the militants. The former knew that secur-ing or blocking legislation on a wide range of policy issues would require dealing with a powerful conservative coalition of Republicans and southern

Democrats. Moreover, while the election of 1948 marked the establishment of the civil rights issue on the political agenda of the two main parties, it also signalled its subordination to the question of anti-communism.[47]

While deploring this outcome, the proponents of the 'lost opportunity' thesis rarely suggest how the radicalism they uncover at the grassroots might have triumphed over liberalism in national Democratic circles. They lament that the solidarity of the labour movement was too weak and imply that the subsequent civil rights movement was always too removed from the workplace and the realities of class relations. The bi-racial working-class organizations they describe are an important corrective to the orthodox portrait of American labour as intrinsically hostile to black advancement, but the unearthed local successes have not yet been fitted into the national pattern. Perhaps it will prove a matter of generational succession after all. The black workers who secured better jobs, pay and conditions through labour activism in the 1940s were better placed to send their children to college in the 1960s and to support activist clergy in their local churches. In this way, the black labour gains of the 1940s fuelled the later movement.

The Dangers of White Allies

Let us now turn to an alternative critique of the development of the civil rights movement. Whereas the new labour history points to a bi-racial class consciousness, black nationalists stress the fundamentality of racial consciousness and deplore the movement's misguided commitment to the ideal of racial integration. Like the labour historians, proponents of this view regard the alliance with white liberals as the strategic error of the 1950s protest movement, and the ultimately disappointing performance of such liberals encourages this verdict. Let us begin therefore with the liberals.

Northern urban liberals had embraced sociologist Gunnar Myrdal's oversanguine assessment of the prospects for improved race relations based on the modernization of the southern political economy, the world leadership role of the United States and, in particular, the moral imperatives of the so-called 'American Creed'.[48] Truman himself had echoed Myrdal's reasoning in his February 1948 message to Congress. 'There is a serious gap between our ideals and some of our practices', Truman told Congress. 'This gap must be closed.' In the wake of the Nazi holocaust many liberals saw prejudice as a virulent infection which, left untreated, might culminate in fascism. As the GI bill made college accessible to Americans in unprecedented numbers, liberals looked to education as a way of reducing prejudice and providing opportunities for the disadvantaged. Moreover, as Myrdal had anticipated and Truman confirmed, the international position of the United States made racial prejudice profoundly embarassing in the propaganda battle for allies. After 1947 this

Cold War mentality urged Americans to set their own house in order to ensure victory in the propaganda war with international communism. In a major campaign speech in Chicago, Truman declared that when citizens were deprived of the right to vote and 'other basic rights and nothing is done about it that is an invitation to communism'.[49]

Mesmerized by the continuing prospect of presidential support and favourable judicial decisions, national civil rights leaders like Randolph and White hesitated to break with Truman and were therefore inclined to be more supportive of the Korean War. The hysteria of the Red Scare stifled attempts to emulate the Double V campaign of World War Two, which had used the pressure of emergency conditions to gain concessions. However, Truman's dependence on white southern congressional support for the Cold War effort, a political reality which Myrdal had not anticipated, meant that he did not give priority to a civil rights legislative programme: FEPC, anti-lynching and anti-poll tax bills languished in the Senate. With federal action blocked, northern liberals turned to state and local campaigns. Northern and western states and cities passed FEPC laws, and eighteen states desegregated public accommodation. There was also a wave of educational campaigns designed to extirpate prejudice, particularly among whites, as Myrdal had stressed that race was essentially a problem in the minds of the white majority. However, Myrdal had overestimated the daily influence of the American creed. Robert Merton suggested as early as 1949, and Nahum Medalia affirmed strongly in 1962, that generalized beliefs seldom determine conduct in specific situations. In the North, the same person might shop with blacks without concern, might belong to a union like the UAW or the packinghouse workers which strongly endorsed a policy of non-discrimination, yet still be deeply opposed to the idea of blacks buying a house in his neighbourhood. Just such varying levels of prejudice in different contexts, Medalia concluded, would come to the South as it became more urbanized and industrialized.[50] Contrary to liberal assumptions, modernization would not lead inevitably to improvement but to a more homogeneous national pattern of *de facto* segregation and institutional racism. Gradualism, the liberals' instinctive preference, was thus misguided and their promise of progress through consensual bargaining was a confidence trick.

The rank-and-file militants – often communists who had struggled to establish unionism among black and white workers – were sacrificed by liberals during the Red Scare partly because a faith in gradualism persuaded national leaders that the long-term interests of their organizations were best served tactically by a period of accommodationism which would protect existing gains in readiness for the next progressive phase. Such figures placed their faith in education and the rationalism of modernity. Studies had shown a definite correlation between prejudice and low levels of education, and as racial prejudice was seen by modern authorities such as Myrdal as primarily attitudinal rather than economically functional, education would eliminate prejudice by changing individual attitudes. Southern-style segregation was also regarded as a product of the region's general backwardness, and in this respect its eradication was predicted as the South industrialized and urbanized. Such faith in long-term trends often inclined white liberals to gradualism. Moreover, racial equality was not the undisputed burning issue among the white intelligentsia.[51] In 1950, the war in Korea and the use of Red-baiting to secure office (as in the case of freshman Senator Richard M. Nixon of California) or to unseat an incumbent (as in the case of Senator Millard E. Tydings of Maryland) gave white liberals additional concerns. For those concerned with racial issues, the election of segregationist James F. Byrnes as governor of South Carolina, the re-election of Herman Talmadge as governor of Georgia, and the defeat of prominent New Deal Senators Claude Pepper of Florida and Frank P. Graham of North Carolina cast a shadow.[52] There were also gains however: the NAACP's twin victories over segregated graduate school education, via *Sweatt v Painter* and *McLaurin v Regents of Oklahoma*, and the implementation of desegregation in the armed forces, albeit under the exigencies of actual combat. The struggle for black rights at the local level, such as the campaign to desegregate public accommodations in Washington D.C., continued to include public protest just as the struggle to secure workers' rights continued to involve shopfloor militancy, but in both instances national organizations and spokespersons strove to preserve a reputation for moderation and legality.[53]

The national civil rights establishment saw successful litigation and unobtrusive but effective lobbying of the President as the main parts of its strategy. In the summer of 1950, Thurgood Marshall led a strategy meeting of the NAACP's Legal Defense Fund which decided that the Association would no longer pursue so-called equalization suits, cases in which blacks used the *Plessey* doctrine of separate but equal facilities to argue that segregation, as currently practised, infringed the Fourteenth Amendment's guarantees of equal treatment. As the Supreme Court itself indicated in its ruling of 1954, this shift of strategy followed logically from the NAACP's victories in the *Sweatt* and *McLaurin* cases. In both instances, unquantifiable deficiencies in segregated educational provision had persuaded the court to order integration at the graduate school level. Four years later, the court accepted social psychologist Kenneth B. Clark's evidence of damage to the self-esteem of black grade-school children and cited Myrdal's *An American Dilemma* to overturn the *Plessey* doctrine.

The *Brown* decision represented the culmination of a long-standing NAACP campaign against segregated education and was in keeping with an emphasis in mainstream liberalism on education as a crucial sphere for positive social engineering. But as southern liberals exclaimed in May 1954, it was not gradualist. The initial judgement did seem to represent a dramatic assault on what Herbert Blumer has defined as the 'inner' as opposed to the 'intermediate' and 'outer color line'. Writing in 1965, Blumer explained that 'as a metaphor, the color line is not appropriately represented by a single, sharply drawn line but appears rather as a series of ramparts, like the "Maginot Line", extending from outer breastworks to inner bastions. Outer portions of it may, so to speak, be given up only to hold steadfast to inner citadels'.[54] The outer line ensured 'the segregated position of Negroes in the public arena'. It denied blacks 'free access to public accommodations and public institutions, the enjoyment of the franchise, the equal protection of the laws, and equal rights as consumers'. The intermediate colour line related to black economic subordination and opportunity restriction. And the inner citadel concerned intimate friendships between whites and blacks, an area which can be seen as one properly outside of formal governmental control.[55]

The public school system was a point of intersection for the different 'color lines', but to the parents of children involved it clearly threatened the inner citadels of prejudice. The local school was a major public institution. Indeed, Chief Justice Warren took the view that 'education is perhaps the most important function of state and local government'. Education was also crucially conceived as the foundation of opportunity and economic advancement. To quote Warren's opinion in the *Brown* decision again, 'it is doubtful that any child may reasonably be expected to succeed in life if he is denied the opportunity of an education'.[56] However, schools, particularly high schools in the 1950s, were key institutions of social interaction in which being popular, making the football team, and finding a 'date' were vital concerns to students, and precisely those concerns which agitated parents at the visceral level of the 'inner color line'. Chief Justice Warren recalled that Eisenhower once told him that southerners 'are not bad people. All they are concerned about is to see that their sweet little girls are not required to sit in school alongside some big overgrown Negroes'.[57] Consequently, southern moderates accurately predicted a stormy reception. Justice Hugo Black from Alabama warned his colleagues that a decision striking down segregation would 'mean the end of southern liberalism for the time being'.[58]

Gunnar Myrdal had tried to reassure Americans of the possibility of progress on the race question by a chart of the rank order of discrimination which suggested that what whites feared the most – the personal interracial intimacy symbolized by miscegenation – was what blacks least desired. Conversely, what blacks wanted most – legal protection and political and economic opportunity – whites claimed to be most willing to concede.[59] Yet such declarations of principle were, like the American Creed, contradicted by actual practice. The continuing defeat of anti-lynching legislation by the southern Congressional bloc frustrated hopes that the South would be compelled to reform its racist policing practices. Meanwhile, police in northern ghetto areas were feared and detested for their brutality. Equally, the defeat of federal fair employment legislation by conservative Republicans, anxious to preserve employers' rights, and southern Democrats anxious to preserve not simply the 'intermediate color line' but the attractiveness of their native region to business as an area of low wages, low taxes, low unionization and minimum governmental interference, dampened prospects for improved black economic opportunity.

On the voting issue, although the Supreme Court had struck down the white primary in 1944, this was given little cognizance in the Deep South. However, disenfranchisement was a vulnerable issue, especially when its instruments – like the poll-tax – denied the vote to poor whites as well as blacks. Governor James Folsom of Alabama, 'the little man's big friend', called for repeal of the poll tax. This, along with other populistic causes, made him the overwhelming choice of poor whites in the hills, the wire-grass, and the urban working-class districts, and also of the small and largely urban black electorate. Conversely, Folsom alienated the county bosses of the black belt.[60] The latter cherished and exploited the key instruments of disenfranchisement, the literacy and understanding tests and other procedures which were applied at the discretion of local registrars. Neither Truman's expansion of the Justice Department nor Lyndon Johnson's hard-bargained-for Civil Rights Act of 1957 or that of 1960 effectively answered black complaints about the virtual annulment of the Fifteenth Amendment in the Deep South. These injustices would not be addressed until the Voting Rights Act of 1965.[61]

Thus, Myrdal's hope that the vicious circle of cumulative causation in American racial inequality could be broken came to rest on the issue of school desegregation. The Warren Court judged that to separate Negroes 'from others of similar age and qualifications solely because of their race generates a feeling of inferiority as to their status in the community that may affect their hearts and minds in a way unlikely ever to be undone'.[62] It ruled that separate educational facilities were inherently unequal. The only cure for the damage done to black self-esteem was desegregation.

The Court thus rejected the reasoning of John W. Davis, counsel for the South Carolina white defendants in the schools cases. Davis asked the court to consider the likely consequences of court-ordered integration in a county with 2,800 black pupils and 300 white ones:

> If it is done on the mathematical basis, with thirty children as a maximum ... you would have twenty seven Negro children and three whites in one schoolroom. Would that make the children happier? Would they learn any more quickly? Would their lives be more serene?
>
> Children of that age are not the most considerate animals in the world, as we all know. Would the terrible psychological disaster being wrought, according to some of these witnesses, to the coloured child be removed if he had three white children sitting somewhere in the same schoolroom?
>
> Would white children be prevented from getting a distorted idea of racial relations if they sat with twenty seven Negro children?[63]

What added pungency to these words was the fact that South Carolina under Governor James F. Byrnes was so desperate to keep segregation that it had set up a massive programme to bring black schools up to equality in quantifiable terms. According to Harold Cruse, this was a missed opportunity. The tragedy for southern blacks, he claims, was that the NAACP had become so wedded to what he terms 'non-economic liberalism' that it underestimated the benefits to be obtained under a genuine equalization programme in terms of the development of black communal resources. Following Myrdalian liberalism, the NAACP regarded segregation as the primary evil, and thus sought court-enforced integration as a protection against discrimination. Cruse, on the other hand, argues that equalization would have strengthened blacks as a group, enabling them to compete in America's pluralistic political economy. Thurgood Marshall was mistaken to see equalization as simply a tactic in the battle for integration, a lever with which to swell the fiscal costs of maintaining segregation to unacceptable levels. Instead, the NAACP should have insisted on genuine measurable equality which would have given southern black communities additional resources yet preserved their control over their local schools.[64]

While the subsequent history of school desegregation has proved so troubled that few liberals would regard the *Brown* decision with the fervent enthusiasm with which they greeted it in 1954, it seems that Cruse's harsh judgement typifies the pitfalls of historical interpretation from an uncritically presentist perspective. While black Americans in the 1990s argue the merits of separatist institutions within a framework of protective legislation, the appeal of their critique (particularly from the perspective of contemporary metropolitan ghettos) should not distort the historical assessment of past strategies for racial advancement. Cruse, for instance, greatly exaggerates the autonomy of black school leaders in the South under segregation. Whatever their private sentiments, few teachers were as bold as Septima Clark in their challenge to white superiors. Instead, the Booker T. Washington tradition of interracial diplomacy was the dominant one among black school administrators. Even at the college level, instructors like Jo Ann Robinson knew the pressures that could be brought to bear on their college principals. Consequently, when Robinson and her fellow members of the Women's Political Council used the local Montgomery college mimeograph to copy handouts urging a boycott of local buses in 1955, they did so secretly so that the principal could legitimately deny all knowledge of such action to white authorities.[65] Wherever the movement campaigned in the 1960s, it secured relatively little active support from teachers and principals because of their economic vulnerability. Principals, in particular, were threatened with financial cuts and loss of programme accreditation if they failed to discipline both faculty and student participants in civil rights protests.

Moreover, educators, like the majority of the black clergy, were members of a black bourgeoisie whose relationship to segregation was ambivalent. While the colour line deeply wounded the self-esteem of educated middle-class blacks by its denial of status expectations, it maintained the elite position of such individuals in the closed world of Jim Crow. Integration of schools threatened black teachers with a loss of status, authority or even employment, since only a minority of black educators had had the educational and professional opportunities to compete with their white counterparts in terms of formal qualifications. Cruse bemoans the effects of integration upon black communal resources, largely one suspects from a northern metropolitan perspective derived from the fact that ambitious black teachers in an integrated school system sometimes prefer to work and live in suburbia rather than struggle in the *de facto* segregation of ghetto life. Given the ability of white southern elites to eviscerate the integration imperative within *Brown* in the first decade of implementation, it is not extravagant to conclude that a decision that re-affirmed *Plessy* in terms of its acceptance of separation would have produced the same evasion of the principle of equal opportunity in the long term.[66] For instance, giving the same capitation payment per student and even the same capital allowances to schools with vastly different socio-economic constituencies does not ensure equality, it simply formalizes the difference between one area in which most parents can afford to make supplementary voluntary provision and other areas where parents cannot.

While one may question the sincerity of South Carolina's commitment under Governor Byrnes to the principle of equal educational opportunity, and regard the proposed increase in funding for black schools as a strategem to maintain the substance of segregation in the context of overwhelming black economic subordination, one cannot dismiss so readily John W. Davis's doubts about the therapeutic benefits of integration. Subsequent study of the children who experienced desegregation fails to show substantial benefits, and in the light of the massive resistance which greeted the token number of students, such as those at Little Rock's Central High school, the psychological trauma of integration seems as grave as anything likely to arise from attendance at an all-black but adequately funded high school.[67]

While the eighty years old Davis seems to anticipate the disdain of the Black Power advocates of the 1960s in his incredulity at the notion that what coloured children needed was the comforting presence of white students, his scenario of a tiny trio of whites in an overwhelmingly black class presages far more the anxieties of white opponents of busing, both North and South. In reality, if children were to be the catalyst for integration, the leaven would be black. Like other exponents of non-violence, the children of 'Black Monday', it might be argued, received a very direct and gruelling education in the politics of citizenship and self-respect.[68] While King's bus boycott is usually seen as the event that placed non-violence at the centre of the civil rights protest, one can also point to the individuals who integrated southern education as powerful examples of such tactics. Indeed, in 1956 press attention was drawn to Alabama initially not by the unknown Montgomery preacher but by

Autherine Lucy and her steadfast attempts to enroll at the state university. Similarly, in Little Rock what triggered federal intervention was the media coverage of a peaceful black quest for the implementation of a federal court order in the face of white violence with tacit local state support.

If the implementation phase of the NAACP's legalistic strategy led inexorably to a form of non-violent direct action, how far did the Montgomery bus boycott mark the emergence of a new movement, and how far did that movement represent an abandonment of what proponents regard as the lost promise either of the labour alliance or of a nationalistic black mass mobilization? The threat of a bus boycott had been discussed in Montgomery for several years. Black political activists like E.D. Nixon, who ascribed his political education to his involvement in Randolph's Brotherhood of Sleeping Car Porters, and the members of the Women's Political Council, who were particularly incensed by the disrespectful treatment they received from white bus drivers, had debated how to secure concessions from a divided city commission.[69] While one could try to magnify Nixon's significant role in the formation of the Montgomery Improvement Association (MIA) and the instigation of the boycott in support of the view that the labour movement of the 1940s was a vital seed-bed for the movement, it may be more revealing to stress that the boycott was a consumers' rather than a workers' protest. One might even tentatively suggest that this use of consumer power reflected much more the selective buying campaigns advocated by W.E.B DuBois among others in the 1930s, which Harold Cruse sees as essential to black advancement.[70]

Aldon Morris has stressed the importance of black communal mobilization as the principal source of the civil rights movement. The growth of communal resources in cities across the South in the 1940s provided a new potential for sustained protest. Within communities, black churches and colleges and a larger black middle class grew by serving the needs of the increased black population. These institutions and personnel might undertake protest at less risk to themselves than was the case for an isolated sharecropper. Morris also points to the neglected connections between protest centres. The earlier Baton Rouge bus boycott was a source of operational guidance for the MIA. This demonstrated how the black ministerial network operated as a disseminator of protest techniques even before the formation of the Southern Christian Leadership Conference.[71] Other scholars have pointed to other external factors in the development of the Montgomery boycott. J. Mills Thornton notes that shortly before the boycott the Reverend Adam Clayton Powell, Jnr., experienced organizer of selective buying and bus boycotts in Harlem, gave a speech to Nixon's Progressive Democratic Association in which he warned the newly formed white Citizens Council that their use of economic intimidation 'can be counter met with our own economic pressure'. Powell also organized a National Deliverance Day of Prayer on 28 March 1956 and sent $2,500 to the MIA.[72] Similarly, Morris notes that prior to her arrest for refusing to surrender her seat, Mrs Rosa Parks had attended a workshop on political activism at Myles Horton's union-sponsored Highlander Folk School. Despite the role of such places – what Morris terms movement halfway houses – the strongest influences were indigenous to the local black community.[73]

Martin Luther King, Jnr's account of the Montgomery bus boycott angered several local leaders by failing to mention earlier protest efforts and by exaggerating the influence of Gandhian non-violence.[74] Indeed, it is questionable whether the Montgomery bus boycott was conceived within the philosophical framework of non-violent direct action. A. Philip Randolph's March on Washington and CORE's Journey of Reconciliation were both far more consistent with Gandhian methodology, since they represented action which required positioning oneself in defiance of a socially unjust situation so as to compel the white power holders to acknowledge and respond to one's demands. The boycott was a withdrawal from the point of confrontation which exerted pressure because blacks made up the bulk of the bus company's clientele. Moreover, although they were among the economically most protected group in the black community, King and the other ministers did not envisage a prolonged campaign but a dramatic gesture – a one-day boycott – followed swiftly by a negotiated settlement in which the bus company and city officials granted greater civility within segregation, leaving desegregation for the courts and legislature to decide. It was the strength of popular support and the intransigence of white authorities that expanded the boycott.[75]

Thus, the recent scholarship on the boycott shares the new emphasis on the contribution of the earlier alliance with organized labour and the primacy of black solidarity. While this may seem like another Old Left attempt to claim the laurels or an ironic recruitment of the slain integrationist to the ranks of Black Power, in practice what is more striking is how much more fragile and uncertain the campaign was than earlier accounts suggested. Martin Luther King, Jnr. was just twenty seven years old in early 1956, so his limitations as a leader should not be surprising, although the charge that he was a poor negotiator would be repeated throughout his career, notably in Chicago in 1966. Notwithstanding his training for the ministry and the committees he set up on his arrival at Dexter Avenue church, he was also inexperienced in organizing collective action and even perhaps temperamentally unsuited to administration. This may explain why the MIA had to surmount a scandal over the use of donations and it certainly explains the slowness with which the SCLC developed following its foundation in 1957; Birmingham 1963 was the SCLC's first major success.[76]

Yet these are the common deficiencies of charismatic leadership and they are evident in other protest movements during their early growth. Equally striking is the initial disinterest of the civil rights mainstream. In 1955 its focus was still school desegregation, as black leaders awaited the Supreme Court's implementation ruling and prayed that Eisenhower would embrace the *Brown* decision publicly in the same way that Truman had endorsed *To Secure These Rights*. Civil rights leaders were to be disappointed on both counts. Rejecting the NAACP's call for a tough, precise schedule for school desegregation, the Supreme Court in *Brown II* turned implementation over to local courts with no more specific timetable than 'with all deliberate speed'. Meanwhile Eisenhower refused to be drawn publicly on his own feelings and thereby gave tacit encouragement to Southern resistance.[77] In this context, the Montgomery bus boycott was an ill-timed distraction for the NAACP, given its increasingly desperate struggle to overcome the South's massive resistance to *Brown*. In Alabama in particular, the Association was fighting for survival as the white political establishment attacked it as a subversive organization.[78] Its New York-based leadership did not want to get involved in ameliorating segregated seating arrangements in the cradle of the Confederacy, though ironically white Alabamans remained convinced that the NAACP lay behind the boycott.[79]

Similarly, A. Philip Randolph and the blacks-with-labour coalition were also preoccupied more with preserving some impetus in a campaign for inter-racial unionism following the merger of the CIO with the American Federation of Labor (AFL) in 1955. This fight to make black rights a priority produced angry clashes between Randolph and AFL-CIO president George Meany. From Meany's perspective, trade unionism was weak enough in the South without alienating existing locals by insisting on racial integration.[80] As mentioned earlier, the MIA's insistence on the hiring of black drivers aroused fierce opposition from the AFL white drivers' union, whose contract stipulated that all drivers had to be hired from the union driving school and which had never admitted a black man for training. Furthermore, as drivers earned a bonus on busy routes and the busiest routes were those serving the black district, drivers were assigned these routes on the basis of seniority, giving little prospect of black drivers on predominantly black routes.[81] Despite E.D. Nixon's Pullman porters' connection, there is no evidence that the MIA drew much guidance from that quarter. The caution of each established group seems to confirm the argument that organizations tend to become so intent upon ensuring their institutional survival that they lose sight of their original objective.[82] In this instance, the Montgomery protests were in a sense a nuisance to the NAACP and black workers' demands an embarrassment to the AFL-CIO.

Indeed, as Ray Arsenault recently observed, it was only the most marginal of civil rights figures from the 1940s – Bayard Rustin – who perceived the significance of the early Montgomery campaign. A former communist, pacifist and convicted homosexual, Rustin had by 1955 become as much an embarrassment as an asset to a civil rights establishment anxious to appear free from the 'unAmerican' attributes with which their opponents regularly smeared them. Rustin believed that the Montgomery campaign had potential, but his first encounter with the MIA leadership also confirmed his opinion that they had no conception of non-violence. King, for instance, was so new to the principles of non-violence that he had accepted friends' advice, as the whites turned to violence, and had taken out a gun permit. When Rustin arrived a loaded hand gun lay on a chair in the young preacher's sitting room![83] Although King's non-violent response to the bombing campaign and his moving sermons highlighting the Christian non-violent aspects of the protest campaign excited national sympathy via the press in 1956, his knowledge of non-violent direct action did not match that of A.J. Muste's disciples at CORE. Thoreau's essay on civil disobedience was scarcely enough.

Thus Rustin, who had left the Communist Party in the early 1940s, who had condemned Randolph's cancellation of the March on Washington as premature in 1941, and who had served time on a South Carolina road gang for his part in the Journey of Reconciliation in 1947, became, after a period in the wilderness, a conduit by which a local movement interacted with the national civil rights leadership. Once the issue became desegregation of intrastate transit, the beleaguered NAACP felt compelled to assist the MIA, though it eyed King, as it did all 'free-lancers', as someone who might divert energies and funds away from the NAACP. While King endeavoured to placate Roy Wilkins by insisting that the SCLC did not seek to compete with the NAACP but to complement its activities, Wilkins remained sceptical, especially when the SCLC switched its attention from de-segregating transit to voter registration.[84]

Rustin was also able to introduce King to A. Philip Randolph, who had remained more active in campaigns against the outer and intermediate colour line issues of disenfranchisement, lynching, and employment discrimination rather than those pertaining to school desegregation. When King shot to national prominence, his association with Randolph came first in 1957 with the so-called Prayer Pilgrimage for Freedom, a mass rally in Washington, D.C. to highlight the continuing disenfranchisement of southern blacks. Randolph probably hoped that King's ministerial network might provide the mechanism for the grassroots mobilization which voter registration campaigns required.[85] However, in the late 1950s this was simply not the case. The SCLC was an administrative shambles whose survival rested upon the fund-raising capabilities of King's eloquence, a foundation threatened by King's near-fatal stabbing in 1958. During these largely fallow years between 1957 and 1960, the faltering potential of SCLC as a protest vehicle was preserved largely due to the efforts of another 1940s veteran, Ella Baker, whose attempts to discipline the male ministerial clique around King at SCLC proved embittering.[86]

The SCLC's decision to switch its energies from the desegregation of transportation to voter registration was logical in some respects. Disenfranchisement was arguably the least defensible area of the outer colour line. Its blatant character offended northern sensibilities and embarrassed the US government overseas. However, the insubstantial character of the Civil Rights Act of 1957 meant that voting rights still had to be secured by agonizing personal efforts on the part of southern blacks. Since King's attempts to transfer the techniques of the bus boycott from Montgomery to other SCLC affiliates had not been successful in either Tallahassee, Florida or Rock Hill, South Carolina, voter registration was seen as the means whereby to oust white supremacist rule, as King indicated in his 'Give Us the Ballot' speech at the Prayer Pilgrimage rally. It was also an issue appropriate to the kind of national figure that King had by then become. However, by choosing voter registration, SCLC selected for itself as arduous a task as had the CIO in 1946 when it launched Operation Dixie. Given that the fate of the latter hinged in practice on the outcome of factory elections on whether the union should be accepted by the National Labor Relations Board as the workers' chosen representative, Operation Dixie did resemble a voter registration campaign.[87]

Like Operation Dixie before it and the Voter Education Project after it, the SCLC's Crusade for Citizenship disappointed its initiators in quantifiable terms, especially in the rural black belt. However, in all three cases, one should not discount a longer-term politicizing effect. Indeed, scholars like Aldon Morris have stressed the importance of this role of the early SCLC, its local affiliates and of local NAACP branches, especially the youth councils, in the late 1950s in preparing the movement centres from which the protests of the 1960s sprang.[88] Nevertheless, one can suggest that it would have been equally logical for SCLC to move its desegregation efforts from transportation to public accommodations in general. Given King's reluctance to get involved in the later sit-ins in Atlanta and his role as mediator between student activists and the black political establishment there (which included his father), one can speculate that King's move to Atlanta played a part in the change of strategy, since voter registration was quite acceptable to the black Atlanta elite and its white allies, anxious to strengthen their mutual bargaining power and to over-turn the hostile influence of the white supremacist black belt within Georgia politics.[89]

Conclusion

Thus, at the end of the 1950s, as at the close of the previous decade, moments of democratic promise were perceptible. In the 1940s, these instances had been particularly vulnerable in the South, but with the emergence of a movement more clearly rooted in the indigenous institutions of the black South, particu-larly its churches, the potential for sustained action had increased. However, the passage of knowledge from the predominantly northern labourite movement of the 1940s to the southern quasi-religious movement of the late 1950s and from generation to generation was difficult and partial. For a majority, one sus-pects, education for activism came principally from participation. Thus, to stress the strands of continuity between the protest movements of the post-war decades can ultimately prove misleading. Veterans of earlier movements like Bayard Rustin or Ella Baker or A. Philip Randolph had their greatest impact when they confirmed the inclinations and preferences of current protest leaders. Equally misleading are critiques of past strategy from the perspective of values whose appeal is derived from the postulates of past achievements; *separate but plural* attracts because of the victory over *separate but equal*. Thus, to see the 1940s as the 'daybreak of freedom'[90] or the 1950s as the closing in of a doomed long night of obsessive integrationism and non-economic liberalism are potentially distortions.[91] Yet future historians will doubtless feel impelled to search the twilight of the past for beginnings and endings, to use the metaphors of dawn and dusk as more than literary conventions, and in the black protest movement of the 1950s, they will, of course, find both.

Notes

1. For details of these developments, see Richard Kluger, *Simple Justice: The History of Brown v Board of Education and Black America's Struggle for Equality*, 2 vols. (New York: Alfred A. Knopf, 1975); David Garrow (ed), *The Walking City: The Montgomery Bus Boycott, 1955-1956* (Brooklyn, N.Y.: Carlson Publishing, 1989); and T. Freyer, *The Little Rock Crisis: A Constitutional Interpretation* (Westport, Conn.: Greenwood Press, 1984).
2. Eric Foner, *Reconstruction: America's Unfinished Revolution, 1863-1877* (New York: Harper & Row, 1988), p. 603.
3. A. Pinkney, *The Myth of Black Progress* (London: Cambridge University Press, 1984); cf. A. Hacker, *Two Nations: Black and White, Separate, Hostile and Unequal* (New York: Scribner, 1992).
4. R. Farley, *Blacks and Whites: Narrowing the Gap?* (Cambridge, Mass.: Harvard University Press, 1984), p. 40.
5. R.M. Dalfiume, 'The Forgotten Years of the Negro Revolution', *Journal of American History*, 55 (November, 1968); reprinted in B. Sternsher, *The Negro in Depression and War: Prelude to Revolution, 1930-1945* (Chicago: Quadrangle Books, 1969), pp. 298-316.
6. R. Korstad and N. Lichtenstein, 'Opportunities Found and Lost: Labor, Radicals and the Early Civil Rights Movement', *Journal of American History*, 75 (1988), 786-811.
7. J.B. Kirby, *Black Americans in the Roosevelt Era: Liberalism and Race* (Knoxville: University of Tennessee Press, 1980).
8. R. Arsenault, 'Bayard Rustin, National Civil Rights Organizations and the Freedom Struggle', unpublished paper, Civil Rights session, British Association for American Studies Annual Conference, Wolverhampton Polytechnic, 1991.
9. L.E. Lomax, *The Negro Revolt* (New York: Harper & Row, 1962); L. Killian, and C. Griggs, *Racial Crisis in America* (Englewood Cliffs, N.J.: Prentice-Hall, 1964); and A. Lewis et al., *The Second American Revolution: A First-Hand Account of the Struggle for Civil Rights* (London: Faber & Faber, 1966).
10. Carol Mueller, 'Ella Baker and the Origins of Participatory Democracy', and G. Jordan McFadden, 'Septima P. Clark and the Struggle for Human Rights' in V.L. Crawford et

al. (eds), *Women in the Civil Rights Movement: Trailblazers and Torchbearers* (Brooklyn, N.Y.: Carlson Publishing, 1990).

11. Garrow, *Walking City*.
12. A. Meier and E. Rudwick, *CORE: A Study in the Civil Rights Movement, 1942-1968* (New York: Oxford University Press, 1973).
13. C. Green and B. Wilson, *The Struggle for Black Empowerment in New York City: Beyond the Politics of Pigmentation* (New York: Praeger, 1989), p. 12.
14. P.E. Pfeffer, *A. Philip Randolph: Pioneer of the Civil Rights Movement* (Baton Rouge: Louisiana State University Press, 1990).
15. H. Garfinkel, *When Negroes March: The MOWM in the Organizational Politics for FEPC* (Glencoe, Ill.: The Free Press, 1959).
16. M.E. Reed, *Seedtime for the Modern Civil Rights Movement: The President's Fair Employment Practices Committee, 1941-1946* (Baton Rouge: Louisiana State University Press, 1991).
17. R.M. Dalfiume, *Desegregation of the US Armed Forces*, (Columbia, Mo., University of Missouri Press, 1969), p. 33.
18. Pfeffer, *Randolph*, pp. 65, 57.
19. Pfeffer, *Randolph*, chapters III & IV.
20. D.R. McCoy and R.T. Ruetten, *Quest and Response: Minority Rights and the Truman Adminstration* (Lawrence, Kans: University of Kansas Press, 1973), pp. 26-29, 130-31.
21. W. Harris, *Keeping the Faith: A. Philip Randolph, Milton P. Webster and the Brotherhood of Sleeping Car Porters, 1925-1937* (Urbana, Ill.: University of Illinois Press, 1977).
22. D. Capeci, 'From Harlem to Montgomery: The Bus Boycotts of Adam Clayton Powell Jnr. and Martin Luther King Jnr.', in Garrow, *Walking City*, pp. 303-22.
23. H. Sitkoff, 'Racial Militancy and Interracial Violence in the Second World War', *Journal of American History*, 58 (1971), 661-88.
24. Capeci, 'From Harlem to Montgomery', pp. 239-40.
25. G.B. Tindall, *The Emergence of th New South, 1913-1945* (Baton Rouge: Louisiana State University Press, 1967), pp. 713-16.
26. A. Meier and E. Rudwick, *Black Detroit and the Rise of the UAW* (New York: Oxford University Press, 1979), pp. 188-89, 109-10, 192.
27. Meier and Rudwick, *Black Detroit*, p. 178.
28. Meier and Rudwick, *Black Detroit*, pp. 201-07.
29. P. Daniel, 'Going among Strangers: Southern Reactions to World War II', *Journal of American History*, 77 (1990), 893.
30. Daniel, 893.
31. Dalfiume, *Desegregation*, pp. 132-33.
32. McCoy and Ruetten, *Quest and Response*, pp. 44-5, 48.
33. P. Robeson, *Here I Stand* (New York: Othello Associates, 1958).
34. G. Horne, *Communist Front? The Civil Rights Congress, 1946-1956* (London: Associated University Presses, 1988), pp. 14, 89.
35. Horne, pp. 97, 142.
36. D.M. Oshinsky, 'Labor's Cold War: The CIO and the Communists', in R. Griffiths and A. Theoharis (eds), *The Specter: Original Essays on the Cold War and the Origins of McCarthyism* (New York: Franklin-Watts, 1974), pp. 116-51.
37. D.F. Crosby, S.J., 'The Politics of Religion: American Catholics and the Anti-Communist Impulse', in Griffiths and Theoharis, *Specter*, pp. 18-39.
38. Meier & Rudwick, *CORE*, pp. 11, 19.

39. C. Barnes, *Journey from Jim Crow: The Desegregation of Southern Transit* (New York: Columbia University Press, 1983).
40. Meier & Rudwick, *CORE*, pp. 35-39.
41. B.S. Griffith, *The Crisis of American Labor: Operation Dixie and the Defeat of the CIO* (Philadelphia: Temple University Press, 1988), p. 20.
42. J.C. Cobb, *Industrialization and Southern Society, 1877-1984* (Lexington, Ky.: University Press of Kentucky, 1984), p. 83.
43. Griffith, *Crisis of American Labor*, p. 76.
44. Griffith, *Crisis of American Labor*, pp. 81, 74-5.
45. E. Halpern, '"Black and White, Unite and Fight": Race and Labor in Meatpacking, 1904-1948', Ph.D. Thesis, University of Pennsylvania, 1989, (UMI: 51:270A, DA9015101), pp. 496, 539, 541.
46. N. Bartley and H.D. Graham, *Southern Politics and the Second Reconstruction* (Chapel Hill: University of North Carolina Press, 1975), p. 85.
47. H. Sitkoff, 'Harry Truman and the Election of 1948: The Coming of Age of Civil Rights in American Politics', *Journal of Southern History*, 37 (1971), 597-616.
48. G. Myrdal, *An American Dilemma: The Negro Problem and Modern Democracy*, 2 vols. (New York: Harper & Brothers, 1944).
49. W. Jackson, *Gunnar Myrdal and America's Conscience: Social Engineering and Racial Liberalism, 1937-1987* (Chapel Hill: University of North Carolina Press, 1990), p. 277.
50. Jackson, *Myrdal and America's Conscience*, pp. 279, 301-02.
51. J.T. Kneebone, *Southern Liberal Journalists and the Issue of Race* (Chapel Hill: University of North Carolina Press, 1985).
52. Bartley and Graham, *Southern Politics*, p. 52.
53. B. Jones, 'Before Montgomery and Greensboro: The Desegregation Movement in the District of Columbia, 1950-1953', *Phylon*, 43 (1982), pp. 144-54.
54. Blumer in McKinney and Thompson (eds), *South in Continuity and Change*, p. 323.
55. H. Blumer, 'The Future of the Color Line', in J.C. McKinney and E.T. Thompson (eds), *The South in Continuity and Change* (Durham, N.C.: Duke University Press, 1965), pp. 323, 328, 335.
56. P. Escott and D.R. Goldfield (eds), *Major Problems in the History of the American South*, vol. 2 (Boston: D.C. Heath, 1990), p. 540.
57. J. Harvie Wilkinson III, *From Brown to Bakke: The Supreme Court and School Integration* (New York: Oxford University Press, 1979), p. 24.
58. R. King, 'Justice Black, Dr. King and the Public Forum', in R. Kroes and E. Van Bilt (eds), *The US Constitution After 200 Years* (Amsterdam: Free University Press, 1988), p. 102.
59. Myrdal, *American Dilemma*, vol. 1, pp. 60-61.
60. Bartley and Graham, *Southern Politics*, pp. 38-40.
61. Steven F. Lawson, *In Pursuit of Power: Southern Blacks and Electoral Politics, 1965-1982* (New York: Columbia University Press, 1985).
62. Escott & Goldfield (eds), *Major Problems*, vol. 2, p. 541.
63. H. Cruse, *Separate But Plural: A Critical Study of Blacks and Minorities in America's Plural Society* (New York: Morrow, 1987), p. 254.
64. Cruse, *Separate But Plural*, Part 4.
65. Garrow, *Walking City*, pp. 607-20.
66. E. Black and M. Black, *Politics and Society in the South* (Cambridge, Mass.: Harvard University Press, 1987), chapter 7.

67. G.J. Powell, *Black Monday's Children: A Study of the Effects of School Desegregation on the Self-Concepts of Southern Children* (New York: Appleton-Croft, 1973), Part 3.
68. R. King, 'Citizenship and Self-Respect: The Experience of Politics in the Civil Rights Movement', *Journal of American Studies*, 22 (1988), 7-24.
69. Garrow, *Walking City*, pp. 607-20.
70. Cruse, *Separate But Plural*, passim.
71. A. Morris, *The Origins of the Civil Rights Movement: Black Communities Organizing for Change* (Baton Rouge: Louisiana State University Press, 1984).
72. J. Mills Thornton III, 'Challenge and Response in the Montgomery Bus Boycott of 1955-1956', in Garrow (ed), *Walking City*, pp. 343, 312.
73. Morris, *Origins of the Civil Rights Movement*, chapter 7.
74. Martin Luther King, Jnr., *Stride Towards Freedom: The Montgomery Story* (New York: Harper & Row, 1958).
75. A. Fairclough, 'The Preachers and the People: The Origins and Early Years of the SCLC, 1955-1959', *Journal of Southern History*, 52 (1986), 403-40.
76. David Garrow, *Bearing the Cross: Martin Luther King, Jr. and the Southern Christian Leadership Conference* (New York: Morrow, 1986), pp. 50, 78.
77. R.F. Burk, *The Eisenhower Administration and Black Civil Rights* (Knoxville: University of Tennessee Press, 1984).
78. Morris, *Origins*, pp. 26-39.
79. Arsenault, 'Bayard Rustin'.
80. Pfeffer, *Randolph*, pp. 207-8.
81. Capeci in Garrow (ed), pp. 239-40.
82. Frances Fox Piven and Richard A. Cloward, *Poor People's Movements: Why They Succeed, How They Fail* (New York: Vintage Books, 1979).
83. Arsenault, 'Bayard Rustin'.
84. Garrow, *Bearing the Cross*, pp. 91, 97-8, 100-03.
85. Pfeefer, *Randolph*, pp. 176-85.
86. Mueller in Crawford et. al. (eds), *Women in the Civil Rights Movement*.
87. Griffith, *Crisis of American Labour*.
88. Morris, *Origins*, pp. 124-5, 188, 192-4.
89. C.N. Stone, *Regime Politics: Governing Atlanta, 1946-1988* (Lawrence, Kans.: University Press of Kansas, 1989), pp. 52, 54.
90. R. Korstad, '"Daybreak of Freedom": Tobacco Workers and the CIO, Winston-Salem, North Carolina, 1943-1950', Ph.D. Thesis, University of North Carolina-Chapel Hill, 1987, (UMI 49:2788A, DA8221486).
91. Cruse, *Separate But Equal*.

Is he a Bedouin? Post-war American and French Responses to North Africa in the Work of Paul Bowles and Albert Camus

Marzia Balzani and Clive Bush

Comme les plus grands artistes, Melville a construit ses symboles sur le concret, non dans le matériau du rêve. Le créateur de mythes ne participe au génie que dans la mesure où il les inscrit dans l'épaisseur de la réalité et non dans les nuées fugitives de l'imagination.

Camus, 'Herman Melville.'[1]

To this day they have not discovered at the Indies any mediterranian sea as in Europe, Asia and Affrike.

Joseph Acosta, *The Naturall and Morall Histories of the East and West Indies* (trans. E.G.), London: 1604.[2]

In some ways they could not have been more different. The North Africa that came under their scrutiny would emerge from a radical dissimilarity of background, sense of place, culture, political experience, nationalist sensibility, and ideology. But the fact that they were novelists working in the same post-war period meant that structure and literary legacies overlapped and the historical experiences of the thirties and forties were, in the most general sense, shared.

Both were in some senses displaced persons. The position of *pied noir* for Camus in Algeria involved experiencing the contradictions of a culture within a culture as a given, not as a sought-for, condition. In Algeria he was a colonial with the sensibility of a native inhabitant divorced from the culture of the majority of native inhabitants, in France an immigrant but a French writer accepted by the French as part of the French tradition.

As for Bowles, he was a New Englander and an American whose first inclination, in the grand tradition of other American writers like Stein, Pound,

Hemingway, Miller, and Fitzgerald, was to join the literary expatriate community in Paris. These writers were to a greater or lesser degree involved in French culture. Pound's involvement with Provençal culture and the poetry of Mallarmé and Laforgue, and Miller's use of the surrealist experience are cases in point. Like other American writers from the nineteenth century onwards, Bowles sought a world elsewhere. He was to invent a North Africa from 1947 onwards (preceded by Mexico) in the way Henry James and T.S. Eliot invented London, or Hemingway invented Spain. The writers felt a need to distance themselves from the high technological and materialist culture typified increasingly by twentieth century America. For Camus in *L'Homme Révolté* it was part of a political analysis which had begun to take shape as early as 1937:

Les illusions bourgeoises concernant la science et le progrès technique, partagées par les socialistes autoritaires, ont donné naissance à la civilisation des dompteurs de machine qui peut, par la concurrence et la domination, se séparer en blocs ennemis mais qui, sur le plan économique, est soumise aux mêmes lois: accumulation du capital, production rationalisée et sans cesse accrue.[3]

In part it was a reflection of comparative wealth (with favourable exchange rates for the dollar in the Paris of the 1920s), in part an inheritance of the English writer's predeliction for travel, in part a search for an often 'imagined', coherent and timeless culture of long historical duration to balance a world in which the future drove out the present, with its poorly imagined and terrifying expectations, and in which multiplicity, as Henry Adams had noted, replaced unity. The cultures of Mexico, North Africa, and even rural France for someone like Gertrude Stein preserved a sense of communal daily common life which appeared under threat in America. French writers, however, had also felt the pull, and travel writing which bore the ultimately romantic need for a world elsewhere had a long and established tradition in France from Flaubert, through Montherlant and Gide.

'Displacement' was the social result of the political changes of the First World War. It was also an interior condition. The transition from political to economic colonialism which both Camus and Bowles were to experience after the Second World War in North Africa was to intensify that experience and to provide a great deal of the material for their writing. There was both freedom and constraint inside that displacement. Camus's biographer actually makes the comparison with the American cultural experience in describing the French writer's inheritance as a French Algerian: 'They could be what they made of themselves. It was happening at the same time and in the same way in the United States of America but was then no longer possible in old Europe.'[4]

The main difference between the two men in terms of their 'displacement' was that in Camus's case it was involuntary. Algeria was as 'native' for

Camus as it was for the Arabs, and as a radical 'European' writer of this period he was committed to politics in a way Bowles would never be. The point was summed up in the American's statement: 'I have no reason for being anywhere that is certain.'[5] Yet paradoxically the metaphysical *double entendre* one could ring on the statement points, in its moral tone and emotional content, to an experience of *ennui* which Camus would have understood.

The differences in education were marked. Yet in spite of them Camus and Bowles shared interests in the grand narratives of religious culture and discourse. Bowles was as ambiguous about Islam as Camus was about Christianity. Bowles had no important mentor in literature and philosophy like Jean Grenier, but Aaron Copland and Gertrude Stein were teachers by the seriousness of their commitment to art. Both men, Bowles through music, Camus through writing plays and as a producer, were deeply involved in the theatre. Both men were very reticent about their private lives. Both had difficult marriages. However, Bowles, the New Englander, seemed relatively uninterested in sex with either men or women, though he had strong creative friendships with men. Camus was something of a romantic existential seducer but he was clearly also capable of serious friendships with women.

One of the rationales of this essay in 'comparison' is the degree to which both Camus and Bowles were engaged in the literature of each others' countries. This cross-exchange is a fact of both French and American culture of the 1950s. As late as 1957 Norman Mailer was to attempt to create an American existentialist hero in his essay 'The White Negro', and to a degree the literature of the Beats carried European political existentialism into a critique of social values and an anarchist attack on the domestic bourgeois values of the Cold War. As late as the Fall of 1968 Bowles was teaching the French 'existential novel' at the University of San Fernando, where he taught Camus's *L'Etranger*, Sartre's *La Nausée*, 'Intimité', and Simone de Beauvoir's *Le Sang des Autres*. Like Camus, Bowles was deeply influenced by Gide, and like Camus met him briefly. A school-teacher had introduced Bowles to French literature, and the interest so stimulated played at least a part in his first escape across the Atlantic from home and America, reading Gide's *Journal des Faux Monnayeurs*.[6] Later he would translate Sartre's *Huis Clos*, and Mohamed Choukri's memoirs, *Jean Genet in Tangiers*. Paris exerted a considerable pull for everyone in the arts. At the time Camus was drawn to it, it was also the Paris of Pound and Joyce, of *Transition*, of Sylvia Beach, Hemingway, Fitzgerald, Stein and Henry Miller.

American literature arrived seriously in France long before it arrived in Great Britain, with the solitary exception of D.H Lawrence's *Studies in Classic American Literature* of 1924. Sartre was to write essays on Faulkner and Dos Passos,[7] a writer whom Henri Hell invoked in discussing *L'Etranger*.[8] Simone de Beauvoir was swept off her feet by Nelson Algren.[9] From Baudelaire's discovery of Poe (indeed from Jefferson's reading of the Encyclopaedists) to the existentialist writers' welcome of Richard Wright, French and American literature had taken creative measure of each others' strengths. After the war Camus told a New York audience that he had read American literature from Dos Passos to Faulkner, and expressed a worry that the absolute rejection of literariness might impoverish the novel's resources.[10] On the whole he preferred the nineteenth century works of Melville and James.

Camus's essay on Melville shows him to be a sophisticated interpreter of a writer whose use of the ancient resources of epic, and whose sensitivity to the grand moral drama of stories like *Billy Budd*, could echo his own. Both would use the grand themes of the Greeks, and signal in their works a movement out of Romanticism towards the more existentialist dilemmas of the twentieth century. Both were aware that a tragic view of life, an awareness of what Melville called 'Cartesian vortices', was close to the deepest resources of the artist.[11] The only *American* dramatist Camus knew was O'Neill, who in the forties had written his own 'Greek Trilogy'. Shortly before his death Camus was deeply engaged in negotiations with Malraux over a new theatre, and one of the plays which was scheduled to be performed was O'Neill's *Strange Interlude*.[12]

In political terms their worlds seem wide apart, yet in both there is a tendency to place a view of culture *before* political fact, and both the weaknesses and the strengths of their work would derive from a synchronic moral engagement with the experience of cultural and political change.

Camus's political affiliations and activities are well known and documented. Up to 1936 Camus was a communist inside the Popular Front. He wrote to Grenier in 1936 on Gide's joining of the Communist Party that

the artist having suddenly become conscious of his own misery and of human solidarity, suddenly joins a party, simply to get outside himself, just as girls used to decide hastily to marry in order to escape their families. But that makes for unhappy households. It is very possible, therefore, that Gide's marriage with Communism will turn out badly.[13]

And, famously, he said: 'I shall always refuse to place a volume of *Capital* between life and mankind.'[14]

The Algerian Arab communists were poised uneasily between French Colonialism and the Muslim nationalists, a situation that Bowles would exploit in his novel *The Spider's House*. It would be a situation which threatened Camus from both sides. As a Frenchman he would be exposed to Nazism and Fascism in a 'European' sense, as a radical *pied noir* he would loathe colonialism yet not suffer as a Muslim victim of French power, as a 'communist' he could perceive in a way neither Muslim nationalist, nor Algerian communist, nor French colonial officer, the political connections between these systems of oppression. Not to be naively nationalist, naively internationalist, naively colonialist would alienate him from Arab Algerian, colonial Algerian, the world of the *pied noir*, and the world of the communists more or less equally.

There is a sense in which he was *driven* to the high ground of Enlightenment moral and humanist impartiality. Camus was largely ignorant of the details of the nationalist struggle in Algeria, but he risked his life for them nonetheless.[15] However, as his *Actuelles III* show in the eight articles he wrote for *Combat*, his actual non-involvement with the Nationalist movement did not preclude a clear-sighted and detailed understanding of the actuality of Algerian colonial oppression.

The break with Sartre gives further clues to Camus's political position. Partly ostensibly and partly in fact it was a clash between idealist and moralist, and socialist-communist engaged with reforming Stalinist State communism from within. Jeanson's attack was philosophically simplistic, Camus's replies and Sartre's rejoinders showed neither writer at the height of their critical powers. The sadness is that Sartre's famous obituary emphasized just the grand moralist which Jeanson's original article attacked. But the weakness of Camus was nonetheless signalled. What levels of the representations of the particularity of complex reality would be missing in the often splendid and necessary rhetoric of a complex moral discourse which used the literary traditions of the romantic convergences of landscape and psychological description, of moral philosophy, and the nineteenth century novel's generic traditions of the representation of solitude and sexual tragedy? Camus's works cannot in fact be taken simply as representative of some anti-historical position coded in the synchronic terms of the moralist, neither can they simply be seen as imperfect allegories of actual political events to which they are nonetheless related. This essay will not reconcile these contradictions, which additionally involve difficult questions of the relation of political representation to literary genre, but will attempt to find a criticism in which they might be seen more complexly in play.

Certainly Camus and Bowles converge in many ways within the generalised anarchist stance of the *libertaire*,[16] but such a convergence does not distinguish sufficiently the very much more politically-engaged Camus. Slow to respond to the F.L.N.'s drive for political independence, and deeply aware that over a million Algerians of French descent living in company with nine million disenfranchised Moslems complicated the political scene, Camus broke with *L'Express*. But complexity is the first victim of armed struggle, given the absolutely necessary violence of the endlessly-exploited and betrayed Algerian Muslims, and Camus's words quoted by Roget Quilliot have a special and highly contradictory relevance in 1992 when Islamic 'fundamentalists' voted to overthrow a corrupt one-party communist State, and were then denied the fruits of their victory:

> Une Algérie constituée par des peuplements fédérées, et reliée à la France, me paraît préférable, sans comparaison possible au regard de la simple justice, à une Algérie reliée à un empire d'Islam qui ne réaliserait à l'intention des peuples arabes qu'une

addition de misères et de souffrance et qui arracherait le peuple français d'Algérie à sa patrie naturelle.[17]

Here 'la simple justice' moves two ways. Positively it affirms the Enlightenment tradition of democratic thought and practice. At the same time, however, it rules out for ever that very possibility in the prejudiced generality of the 'empire d'Islam'. The real issue is monarchy, or oligarchy, co-opting Islam, versus capitalist democratic practice parading its moralism on the basis of actual superior power. In this context Camus's work for a civil truce, and his general refusal to comment on the Algerian war, are inevitably seen as signs of political weakness.

Sartre's trenchant secularism illuminates the downside of enlightenment universal value:

> for with us there is nothing more consistent than a racist humanism since the European has only been able to become a man through creating slaves and monsters. While there was a native population somewhere this imposture was not shown up; in the notion of the human race we found an abstract assumption of universality which served as cover for the most realistic practices.[18]

Yet there are problems with that 'abstract assumption of universality' with which Sartre weights the dice against Camus's position. Universalities do not automatically appear in the guise of abstract assumptions. There are plenty of universals within dialectical materialism, for example. That Camus's universals included the nature of subjectivity, personal ethics in relation to political choice, marked him, not least in a dialectical sense, as able to criticize the materialist scientism of the Marxist and the reductionist parameters of their praxis, as well as being vulnerable to the obvious dangers of the charge of humanist moralism. For the irony is that the *a priori* declaration of universal human rights (chief among which is the right to difference) of the Enlightenment is also the basis of Sartre's protest against abstract racist humanism. At one level of politics ideological particularity has to be transcended by the recognition of *a priori* 'humanist', 'Enlightenment' common universalist value – whatever the obvious dangers signalled across the board by cultural relativists and anthropologists.

In this sense Camus condemned the Stalinist Soviet Union long before Sartre, and broke with the communists precisely over the Arab question. Camus felt that the anti-Nationalist line of the Communist Party in the independence struggle was too simplistic and too unaware of the complexities of Algerian Arab and Muslim culture.[19]

Bowles's politics are more easily discussed because much less engaged. Like Camus, and at a level where American anarchist sympathies met French, his values were measured by the freedom of the artist to create. His way into the culture of the dispossessed in America and Africa was through music: jazz in the case of black culture, and ethno-musicology in the case of North Africa. Was he, therefore, merely like a typical white leftish aesthete entranced by the Harlem Renaissance before that movement became more politically serious? The answer to that must lie in a close examination of his texts.

The American Communist Party in the late thirties was more Stalinist than Stalin himself, and Bowles, in 1937 following the party line, had some 15,000 anti-Trotskyite posters printed to take to Mexico. He tried to resign, however, from the Communist Party in 1940, but he was informed that he could only be expelled. Critics have argued that Bowles's *The Spider's House* is not a political novel (a dubious claim which depends on a very narrow definition of 'political').[20] Even more than for Camus, the upheaval in North Africa filled Bowles with pure dismay, and he records, not very subtly, a personal and somewhat lofty disbelief in the Moroccan political independence struggle:

> It isn't even amusing for the Arabs, who want nothing more than to see great bloodshed, and spend their time moping around the house in hunger strikes and ripping pictures of Mendès-France out of the papers after which they either spit on them or, which is more likely, put them into their mouths and chew them up, grinding the saliva-soaked paper between their teeth until it's nothing but paste. It's not amusing because it's not going anywhere and can never make anything.[21]

This is the loftiness of colonialist distance. It does not, however, do justice to the much more politically acute representation of American/European/ Moroccan encounters in his actual novels, nor does it indicate the kind of political comment Bowles could make when he had a mind to.

Bowles's 1957 article for *The Nation* on the Mau Mau in Kenya is a case in point.[22] More radical abroad than on his own territory (as is so often the case), Bowles savagely condemned the British Imperialists for continuing in Kenya the absolutist practices they had been forced to abandon in India. He pointed out that Kenyans had little control of their own commerce and that the Kikuyu had been pushed into violence by poverty, discrimination and hunger. Africans earned a fifth of what Asians earned, and both fell far below the incomes of their white colonial masters. Bowles observed that 'any African can be picked up at any moment and imprisoned without trial in one of the vast detention camps, or arbitrarily deported from wherever he is to his reserve' ('Letter from Kenya', p. 466). Three thousand Africans a month were being detained, forty-four thousand were in the detention camps. A pass book system created an apartheid system like that of South Africa. Bowles noted that the wild animals seemed better off, and he continued unsparingly to condemn this 'land of barbed wire and watch towers' ('Letter from Kenya', p. 467). As in Algeria, the whites who were killed were avenged a thousand times over by killings of the indigenous population. Bowles further adds that while the British lost perhaps about fifty people, the counter-terror of the British involved the deaths of over a hundred thousand Africans. In addition, from October 1952 to March 1956, one thousand and fifteen dissidents were executed, an average of one a day ('Letter from Kenya', pp. 447-8).

But for both writers the use of North African, or more strictly Maghreb, materials falls within several traditions. These include travel topographies; psychological narratives involving a topographical symbolism, a landscape iconography of desert, sun, and sea whose roots go back to classical and biblical times; the naturalist genre in which extreme situations within nature structure (with a degree of fatalism) personal and psychological crises; and finally the nature of the exotic: what Said called for countries farther to the East, at least from the European's standpoint, 'orientalism'.[23] Both Camus and Bowles will structure their novels at an edge between the codifications of dream as cultural expectation, the naive literary expectations of the imperial exotic, and the representation of the difference of the actual encounter.

For Camus, under the precedents set by Montherlant and Gide, was to create his own ideology of the Mediterranean. His view would, of course, be his own: '... je ne dirai pas ce qui manque à Gide et à Montherlant, c'est d'avoir des réductions sur les trains qui les contraignent du même coup à rester six jours dans une même ville. Mais je sais bien que je ne puis au fond voir les choses comme Montherlant ou Gide – à cause des réductions sur les trains.'[24]

Yet at the most profound level, Camus's Mediterranean is compounded with his classicism. His great good place is the ruins of Tipassa. Here the long sense of time of Mediterannean culture, the old romantic theme of ruins and nature, is coupled with a Nietzschean sense of heroic vitality and a visceral sense of the Mediterranean climate. Culture follows climate in an almost Montesquieu-like sense. Nor was Camus the only artist coming out of the earlier part of the twentieth century to return to the classics for a sense of stability and an almost nineteenth-century pseudo-historical sense of 'original' value. One thinks of Picasso's pictures of the 1920s or the American H[ilda].D[oolittle].'s poetry. Not the least complex aspect of Camus's 'Mediterannean' is that the Stoic, the Nietzschean hero, the Christian-Marxist conscience, and the romantic lover predicating creativity itself on the senses, all lend their perspectives and values to the definition of landscape.

Camus would also have agreed with Braudel: 'So what is civilization if not the ancient settlement of a certain section of mankind in a certain place?'[25] The late twentieth-century tragedy is that actual displacement seeks this very idea in the banalities of commercial tourism:

Quinze ans après, je retrouvais mes ruines, à quelques pas des premières vagues, je suivais les rues de la cité oubliée à travers des champs couverts d'arbres amers, et, sur les coteaux qui dominent la baie, je caressais encore les colonnes couleur de pain. Mais les ruines étaient maintenant entourées de barbelés et l'on ne pouvait y pénétrer que par les seuils autorisés.[26]

Yet for all the complexities of Camus's responses there is also the simple joy of that region. In 1949 Braudel published his great work, *The Mediterannean and the Mediterrananean World in the Age of Philip II*. In a manner altogether strange to modern historians, and with the romantic passion of a Michelet, Braudel began with a declaration of love:

> I have loved the Mediterranean with passion.... In return, I hope that a little of this joy and a great deal of Mediterranean sunlight will shine from the pages of this book.... The reader who approaches this book in the spirit I would wish will do well to bring with him his own memories, his own vision of the Mediterranean to add colour to the text and to help me conjure up this vast presence.... My feeling is that the sea itself, the one we see and love, is the greatest document of its past existence.[27]

From the beginning, as with Braudel, Camus's Mediterranean was a collectivity of experiences, not the narrow folk regionalism of the right. It comprised countries and histories and even seas which had a contemporary and historical shape. At one end it brought together East and West: at the other it opened out through the gates of Hercules to the Atlantic and the New World.[28]

Camus's view would deepen and shift about his elements of sea, sun and ancient land. The Camus of the mid-fities would clearly bring a reading of Melville into his writing about the sea. Here are to be found that bitter ecstacy which the romantic and bourgeois tradition has always drawn around the sea; the poverty of the common sailor and the greed of owners, the contrast between sea and land, adventure, mysticism, promise, solitude and desolation. In 1952 Camus wrote on Melville; in 1954 he opened his 'log':

> J'attends longtemps. Parfois je trébuche, je perds la main, la réussite me fuit. Qu'importe, je suis seul alors. Je me réveille ainsi, dans la nuit, et, à demi endormi, je crois entendre un bruit de vagues, la respiration des eaux. Réveillé tout à fait, je reconnais le vent dans les feuillages et la rumeur malheureurse de la ville déserte. Ensuite, je n'ai pas trop de tout mon art pour cacher ma détresse ou l'habiller à la mode.[29]

There was also another American component which coincided with and strengthened Camus's 'Mediterannean'. It was his admiration for Faulkner, a novelist similarly trapped in a 'colonized South' and who also turned to the classicizing vocabulary of the grand moral tradition with its symbolism of elemental climate. In his note on Faulkner's *Requiem for a Nun*, Camus said, 'Ses personages sont d'aujurd'hui et ils sont affrontés pourtant au même destin qui écrasait Electre ou Oreste. Seul un grand artiste pouvait tenter ainsi d'introduire dans nos appartements le grand langage de la douleur et de l'humiliation.'[30]

It is not without irony that Bowles's first view of North Africa was Oran, the home of Francine Faure, who became Camus's second wife and whose grandfather had built part of the harbour. It was also, of course, the town of *La Peste*, the town of tedium that had turned its back on the sea. For Bowles it was at once both 'beautiful and terrible'.[31] What had begun for Bowles as a light-hearted adventure turned out to be a life-time's love affair. The response was immediate. Approaching Oran Bowles felt an excitement:

> ... as if some interior mechanism had been set in motion by the sight of the approaching land. Always without formulating the concept, I had based my sense of being in the world partly on an unreasoned conviction that certain areas of the earth's surface contained more magic than others ... a secret connection between the world of nature and the consciousness of man, a hidden but direct passage which bypassed the mind.[32]

The world of North Africa and more especially Morocco was indeed to become a space of both beauty and terror.

Bowles's other interest was ethno-musicology, a cultural interest spurned by colonial, revolutionary, Muslim and Nationalist alike, and his magnificent collection still lies in silence in the Library of Congress. Marxists, Muslims, and French officers exhibited a totalitarian puritanism in relation to the traditional ethnic culture, and had taken to heart Fanon's words: 'It is around the peoples' struggles that African-Negro culture takes on substance, and not around songs, poems, or folklore.'[33] Culture is in essence opposed to custom.[34]

The cultural and political battlegrounds of the day had perhaps inevitably a certain simplistic duality: internationalism versus regionalism, revolutionary literature versus folk-lore. For the practising musician and poet there was no obvious place in the revolutionary struggle.

Yet for all the pseudo-colonial distance, Bowles was strangely both aware and unaware of the culture into which he had suddenly come. The friendships with men like Ahmed Yacoubi were long lasting, and his more general comments show that he had sufficient knowledge, at least, to declare he did not feel at home in the culture: 'I don't think we're likely to get to know the Moslems very well,' he said in 1952, 'and I suspect that if we should we'd find them less sympathetic than we do at present. And I believe the same applies to their getting to know us'.[35] Indeed the mutual distrust, the confrontation of the blind eyes of the colonial with the completely other world of the Muslim, was a major theme of his novels perhaps even more than it was for Camus.

Yet Bowles also had what anthropologists call a 'salvage' view of North African culture. He saw it as 'doomed', and hence attempted to 'salvage' just those parts of it which a Fanon would reject: 'the religions, the music and the dances of the doomed African cultures! How much, if we wished, we could learn from them about man's relation to the cosmos, about his conscious connection with his own soul. Instead of which, we talk about raising their standard of living.'[36] In Fanon's terms, this is counter-revolutionary aesthetic sentimentalism. But it has to be said also that Fanon's capacity for dialectical political analysis did not extend to the arts in any sophisticated way.

It depended where you were coming from. Bowles could not transform himself into a member of the Islamic proletariate any more than Camus, nor indeed Fanon himself. Bowles had fled the material industrial culture of America with an absolute horror, and as a skilled musican found in Moroccan music a resource, an art form in all its difference, as well as 'folk essence'.

In more positive terms, Fanon's political prescriptions for the artist had the merit of pleading for cultural innovation and life against an art legitimated *a priori* by its revelation of the folk soul and by that reduction of ethnic art to static repetitions dear to the eye of the aristocratic connoisseur (and the ethno-collecting liberals who haunt the academy these days), but at the same time it tends dogmatically to rule out of court the resources of the past. The unforgiving oppositions of 'folk' and 'modern' rule out the very process of transformation itself and the possibility of new art.[37] The fact is that Bowles as a musician was as sensitive to Maghreb music as Bartok was to the folk songs of the Hungarian plain, or Ravel to the Auvergne.

Nonetheless, it is how you deal with the past that is crucial.[38] The mummification of the past is not to be confused with the fact that there is a past whose legacies need discrimination as the basis for creative renewal. In the end it is the autocracy of social-realism predicated on correct progress that is counter-revolutionary, for it rules out that necessary interaction between so-called high and low culture, and between tradition creatively understood and the present necessity, which is always the hallmark of great art.

Bowles chose to live in Morocco, through laziness or weariness as he said, and because Tangier seemed less afflicted by the evils of other western or westernizing cities.[39] Bowles, as an American, came into North Africa at the point of the collapse of the European empires. As an American he was an ally of the colonial powers without the stigma (at least in this part of the world) of actual colonization. In his 'colonial' life as permanent exile, or permanent tourist, or settler, or immigrant – categories with their own nuances of particular possibilities of interaction – two contradictory levels of consciousness are immediately apparent: the first, a white participant/onlooker in a politics of decolonialization; and the second, a white with greater access, socially, to Moroccan culture because of no *personal* political need for distance. All the novels and short stories about Morocco portray the anxieties of the clash of cultures, and the contradictions of the three intermeshed levels: political, social and personal.

In the larger political world the United States was beginning to fill the vacuum left by the British and French Empires. In North Africa, United States foreign policy pursued decolonialization in name but the retention of French influence in fact. The actual situation could be quite complex. For example the Coca-Cola company would support the Nationalists, and the U.S. government would back French advocacy of restriction on American businessmen. European recovery was essential to American interests in its stand against communism.[40] The politics of oil were to make North Africa a major focus in a new global American foreign policy. For example the new 'cultural relations policy', as defined by Mortimer Graves in 1950, included the attempt to acquire 'every significant publication in every important Near Eastern language published since 1900', an attempt 'which our Congress ought to recognize as a measure of our national security'.[41] This strategic rationale was the key. As late as 1967, as Said witheringly points out, Middle East sociologists like Monroe Berger were affirming a long standing 'orientalist' attitude towards the actual cultural achievements of the region: 'The modern Middle East and North Africa is not a center of great cultural achievement nor is it like to become one in the near future.'[42] Bowles's serious cultural interest in North Africa, in its storytelling and in its music, should be revalued in the light of this nonsense.

Bowles's novels are in fact much more sophisticated about Morocco than most of his direct statements about the culture. *The Sheltering Sky*, for example, is merciless in its sardonic judgements. They are there in the staggering banality of the *ménage à trois* for which the North African scene is in part a naturalist, psychological analogue of its relation. Kit says, for instance, immediately after landing: 'The people of each country get more like the people of every other country. They have no character, no beauty, no ideals, no culture – nothing, nothing.'[43] And later, when finally the desert obligingly replaces rocks with sand and some 'dark men mounted on mehara' are seen, their 'kohl-larded faces ... fierce above the draped indigo veils that hid their faces', she bursts out with chilling ineptness: 'it *is* rather wonderful ... to be riding past such people in the Atomic Age' (*Sheltering Sky*, pp. 175-6).

Port, her husband, is, to a degree, more introspective:

> How friendly are they? Their faces are masks. They all look a thousand years old.... Are they Moslems or Christians? They don't know. They know money, and when they get it all they want is to eat. But what's wrong with that? Why do I feel this way about them? Guilt at being well fed and healthy among them? ... The Spanish maid at the hotel had said to him that noon: 'La vida es pena.' 'Of course', he had replied, feeling false even as he spoke, asking himself if any American can truthfully accept a definition of life which makes it synonymous with suffering.... For years it had been one of his superstitions that reality and true perception were to be found in the conversation of the labouring classes. Even though now he saw clearly that their formulas of thought and speech are as strict and as patterned, and thus as far removed from any profound expression of truth as any other class, often he found himself still in the act of waiting, with the unreasoning belief that gems of wisdom might yet issue from their mouths. (*Sheltering Sky*, p. 18)

The paranoia is that of the colonial: the attempted self-reassurance of a cash-nexus value relation is American: the notion of 'squandering' money on food is a class judgement predicated also on the relation of money and time, and there is a further over-riding irony in the fact that buying food hardly provides the content of luxury the turn of phrase demands. The Puritan reassurance of the hero about suffering is torn apart by Puritanical introspection, and Bowles adds another American sarcasm which relies on knowing that the word happiness is built into the Constitution, and has degenerated into a culture of uplift. Finally there is despair when the Moroccan poor are imaged as Marxian proletarians, but the despair is at the level of language not politics. In other words it is here an aesthetic despair attempting to over-ride a political despair. To that extent it is shown to be hypocritical.

Let it Come Down was begun in 1949 and published 'early in 1952, at the very moment of the riots which presaged the end of the International Zone of Morocco. Thus, even at the time of publication the book already treated of a bygone era, for Tangier was never the same after the 30th March 1952'.[44] Was then Bowles's Morocco merely a nostalgia for a 'bygone' vision of a politically-arrested culture? Love of the past there was certainly. Nostalgia is an inadequate word for the traveller who seeks the need to shift the attention from immediate modernity to the achievements of the past for a break from the disasters of the twentieth century.

Certainly in *Let it Come Down*, there is little peace or comfort for European, American or North African. Politically the 'International Zone' of Morocco is as corrupt as anything in the post-war Germany of Pynchon's *Gravity's Rainbow*. It also became a space of corruption for another American writer, William Burroughs, as his early essay called 'International Zone', the predecessor of that urban 'Interzone', the main scene of his fiction, indicates:[45] 'It was one of the charms of the International Zone that you could get anything you wanted if you paid for it. Do anything, too, for that matter – there were no incorruptibles. It was only a question of price' (*Let it Come Down*, p. 26). The perspective is of course the one held by those who do possess the means. The relation between money and cultural consciousness is always a strong strand in Bowles's work. Here the cash-nexus reduction is not an absolute statement about Morocco but part of the self-deception within the American's gaze.

One of the most brilliantly critical and sardonic moments of *Let It Come Down* is where a rich American woman, Eunice Goode [sic], having bought a young Moroccan woman as sexual partner from the local brothel, reflects on her emotions and then writes her diary:

She did not hope Hadija would be able to share her sensations; she asked only that the girl act as a catalyst for her, making it possible for her to experience them in their pure state. As a mainspring for her behavior there was always the aching regret for a vanished innocence, a nostalgia for the early years of life.... At daybreak, while Hadija was still asleep beside her, she sat up and wrote in her notebook: 'A quiet moment in the early morning. The pigeons have just begun to murmur outside the window. There is no wind. Sexuality is primarily a matter of imagination, I am sure. People who live in the warmer climates have very little of it, and so society there can allow a wide moral latitude in the customs. Here are the healthiest personalities. In temperate regions it is quite a different matter. The imagination's fertile activity must be curtailed by a strict code of sexual behavior which results in crime and depravity. Look at the great cities of the world...' But of course all cities are points of infection, like decayed teeth. The hypersensitivity of urban culture (its own virtue) is largely a reaction to pain. Tangier has no urban culture, no pain. I believe it never will have. The nerve will never be exposed. (*Let it Come Down*, pp. 58-9)

Like Scott Fitzgerald, Bowles is most effective when mercilessly and unself-pityingly writing close to his own obsessions: the search for a non-mechanized urban milieu, a less-policed, more erotic world, the great, good, non-American place. In this passage the sexual Mecca of the other turns on Eunice Goode's own narcissistic egoism which is dependent on her simple western economic power. The legitimations of Goode's obscene behaviour (herself the American woman as fat pink puffy gin-sodden body of 'Oriental decadence') obliterate political reality for reasons of 'climate', a reductive orientalist mind-body split, and psycho-medical explanation.

Politics and religion are more directly invoked in *The Spider's House*. The American Stenham is the innocent abroad, all the more dangerous for a little knowledge of the culture of Fez. The walk through the city which opens the book in virtuoso style gathers the American's thoughts into a dazzling sequence of Orientalist misconceptions and assumptions. Taking leave of his Moroccan friends Stenham comments 'Their adieux were always lengthy and elaborate, as if he were leaving for the other side of the world rather than the opposite end of the Medina and he consciously liked that, because it was part of what he thought life in a medieval city should be like'.[46]

The dramatic 'irony' is that the city is on the verge of political revolutionary violence paralleling the violence (in which hundreds of Moroccans lost their lives wholly disproportionately to French lives) of the actual events immediately preceding and following Bowles's actual writing of the book, from the banning of the Istiqlal in December 1952, through the 'abdication' of Sidi Mohammed ben Youssef the following August, to his restoration in the summer of 1955, to independence from France in May 1956. Indeed what things 'should be like' equates Stenham's consciousness with that of the sophisticated and more savvy, but distinctly British, colonialist, Moss, whose culturally chic explanations are just as imperialist as the American's psychological judgements: 'How these people love games, he [Stenham] thought. This one's playing cops and robbers now; they're always either stalking or being stalked. "The Oriental passion for complications, the involved line, Arabesques," Moss had assured him, but he was not sure that it was that' (*The Spider's House*, p. 5). Stenham is always on the verge of edging out of Orientalist judgements. But he is a type of liberal whose even-handedness and tolerance is a form of blindness. The cultural love of Fez, the friendships with Moroccans, are separated by an absolute gulf from his own half-consciousness of the actual political situation:

Ever since that day a year ago when the French, more irresponsible than usual, had deposed the Sultan, the tension had been there, and he had known it was there. But it was a political thing, and politics exist only on paper; certainly the politics of 1954 had no true connection with the mysterious medieval city he knew and loved (*The Spider's House*, p. 10).

Stenham wishes for a mummification of the city, preserved outside himself, into which he can dip for aesthetic, escapist, transcendental experiences. For him, too, the violence of the other is without theme, as it always is in the colonial consciousness (*The Spider's House*, p. 199). In addition to Stenham's deliberations, Bowles finds many other ways to prod the weaknesses of French colonialism, Moroccan Nationalists, and the Istiqlal alike. If the authorial viewpoint finally has the weakness of an anarchistic position, it also has the strength of powerful satire. Stenham is shown to *equate* French and Nationalist movements in the conflicts imagined as a struggle for politically undifferentiated power. But the satire is finally founded upon a false universalization of human value. There is no equivalence, and therefore no equation is possible, between unequal powers: such as the French and the Nationalists in the early 1950s.

In fact Moroccan nationalism rose in opposition to attempts by the French increasingly to centralize imperial power. The Istiqlal also relied on an uneasy relationship with Muslim Nationalist support, as Bowles's book actually shows. Bowles's political weakness is ultimately that of the 'invisible spectator', the man of no country by virtue of voluntary ex-patriotism whose even-handed criticisms are not embedded in committed political decisions with their consequences inside the culture he inhabits. Yet there is an important sense in which for Bowles this is involuntary. It is also perfectly possible to be a tourist in your own country, and to that extent Bowles is more involved in Morocco than many Moroccans. He is in the position of Sartre's 'technician of knowledge', with the potential to cross the line to intellectual. Indeed by his very creativity there is an important sense in which Bowles does cross that line, for his stories present a rivalry to the status quo of his characters' self-legitimated beliefs again and again. He is suspect because he is 'forever saying no'.[47]

In fact Bowles does question the inevitability of that Marxist-Leninist route which, in the post-war Stalinist version, would seem with hindsight to replace one centralized autocracy with another (*The Spider's House*, p. 155). Bowles shows Stenham, in his soliloquies, always too quick to move from politics to a universalist quasi-existential questioning which itself has the political content of fatalism. And finally, like so many good American writers before him, Bowles inscribes the very ambiguous position of the writer into the general moral thematics of the text, for he makes quite clear that 'writing' buys Stenham dinners and keeps him out of trouble.

Thus, though more complex, Stenham is scarcely more morally admirable than a kind of latter-day Henrietta Stackpole, the tourist journalist of Henry

James's *Portrait of a Lady*. Polly Burroughs, who absurdly looks for 'the cult of Pan' among 'these people' (always the give-away phrase) in 'untouched regions', thus complements his own attitudes more than he knows (*The Spider's House*, pp. 310-11). But the tourist gaze is most notably demonstrated in the comic scene which links the narratives of Muslim and American and in which Amar 'deconstructs' Polly Burroughs and Stenham talking together in a café.

Bowles must not be confused with Stenham. Stenham's political philosophy is scarcely sophisticated and is shown as such: 'To him wisdom consisted in the conscious and joyous obedience to natural laws' (*The Spider's House*, p. 156). To which Moss replies that knowledge, not wisdom, is now needed. A very American split between piety (aesthetic obedience) and pragmatic instrumentalism is thus signalled, and a more sophisticated reading of Bowles's story would suggest that it is the mutually supporting elements of this double bind that is the object of his satire.

Amar, too, is satirized gently but firmly throughout the book, mainly through his beliefs about himself, mediated through a religious consciousness of himself as a *Cherif*. The struggle of the son against the father, the beating of Amar by the father, the brother who rebels by smoking kif, thematically recall Baldwin's *Go Tell it on the Mountain* (1953), where Christian belief and parental control mirror a world of violence inside the family which is sustained by a very self-conscious distancing of itself from the political oppression without. Amar, too, is a self-willed innocent, conscious of his destiny, which he seeks by signs, wandering between competing ideologies. Bowles parallels Moroccan with American, for Stenham, too 'had lived in solitude and carefully planned ignorance of what was happening in the world. Nothing had importance save the exquisitely isolated cosmos of his own consciousness' (*The Spider's House*, p. 195). Bowles signals the very poverty of American individualistic philosophy: Stenham falls back on the senses and the predication of critical difference on psychology: 'Discussion was nothing more than the clash of personalities' (*The Spider's House*, p. 210).

It is imposssible to sum up the differences between the two writers and their representations of cultures, one lost and the other barely found. Camus was exiled from Algeria by the actual contradictions of imperialist politics. As an American tourist of the post-imperialist age Bowles entered the world of Morocco, drawn through its difference from America and by its perceived exoticism. Camus's works do not deal with sexual encounter between races. Bowles's works do, but they use it to analyse the inmost recesses of a new totalitarian psychology of power between strong and weak, between different cultures, between men and men and women and women, at the level of the erotic. Both mercilessly parody the mind and habit of colonialism in terms of the psychopathology of everyday life. Camus was sophisticated at the political level, Bowles at the social. Camus's lack of inwardness with Islamic culture blinded him (largely from the impossibility of his position as a *pied noir*) to the strengths of Nationalist feeling arising out of violent colonial rule, yet his very distance made him clearly aware of complexities which the heat of revolutionary revenge could not, and still cannot, cope with.

Bowles, the writer aesthete, might have longed for a Tangier which never in fact existed (an American's never-neverland of that untouched world elsewhere), and was by reason of ex-patriotism not politically involved. Yet through fidelity to detail, to the writer's task, a fearless emotional engagement with actual Moroccans, an extraordinary ability to survive the phoney (because of an uncommitted relation to the larger culture), inward-turning, self-lacerating conditions of expatriate life, Bowles gave an account of what Wilhelm Reich called the 'emotional plague' in that 'Interzone' of 1950s Morocco which has its own political acuteness. For his part Camus knew that his Mediterranean had lost all historical reality and that the great moral insights of the European Enlightenment were being turned into liberal propaganda. And finally, it is clear that Bowles knew that the world might be shrunk to a vision which was to haunt American writers throughout the later fifties and sixties, nations shrunk to a space of homogenous interzone where all details of culture and behaviour would be abstracted by the violence of armed conflict and rates of exchange.[48]

Notes

1. Albert Camus, 'Herman Melville' [originally published in *Les Ecrivains célèbres* Tome III, (Paris: Editions Mazenod, 1952)] in *Récits Nouvelles Théâtre*, ed. Roger Quilliot (Paris: Pléiade Gallimard, 1962), pp. 1909-10. 'Like the greatest artists, Melville constructed his symbols out of concrete things, not from the material of dreams. The creator of myths partakes of genius only in so far as he inscribes these myths in the denseness of reality, and not in the fleeting clouds of the imagination.' [This translation from Albert Camus, *Selected Essays and Notebooks*, ed. and trans. Philip Thody (1970; rpt. Harmondsworth: Penguin Books, 1979), p. 181]. Other translations are the authors' own unless otherwise indicated. Only Camus's own words will be cited in French in the text.
2. Fernand Braudel, *The Mediterranean and the Mediterranean World in the Age of Philip II*, trans. Sîan Reynolds (London: Fontana/Collins, 1975), frontispiece.
3. Albert Camus, 1951 *L'Homme Révolté* in *Essais*, ed. R. Quilliot (Paris: Editions Gallimard, Pléiade, 1965), p. 622. 'The bourgeois illusions concerning science and technical progress, shared by the authoritarian socialists, gave birth to the civilization of the machine-tamers which can, through the stresses of competition and the desire for domination, be divided into enemy blocs but which on the economic plane is subject to identical laws: the accumulation of capital and nationalized and continually increasing production.' This translation from Albert Camus, *The Rebel*, trans. Anthony Bower (1953; rpt. Harmondsworth: Penguin Books, 1962) p. 185. For Camus's political

activities c. 1937 see R. Quilliot, 'Politique et Culture Méditerranéennes' in Albert Camus, *Essais*, pp. 1314-1320.

4. Herbert R. Lottman, *Albert Camus: a Biography* (1979; rpt. London: Picador Books, 1981), p. 7.

5. Christoper Sawyer-Lauçanno, *An Invisible Spectator: A Biography of Paul Bowles* (London: Bloomsbury, 1989), p. 296.

6. Sawyer-Lauçanno, p. 67.

7. Cruikshank even argues that in *Le Sursis*, volume II of *Les Chemins de la liberté*, 'Sartre uses a technique ... which closely resembles that of the American novelist John Dos Passos.' John Cruikshank, ed., *French Literature and its background: no 6. The Twentieth Century* (Oxford: Oxford University Press, 1970), pp. 258-9.

8. Lottman, p. 254.

9. Simone de Beauvoir, *Force of Circumstance*, trans. Richard Howard (1963; Harmondsworth: Penguin, 1968), pp. 134f.

10. Lottman, pp. 378-9.

11. See Camus, 'Herman Melville' (1952). For details see note 1.

12. Lottman, p. 468.

13. Lottman, p. 82.

14. Lottman, p. 89.

15. Lottman, pp. 574-5. Camus's visit to Algeria involved at least one difficult moment where he spoke under the protection of Ouzegan and the F.L.N. surrounded by an angry crowd of ultras. See Quilliot on Camus's dangerous visit to Algeria in 1956, especially the incident at le Cercle du Progrès in January. Camus, *Essais*, pp. 1841-2.

16. Lottman, p. 532.

17. Albert Camus, *Actuelles III, Chroniques Algériennnes, 1939-1958* in *Essais*, p. 901. 'An Algeria made up of a federated people and bound to France seems to me to be preferable in terms of plain justice, to an Algeria bound to the Islamic Empire which would accomplish nothing, insofar as the Arab people are concerned, except to increase their poverty and suffering, and which would tear the Frenchmen of Algeria from their native land.' This translation cited in an essay by Roget Quilliot, 'Albert Camus's Algeria', in Germaine Brée, ed., trans. Emmet Parker, *Camus: A Collection of Critical Essays* (Englewood Cliffs, N.J.: Prentice-Hall, 1962), p. 46.

18. Jean-Paul Sartre, introd. to Franz Fanon, *The Wretched of the Earth* [*Les Damnés de la Terre*, 1961] (Harmondsworth: Penguin, 1967), p. 22.

19. Lottman, pp. 156-7. Camus was accused of being a Trotskyite by Robert Deloche.

20. Sawyer-Lauçanno acknowledges it has 'political overtones' but regards it in generalized humanist terms as 'a depiction of how people respond to stress'. See *The Invisible Spectator*, p. 326. Given that the novel was written under the direct pressure of the most dramatic political events Morocco had seen, and the conflicts between communist and Nationalist and religious issues of the time are directly dramatized in the novel, this judgement seems mildly evasive.

21. Sawyer-Lauçanno, p. 316.

22. Paul Bowles, 'Letter from Kenya', *The Nation*, 184, 21 (1957), pp. 448, 466-8. Further references, all to this source, are incorporated in the main text.

23. In this respect Morocco was often compared with the Ottoman Empire. See F.V. Parsons, 'Late Nineteenth-Century Morocco through Foreign Eyes', *The Magreb Review* III, nos. 5-6 (Jan-April, 1978), 1-5.

24. Albert Camus, *Carnets d'Albert Camus* (Paris: Gallimard, 1962), [21 octobre, 1937], p. 93. 'I wouldn't go so far as to say that what is lacking in Gide and Montherlant is

the fact that they have never travelled on a cheap ticket which compelled them to spend six days in the same town. But I am perfectly certain that basically I can never see things as Gide or Montherlant do – because of the cheap tickets.' This translation Philip Thody, ed. and trans., *Camus: Selected Essays and Notebooks* (Harmondsworth: Penguin, 1970), p. 244. On the French tradition of attitudes to the 'Orient' in Nerval, Chateaubriand, Lamartine, Flaubert (who parodied it in *Madame Bovary*) and Gide, see E.W. Said, *Orientalism* (1978; rpt. Harmondsworth: Penguin, 1985).

25. Fernand Braudel, *Capitalism and Material Life,* trans. Miriam Kochan (1967; London: Fontana, 1974), p. 443.

26. Albert Camus, 'Retour à Tipasa', in *L'Eté* [1954] rpt. in *Essais*, ed R. Quilliot (Paris: Pléiade, 1965), p. 870. 'Fifteen years afterwards I found my ruins again, a few steps from the first waves. I followed the streets of the forgotten city across the fields covered with bitter trees, and, on the hills overlooking the bay, could still caress the breadcrust-coloured pillars. But now the ruins were surrounded by barbed wire, and could be reached only through official entrances.' This translation from Philip Thody, ed. and trans., *Camus: Selected Essays and Notebooks* (Harmondsworth: Penguin, 1970), p. 148.

27. Fernand Braudel, *The Mediterranean and the Mediterranean World in the Age of Philip II*, trans. Sîan Reynolds (1949; London: Fontana/Collins, 1975), p. 17.

28. Lottman, p. 131. For particular problems relating to Algeria in terms of how culture biases the very association of geographical areas, see Jacqueline Kaye and Abdelhamid Zoubir, *The Ambiguous Compromise: Language, Literature and National Identity in Algeria and Morocco* (London and New York: Routledge, 1990), p. 75: 'It should also be observed that the partition of the world into such cultural compartments as the mythical West and its oriental counterpart is detrimental to the understanding of Algerian culture insofar as the latter is embedded in spatial limits that are closer to the geographical west than Italy itself. This is not said in order to subtly identify Algeria with the west, but rather to suggest that Saint Augustine's Algerianness could easily be denied on the grounds of these cultural compartments, whereas Feraoun's could be stripped of its positive attributes on the grounds of his permeability to cultural cross-purposes.'

29. 'I have been waiting for a long time. Sometimes, I stumble, I lose my touch, success evades me. What does it matter, for I am then alone. It is thus that I wake up at night, and, still half-asleep, think I hear the sound of waves and the breathing of the waters. Fully awake, I recognize the wind in the trees and the sad murmur of the empty town. I then need all my art to hide my distress or clothe it in the prevailing fashion.' For this translation see Thody, p. 155.

30. Albert Camus, *Théâtre, récits, nouvelles*, Préface Jean Grenier, ed. Roger Quilliot (Paris: Éditions Gallimard, 1962), p. 1865. 'His characters belong to our own day, and yet they confront the same destiny which crushed Electra or Orestes. Only a great artist could thus attempt to introduce the great language of pain and humiliation into our apartments.' This translation, Thody, p. 183.

31. Sawyer-Lauçanno, p. 110.

32. Sawyer-Lauçanno, p. 110.

33. Fanon, p. 189.

34. Fanon, p. 180.

35. Sawyer-Lauçanno, p. 310.

36. Sawyer-Lauçanno, p. 327.

37. It is instructive in this respect to note that current *Rai* music, a mix of Western pop, jazz, and reggae influences which originated in Oran is now banned as degenerate by

the Algerian government. In this context, the authors strongly disagree with Jacqueline Kay and Abdelhamid Zoubir in their book *The Ambiguous Compromise: Language, Literature, and National Identity in Algeria and Morocco* (London: Routledge, 1990). The argument against Bowles's translations of Moroccan literature as 'the authorial transcription of illiterate storytelling' seems to us theoretically naive, and not a little pompous. To picture a Platonic heaven ('authentic oral reality') of oppressed communal oral purity in Manichean opposition to literate individualist corruption is commonplace in academic courses on colonialism these days. Unfortunately it is sometimes histor-ically inept, for it obliterates any possibility of a creative relationship between oral and literate cultures. Kaye/Zoubir misapply *auteur* theory, and strangely right-wing Ongian/McLuhan [Catholic] arguments against writing [as if Islam itself were not founded in part on the 'Book'!] to accuse Bowles of what he never set out to do. Boazian ethnographic detail about the linguistic source was not required. Doubtless it would be better if readers were aware of all the subtleties of North African languages but in that case Kaye/Zoubir should have written, or better spoken, in Arabic. Their point we take it is to introduce English readers (as *auteurs/writing/English*) to the sadly neglected literature of Algeria and Morocco, which is precisely what Bowles with his wicked and technologically-corrupt tape-recorder also set out to do. As far as translation and its problems go (from linguistic to politico-cultural), the reader is recommended the Pre-face to Jerome Rotherberg's *Shaking the Pumpkin: Traditional Poetry of the Indian North Americas* (New York: Doubleday & Company, 1972).

38. Typically, the current Moroccan view is that this music is 'degenerate'. Sawyer-Lauçanno, p. 349.
39. Paul Bowles, *Without Stopping*, p. 366.
40. Egya N. Sangmuah, 'Interest Groups and Decolonization: American Businessmen and Organized Labour in French North Africa, 1948-56', *The Magreb Review*, XIII, 3-4 (1988), 161-174.
41. Said, p. 295.
42. Said, p. 288.
43. Paul Bowles, *The Sheltering Sky* (London: John Lehmann, 1949), p. 13. Further refer-ences, all to this edition, are incorporated in the main text.
44. Paul Bowles, *Let it Come Down* (1952; rpt. Santa Barbara, Black Sparrow Press, 1980), [1980 Preface], p. 7. Further references, all to this edition, are incorporated in the main text.
45. Michelle Green, *The Dream at the End of the World: Paul Bowles and the Literary Renegades in Tangier* (London: Bloomsbury, 1991), p. 148.
46. Paul Bowles, *The Spider's House* (1955; London: Arena, 1986), p. 4. Further references, all to this edition, are incorporated in the main text.
47. Jean-Paul Sartre, 'A Plea for Intellectuals', in *Between Existentialism and Marxism*, trans. John Matthews (New York: Morrow Quill Paperbacks, 1979), p. 243.
48. See William S. Burroughs, *Interzone*, introd. James Grauerholz (London: Picador, 1989). Grauerholz writes of one of the sections called 'International Zone': 'The name of the piece refers, of course, to the quadripartite administration of Tangier, divided between the U.S., French, Spanish, and English sections' [xvii].

Conscience of a Decade: Arthur Miller

Karl-Heinz Westarp

> The country clutched corruption to its breast while it sent its sons to cleanse the earth eight thousand miles away in Korea.
>
> Arthur Miller, *Timebends*

The 1950s was a decade of great international and domestic turmoil for the United States. Among the important developments one need only think of the Korean War and Senator McCarthy's anti-communist machinations. Before the start of the decade Arthur Miller had already come into his own as one of the country's leading dramatists with his plays *All My Sons* (1947) and *Death of a Salesman* (1949). This status was questioned in the light of both his less successful adaptation of Ibsen's *An Enemy of the People* (1950) and the feelings of political unease created by his play *The Crucible* (1953). In common with other artists, Arthur Miller had the era's anti-communist spotlights trained on him. He had after all sympathized with communist ideas, had in 1947 been to five or six Communist Party writers' meetings[1] and had in 1949 attended the Waldorf-Astoria Hotel pro-Soviet 'Cultural and Scientific Conference for World Peace',[2] all of which finally brought him before the House Un-American Activities Committee on 21 June 1956.

Because of his basic convictions about human freedom of expression, Arthur Miller stood up against the injustices inflicted upon his fellow artists. He thus acted in his own life as the 'bad' conscience of American society at that time, and his convictions shine through in his writings. When *The Crucible* reached Broadway in 1953, the Salem witch-hunt of the play was immediately connected by audiences and critics with McCarthy's modern form of witch-hunting. Though Miller was irritated that it was interpreted in this way, both discussions about the play and Miller's other statements of the period contributed to a growing consciousness of the shortcomings of the decade: in short Miller can be said to have acted as the conscience of the decade.

In the following I shall try to show how Miller managed to live through the most turbulent years of his life fighting relentlessly for sincerity and personal dignity. After that I shall adduce some of the most prominent means and arguments employed by Miller in his attempt to bring America back upon what he considered the right track.

'His sense of personal dignity'

Arthur Miller fought for his deeply felt human concerns and for his passionate belief in social responsibility not only with words but also in deeds, paying no attention to the way in which this might affect his artistic career. In his 1949 discussion of Willy Loman as tragic common man, Miller had already delineated the connection between tragedy and personal dignity: 'Tragic feeling is evoked in us when we are in the presence of a character who is ready to lay down his life, if need be, to secure one thing – his sense of personal dignity.'[3] Yet Miller's confessions in *Timebends* witness that it was an almost superhuman struggle to achieve such dignity in his own life. He was fully aware that all issues in contemporary American society were colored by the premises of American Cold War politics, which had been laid down in 1946-47. Since 1948 the conservatism of the Truman administration had encouraged anticommunist investigations, and the communist issue held great prominence in Eisenhower's election campaign that ensured him the presidency in 1952. Though HUAC, the House Committee on Un-American Activities, had existed since 1938, it became a powerful instrument only in the anti-communist investigations of the late 1940s and early 1950s. Senator Joe McCarthy's charges in 1950 against the State Department, his rise to power as Chairman of the Senate Committee on Government Operations and his 1954 Army hearings can also only be understood as a result of the anti-communist atmosphere that characterized the period. Arthur Miller was aware that the 'air was growing hot with belligerence [against the Soviets]. I thought one must either speak out against it or forfeit something of honor and the right to complain in the future' (*Timebends*, p. 234). Miller reached the conclusion that 'the country was intending to become a philosophical monolith where no real differences about anything important would be tolerated' (*Timebends*, p. 330). Though there were others who defended McCarthyism as 'a program of action against those in our land who help the enemy',[4] Miller felt that he was living 'in an occupied country where anyone at all might be a spy for the enemy' and where, he came to realize, a 'blanket of suspicion was really smothering any discussion at all' (*Timebends*, pp. 311-12). To this extent he believed that the incrimination of people who maintained liberal principles – such as having and defending one's own opinion – was being turned into a hunt for the 'alienated' who did not want to accept the gospel of conformity. Miller saw how people, often close friends, who had had no political leanings other than perhaps a wish to embrace 'the Russian Revolution as an advance for humanity'

125

(*Timebends*, p. 330) were incriminated and forced – at least morally – to speak out against their own consciences and defame themselves and others. He was shocked to find out that even Hemingway would write 'A man alone ain't got no bloody fucking chance', and Miller added: 'Amazing recognition from a professional loner that a new kind of hero had walked on the scene, a man whose self-respect demanded solidarity with his fellow men' (*Timebends*, p. 265). Miller was deeply disappointed with the lack of stamina and commitment he found in his fellow writers. 'Guardedness, suspicion, aloof circumspection – these are the strongest traits I see around me, and what have they ever had to do with the creative act?'[5] When his director and close friend Elia Kazan confessed before HUAC, Miller was profoundly shocked and said he was 'experiencing a bitterness with the country that I had never even imagined before, a hatred of its stupidity and its throwing away of its freedom' (*Timebends*, p. 334). Miller was aware of the fact that after the Republican victory of 1952 McCarthy 'was to have authority in his own hands to summon witnesses, issue subpoenas, push for contempt citations, refer matters to the Department of Justice, probe, press, pry, push, and explore "evil" which had been the theme of so many speeches, clangorous and foreboding'.[6] The production of *The Crucible* and its reviews focussed the searchlights upon Miller and, he confesses, he 'was possibly more scared than others because I was scared of being scared' (*Timebends*, p. 322-23). In 1954, when the State Department refused to issue him a passport in connection with the opening of *The Crucible* in Brussels in March, Miller received a clear warning that something was being planned against him. Though McCarthy had been ousted from his powerful chairmanship thanks to a Senate resolution passed on 3 August 1954, and had been 'condemned' by the Senate on 2 December 1954 for 'contempt' and 'unsenatorial behavior', investigations continued. Miller was at that time deeply involved in the writing of a film-script for the New York City Youth Board; the project was suddenly cancelled, apparently because investigations about him were being carried out. As he formulates it in his autobiography:

> While I still held some cards in this game of Let's Kill Miller, I had no illusions about the fact that powerful people had me in their sights and were only awaiting a clear shot. ... I now had no reason to doubt that should the [American anti-communist] Legion decide to picket my next play to death, I could look for no meaningful defense from my fellow playwrights [i.e. of the Theatre Guild], for these were the most powerful names in the theatre and they were either scared or bewildered about how to act (*Timebends*, pp. 316, 322).

Things came to a head in 1956 when Miller was brought before the House Committee on Un-American Activities on 21 June. Now he was to demonstrate to himself and his fellow artists whether he was simply a man of words only or if he could withstand the pressure of the questioning. He clearly stated that he was 'never under Communist Party discipline' (Bentley, p. 797) but he admitted that he had contributed to front groups, criticised HUAC activities and signed an advertisement denouncing measures against the Communist Party. But when it came to limiting literary freedom and to giving the names of others, Arthur Miller firmly withstood the tribunal's pressure. In connection with accusations of subversive activities under the Smith Act, passed in 1940 as a safeguard against the overthrow of the US Government, Miller said: 'I am opposed to the laying down of any limits upon the freedom of literature' (Bentley, p. 808). He was asked to point out others who had taken part in meetings of the Communist Party at which he himself admitted to having been present. His reaction was: 'I could not use the name of another person and bring trouble on him. These were writers, poets, as far as I could see, and the life of a writer, despite what it sometimes seems, is pretty tough. I wouldn't make it any tougher for anybody. I ask you not to ask me that question' (Bentley, p. 820). The questioners, however, were not satisfied with this answer and threatened: 'We do not accept the reasons you gave for refusing to answer the question, and it is the opinion of the Committee that, if you do not answer the question, you are placing yourself in contempt' (Bentley, p. 822). Miller did not give in and as a result, on 31 May 1957, was convicted of contempt of Congress for refusing to name suspected communists. This conviction was, however, unanimously reversed by the Supreme Court in August 1958.

Though the outcome of Miller's individual fight for dignity and personal integrity was not 'disastrous', as it is for many of his characters, he was clearly aware that time was running out for traditional American culture and that the machinations of the Committee were manifestly anti-democratic and in contempt of basic American rights. He tended to believe with John Stuart Mill that in a political society 'there ought to exist the fullest liberty of professing and discussing, as a matter of ethical conviction, any doctrine, however immoral it may be considered'.[7] He was shocked by the notion that 'conscience was no longer a private matter but one of state administration'.[8] But Miller saw personal freedom endangered not only by the anti-communist investigations of HUAC. He saw as possibly even greater dangers the socio-economic relations which forced man into an acceptance of a certain uniformity, and which in the final analysis lead to frustration, discontent, alienation and the experience of the absurdity of life. To obviate this experience was Miller's major objective. In his essay 'On Social Plays' Miller addresses himself to this issue:

> The deep moral uneasiness among us, the vast sense of being only tenuously joined to the rest of our fellows, is caused, in my view, by the fact that the person has value as he fits into the pattern of efficiency, and for that alone.... So long as modern man conceives of himself as valuable only because he fits into some niche in the machine-tending pattern, he will never know anything more than a pathetic doom.... There is a kind of perverse unity forming among us, born, I think, of the discontent of all classes of people

with the endless frustration of life. It is possible now to speak of a search for values, not solely from the position of bitterness, but with a warm embrace of mankind, with a sense that at bottom every one of us is a victim of this misplacement of aims.[9]

This issue was certainly much more difficult to tackle, but Miller took it up again and again in his plays. His protagonists realize their duty to society, the fact that they can only live fully if they live true to themselves but at the same time are willing to fulfil their social functions as part of the process of self-realization. Miller himself was conscious of this duty in his own life and in his art. Dennis Welland has aptly summarized this. Miller's central theme, he writes, has always been 'the integrity of the individual towards himself and towards his fellows – but the cost of that integrity for most of his characters has been life itself'.[10] According to Welland, Miller's is 'an almost Transcendentalist insistence on the individual's duty to his own conscience ... widened by the non-Transcendentalist recognition that his conscience may mislead him'.[11]

'"Duty" to society ... implies sacrifice and self-deprivation'

Miller, the artist, regards it as his duty to society not only to write plays but also to formulate his ideas in critical essays and introductions. The plays produced in the 1950s were his adaptation of Ibsen's *An Enemy of the People* (1950), *The Crucible* (1953), *A Memory of Two Mondays* and *A View from the Bridge* (1956), of which *The Crucible* holds most interest in our context.

Miller was not enthusiastic about the idea of adapting Ibsen, but he came to see in the protagonist Dr. Stockmann a person who fights relentlessly for his right to stick to the truth as he sees it, and to inform society about this truth. This conviction is essentially Miller's own as he described it in the Preface to the play: 'It is the question of whether one's vision of the truth ought to be a source of guilt at a time when the mass of men condemn it as a dangerous and devilish lie.'[12] One can see that Dr. Stockmann's conviction can be held with equal rights by a man on the political left and by a political right-winger. Miller was understandably irritated when the play was badly reviewed because, among other things, it was classified as pro-Marxist.

Miller's restless social conscience is focused in another way in *A Memory of Two Mondays*, which portrays a group of characters in the meaningless day-in-day-out traffic of an automobile spare-part shop. Bert, who is the only character who enters and leaves the environment on his way to a college education and who therefore stands at a distance from the meaninglessness of the job, recollects in his memory 'the predicament of characters who are unable to understand or combat oppressive influences in their society'.[13] In this almost static play, a form of 'still life', Miller warns the audiences of the 1950s – and indeed us today – against the danger of alienation and depersonalization becoming the shocking result of job-slavery in industrialized society. Faced with such experiences of meaninglessness in his own life and in the surrounding society, Miller tended to discover and present this truth about that society in a realistic manner. However, at times he felt tempted, with Sartre, Camus and Beckett, to change to the mode of absurdity: 'Had I really obeyed the logic of my daily observations, however, I would have been an absurdist myself, for most of the time I was shaking my head at what was going on and laughing the dry laugh of incredulous amazement' (*Timebends*, p. 314).

Yet *A View from the Bridge* is presented in an intensely realistic form, based as it is on Miller's own experience of racial and social clashes in New York. Italian immigrant Eddie Carbone fights against the injustice of the surrounding society, and in his attempt to retain his good name he blindly forgets himself and loses his only chance to survive. The central struggle in the play is certainly initiated by social injustice and lack of empathy, but the conflict is so deeply personalized that it appears as an instance of Miller's own position that he 'does not look towards social or political ideas as the creators of violence but into the nature of the human being himself'.[14]

The Crucible presents a study of the close interrelationship between powerful social mechanisms and the individual's fight for humanity and personal dignity. Miller had known of and carefully studied the documents of the 1692 Salem witch hunt, but as he says in his autobiography: 'At first I rejected the idea of a play on the subject. My own rationality was too strong, I thought, to really allow me to capture this wildly irrational outbreak. A drama cannot merely describe an emotion, it has to become that emotion' (*Timebends*, p. 331). Miller's treatment of the emotional turmoil of the play's climax in the court scene (Act III) in the Salem meeting house clearly proves that he succeeded in creating such emotion. The spine-chilling hysteria of the children is ingeniously counterbalanced by the quiet and mature passion in the relationship between Proctor and his wife Elizabeth, with Abigail as the connecting pivot between the public madness and the private struggle for human dignity. In his otherwise not very favourable review of the play, David Levin summarizes Proctor's conflict: '*The Crucible* dramatizes brilliantly the dilemma of an innocent man who must confess falsely if he wants to live and who finally gains the courage to insist on his innocence – and hang.'[15] Proctor's personal tragedy is brought about by his wish to stay honest and keep his good name. At the same time he wants to save his wife and all the other innocents from the accusations of witchcraft, which are, as Proctor sees it, the result of Abigail's sexual revenge. Proctor is in the play one of those people who 'have such a belief in themselves and in the rightness of their conscience as to give their lives rather than say what they thought was false'.[16] Or, as Dennis Welland has formulated it, Miller insists on 'the human vulnerability of a man who is not a saint, ... but just a decent man trying to understand and to translate into action the dictates of his conscience, trying to do, not what he feels, but what he thinks is right'.[17]

This was the kind of character Miller placed before his contemporaries in the 1950s, particularly in the Red Scare years, to encourage them to take a stand at a time when social, economic and political pressure seemed to encourage the opposite. Though *The Crucible* has much wider relevance, it is not surprising that his first audiences in 1953 saw the play as an allegory about their own time, however much he himself detested this reading. The text certainly invites this kind of historical identification, because it includes remarks which are directly applicable to the methods of McCarthyism. To mention only a few obvious examples, there are Parris's demands for names (*Crucible*, p. 47); Proctor's question to Hale, 'Is the accuser always holy now?' (*Crucible*, p. 77); Danforth's New-Testament-like defence that 'a person is either with this court or he must be counted against it' (*Crucible*, p. 94); Giles's 'I will not give you no name', alongside Danforth's threat 'to arrest [him] for contempt of this court' (*Crucible*, p. 97); and finally Proctor's 'How may I live without my name? I have given you my soul; leave me my name!' (*Crucible*, p. 143). There seems little doubt, I think, that Miller must have been fully aware of the contemporary dimension of those remarks and indeed of the entire play. His downright denial may be explained by his well-founded fear of being labelled pro-Marxist, with a resulting lesser degree of artistic freedom. In his autobiography he confesses that *The Crucible* was 'the only Broadway play to take on the anti-Communist hysteria' and that he was furious because 'Odets denigrated it to Kazan as "just a story about a bad marriage"' (*Timebends*, p. 236). Years before *Timebends*, there was a critical consensus that *The Crucible*, which 'pillories the ignorance that mass hysteria can foment, was Miller's bold reply to the McCarthy investigations'.[18] In connection with the first American revival of the play in 1958 Miller had already conceded that *The Crucible* was written 'not merely as a response to McCarthyism',[19] but that it had much wider implications.

The history of *The Crucible*'s reception shows its great popularity all over the world, both among audiences and performers. This seems to me to prove that Miller has succeeded in communicating his appeal for personal freedom and personal responsibility when confronted with centralized state manipulation. It is difficult to prove whether the play had any direct effect upon the final downfall of McCarthy, but the growing awareness in the United States towards the end of the 1950s and especially in the 1960s of the importance of taking a personal stand in accordance with one's conscience can only be seen as a new awareness which was partially due to Miller's unremitting fight for these values, both in his own life and in society at large.

Notes

1. Eric Bentley, ed., *Thirty Years of Treason*, Excerpts from the Hearings before the House Committee on Un-American Activities, 1938-1968, (New York: Viking, 1973) p. 819. Further references, all to this edition, are incorporated in the main text.
2. Arthur Miller, *Timebends* (London: Methuen, 1987), p. 4. Further references, all to this edition, are incorporated in the main text.
3. In Robert A. Martin, ed., *The Theater Essays of Arthur Miller* (Harmondsworth: Penguin, 1978), p. 4.
4. William F. Buckley and L. Brent Bozell, 'The Question of Conformity' in Earl Latham, ed., *The Communist Controversy in Washington* (Cambridge, Mass.: Harvard University Press, 1966), p. 53.
5. 'Many Writers: Few Plays' in *Theater Essays*, p. 25.
6. Latham, ed., p. 321.
7. Cited in Roy Cohn, 'History will vindicate him' in Thomas C. Reeves, ed., *McCarthyism* (New York: Kreiger, 1978), p. 66.
8. Dennis Welland, *Miller, A Study of His Plays* (London: Eyre Methuen, 1979), p. 56.
9. Martin, ed., *Theater Essays*, pp. 59, 60, 62.
10. Dennis Welland, *Arthur Miller* (London: Oliver and Boyd, 1961), p. 26.
11. Welland, *Arthur Miller*, pp. 104-105.
12. 'Preface to an *Adaptation of Ibsen's An Enemy of the People*' (New York: Viking, 1951) p. 17.
13. Leonard Moss, *Arthur Miller* (New York: Twayne, 1967), p. 71.
14. Allan Lewis, 'Arthur Miller – Return to the Self' in *American Plays and Playwrights* (New York: Crown, 1965), p. 37.
15. 'Salem Witchcraft in Recent Fiction and Drama' in Arthur Miller, *The Crucible*, ed. by Gerald Weales, (Harmondsworth: The Viking Critical Library, 1977), p. 250. Further references, all to this edition, are incorporated in the main text.
16. Arthur Miller, 'Journey to *The Crucible*' in Martin, ed., *Theater Essays*, pp. 29-30.
17. Welland, *Miller: a study of his plays*, p. 58.
18. Lewis, p. 48.
19. Martin, ed., *Theater Essays*, p. 172.

San Francisco: Arts in the City that Defies Fate

Eric Mottram

On the back cover of Grove Press's *Evergreen Review*, No. 2 (Summer, 1957), editors Donald M. Allen and Barney Rosset announced the news that had already emerged in less concentrated ways: 'A vigorous new generation of writers, painters and musicians in the Bay Area is revolting against the sterility of American "academicians". Brought together for the first time are the leading figures of the "San Francisco Renaissance".' For documentation in a beautifully pictorial and enthusiastic way, Lawrence Ferlinghetti and Nancy J. Peters' *Literary San Francisco* (1980) remains a first-rate entrance into the range, not only of that scene but also of the lively history of the area's broader cultural activities: from the Costanoan Indians to Ishmael Reed, shown to the right of the founders of the *Before Columbus Foundation* in the final (circa 1974) photograph.[1]

In a country as huge and varied as the United States, those intercommunications that, beyond isolated struggles, shape into a cultural phase with historical as well as geographical location and meaning, are still not easy to maintain. American writing, painting and jazz tend to accumulate by drift and personal attraction cityward, before they centre, are stabilized by employment, and – by both serious and irresponsible publicity and with something akin to relief – are called a 'renaissance'. One instance for the arts is Chicago in the time of Harriet Monroe's *Poetry* (which published Carl Sandburg and Edgar Lee Masters alongside William Carlos Williams, D.H. Lawrence, Wallace Stevens, Vachel Lindsay and many other major poets of the years after World War One), and the first great creative period of jazz focused there in King Oliver and Louis Armstrong. Another is the way in which Black Mountain College in North Carolina drew together a range of American and recent European arrivals among artists, writers and teachers in the 1950s. A third is New York, which in the late 1940s and in the 1950s became a generative site for writers, musicians and visual artists. The assemblage in San Francisco may exemplify how the national culture focuses, but also how such a property-owning, capitalist democracy, with its blatant official culture, considers its avant-garde, with and without suspicion, violent denigration and neglect, once it has been discovered through the mass media.

The idea of a 'renaissance of the arts' in this north-west city might suggest a self-appreciative provincialism, backed by publicity. But in the 1940s and 1950s, a revival of painting and poetry centred here that reflected major changes in post-war American arts. To the North and South of the Californian hill port, other western cultural developments were prominent. To the North, in Seattle, the painters Mark Tobey and Morris Graves, and the poets Theodore Roethke and Caroline Kizer, formed a group with other figures at the University of Washington, part of a recharging of north-western culture since the war. The earlier *Rocky Mountain Review* and *Western Review*, with Ray B. West behind them, merged into *Contact*, a leading outlet for writing and criticism. To the South, Ivor Winters, poet and university critic, worked from Stanford University; at Venice West in the Los Angeles area, Lawrence Lipton, poet, representative of the Beat Generation, and author of *The Holy Barbarians* (1959), lived and worked. Henry Miller was a long-term resident of the Pacific settlement of Big Sur. William Saroyan and John Steinbeck were Californian, and the major poet Robinson Jeffers lived for many years at Point Sur.

In San Francisco itself, writing already flourished in the later 1930s and early 1940s through Miller, Kenneth Rexroth, Kenneth Patchen and Robert Duncan, with other active poets. Then a second impetus developed from about 1944 onwards. Rexroth and Duncan were still leaders, but with them were Brother Antoninus (William Everson), Jack Spicer and Philip Lamantia. From 1944 to 1948, George Leite published the magazine *Circle* from Berkeley, the university town across the bay from the city. Around these figures, and a number of first-rate small publishing presses, the writing arts flourished and drew an audience of size and talent unknown except perhaps in New York. The scene remained; talent dispersed and changed, but the value level remained more or less constant, and a third impetus occurred with major developments in painting, jazz and poetry, and with the arrival of Beat writers from the East from the early 1950s onwards.

The older West coast painters Mark Tobey and Morris Graves were well-known and appreciated before this period, and their example – their interests in the Oriental (they had both visited the Far East), in calligraphy, in the non-figurative control of space and volume on the plane, and in mysterious and magical images – had become seminal. Between 1945 and 1952, action painting and abstract expressionism emerged in the work of Hans Hofmann, Jackson Pollock, Adolph Gottlieb, Clyfford Still, and many other artists. Out of Bauhaus principles, Cubism, Dada and Surrealist examples came an American painting. Painters in San Francisco emphasized the large spatial area, the controlled surface movements at work on a plane, and a distinctive figurative concern. The critical work, around 1948, shows the painters incorporating something of the open stretches of the Pacific and the Sierras, the deserts and colour luxuriance of the region, as well as the strong Chinese sign culture of the city and the intense personal detail of Beat Generation writing. Clyfford Still's paintings, as in a kindred sense Mark Rothko's, contain a saturated planimetric force, quiet and tremendous: a massive and incandescent but meditative power. For a time, the focus became the California School of Fine Arts, under Douglas McAgy. A San Francisco body of painters materialized, part of which merged after about 1952 into contemporary American painting. The large plane is treated as a space in which to make personal gestures, creating an existence of emotions and movement in pigment; or it situates human figures in space both intimate and opening into the vast. Local light, sky distances, and sea are transmuted. Rothko taught at the School in 1947 and 1949; Still from 1946 to 1950 (his first exhibition came at the San Francisco Museum of Art in 1943). Lawrence Calcagno was at the School with Rothko and Still from 1947 to 1949, Edward Dugmore was there from 1948 to 1950, and Sam Francis (born in California and educated at Berkeley) began serious painting there in about 1946. Oregon-born Richard Diebenkorn, a major figurative painter, studied at Stanford University and at the University of California, and lived, studied and taught at the School from 1946 onwards. One of the founders of contemporary American painting, Hans Hofmann, taught at Los Angeles and Berkeley in the 1930s; Robert Motherwell was at the School as early as 1932.[2]

San Francisco jazz has a more mixed recent history, necessarily.[3] At the 1939 San Francisco World's Fair, Lou Watters (trumpet) hired Bob Scobey (trumpet) and Turk Murphy (trombone); together they reconstructed the old King Oliver numbers and recorded them in 1941. By then their Yerba Buena band (named after the old Spanish name of the city) had inaugurated a traditionalist revival. A band of good vitality and hearty sound, they recorded again after the war – and now called it the San Francisco Style. But in the later 1940s the cooler sounds of Gerry Mulligan, Stan Getz and Dave Brubeck developed there. Universities and colleges were offering jazz courses and workshops; Earl Hines played piano at the Hangover club; and at Turk and Hyde streets in the night club area the Black Hawk crammed in a capacity audience of two hundred. The owners, Guido Cascienti and his friend Johnny Naga, had bought a bankrupt club in 1949. Cascienti's wife Eleanor ran the cash register; Naga married the head waitress. Despite the fact that he was hard of hearing, and despite his claim that 'I've struggled to keep this place a sewer', Guido booked Brubeck, Mulligan, Chet Baker, Miles Davis and Erroll Garner – and soon had to take the bells off the cash register. By 1959 the Black Hawk had become a centre for modern jazz, and safe enough for *Time* magazine to write up. Paul Desmond played with Brubeck; Cal Tjader concentrated on Latin-American sounds. As jazz columnist Ralph Gleason wrote in the *San Francisco Chronicle*: 'It's the club musicians like best. First, the owners don't tell them what to do. They can't – they can't communicate. Second, the audience is best. Why else except to listen would anyone endure these conditions?' He recalled Art Blakey one night hitting his cymbal so hard it bounced into a table where 'two worshippers were sitting with eyes closed. They went six feet into the air straight up'. In 1958, Naga sold their interest to Max Weiss, secretary-treasurer of the local Fantasy Records label, one of the finest. The Jazz Workshop opened at 473 Broadway, and in 1957 at The Cellar the poets Kenneth Rexroth and Lawrence Ferlinghetti held their highly successful poetry and jazz sessions, the first revival of an art tried out by Vachel Lindsay, Langston Hughes and a few others. At the Coffee Gallery, 1353 Grant Avenue, North Beach, a very good trumpeter named Pony Poindexter became almost a local custom; late at night and in the early morning a black club at 1690 Post Street called Jimbo's Bop City produced fine, vigorous jam sessions – Charlie Parker played there in the early 1950s.

In 1953, the comedian as social critic hit San Francisco.[4] Mort Sahl had been discharged from the Army in 1947 (one of his best routines debunked the Korean war); he obtained a bachelor of science degree at the University of Southern California, and began a master's thesis on traffic flow. Feeling resistance, he went into the theatre. He fell in love with a teenage girl in Los Angeles, followed her to Berkeley, attended some lectures at the University of California there, reportedly slept mainly in his Chevy – and had his appendix out. In the Autumn of 1953, at his girl's suggestion, he auditioned before a live audience at the hungry i club, and the proprietor Enrico Banducci hired him. (Sahl was a friend of Paul Desmond, and sponsored by the jazzman Stan Kenton). His jokes were anti-McCarthy and anti-Eisenhower, and the audience needed the break. This proved to be Sahl's major shaping period, in the Bay Area Beat life he recalls nostalgically. A social critic raised in Los Angeles with the Californian's mistrust of the East, he became a leader of dissent responsive to the need to satirize the assumptions of an affluent and confused middle class. He nevertheless also became, at the age of thirty four, a friend of both John F. Kennedy and Adlai Stevenson. He wore two wrist-watches, one set permanently to Los Angeles time. His non-Marxist irreverence and scepticism was about as far to the Left as most Americans are prepared to shift.

In more extensive and necessarily more prepared ways, strong traditions of dissent provided the grounds for the establishment of the Pacifica Foundation and the FM radio station KPFA, which was run on a shoestring subscription system as a non-profit making organization. The station's programming basis was excellence in political and cultural information, with every subject open to discussion, citizens broadcasting for themselves, and talks by members of the local universities (among them Albert Guerard, Josephine Miles and Seymour Lipset) and writers (Ray Bradbury, many of the new poets, and, regularly, Kenneth Rexroth). KPFA used BBC transcriptions of the Goon Show, among other programmes. Coverage of the civil rights and free speech protests was exemplary, and now constitutes a major resource for cultural history. Long sessions of every kind of good music formed a basis of pleasure and information second to none. And the station became a model for others in the United States.[5]

Within the thriving forms of theatre in the city, a few may be invidiously selected. Between 1952 and 1960 the Actors Workshop increased its annual attendance figures (excluding foreign tours) from ten thousand to fifty-five thousand. The managing director was Jules Irving and the consulting director Herbert Blau; their productions included Osborne's *The Entertainer*, Williams' *Camino Real* and *The Garden District*, Beckett's *Waiting for Godot*, Miller's *The Crucible*, and the American premier of Brecht's *Mother Courage*. The Interplayers, founded in 1946 by Joyce Lancaster (a very successful school-teacher), her husband, Adrian Wilson (a distinguished historian of typography and printing), and two colleagues, is the city's oldest independent theatre, celebrating its fifteenth anniversary in 1961. Productions between 1956 and that year included work by Anouilh, Saroyan, Lorca, Giraudoux, Shaw, Lillian Hellman, Arthur Miller, Thornton Wilder, Sardou, Behan, Wycherley and Shakespeare.

Public poetry readings in the city reached the proportions of an oral revival in the 1950s, and were a major part of the third impetus of the renaissance. Two interrelated events lead to the changes. San Francisco State College's Division of Humanities and Language Arts included not only distinguished teachers such as Samuel I. Hayakawa, James Schevill, Ray B. West and Walter Van Tilburg Clark, but also the Poetry Centre, founded by Ruth Witt-Diamant in 1954-55 with the assistance of a $5,000 Rockefeller grant and the help of W.H. Auden. With a subscription membership as well, the Poetry Centre's activities were by 1960 part of the College's curriculum, with workshops, seminars, and readings by a wide range of poets. The 1959 programme included Rexroth, Caroline Kizer and the British poet George Barker. Spring 1960 featured Richard Eberhart, Stanley Kunitz, and Louis Simpson; in the Summer John Crowe Ransom, Cid Corman, Madeleine Gleason and James Broughton – who called the Poetry Centre 'a gymnasium of poetic forms' – gave readings.

The second event was the advent and establishment of new writers, both locals and recent arrivals from the East. Jack Kerouac arrived as early as 1949 (his most famous novel *On the Road* was published in 1957 but he wrote it some time before 1951). Lawrence Ferlinghetti came in 1951, and in June 1953 founded the City Lights bookshop at 261 Columbus Avenue in collaboration with Peter Martin. Such was his subsequent identification with the city's culture that in 1975 San Francisco proclaimed a Lawrence Ferlinghetti Day in honour of a fine poet, an enterprising publisher and a tireless promoter of civil rights in the great anarchist traditions of the north-west United States. Allen Ginsberg arrived in 1954 and the following year met up in Berkeley with Gary

Snyder. These poets were followed in 1956 by Gregory Corso, who stayed five months, reading with Ginsberg. (Most of his *Gasoline*, the eighth of Ferlinghetti's City Lights *Pocket Poets* series, was written later in Mexico). In 1955, Ferlinghetti published his own poems, *Pictures from a Gone World*, and Ginsberg's *Howl and Other Poems* as numbers one and four of *Pocket Poets*. Numbers two and three were by Rexroth and Patchen respectively, and these were followed by editions of work by Robert Duncan, William Carlos Williams and Denise Levertov.

Other poets who read and were published in the Bay Area at this time included Michael McClure, Philip Whalen, David Meltzer, Jack Spicer, John Wieners, Thomas Parkinson, Ebbe Borregaard and Kirby Doyle. In 1956 the older East Coast poet, Richard Eberhart, wrote in the *New York Times* for 2 September 1956: 'Poetry here has become a tangible social force, moving and unifying its audience, releasing the energies of the audience through spoken, even shouted, verse, in a way at present unique to this region.'

In his *The Holy Barbarians*, Lawrence Lipton emphasized the effect of Dylan Thomas's public readings in the bardic manner on poetry performance outside the classroom and the study. He cites Robert Duncan's opinion that:

> the poet must have some urge for a large audience, which is also a social urge. What that audience is to be is not clear yet – to me, at least – but that social urge must certainly be to transform the nature of the audience. Not only to find his audience, but the audience must find him, and finding his audience he would also find the ritual conditions necessary to transform the audience. At the present time when we have poetry readings at a Poetry Center, rising out of universities, the poet's urge is disruptive, actually, of these institutions.... Poets have not yet learned to distinguish between the intimate poem and its intimate audience and the public poem.[6]

Writing in *Downbeat* for 2 May 1957, Gleason recalls Rexroth thinking of jazz and poetry as a way of getting new and good lyrics for the music. The first session at The Cellar became a problem of fitting preconceived poem to improvised music. Ferlinghetti worked in the same way; so too did Kenneth Patchen with the Chamber Jazz Sextet at the Black Hawk. In *Downbeat* for 14 November 1957, Gleason wrote:

> Mostly the poets are slumming. Jazz already has its audience and they don't. They're cashing in on the jazz audience but they won't try to learn anything from jazz or listen to it or try to allow the natural jazz rhythms they have to come out.... Not until a poet comes along who learns what jazz is all about and then writes poetry will there be any merger.

But the revival of an oral tradition of performance for skills in voice and music, whether using the instance of Dylan Thomas's recordings or not, was vital, and clearly Rexroth and Ferlinghetti looked for a way of restoring poetry as a social art, allied to music and using jazz as a peculiarly American musical language. The poem written as a score for performance substantiates the dimension of sound and voice; and it is there too, vitally, in Kerouac's recording of part of his *The Subterraneans* (1958): the tape has become text.

Following World War Two, there was also an exceptional flourishing of little presses and literature magazines for the academically-termed 'avant-garde', with editors of the calibre of Jonathan Williams, Cid Corman, Robert Creeley and others; their magazines and presses (*Jargon, Origin, Black Mountain Review*); and much more. San Francisco became a main focus, largely decentralized away from capital and its market place. Writers the academic, and therefore timid, presses could not countenance had a publication scene of considerable reputation and power. Local fame in this case was not provincial. But the city itself was certainly an attraction, for reasons which are usefully documented in Daniel Wolf and Ed Fancher's *Village Voice Reader* (1962).[7] In February 1957, the *Voice* recorded that Ginsberg and Corso had returned from San Francisco and were off to Tangier. Ginsberg said: 'We want everyone to know that we had to leave the Village to find fulfilment and recognition'; Corso added: 'There is no room for youth and vitality in New York. It is a city full of guilty academicians.... We wanted to get away from the cliques and snobbery here. The poets in the Village are disorganized and isolated.' Fresh from being photographed for *Life*, he proclaimed: 'Right now we're hot.' In September, Kerouac was saying he had to become a San Francisco writer in order to be famous. Recognition came in the West. Why? 'One thing. Rexroth. A great man. A great critic. Interested in young people, interested in everything.' Later he had kicked Kerouac out of his house as an objectionable loafer, but Kerouac held no grudge, and apparently obtained some pleasure from the event. By this time his part in the city's renaissance was over. That same year the *Evergreen Review* had devoted its second number to 'the San Francisco Scene', and the success of this issue assured a wide distribution of information. But throughout 1957 Ginsberg's 'Howl' was on trial for (and finally exonerated from) obscenity charges. Much of the pyrotechnic force of the 1950s calmed into steady creativity in place of the packed, excited readings, the shock dissent tactics of the Beat writers, and the jazz and poetry sessions that had by then practically ceased. The scene so well evaluated by Rexroth in his essay 'Disengagement: the Art of the Beat Generation' in 1957 had nearly become part of recent history.[8]

Rexroth begins by recording the post-war migration of what was left of the avant-garde to northern California, meeting part of the old guard already there, including Henry Miller and himself: 'San Francisco today is the seat of an intense literary activity not unlike Chicago of the first quarter of the century. A whole school of poets has grown up – almost all of them migrated here from somewhere else.'[9] The development of poetry readings at the Poetry Centre, in galleries and in private homes means that poetry has become an actual social force – something which has always sounded hitherto like a Utopian dream of the William Morris sort. It is a very thrilling experience to hear an audience of more than three hundred people stand and cheer and clap, as they invariably do at a reading by Allen Ginsberg, certainly a poet of revolt if there ever was one. There is no question but that the San Francisco renaissance is radically different from what is going on elsewhere. There are hand presses, poetry readings, young writers elsewhere – but nowhere else is there a whole younger generation culture pattern characterized by total rejection of the official high-brow culture – where critics like John Crowe Ransom or Lionel Trilling, magazines like the *Kenyon*, *Hudson* and *Partisan* reviews are looked on as 'The Enemy' – the other side of the barricades.

There is only one trouble about the renaissance in San Francisco. It is too far away from the literary market place. That, of course, is the reason why the Bohemian remnant, the avant garde, have migrated here.... Distance from New York City does, however, make it harder to get things, if not published, at least nationally circulated.... Social disengagement, artistic integrity, voluntary poverty – these are powerful virtues and may pull though, but they are not the virtues we tried to inculcate – rather they are the exact opposite.

And by 'we' he means 'my generation'. The city's police became a nuisance, writers drifted away, tourists and 'beatniks' took over. In September 1962 Kerouac published *Big Sur*, a restless, searching narrative of disillusion with the Beat way of life in his New York and San Francisco years. At the 1962 Poetry Centre festival, the local excellence came mainly from Ferlinghetti's play *The Alligation* and the poems of Brother Antoninus. Ginsberg and Corso were not in America, and Duncan did not read. The poetry came from Whalen, Broughton, Rexroth, Jack Gilbert and other local figures. In 1961 the statue of Saint Francis that Ferlinghetti had celebrated in one of his best poems was removed from its church porch on Vallejo Street. The following year, the poet said that 'in the city that once jumped with café poetry readings, due to "police harassment" the jumping has slowed to a crawl'. 'The beats', he added, 'are middle-aged men in dungarees.' The Bohemian communities – from the Golden Gate to Greenwich Village – kept changing, and the Beat would presently be followed by something else: 'If I knew what it would be, I'd publish it.'

In a 1949 issue of *Contact,* a San Francisco collection of new writings and essays on art and ideas, Walter Van Tilburg Clark delineated some of the auspices of the culture. As late as the 1920s, the flowering of the arts in the West was still considered subservient to a basis of cowboys and the Klondyke, Bret Harte, Zane Grey and Jack London's roughs. But then Robinson Jeffers and John Steinbeck became nationally known figures, living in California. Little was considered in the Rockies and Sierras or the north-west, however. One rectifier was Ray B. West. Teaching in a high school in Murray, Utah in 1935, he began to plan for the first issue of the *International Review of English and Speech* (1936), a journal which in 1945 became the *Rocky Mountain Review*, then (when West moved via the University of Kansas to the

139

University of Iowa) *The Western Review*, and subsequently part of *Contact*. Clark concluded:

> There is a great deal of similarity between this decade and the twenties, and much of it goes deeper than the obvious revival or imitation of clothes, jazz, dances, and automobiles. There is for one thing, a comparable ferment in literature, another questing for values and for the forms that can embody them effectively. And this time the ferment seems to be most active in the West and to have its centre in San Francisco.

In the San Francisco number of *Esquire*, the cultural historian Lynn White traces the city culture further back, to the trek westward of European intellectuals after the 1848 revolution failures. White believes that the place remained surprisingly continental European. The Protestant culture was slacker, and, with the subsequent arrival of Japanese and Filipinos (after the earlier Chinese), subject to less racial cleavage.

Albert Parry reminds us San Francisco also had an early Bohemia: that, for instance, Ada Clare was in San Francisco in 1864 and wrote for the *Golden Era*, where Bret Harte and, later, Joaquin Miller and Mark Twain also appeared.[10] Clare criticized books, theatre, life and manners in the West, hated it, sailed for Hawaii, and then returned to San Francisco, where, helped by Tom Maguire, she revived her stage career. She played Camille, was greeted with catcalls and sniggers, and then left for New York. In 1863 the Oakland *Amateur Bohemian* carried one of Jack London's earliest contributions, while in San Francisco Daniel O'Connell issued the *Illustrated Bohemian* in 1865. Bret Harte, the archetypal Bohemian or 'Murgerite', published *Bohemian Papers* and *Bohemian Days in San Francisco*: records of gambling saloons, the Chinese quarter and carefree miners, as well as the pioneer life. In the 1860s there were enough 'Latins' for a Latin Quarter. Writers on the *Chronicle* and the *Examiner* formed a Bohemian Club of determined nonconformists which included Ambrose Bierce. Perry records that when they moved headquarters to Pine Street in 1877, their pet owl, Dick, was carried in the procession in a cage on a litter, and on arrival immediately laid an egg. This was taken as a tremendous omen as well as a steady talking point. In 1873 Bret Harte and Mark Twain were elected honourary members. There were continuous parties, what used to be called 'high jinks', and celebrations for visiting artists. Their motto was 'Weaving Spiders Come Not Here'; in 1882 their patron saint became St. John Nepomuck, a Czech from Bohemia who died rather than tell a woman's secret. In 1880 a break-away group, who thought the once-bold club had become dainty and commercial, formed the Pandemonium in rooms over a grocery store, where they smoked clay pipes and gorged on beer and sandwiches. *The Lark*, which lasted for two years from 1895, entertained 'no advertisements, no criticism; no timeliness and no women contributors', and proclaimed 'it is the luxuries that are necessary'. It was printed on Chinese bamboo paper. The earthquake of 1906 disastrously curtailed these activities.

Bret Harte had called the city 'serene, indifferent to Fate'. Now it had to be scornful of Fate. In 1895, the 'Balclutha', last of the Cape Horn square-rigged sailing fleet, was given permanent moorings at Pier 43 on Fisherman's Wharf. At North Beach were located the first docks (at the foot of Broadway, where early immigrants landed) and the first colonies (at the base of Telegraph Hill). Writers and artists later lived on the hill's slopes, and in the surrounding multi-racial areas. But it was also an early lookout, or semaphore signal station, informing approaching ships passing through the Golden Gate. Coit Tower, which stood at its apex, was a memorial to San Francisco's early volunteer firemen. Lilly Hitchcock Coit, a young lady who enjoyed chasing fires, left part of her fortune to establish it. Inside, it features 1930s murals by San Francisco artists.

Part of the reason for the renaissance remained the pleasantness of the city as a place to live with a history of liberal encouragement for the arts. So that there was a specific place for Berne Porter publishing Duncan at Berkeley in 1947 and 1949, and Philip Lamantia's *Erotic Poems* in 1946. Jonathan Williams' Jargon press published McClure's *Passage*, his first book, from Big Sur in 1956, and Robert Creeley's poems between 1953 and 1959. The Auer-hahn Press published Lamantia, McClure, Whalen and John Wieners in 1958 and 1959. Discovery published David Meltzer, Centaur published Duncan – the list could be lengthily extended. And the little press magazines were also an essential vanguard. In the words of Thomas Parkinson, a poet and a teacher at Berkeley:

> The poetry they wrote and liked was deeply religious in tone, personalist in dramaturgy, imagist in iconographic habit, and experimentalist in prosody. With this poetics was associated a loose cluster of concerns and attitudes – anarcho-pacificism in politics, relatively conservative (especially Roman Catholic) religious preoccupations, a generally receptive attitude toward Eastern art and thought that grew naturally out of the Pacific Basin orientation of the great port of San Francisco, intensive interest in the traditions of European experimentalism, and perhaps above all a very deep elegiac sense of the destruction of both the natural world and the possibilities of the American dream (its waste in the great wars and the frozen polity of the postwar period) dramatized in the brutal exploitation of California as its population swelled.[11]

The renaissance formed round senses of community, that particularly American sense of community based on an altruistic dream within a vast, competitive, market economy. The poetic community around Duncan, George Leite and Kenneth Rexroth, and *Circle* magazine, drew in Josephine Miles (a poet and university teacher of distinction), George P. Elliott and Brother Antoninus (the poet William Everson, who entered the Dominican order as a lay brother without vows in 1951). Their variety is connected by their resistance to official culture. Rexroth was not a great poet, but a man of communication, of ideas, and of sympathy for younger writers, His technical knowledge was excellent, and he really knew and promoted the work of Lawrence, Blake and Yeats, the philosophy of Martin Buber, the anarchists, Thoreau, and twentieth-century French poetry from Apollinaire to Reverdy. People who came to his discussions and readings were among the founders of KPFA and the Pacifica Foundation: 'I write poetry to seduce women and overthrow the capitalist system.'[12]

Robert Duncan was a great poet as well as a centre, a local man organizing discussions and readings, drawing in the post-war student and writer population as it rapidly increased. At one time he co-directed the Poetry Centre, and through him the local was fertilized by work associated with Black Mountain College and the *Black Mountain Review*, edited by Robert Creeley, whose first number (appearing in Spring 1954) contained work by Charles Olson, Irving Layton, Paul Blackburn, and Creeley himself. The contributing editors were Blackburn, Layton, Olson and Rexroth – although the latter left not long after as a result of a row about Dylan Thomas and Theodore Roethke, both of whom he admired. These poets inherited and developed the work of Pound, William Carlos Williams and the Objectivists, including Louis Zukofsky, and the standards of cultural relevance and open field, open form poetics.

Duncan's poetry, in the words of Jack Spicer in *After Lorca*, 'is a collage of the real.... Things don't connect; they correspond. That is what makes it possible for a poet to translate real objects, to bring them across language as easily as he can bring them across time'. His play or 'comic masque' *Faust Foutu* was first performed at a reading in the Six Gallery in January 1955. The readers were himself, Spicer, Michael McClure, Helen Adam, and the artist Jess Collins. Of the play Duncan wrote: 'Writing is compounded of wisdom and intuition. Faust seeks to wrench himself free from the world of wisdom and to achieve pure intuition. My lot is not Faust's lot, but the play's lot: this conflict unresolved ... a play is a play here – a prolonged charged aimless, constantly aimed, play ground.' Duncan once spoke of the poem as 'a spiritual urgency at the dark ladders leaping', and said that he 'questions the whole basis of an unbroken continuum in poetic language and tries to force a new sense of interrupted movement'. The results needed the kind of audience engendered in San Francisco, and he situated himself carefully within that orbit. He worked in Berkeley between 1946 and 1950 with Spicer, whom he called his mentor, censor and peer. In 1950, he says, Pound's *Pisan Cantos* and Williams' *Paterson* provided the 'measure', and the painters 'displayed new organizations allowing for discontinuities in space, for more vitality then (variety of impulse) than I had in my work in poetry'. The next recognition came from the Black Mountain poets and Spicer's *After Lorca*, published by the White Rabbit press in San Francisco in 1957. Duncan awakened to what he called 'a multiphasic experience sought as multiphasic form' through Olson's poems and theory, and the painter Jess Collins. In his *Mayan Letters* Olson was saying 'I keep thinking, it comes to this culture displacing the state'. Duncan shared this belief, and in 1959 developed a sense of the necessity whole:

> There is a wholeness of what we are that we will never know; we are always, as the line of the phrase or the word is, the moment of that wholeness – an event; but it, the wholeness of what we are, goes back into an obscurity and extends to and into an obscurity. The obscurity is part too of the work, of the form, if it be whole.

In the 1940s and 1950s it had become necessary for some poets to peel off custom, to disaffiliate from the 'criticism-poetry' of the recent past. San Francisco offered a place for the dissent to take place in communities: Miller's at Big Sur; around Telegraph Hill and Coit Tower in the city's North Beach area; groups further South in Venice West, Los Angeles; and elsewhere. But as Ferlinghetti insisted, it was not simply a matter of disengagement. He distinguishes between Beats and poets. Poets are not disengaged: 'Only the dead are disengaged. And the wiggy nihilism of the Beat hipster, if carried to its natural conclusion, actually means the death of the creative artist himself. While the non-commitment of the artist is itself a suicidal and deluded variation of the same nihilism.'

Kerouac's 'October in the Railroad Earth' tells of his working on the railroad, living on Third Street, San Francisco, and obtaining some of the necessary freedom from the limited independence his job affords.[13] He writes in long-breathed sentences and cadences in the traditions of Thomas Wolfe and Henry Miller, calling it 'spontaneous bop prosody' after developments in jazz during the late 1940s and early 1950s. Beginning his Jargon press series in the city in 1951, Jonathan Williams said of his vocation as publisher as well as (excellent) poet:

> There are certain kindred spirits at work in this country, and it is to make coherence of these that *Jargon* exists. It does not represent an armed camp. The avant garde is never anything but a community of particular sympathy. I have attempted to know it in a number of areas because it is the total locale of America that produces the culture. [Edward] Dahlberg asks whether a civilization can be produced on a landscape vaster than the body of a Titan. It is our business to try.

The most intense publicity surrounded Allen Ginsberg, fresh from revolt against Columbia University, New York, and the literary quarterlies world. His first major poem 'Howl' was composed in San Francisco in 1955: 'I suddenly turned aside in San Francisco, unemployment compensation leisure to follow my romantic inspiration – Hebraic-Melvillean bardic breath.' He began to use Whitman's long-breathed linear structures to develop his own 'large organic structures'. Part Two of the poem is a rhythmic denunciation chant against Moloch, god of war, and, by extension, of money, greed and organized industrial-mechanized society:

I had an apartment on Nob Hill, I got high on peyote, & saw an image of the robot skullface of Moloch in the upper stories of a big hotel glaring into my window; got high weeks later again, the Visage was still there in red smokey downtown Metropolis. I wandered down Powell street muttering, 'Moloch, Moloch' all night and wrote *Howl* II ... deep in the hellish vale.[14]

It was the local response to Ginsberg reading this poem that impressed Rexroth as a new poetic sociality. *Howl and Other Poems* was in fact printed in England. In 1957 the Collector of Customs denounced the poem as obscene, a charge contested by the American Civil Liberties Union. The *San Francisco Chronicle* invited Ferlinghetti to defend the poem he had published: 'It is not the poet but what he observes which is revealed as obscene. The great obscene wastes of *Howl* are the sad wastes of the mechanized world, lost among atom bombs and insane nationalisms.' But he was arrested by the police. The *Chronicle*'s headline ran 'The Cops Don't Allow No Renaissance Here'. In fact Judge Clayton Holmes had cleared the work of the obscenity charge, and it was the second printing that the Collector, Chester MacPhee, had attacked. The local United States Attorney refused to institute condemnation proceedings against the poem. The trial proceeded through the summer of 1957, and included critical support for the poem from University of California professors, Herbert Blau of the Actors Workshop, Kenneth Rexroth, Vincent McHugh (Ferlinghetti's colleague) – these actually in the witness box – as well as Robert Duncan, Ruth Witt-Diamant, Kenneth Patchen, James Laughlin of New Directions and many others. *Howl* was finally cleared; the judge's summing up is in fact a good analysis of the poem – and he was re-elected to office.[15] In 1959 Ginsberg wrote that the

poetic renaissance glimpsed in San Francisco has been responded to with ugliness, anger, jealousy, vitriol, sullen protestations of superiority. And violence. By police, by customs officials, post-office employees, by trustees of great universities. By anyone whose love of Power has led him to a position where he can push other people around over a difference of opinion – or Vision.[16]

The *Howl* trial typified the conflicting responses to the San Francisco renaissance, both in the United States and in Europe, especially Britain. Frank J. Donner's *The Un-Americans* (1961) excellently details the attack on the liberties articulated by the renaissance, which led to the violence of authoritarian America during the 1960s. On 13 May 1960 about one hundred policeman and a squadron of motorcycle cops attacked about two thousand students with hoses as they demonstrated in front of San Francisco City Hall. The seated students were beaten up and dragged away, some feet first, heads bumping on the marble steps. A *New York Post* journalist reported: 'Never in twenty years as a reporter have I seen such brutality.' An appalling description followed. This was the climax of three days' protest against the House Un-American Activities Committee (HUAC) by Bay Area students, their parents, professors, ministers and other alarmed citizens. They demanded the Committee's abolition, challenged its legality and denounced its abuses. J. Edgar Hoover, the FBI chief, of course denounced the protest as 'communist-instigated' and so forth, with no evidence offered, as usual. Charges against sixty-three of the sixty-four people arrested were dismissed; fifty-eight of them issued a statement: 'Nobody incited us, nobody misguided us. We were led by our own convictions and we still stand firmly by them.'

It was the fourth visit of HUAC to the city, following earlier appearances in 1952, 1956, and 1957. The 1957 hearing had been darkened by the suicide of William Sherwood, a subpoenaed scientist. His suicide note said he could not face the ordeal of televised hearings. Protest increased with the subpoena served by HUAC on 110 school-teachers, after which the committee was forced into retreat by public outrage from the Democratic Party, local churches, organized labour, educators, students and part of the press. The 1959 hearings were cancelled, but in 1960 HUAC returned. Most of the students attacked were members of the University of California's Students for Civil Liberties group. Beat had given way to Protest. HUAC had chosen to dub subversive the NAACP, the National Council of Churches, SANE, and other organizations protesting against the government's imperialist and anti-civil rights policies. The televised news spread round the world.

But the image of San Francisco as a focus of social and political conflict and demonstrations of artistic and political excellence in revolt produced classic responses throughout the 1950s and 1960s. In *Esquire* magazine for February 1958, John Clellon Holmes, a leading chronicler of the Beat Generation writers, described San Francisco as 'in many ways, the Paris of this generation'. By this time, the news had spread to Britain. On 23 November 1958 Al Alvarez wrote in *The Observer* of the Beat writers and the associates: 'The simple fact [is] that they are the only group in America whose whole way of life is based on a kind of a-moral sales resistance. They deny Eisenhower's Peace-and-Prosperity by ignoring its most efficient proselytizing, the advertisement. The Beats are, by programme, the have-nots and the indifferent.' He added that their passivity was supported by Oriental religion, genuine or weak, and sometimes maintained through drugs. This journalistic generalization barely entered the scene, but it was typical. But in the *New Statesman* for 14 February 1959, Marcus Cunliffe, the distinguished pioneer of American Studies in British universities, wrote of San Francisco:

The elements in the situation include a shoddy Bohemia; a half-genuine, half-commercialized tincture of the Orient; a too-rapid spread of population and industry; and yet a city of rare felicities: the magnificent shock of the Pacific challenging the California coastline; the clean, extraordinary solitudes of California mountain country. It is an amalgam of camping, wine-drinking, hi-fi, Mort Sahl, sports cars, intellectualism, vulgarity. The sun is benign, the fog harmless, the night sky packed with stars, the day sky scored with fighter-trails. Physical well-being – sheer sensation, and a good thing too –

combines cynicism, guilt, the feeling that one cannot remember what yesterday was like and cannot be sure of tomorrow. Something of the mood has been evoked by Jack Kerouac. Mr. Rexroth states it better, with intelligence, sensibility and considerable precision ... an honest and diversified guide to one of the most lovely, privileged, important and uneasy corners of our world.

The theatre critic and dramaturge Kenneth Tynan told *Observer* readers on 1 September 1959 that it was 'a haven of tolerance', and refered to the listener-sponsored radio station KPFA (he had been particularly impressed by its four-hour programme of marijuana interviews), Mort Sahl and Lenny Bruce, and Alan Watts' advocacies of Zen Buddhism. He cited Rexroth: 'We had our renaissance twenty years ago' – meaning himself, Henry Miller, Kenneth Patchen and Robert Duncan. Ralph Gleason had reported that Pierre de Lattre, a young Congregationalist minister who ran the Bread and Wine Mission (now a laundromat, and the address of *Beatitude* magazine), got tired of being on call day and night and retired to the country to write a novel. Tynan added: 'He says he likes the Beats because they live a communal life more selfless and unworldly than he had ever seen outside purely religious groups', one dedicated to a poverty of bare necessities, hatred of violence and the Bomb, engaged in contemplation, and doing no harm except perhaps to themselves. By 25 March 1961, W.J. Weatherby was bringing the good news to *Guardian* readers: 'an easy-going place in handsome surroundings with no man his neighbour's watcher'. This city could be a good place for nonconformist living and writing. At least one Briton made a name there. *The Kensington Post* for 1 January 1964 reported how Michael Jackson, son of a Bayswater (London) publican, began as a disc jockey in the Bay Area, and then from his inter-disc patter and phone-in calls built up a public service:

> While he was working on the RKO station KHY, San Francisco, Mort Sahl called him the 'all-night psychiatrist'. He held public telephone conversations with private citizens in the small hours of the night about their problems, and had an answer for everything, from desperate queries from pregnant 15-year-olds ('tell your parents') to juvenile delinquents with a stolen car ('don't take it over the State boundary').
> Nine months ago the Hollywood station KEWB bid for his services, and he has been doing a similar programme there during the peak listening hours of 7 p.m. to 10.30 p.m. This month he received the premier accolade of the *Los Angeles Sunday Times*.

But San Francisco authorities were not as liberal as some of these reports maintained. When Benny Bufano's statue of St. Francis was removed from the porch of the church of St. Francis and transported to Oakland, Lawrence Ferlinghetti commented to the *San Francisco Chronicle* for 16 March 1961: 'They have driven away the creative people, so now they remove the statue of their saint.'[17] Ralph Gleason had noticed the moves the previous year, in *Contact* magazine. He begins 'The Comedy of Dissent' by noticing the growth of satire as a total assault on cultural taboos, assumptions and stereotypes in the night clubs and jazz clubs: Sahl against Eisenhower, Nixon and McCarthy, alone at one time, and creating his audience. Then he adds:

> The mass communications media and the San Francisco police department were being logical when they campaigned against the beatniks (that well-meaning but misguided group on the periphery of the jazz world).... The captive poets in the universities are correct in damning Ginsberg. And the spokesmen for the vested interests, literary or otherwise ... are correct in adding their voices to the derisive chorus. All of the forces of status quo have reacted correctly and instinctively in self-preservation....
>
> As jazz was a dissent from the classics, Kerouac, Rexroth, Ginsberg, Ferlinghetti and the rest are a dissent from the Madison Avenue of literature, on the road, perhaps, in a world they never made, but what is more important, ON THE MOVE. And it is all part of the same thing – the total dissent including the wit of Lenny Bruce.
>
> Comedy, satire and humour in this country – from the time of Mark Twain on down – has been characterized by the wisecrack, the quip and switch on the old joke. The depression gave it guts enough to become really socially useful as satire. The Moral Depression of the Nuclear Age is doing the same thing again.

But the following year, in the *New Statesman* for 2 June, this San Francisco journalist noted the tourist degeneration of beat into beatnik, and the movement to Big Sur, Monterey, Santa Monica and Venice West; to other San Francisco areas (the Fillmore, Potrero and Russian hills); and upcoast to Bolinas or inland to the Sierra – but mostly to New York. 'The old cafes have become record shops, art-goods shops; the Co-Existence Bagel Shop sells sandals and jewellery; the Jazz Cellar is empty.' The Place, with its notorious 'blabbermouth night' – anyone could get up and speak at will – suffered from the 'psychopathic police department', and, as the owner Jay Hoppe said, 'the cops don't bother the tourists'.

Gleason's mockery of the vested interests world was well-merited. Norman Podhoretz's article in *Esquire* magazine for December 1958 exemplified the panic:

> The San Francisco 'renaissance' and the spread during the last few years of hipsterism, juvenile delinquency, and drug addiction among the young arise from the same central cause: the flabbiness and spinelessness of contemporary American middle-class culture.... The books written by respectable people ... the way of life, the values, and the attitudes shared by the majority of the college-educated Americans ... the class that runs America ... indifferent or even hostile to religion ... favours greater freedom in sexual matters than the older middle class did ... [now] grown defensive and timid about its [liberal and 'enlightened'] values, and has therefore proved unable to assert its authority over the young....

Now the old ways had been replaced by:

> a society where parents are only too happy to let the children 'decide for themselves' because they don't have enough faith in the soundness of the principles and values that are the driving force of their own way of life ... the slogans of rugged economic

147

individualism preached incessantly by politicians and propagandists who themselves know perfectly well that the day of rugged individualism is long since gone; the pretence that we are a pious God-fearing nation ... the insidious attempt by clerics in psychiatric clothing to make the freer sexual mores of a whole population seem disreputable and unhealthy by calling them 'immaturity'.... What juvenile delinquency is to life, the San Francisco writers are to literature – howling at random against they don't know what and making up aesthetic rules of their own that are a rough equivalent in literary terms of the rule of the secret gang, where control and discipline are 'chicken', and subtle or complicated ideas are a lot of bull....

The San Francisco writers, in their hatred of intelligence, their refusal to respect the requirements of artistic discipline, their contempt for precision and clarity, are a perfect reflection of 'the fear of maturity', the fear of becoming a man that [Robert] Brustein finds in American youth at large.

Podhoretz's diatribe is worth re-quoting at length as a classic basis for police and media delinquency, for the licence that civic authorities permit themselves, knowing the kind of ideological analysis they can rely on. The facts required to estimate the value of San Francisco renaissance culture are ignored in order to boost a radical and hierarchical social structure in which the arts are a permanent subject of attack, since their inventive imagination is itself considered to be subversive of all order. Even a cursory glance at the evidence in Don Herron's *The Literary World of San Francisco and its Environs*, Ferlinghetti and Peters' *Literary San Francisco*, Caroline Jones's *Bay Area Figurative Art 1950-1965*, Thomas Albright's *Art in the San Francisco Bay Area 1945-1950*, and Rebecca Solnit's *Secret Exhibition* will vanquish the cultural destroyers, at least temporarily.

Notes

1. Lawrence Ferlinghetti and Nancy J. Peters, *Literary San Francisco* (San Francisco: City Lights Books and Harper and Row, 1980).
2. Caroline A. Jones, *Bay Area Figurative Art 1950-1965* (San Francisco: San Francisco Museum of Modern Art/University of California Press, 1990); Thomas Albright, *Art in the San Francisco Bay Area 1945-1980* (Berkeley: University of California Press, 1985); Rebecca Solnit, *Secret Exhibition: Six Californian Artists of the Cold War Era* (San Francisco: City Lights Books, 1990); Thomas Kellein, ed., *Clyfford Still, 1904-1980* (Munich: Prestel-Verlag, 1992); Richard Armstrong, *David Park* (New York: Whitney Museum of American Art, 1989); *Elmer Bischoff*, with essay by Donald Kuspit (San Francisco: John Berggruen Gallery, 1990).
3. For a brief survey, see Ralph Gleason, 'San Francisco Jazz Scene', *Evergreen Review*, 1, 2 (Summer, 1957), 59-64.
4. For further details, see Eric Mottram, 'The American Comedian as Social Critic, 1950-1970', in this volume.
5. For further details, see John Whiting, 'The Lengthening Shadow: Lewis Hill and the Origins of Listener-Sponsored Broadcasting in America', in this volume.

6. Lawrence Lipton, *The Holy Barbarians* (New York: Dembner Books, 1959), p. 200.
7. Daniel Wolf and Ed Fancher, eds., *The Village Voice Reader* (Garden City, New York: Doubleday, 1962).
8. Kenneth Rexroth, 'Disengagement: the Art of the Beat Generation', rpt. in Thomas Parkinson, ed., *A Casebook on the Beat* (New York: Thomas Crowell, 1961).
9. See also Kenneth Rexroth, 'The New Poetry', in his *Assays* (New York: New Directions, 1961); rpt. in Eric Mottram, ed., *The Kenneth Rexroth Reader* (London: Cape, 1971), pp. 236-45.
10. Albert Parry, *Garrets and Pretenders: A History of Bohemianism in America* (New York: Dover, 1960).
11. Thomas Parkinson, 'Phenomenon or Generation', in Parkinson, ed., p. 281.
12. See also Nick Harvey, *Mark in Time: Portraits and Poetry/San Francisco* (San Francisco: Glide Publications, 1971).
13. Jack Kerouac, 'October in the Railroad Earth', *Evergreen Review*, 1, 2 (Summer, 1957), 119-36; rpt in Parkinson, ed., pp. 31-65.
14. Allen Ginsberg, 'Notes Written on Finally Recording "Howl"', rpt. in Parkinson, ed., pp. 27-28.
15. For details of the trial, see Allen Ginsberg, *Howl. Original Draft Facsimile, Transcript and Variant Versions*, ed. Barry Miles (New York: Harper and Row, 1986), pp. 169-74; for transcripts of court testimony, see Lawrence Ferlinghetti, 'Horn on HOWL', *Evergreen Review*, 1, 4 (Winter, 1957), 145-58.
16. Allen Ginsberg, 'Poetry, Violence and the Trembling Lambs', *Village Voice*, 4, 44 (25 August 1959), 1, 8; rpt in Parkinson, ed., pp. 24-27.
17. *San Francisco Chronicle*, 16 March 1961.

Plurality and the Reproduced: A Selective Approach to American Visual Arts in the 1950s

Allen Fisher

Introduction

Two of the characteristics of American art in the 1950s still prominent today are *plurality* and *simulation*. Plurality results from the changing of boundaries and the quantitative increase in geographical awareness and access. Simulation reproduces the already-reproduced in an age of multi-media that fuels the quantitative spread of mass communication. Plurality was contemporary with an acceptance of uncertainty and an active process of boundary breaking and expansion in which the commodity fetish was transformed then and subsequently into a fetish for techniques and precisions or breakages from them. Simulation was most readily achieved through collage in which more than one reality interacted on the same plane and produced a disrupted spacetime. 1950s American visual art provides part of the rich basis for these characteristics still prevalent in the 1990s. The decade witnessed the development of collage art and processes of recurrence in a period which also saw the transformation of gestural and Expressionist modes into new appraisals of figuration and commercial or brand name images.

Gesture and figuration

Both the range and complexity of artistic practices which arise from the depiction of the human figure in the United States during the 1950s are consequences of the multiplicity of art in Europe and North America that preceded them, of the the new means of disseminating the results of multiple reproduction, and of the difficulties inherent in all figurative art. The range entails a variety of overlapping functions: social, aesthetic, political, entertaining, communicative. On the one hand these functions are akin to the talismanic and prophylactic properties of certain figurative icons, images that may arouse comparison or empathy, adoration or understanding. On the other hand the aesthetic function that dominates the art of the period has direct links to three approaches to composition: firstly, the associations of natural form such as the usual positioning of the human eyes and mouth in the depiction of the head; secondly, ideas about a real world in which the use of artificial perspective and proportions is linked to the artist's studio composition; and thirdly, the need to take care over the execution of the image in order to render it in an acceptable manner: the art-social norm. In some aspects of American art that sought social or political change, the functions of figurative art (both the apotropaic, in the face of social despair, and the aesthetic, with its involvement in living conditions and its need to promote creative innovation) were bridged by both symbolic and Expressionist modes of depiction.

The complexity of figuration is a result of its reliance upon the viewer's production through memory, and this has fed back into the art as a need to facture resemblances and distinctions leaving the picture plane vulnerable to disintegration. The reliance figuration has upon the blurred edge between representational and referral praxis becomes the focus that demands both an efficient use of shape and colour and a reliable understanding of identification in the market place and cultural arena. In American art of the 1950s these requirements shifted in accordance with the simultaneous facture of a non-figurative art: an art with similar, and at times, monumental, aspirations, but equally an art fraught with the difficulties that its need of literature to assist the viewer's production from identifications and statements demands.

The need for literature or other extrinsic information to accompany, or to be explicitly implied in, the visual image has precedents as old as the facture of figurative art. The spectrum may range from, on the one hand, the requirement to know the story the depicted figures illustrate, to, on the other, a need to know the ideas or context for the occasion of the depiction. The middle ground of this spectrum is the reliance of figurative art's report on the living conditions based on the artist's (and the viewer's) direct observation and participation. Both the Expressionist and Surrealist movements relied heavily on such reciprocation. The latter was delivered to America directly in the 1930s and 1940s by magazines, exhibitions, and some of its practitioners in person. André Breton was already in America when André Masson and Max Ernst arrived in 1941. The art that preceded Surrealism also came. The Expressionism of northern Europe continued through the art of Hans Hofmann, who settled in the United States in 1932. The early work of Willem de Kooning already displayed its European origins on his arrival in 1926.

Of less immediate pertinence, but of some importance, is the art of late nineteenth and early twentieth century American Realism (exemplified by Bellows,

Hopper, Sloan and Benton) and Idealism, which provided ground for meticulous life drawing and scenes of everyday life. Such scenes acted as a catalyst to the figurative tradition embellished and elaborated by the growing collections of exemplary European, Modernist art in American public galleries. Figurative art's precision of drawing and verisimilitude overlapped with the formal innovation, ideas of brevity or expression, and the assured autonomy of art confirmed and insisted upon by Braque, Picasso and others after 1906. The monumentality inherent in individual figurative images is offset by the individual psychological symbolism and intended literary or extrinsic elements, which are as prevalent in North America as they are in European art of the period.

The American Modernist tradition, exemplified in its early days by John Marin and Arthur Dove, Georgia O'Keefe and Paul Strand, was as important a precedent for the figurative art of the 1950s in the United States as any other. With the exception of Bradley Walker Tomlin and Jackson Pollock (who died in 1953 and 1956 respectively), most of the important artists of the 1940s continued to work throughout the 1950s. The figurative tradition's predominant elements were concealed or removed by parallel movements towards gesture and Open Field composition. The literary ideas of the figurative artists took precedence over the likeness to living conditions. There was also a simultaneous shift from, for example, the use of a curved line to depict an arm to a use of that curve to describe the arm's motion as it factures the shape. The Symbolist movement and contemporary artists provided precedents for such a practice. The shift from naturalistic colour to heightened and symbolic colour took place at the same time as the revival of the idealized curing and health-giving 'line of Beauty' prevalent in Art Nouveau and its associated movements.

The shift from naturalistic colour and resemblance to the living conditions was also contemporaneous with research into synæsthesia. Gestural facture leads towards an integration of parts, and ideas of wholeness, on the picture plane. Where figurative art individuates and separates different identities, gestural art links them. Where figurative art describes the living conditions through the idealized outline of an appearance, gestural art introduces a sign, a symbol-like reference or a hieroglyph. The latter might allude to the living conditions, but not through appearance. The figures in Pollock's *Male and Female* (1)* of 1942 are painted totems in an atmosphere of shapes that do not describe forms (except possibly the idea of standing figures) and an array of signs that do not describe appearances (except perhaps the algebraic notes on a physics lecture-room blackboard).

Jackson Pollock's gestural works of the 1940s are part of an agreement among painters in the United States that shifts the function of Modernist art

---

*) Figures in brackets refer to works listed at the end of this chapter.

toward ideas of the talismanic and ritualistic or sacred art. Gottlieb's *Forgotten Dream* (2) of 1946 depicts short-hand signs for eyes, teeth and fish. But these are meant to be more like literary signs, mental states, than descriptions of perception. The title suggests a concern with dreams and the unconscious evident in the *First Surrealist Manifesto* (1924) as well as one of the elements of Expressionist praxis apparent in much of the American art of the 1940s and 1950s: the visual description of what cannot be seen – hidden consciousness, feelings, smells, sounds and even micro-biologic or macro-astronomic universes.

Such preoccupations developed at the same time as both a general acceleration in scientific discovery and reviews of Jungian psychology and the idea of a collective unconscious. As Americans looked deeper into outer space so they also looked deeper into inner space. Much art of the period poises on these shifting margins: of intellectual or even occult allusion, or an inner feeling and nervous motor action. It is factured by Americans in a country rich in indigenous sacred art from Hopi to Tlingit, and in the company of many European, Asian and African immigrants. Ideas of psychic automatism, evoked in the drawings of Masson and Arp from the Europe of the 1920s, are reconsidered in the art of Baziotes and Newman. Petroglyphs made by Pueblo nations in the American Southwest, appraised by the German art historian Aby Warburg at the beginning of the century and by Max Ernst in the 1940s, are reappraised by American artists Theodoros Stamos and Richard Pousette-Dart. The move towards abstraction that such reconsiderations and reappraisals represent is both a move to include the sacred and a move towards the monumental in the wake of figuration. (It is heralded in New York in 1939 by the arrival of Kandinsky's show of paintings made on table-tops, partly derived from images of the apocalypse and partly from his collection of Altaic shaman's drums.) These paintings by 1940s Americans, which so clearly celebrate European Modernism in their transformations of it, themselves herald a new wave of art that opens into 'composition by field'.

In the late 1940s and early 1950s, treatment of the picture plane by artists in the United States and Russia (notably Pollock and Rodchenko) led in the former to a different compositional mode described by the poet Charles Olson as 'Open Field'. (Olson, who applied this description to some of the poetry of the period, was at the time working at Black Mountain College, North Carolina. Also at the college during this period were the painters de Kooning, Rauschenberg, Tworkov, Kline, Cy Twombly and Motherwell. I have adapted Olson's term to cover a range of aesthetic practices to which it appears to apply.) In painting, the Open Field mode had two prevalent aspects. The first aspect involved a move from easel painting to painting on the floor from all four sides with decisions about boundaries to be determined after painting has commenced. The second aspect is the shift from European perspectival space and ordering to a compositional mode in which, as Olson put it in his 1951 essay 'Projective Verse' (in Charles Olson, *Human Universe and other essays* (New York: 1967)), 'ONE PERCEPTION MUST IMMEDIATELY AND DIRECTLY LEAD TO A FURTHER PERCEPTION.'

The first aspect of 'Open Field' composition finds its visual precedents in European Expressionism, indigenous sacred art such as Kandinsky's table-top paintings (in which the paper is turned as composition proceeds), and Navajo sand painting (in which the artist moves around and through the composition on the ground). The approach of Kandinsky and others is partly derived from late nineteenth century decorative arts and partly the consequence of an exposure (expressed in the art and collections of Kandinsky and Paul Klee) to 'bird's-eye views' found in the art of naïve painters, Persian garden carpets, children and asylum inmates. Also worth a mention here is the spread of television with its framed screen of shifting contents (in 1950 the U.S. Bureau of the Census recorded four million homes with television; by 1960 it counted forty million). 'Open Field' composition is thus part of a shift in consciousness towards a different apprehension of living conditions. Composition by field led to the use of recurrence as an adjunct to the integrative properties of gestural curves and marks, and encouraged the blurred edge or positive uncertainty. 'Open Field' composition was also adopted in combination with the gestural mode of facture in what Harold Rosenberg was to describe as the field for action painting.

Painters at the beginning of the 1950s factured an action art the leading edges of which either embraced a non-figurative mark-making on an 'Open Field' picture plane or carried figurative art into that 'Open Field' to facture an art particular to the consciousness that this period offered or aspired to offer. This development of the figurative through 'Open Field' composition was the particular preoccupation of those Irving Sandler in 1978 called the 'Second Generation'. These artists (such as Helen Frankenthaler and Larry Rivers) were taught by the 'Abstract Expressionists', either through examples in galleries or, in some cases, directly. Frankenthaler's own art involved a development of Hans Hofmann's gestural style. Her canvases were worked on suspended from studio walls as well as from above onto the floor. She also introduced tipping canvases to control paint runs, which from the 1960s onwards led her to develop an interest in stains and prints.

Like Grace Hartigan soon afterwards, Larry Rivers reintroduced figurative facture onto the gestural and Open Field picture plane. The cohesion projected or implied by Frankenthaler's canvas spaces becomes disrupted in Rivers' canvases, the integrative function of gestural line and paint application giving blurred edges to fragmented figures. Similarly, the disintegrating effects of separate figurations, over a damaged perspectival space in which proportions take third place, are held suspended together by the harmonious effects of his gestural marks and fluffs of apparently casually applied colour. The substance and meaning behind Rivers' use of figuration are both diverse and complex.

154

But in terms of its effect on the perceptive space the shift his art encouraged was startling. The New York art community was often sceptical and dismayed by what some saw as his 'return' to the use of the figure after their long collective struggle to produce an autonomous and abstract art. The facture of this figuration using 'Open Field' composition and gestural techniques must have seemed an added outrage. The figuration dismayed his peers; the gestures alienated the broader public seeking the sort of 'Period Living' style of American figurative art factured by Bellows and others in the early part of the twentieth century. That Rivers heightened the effect of this alienation through the use of what he called 'common reference' will be discussed below. Suffice to say now that this device was slowly extended into a significant reappraisal of Western culture in the 'style' of 'Pop' art, a reappraisal which, with simultaneous moves against artistic alienation, marked a turning point in the shift from Modernist conceptions of 'Being' towards newly pertinent practices of responsible belonging and 'Becoming', a shift which might be described as the first phase of a post-modern position.

The presumption here is that the twentieth century Modernist tradition was predicated before 1945 on a philosophy of 'Being' which permits transcendence and thus admits of alienation or a position of anxious isolation within society. A philosophy of 'Becoming' rejects such transcendence and produces viable alternatives to the sources of alienation. Looking at Larry Rivers' major works in 1992 makes these apparently inflated comments possible. What is clear is that the generation of painters working in the shadow of Hiroshima, Nagasaki and the Holocaust were a very varied bunch, and that Larry Rivers, hot from central Europe, was one of many artists to produce a new art that could confront such conditions with freshness. One of the ways he did so was through his combined use of seemingly opposing modes of facture. The philosophical result was the new, actively-engaged, viewer's gain.

In the 1950s and 1960s, damaged figuration, gestural art that implied the human body, and the negatively capable acceptance of the uncertain synthesis or fraught combination of both, became possible and were realized. They yielded an art that confronted the world at the same time as developments in collage and disruption.

Collage and Disruption

Without doubt, as both compositional process and appearance collage constitutes a major twentieth century form. As developed since the first Cubist *papier collés* of Braque, Picasso, and, more particularly, the inventions of primarily German artists in 1919, collage has carried codes for paradigms of spacetime, consciousness and situations that were invented around the same time as, or in the wake of, those discoveries in physics and mathematics which

155

expressed new paradigms of continuity, certainty and spacetime capable of changing human consciousness. It is no coincidence that these changes occured at the same time as inventions that introduced mass media, changed the speed of communication and long distance travel, and led (partly as a consequence of these inventions and partly as a necessity of the new paradigms) to new complexities of fragmentation and alienation, paralleled by the aesthetics of the early Cubists after 1906.

Many of the developments in collage took place at the same time as the proliferation of repeated images through widely distributed media. This encouraged both an increase in the availability of images as communication and a plurality of cultural exchange. Mass media (a term introduced in the early 1950s to cover a variety of communications forms ranging from magazines and billboards to television) provided a new and multiple fragmentation. Its repetition of images encouraged an at-a-glance reading of image-complexes: a speeded-up (even if in fact reduced in coherence) communication further encouraged by the multiple or shifting screen images familiar in cinema and television. Focused and stable conditions were shifting towards blurred edges, unsettled images and, as a consequence, uncertain or re-coded meanings. Collage, presented two-dimensionally, in relief, or as three-dimension assemblage, became the necessary expressive form capable of presenting multiple images, disruption of spacetime and discontinuity.

America experienced collage art at approximately the same time as the first wave of pre-World War One European inventors, whose Cubist and post-Cubist, Futurist work was exhibited at the New York Armoury show in 1913. Work by Marsden Hartley and Morgan Russell already exemplified developments of these European practices as early as 1914. By the 1920s the disruptive aesthetic was apparent in the work of Stuart Davis and Arthur Dove.

The disruptive aesthetic of collage arose partly in opposition to cultural norms and partly in response to the post-war multiplication of images, which encouraged a repetition of images and motifs in the work of artists like Joseph Cornell. Cornell's relief assemblages (usually in the form of small vertical cabinets), built from the mid-1930s until his death in 1972, on the one hand develop both the European and the American *trompe l'oeil* tradition, and, on the other, continue the European Surrealist presentations of the 1920s. His cabinets vacillate between composite, pseudo-scientific presentation cases of specimens (for instance in his case of corks dated c.1943 in the Bergman, Chicago collection (3)) and his many *Soap Bubble Sets* from 1947 and 1948 (4), with their disparate collage of images that in his assemblies produce new imaginative connections. His Surrealist connections date back to at least 1932 with his Surrealist toys (now in the Smithsonian), cut-out figures and collages exhibited with etchings by Pablo Picasso. Cornell's affinity with the Comte de Lautréamont's famous image from *Les Chants de Maldoror* – 'as beautiful as the chance encounter of a sewing machine and an umbrella on a dissecting table' – is demonstrated in a collage of a fashionable *fin-de-siecle* woman being sewn together on a sewing machine table (described by the gallery owner Julien Levy in *Memoir of an Art Gallery*, 1977), which links him to the Surrealists, who also revered Lautréamont. In his own diaries Cornell both applauds and regrets the attraction to the oddness of Lautréamont's work as a constructed ground for disorientation of thought. His work presents a direct means of breaking the aesthetic of social norms and is at the same time both a child's box of objects and an adolescent's memories of childhood: ordered theatres with various levels of meaning concerned with parts of the European existential condition re-envisioned in the memories and new experience of a quiet American.

Also the subject of Robert Motherwell's work, the existential condition encourages the disruption of aesthetic norms. Motherwell's erudition enabled him to transform an understanding of this subject from a European context. The result is evident in Motherwell's treatment of the picture plane, which is made complex through the doubts Motherwell expresses about European aesthetics (signified by his hesitations and half completed corrections). The uncertainty is articulated in a positive and American spacetime. Motherwell developed an interest in Surrealist theories which he linked to ideas of 'automatism' and French Symbolism. His continued interest in painting focussed on Arp, Klee, Matisse, Miró, Mondrian and Picasso. During the 1940s he was in communication with Baziotes, Pollock, Hofmann, De Kooning, Newman, Rothko and John Cage. In 1944 he became the director of the exemplary *Documents of Modern Art* series, which made available to the American public key texts of the European Modernist tradition.

Motherwell's own work, his engagement with historical and critical theories, and his acquaintances in the 1940s epitomize an American phenomenon that can also be seen in retrospect in the work of his peers in the late 1940s and 1950s. The phenomenon is the rise of American art to a new pitch and coherence. The pitch is given tuning by the radical European arts and the migration of many of its best practitioners to America. The coherence is brought about by the new synthesis American artists effected in the 1940s of French Surrealism and some its Expressionist contemporaries, and European Cubism and Constructivism. The debt to Modernist European arts is exemplified by Motherwell and De Kooning in their use of collage and gestural mark and by Motherwell and Pollock in their use of Surrealist extensions and poetic figurations.

Motherwell uses three forms of collage method which blur, in terms of difference, one into the other: paintings with glued on papers, glued papers, or simply oil paintings on canvas. Two of the methods show Motherwell's interest in paper as a material, the first through a direct use of products (printed papers or packaging) already available to him. Often the papers are unmarked wrappings or papers with drawings, which are undefined because they are torn

157

and pasted as shapes and contributions to the overall shape-complex of the picture. Motherwell seldom uses intact, ready-made images as contributions to his own image-complex. There are exceptions: *View From a High Tower* (5) of 1944 uses a map among other papers with oil paint, but this is not a typical example. In the second type of collage, the paper serves as shape and colour, as on his 1957 collage entitled *The Tearingness of Collaging* (6). This purity of surface is only occasionally disrupted by words, sometimes from the packaging itself (*Pyrenean Collage* (7) of 1961 has 'PRODUCE OF FRANCE' printed on the central pasted paper) but more often from his own painted addition. In the third type of collage, for example in the series *Je t'aime* (1955-57), he writes the painting's title across each canvas. The hand-written words link Motherwell to earlier Dada examples, but more particularly to the tradition of calligraphy in painting apparent in some of the works by Matta, Masson, Walker Tomlin, Baziotes, Tobey, and Pollock in the 1940s, in which the words are part of the active gesture of creativity. The calligraphy, gestures and signatures are part of the larger complex: collage.

The collage method, of glued-on papers disrupting edges, transforming once whole images or shapes into fragments, memories and allusions to their earlier states, is extended in the 1940s by Motherwell's oil painting and in particular by the massive series of paintings, *Elegy to the Spanish Republic* (8) and its many visually associated works. These works differ from the European convention in art products that involve collage. The initial disruption, the 'exploitation of the chance meeting of two distant realities on an unfamiliar plane or ... the culture of systematic displacement and its effects' specified by Max Ernst in *Beyond Painting*, no longer disrupts the aesthetic norm, but has become it. Motherwell's *Elegies* are collages because they simultaneously present his felt thought about the human condition in the Spanish Civil War with its Fascist aftermath, and the reality of his own condition as he factures the work on one disruptive plane.

How are Motherwell's disruptions activated? Through the 1940s and 1950s and well into the 1960s, Motherwell produced a monumental continuity of visual motifs most readily exemplified by his *Elegy* series. Each painting in the series displays large black figures that hang from the top of the picture plane but do not quite reach the base and that are intercepted by oval shapes caught, as if suspended, or as if heads between bars, between the vertical shapes. The overall and repeating motif is that of black paint, bars and oval forms. The size and number of repeated shapes vary, and the backgrounds, which are what every other colour and shape become, vary considerably. They have never been seen hung together – indeed that has been impractical – but when a group of them are hung in the same environment their impact and meaning spreads as a result of their imposing presence, their larger-than-human scope, and the solemnity of their similarity. The disruption Motherwell produces is probably at its most profound in this situation. The collage of recurring motifs and gestures disrupt each other. The expectation of shapes shifts between recurrence and difference. The shapes interfere with each other's integrity and produce in the viewer the sensation of a precise blur where different shapes could have been articulated. The viewer is put into a situation involving both interaction between different paintings of the same series and productive synthesis as the differences begin to cohere as connectedness. The spacetime of the experience becomes a kind of massive existential dilemma broken by the monumental creative intelligence that has disrupted the initial thoughts normalising from repetition. This intelligence has been made visually possible through the use of collage – the use of torn paper studies and more tentative or smaller works – and the stalemate-breaking act of cutting and repasting the human elements of gestured mark and figuration.

Pollock, de Kooning and many others who made use of these methods (albeit in a variety of inventive ways) are now recognized as members of the so-called 'Irascibles' group captured in Nina Leon's 1951 *LIFE* photograph (9) – the photograph includes Stamos, Jimmy Ernst, Pollock, Newman, James Brooks, Rothko, Pousette-Dart, Baziotes, Willem de Kooning, Gottlieb, Reinhardt, Hedda Sterne, Still, Motherwell, and Walker Tomlin – and promoted by critics such as Clement Greenberg as 'Abstract Expressionists'. This catch-all title, needed for their promotion and to encourage coherent statements about 'new' American art in the 1940s, didn't bring together painters of one style, or those using one method or those of similar philosophies – but it did emphasize a tendency, distinct from European art, characterized by large canvases and apparently free or open use of materials and compositional methods. The achievements of Motherwell and his peers in the 1950s produced a substantial American grounding upon which the next generation of Americans could build and disrupt what they built.

Compared to individuals or groups of painters, however, decades cannot as easily be defined or distinguished. Throughout the 1950s the generation that followed the 'Irascibles' were in conversation with them. Learning and complimentarity interacted with disruption and conflict. The best of 1950s American art offers a far broader field for analysis than its precedents from the 1940s. In collage art specifically the former is exemplified by a number of artists, ranging from Cornell, Motherwell and de Kooning to (in the latter part of the decade) Jim Dine, Allan Kaprow and Bruce Conner. A brief survey of a dozen examples should make this clear.

In a photograph taken in his studio in 1950 (10), de Kooning is seen working on the beginnings of his *Woman* series. He is working on a study for *Woman I* (11) which overlaps a second study of the same figure so that the drawings on the two sheets are sometimes continuous in the form of a tone or line and sometimes interrupted by the break in the paper. This working method (apparently invented by de Kooning in the 1930s and presumably derived directly from European Cubism) partly involves continually and abruptly bringing onto one plane a variety of human responses to one concern. In the 1950s it reached one of its most cogent expressions in de Kooning's *Woman* series. Edwin Denby was clear about how the extensions worked when he wrote: 'In two years of work, magnificent ancestors of *Woman I* (12) appeared on the canvas and were painted away by the artist.' Through scraping de Kooning also partly reveals again traces of his former work, thus collaging the underimage 'ancestors' back into the surface text. The finished work comprises hundreds of studies. In one of these (numbered 181 by Cummings) lips have been pasted onto the face and searching array of lines and tones, and the painting (in New York's Museum of Modern Art) still shows evidence of this facial feature.

De Kooning's use of collage is two-fold. The pasting-on of lips at once normalizes and disrupts the composition because of its comic ('common image') or mask associations. It recalls earlier use of 'common image' by Hannah Höch and Max Ernst. The broken pages of the studies, the continuities across them and the breaks made by paper edges that interrupt the flow, are de Kooning's innovation from Braque and Picasso's *papier collés*. The method is clear in much of his work of the 1930s and 1940s; it becomes more assured in the 1950s. In the tiny *Untitled (Matchbook)* (13), an oil and pencil work dated *circa* 1942, the images of common objects (a matchbook and safety pin) are disrupted by tones and lines shifting the recognisable images into compositional shapes. Thus *Woman I* displays a continuity of method in as much as the expectation produced by the use of the 'common image' (the pasted on lips from a magazine cutting) is disrupted by the use of tones and lines which interfere with the normality of the first expectation. Another example of the method's results is *Woman* (14) in crayon and charcoal made from two drawings in *circa* 1952. The top part of the body is separated from the lower by the paper break and this is exaggerated by the blank space left in most of the linkage. In the late 1950s de Kooning extended this method to the juxtaposition of different drawings of similar size and shape abruptly linked together, as they are in parts of his *Black and White* series of 1959-60 (15). In 1961 de Kooning returned to *Woman I* and produced an oil on paper work with a new colourist vigour using a mounted collage from a photographic print of a woman's head cut out of a magazine (16).

Like his contemporary de Kooning, David Smith started his collage art production in the 1930s. In Smith's case the work can be read as an extension of the European Surrealists' proposals of the 1920s and 1930s. His work from the 1930s, such as *Collage circa* 1931 (17), is clearly part of the assemblage tradition in which different and apparently disparate items or fragments are brought together into one plane, one reality. Collage for Smith contributes materially to his overall image production by turning numerous facets into one completed statement or overall image. The resulting spatial normality was first broken by Smith in the mid-1940s. Preceded, as they are, by his *Medals for Dishonour*

(18), completed in 1940, Smith's early *Landscapes* mark a departure from the normalized space into a new space that interacts with it.

Blackburn, Song of an Irish Blacksmith (19) from 1949-50 breaks the normalized space in an array of debris and fragments that make for the viewer an open-ended space. It is a space of signs or images left unclarified against each other except as part of an oval-like configuration or pathway, a journey through the song and thought process of Blackburn over a period of time. *Song of a Landscape* (20) from 1950 and the subsequent *Australia* and *Hudson River Landscape* from 1951 (21 and 22) bring Smith's art to a new spatial coherence as a consequence of these earlier spatial complexities. *Australia* alludes to parts of the bird's-eye view of Australia without making obvious what the symbolic elements of each part are. The latter are honed-down, refined thoughts about these landscapes, and include the mental space in which the selecting and decision-making the process entails are also comprehended.

Smith and de Kooning were part of the leading edge of collage art at the beginning of the 1950s when a later generation started to mature. Larry Rivers is part of that new generation able to use the collage art as a tool towards new figurative ends already partially anticipated by the art of de Kooning and Smith. Rivers takes on board and extends the collage and gestural art of his mentors and celebrates them. His critique is a reappraisal of the image in a new compositional opportunity that the Black Mountaineers in the 1950s named 'Open Field'. This isn't to say that Larry Rivers draws upon the theories of Charles Olson. Rivers' approach is to use the nineteenth century academic compositional method employed by Realist painters like Gustave Courbet, and then to reinterpret this method in a collagist space. Painters like Courbet in the 1850s produced their work from a variety of images (including paintings and photographs they or others had made) which were brought together into one spatial deception. In this way they normalized their production in accordance with their mentors' Idealist and historical paintings. Rivers develops these precedents, using a similar variety of source materials brought together on one picture plane. But Rivers keeps their disparities intact. The spacetime of his paintings is that engendered by collage in which deception or pretence at a spatial realism is rejected. In Rivers' 1953 *Washington Crossing the Delaware* (23) the figure of Washington derives from two of Gilbert Stuart's paintings, the soldiers from a children's book, and the overall idea of the composition from a monumental and historical narrative canvas with the same title made in 1851 by E.G. Leutze (a copy of which is in the Metropolitan Museum in New York). Rivers' figures are placed without regard for their proportions or positions relative to the size and placing of the central figure of Washington. The perspective is also deliberately faulty and the colour is only approximate to the referenced conditions and is, in any case, only partially applied. The work is a marker for a new kind of collage in which the art of composite facture (for example in the work of Leutze) and normalized

Larry Rivers, *Washington Crossing the Delaware* (1953). Oil, graphite and charcoal on linen, 212.4 x 283.5 cm). Collection, The Museum of Modern Art, New York.

Realist space are merged with the gestural facture that painters like Hans Hofmann taught and practiced. The shift from figuration into gestural action in the 1940s and contemporary with Rivers in the 1950s is shifted by Rivers back into figuration, but this time with a different emphasis and regard towards its subject. In the 1950s and 1960s Rivers was to refer frequently to earlier practices as part of his paintings' subjects. His 1956 *The Studio* (24) refers directly to Courbet's 1855 *The Artist's Studio, Real Allegory, determining a phase of seven years of artistic and moral life* (25). Rivers' practice leads towards what might be called simulation, in which each image is reproduced from an image that has already been reproduced. This shift back to re-appraise subjects from the history of art was also matched in the period by Grace Hartigan.

In 1952 Grace Hartigan's work started to use pre-existing images as a compositional and figurative basis. The earliest of these works uses, as Rivers' had, well known historic works. Examples include Albrecht Dürer's engraving *Knight, Death and the Devil* (26 and 27) and Rubens' *The Tribute Money* (28 and 29). Her shift from the Hofmannian aesthetic of the 1940s to simulation was also a shift from collage space into that of Idealist space made strange by the paint application – its apparent rapidity and imprecision. Like Rivers, Hartigan also began using photographs. Her use of a photograph by Walter Silver of a bridal-store window for her 1954 painting *Grand Street Brides* (30 and 31) is exemplary. Her multiplication of the number of source images also leads her back towards a collage space. In *Grand Street Brides* the seven heads of her painting multiplies the two (or three if the shadow of a third is included) of Silver's print: Hartigan is interested in the actual displays on Grand Street or elsewhere – their reflections and ridiculous monumentality. During this period she, like Rivers, made paintings using the poetry of Frank O'Hara. These works stride out into a new territory. They extend the use of word and image from Dada artists and Robert Motherwell into a new space that collages a variety of word sizes, gestural mark making and fragmented figuration. The picture plane becomes an experimental spacetime, a surface carved and re-carved full of traces and blurs. The series uses O'Hara's *Oranges* poems, a poetry already part of a collage tradition and itself full of naturalistic description, transformed quotation and exclamation. Like O'Hara, Hartigan's use of subject shows an excitement with New York: the shop windows (also used in *Giftwares* from 1955 (32)) and sandwich bars, the streets and social life. Rivers, O'Hara and Hartigan form part of a viscous social network in this period, which is part of what their art and life encourage. The use all three have for collage is in turn part of the enlargement of what collage means. It prepares the ground for immediate responses from Robert Rauschenberg.

Rauschenberg in the 1950s limits his materials to those he can find on the block or adjacent blocks in which his studio is situated. This art takes collage back to actual street materials following a constructive method first used by

Kurt Schwitters but now opened and considerably enlarged into an American space. Rauchenberg's first collages use glued papers and cloths as an imageless material and ground for what are effectively visual discussions of structure and ratio. His collages of the early 1950s (33) are to a large extent formal works with almost arbitrary or at best tasteful uses of image. Their strength is formal. These are nevertheless early precedents that anticipate the heterogeneous assemblages and combine paintings that were to follow from late 1953 onwards. The small 1950 *Untitled* collage owned by Jasper Johns (34) displays three distinct columns: one of paint, one of print, and one of glued-on images. The 1952 red paintings, echoing some of their black painting precedents, remain collages beneath paint coded only by the activity of its mark-making and not by extrinsic reference. This method Rauschenberg persisted with into 1954 with *Red Import* (35) and *Red Interior* (36). These latter works overlap with the real shift he effects with *Collection* from 1953-54, *Minutiae* from 1954 (37), *Hymnal* (38), and *Rebus* (both from 1955) (39). *Hymnal* is also contemporary with the first assemblages.

In *Hymnal* Rauschenberg has cut a rectangle in the upper picture plane and hung a Manhattan telephone directory, as if it were a religious reliquary, from the inner space. The lower part of the plane uses coded images including a direction arrow, a fragment from a 'WANTED' poster, wallpapers, a page of notebook scribble, and a newspaper fragment. The fabric surface of the picture plane is a Paisley pattern shawl. In the same year Rauschenberg made the assemblages *Bed*, *Odalisque* (40 and 41) (re-painted in 1958), and *Monogram* (49) (re-made more than once until 1959). This procedure of re-painting and re-working is a trait of the processual nature of Rauschenberg's work during the 1950s; it is also a necessity determined by the rapid deterioration of the fragile surfaces. The works simultaneously combine the coded (reliant on extrinsic information) gestural activities of his mentors in their use of paint (and materials used as if they were paints) and a self-consciousness that denies the autocracy of abstraction. Rauschenberg's early abstract and religious paintings in fact change their conceptual meanings for him in the period. *White Painting* of 1951 (42) shows a shift in Rauschenberg's thought. In 1949 his white ground paintings inscribed with abstract shapes had been titled *Crucifixion and Reflexion*, *The Man with Two Souls*, and *Trinity* (43). In a letter to Betty Parsons written around the time he made the 1951 White Paintings (and cited in Sandler's *The New York School*), Rauschenberg wrote of the appeal of nothingness, of silence, and of absence. Later (for example in his 1959 'Statement' for the Museum of Modern Art *Sixteen Americans* exhibition catalogue) he wrote of the same work as a space for a chance environment in which lights and reflections onto the white plane vary.

Rauschenberg's self-consciousness with regard to this use of coded precedents from his mentors and contemporaries is clearly manifested in his 1957 *Factum I* and *Factum II* (44). Each painting almost, but not exactly, imitates

Robert Rauschenberg. Left: *Factum I* (1957). Combine painting. 156.2 x 90.8 cm. The Panza Collection. Museum of Contemporary Art, Los Angeles. Right: *Factum II* (1957). Combine Painting. The Morton G. Neumann Family Collection.

its pendant: a doubling continued in the imagery: two trees, two heads of Eisenhower and so forth. In both paintings Rauschenberg makes use of coded gestural marks which are duplicated almost exactly in each painting. The apparent spontaneity of the action painter's mark is here subjected to a critique which is implicit in the rhythmic recurrences of some paintings by Pollock and others and in such structural repetitions as the sloping mark in Jackson Pollock's *Blue Poles* (45). *Factum I* and *II* were followed by such combine paintings as *Wager* (46) (re-painted in 1959), *Magician II* of 1959 and *Pilgrim* of 1959 (with its 'striped' chair standing and 'connected' in front of the picture plane) (47).

This break from the frame and European easel is one of Rauschenberg's most distinguished innovations. The works that followed, such as *Canyon* (48), with its stuffed eagle and hanging pillow, remind the viewer of the sculptures, the assemblages of *Odalisque* (with its stuffed rooster) and *Monogram* (49) (a stuffed goat). The emphasis is once again on multiplicity of image and homogeneity of effect. *Bed* from 1955 anticipates this, but the heterogeneous images exemplified in the illustrations for Dante's *Inferno* started in 1959 (50) and *Street Throng* (51) from the same year involve some of the most profound post-1945 uses of collage. Their profundity lies in both their formal innovations and their radiant use of converging imagery. Throughout the work of the 1960s, the links between the American war and space machines, creativity and sexuality are poetically accurate. They are innovative in their initial, apparently incidental, use of random imagery and the eventual cohesion of these images. The Dionysian cathedral produced by the goat through the tyre in *Monogram*, the rooster on the images of women on top of the column that balances on the pillow in *Odalisque*, link directly with the exuberant paint smears and spillages of works like *Bed*. In terms of collage they use their disruptive effects to cohere a disruptive social complexity and in so doing they subvert the artist's own views as much as anyone else's. In aesthetic terms such works also demonstrate the production of a consciousness in the grasp of negative capability and creative necessity against entropy. Theirs is a new spacetime: one exemplified by Rauschenberg's shift of meaning for collage and one shared by many of his contemporaries, the most obvious being Jasper Johns.

Rauschenberg moved into the same studio block as Johns in 1955, the same year in which the latter destroyed all the work he had made and retained. Earlier works still extant – Michael Crichton cites only four – are in the hands of others. The earliest, dated c.1953, is *Untitled* (52) and owned by Edwin Janss. An oil and collage on silk, it has a similar aesthetic plane to that factured by Rauschenberg in his 1952 red paintings. The other three works, all dated 1954 (or 'c.1954'), use objects or are themselves 'constructions'. These works prepared the ground for Johns' creativity over at least two decades. In every extant work Johns uses the spacetime of Cézanne's 'passage' (the picture plane factured by Cézanne in his later life) and Braque and Picasso's extensions as a norm: a verticality rather than a horizontal perspectival imitation. This lead provides the viewer with a meditative spacetime. Unlike Rauschenberg, Johns refuses to present a multiplicity of imagery. He chooses isolated and already heavily coded signs: flags, targets, numbers, letters. He uses packing case stencilled lettering and common objects: forks, spoons, coat hangers. The paint application is, like Rauschenberg's, often vigorous, or apparently vigorous: sometimes using grey with different tonal values, at others unmixed colours direct from the tub or tube. Collage for Johns takes two forms: (i) a ground composed of glued papers over which he builds up encaustic or paint; and (ii) the concise juxtapositioning of very few images. Where Rauschenberg carries collage into a new exuberance involving multiplicities of information, Johns in the 1950s reduces it to a meditative experience. This has oversimplifed Johns' work, but his shift of attention in the 1960s and again in the 1980s is in part anticipated in the late 1950s by the slow overlapping and re-worked care of his number and alphabet works dating from 1955 (such as *Figure 5* (53)) into the 1970s.

Collage in 1950s America is a complex matter. Some works retain their *papier collé* sources, others continue a tradition promoted by Dada. During the decade the disruptive function of collage is broadened by assemblage and then developed into 'Happenings'. Bruce Conner's 1959 *Child* (54) assemblage is continuous with the objects produced by the Dadaists and makes a bridge from them to the work of Edward Keinholtz in the 1960s. The form is produced from the facture of an expectation which is then disrupted through violent or sexually-explicit defiance of normality. The precedents for this kind of disruption may be found in the work of Boccioni, Hausmann, and Grosz. The mannequins shown at the 1938 International Exhibition of Surrealism held in Paris (and illustrated in Seitz's *The Art of Assemblage*) make this explicit. The use of distorted and damaged human forms underlies the formal normality of these works which continues the Expressionist wish to convey feelings of alienation and often distraught existence. An example can be seen in the work of Kienholtz.

In 1959 and throughout the 1960s Kienholtz used a violent, Expressionist and figurative assemblage in works which led towards a sculptured environment. His earlier works like *John Doe* (1959) (55) centre on the single object and figure. In *Illegal Operation* (1962) and *The Birthday* (1964) (56 and 57) the sculpture is part of an environment in which more than one object contributes to the whole work. It is from renewed expressionism that 'Happenings' partly spring. (They are quite different from the 'Happenings' developed from the ideas of John Cage and others, including Rauschenberg as a student, at Black Mountain College.) The happenings of Allan Kaprow and Jim Dine are violent, often funny, actions in a new *Mertzbau* (Schwitters, 1933 and later). As reported in Michael Kirby's *Happenings* (1965), after 1952 Kaprow started to develop what he calls a kind of action-collage technique ... the action-collage then became bigger, and I introduced flashing lights and thicker hunks of matter. These parts projected farther and farther from the wall and into the room, and included more and more audible elements.... I just simply filled the whole gallery up.... When you opened the door, you found yourself in the midst of an entire environment.

Kaprow developed the 'Happening', a scored environment for the visitor, during 1957 and 1958. The terms assemblage and collage, whilst useful to describe elements or precedents, had become redundant for such situations. Kaprow's work was joined by that of other artists: Jim Dine's *Car Crash* (58) and Jean Tinguely's *Homage to New York: A self-constructing and self-destroying work of art* (59), both from 1960; Robert Whitman's *Mouth* (60) and Claes Oldenburg's *The Store* (61), both from 1961. At the same time, Rauschenberg developed his assemblages or three-dimensional combine paintings and Larry Rivers and Jasper Johns extended two-dimensional art into a heightened American statement. The late 1950s and 1960s was an era of simulation in a positive sense, changing the earlier idea of simulation in art. For Aby Warburg in the early part of the twentieth century, simulation equates with the use of quotation in a painting. An example is the use of *grisaille* made by fifteenth and sixteenth century artists like Mantegna who 'quote' from an 'Antique' sculpture in a painting and indicate this by leaving the 'quoted' section in grey or cream under-painting without further colour. In the 1950s the use of quotation becomes subsumed into reproduction of the already reproduced, a development which takes place at the same time as rapid technological improvements in multi-media and print technology.

Simulation in the 1950s is a direct response to the expansion of television and the proliferation of magazines full of coloured reproductions and advertising. Key works by Marshall McLuhan (*The Mechanical Bride: Folklore of Industrial Man*) and his mentor, Harold A. Innis (*The Bias of Communication*) were published in 1951. English translations of Carl Jung's works on archetypes appeared in 1950 and 1954. McLuhan's work for *From Archetype to Cliché* was to follow in the following decade. The use of existing images to produce new images was taking on a new complexity. Simulation's reproduction of the already reproduced became the aesthetic norm throughout American culture and this apparent redundancy began to produce stereotypes: branded products and images of celebrities emblematic of a new society. These images the best of the collagists sought to subvert through their damaged and discontinuous juxtapositioning on planes that, in effect, acted as critiques of such redundancies. The Surrealist project of producing the dream as reality became, for some, a project in conflict with the commodity ethic, the dream apparently made possible, for the hyperreality it in fact presented. Just as the new technological and commodity society made collage art viable, so collage art made the critique of this society its inevitable thesis.

In Rauschenberg's work from this period such a critique is realized through an aesthetic response to the materials, using the latter to produce an image different from their implied meaning. The method of painting over the wording or images on his material becomes a use of the material itself as the medium for the aesthetic statement. The overt meaning of some of his images would be difficult or impossible to ignore: for example the references to loving sexuality in the use of a goat inside a pneumatic tyre in *Monogram*; or the references to aggression in the use of an eagle hanging in front of the plane in *Canyon*. But their underlying meaning may be different. Thus the base to which the goat has been fixed and the plane behind the eagle do not echo the referencing of the overt images. Instead, these grounds (the base and the picture plane) are part of aesthetic statements which have metonymic effects on each work's meaning. The material itself is a discussion of the commodity culture from which it sprang.

Metonymic use of material immediately encourages recall of the direct use of images as if images were materials. In the simulations made by Jasper Johns from such large images as the American flag, it is not the symbolic which provides the meaning of Johns' work, but its metonymic potential as a material that has the most profound effect. In the 1960s both Rauschenberg and Johns would elaborate these issues further, but in the 1950s their metonymic intentions appear to govern their selective acts. Simulation is not, however, the only mode of production developed by artists using collage in the period. The 1950s may also be reconsidered from the perspectives of plurality, recurrence and boundaries.

Plurality of Cultures and Styles: Recurrence of Images and Themes

Like those of earlier imperialist powers, American culture uses and eventually relies upon a great number of images, designs and ideas from a broad range of sources. American technological supremacy requires and is provided with the twentieth century equivalent of Europe's industrial past. Americans tour Europe, Africa and Asia, 'purchase' the treasures of the world and produce, particularly in the years that follow the 1950s, their own composites. Renewed opportunities for the use of this enlarged range of resources are made possible through the art of the 1950s. The tools are provided by a transformed collage method: simulation or reproduction of the already reproduced. What is reproduced derives in the first instance from domestic technologies, the printing press and colour photography, and is exemplified by the global imagery of the *National Geographic* and *LIFE*. The early collages by Pousette-Dart (*Untitled* from 1948 (62)) and the later work by Jess (*Nadine* from 1955 (63)) display a plurality of information from a broad range of geographical sources and a variety of magazines. The scale of collage work in this period also increases, first in Rauschenberg's combine paintings and later in the 1960s when James Rosenquist's work simulates public billboards and hoardings. The images are compounded by other images until the sources and meanings overwhelm cohesion and become incoherent structures. Like Cotterill's illustration of Victorian architecture, with its Renaissance, Greek, Egyptian and Gothic designs, American art and artifacts become international in content, become plural without grasp of the substance of their materials, until the new artists take a new measure – a new understanding of their situation – and produce a new art: the art that is American. Definition of this phrase no longer rests on ideas of the plural. The art embedded in the plural and simulation generates an art of recurrence and uses recurrence and transformed repetition as its American aesthetic.

Throughout the work of American artists of prominence in the 1950s, recurrence itself becomes a theme and a method. The recurrent thematics of de Kooning's *Woman* paintings, the repeating eagle in the work of Rauschenberg, Johns' *Flag* (64), *Target* and alphabets are interfaced by the actuality of recurrence as the artist's method of simulation: the use of existing reproductions. The latter is echoed by the reproduction process itself, the repeated printing of the same image, the multiplication of images on every television in every home, the identity of images repeated and repeated. In retrospect the art that becomes the art of Warhol and Lichenstein was inevitable. The images do not begin the decade with boldness but are half-concealed beneath skins of polyethylene plastic and acrylic paints. The boldness of the 'Irascibles' (promoted as 'Abstract Expressionists') at the beginning of the decade is the overall composite image itself. It takes Johns in mid-decade to take that boldness of the American image and bring to it a new interpretation which he then continues to reinterpret in the later 1950s and 1960s. It takes the boldness of Rauschenberg to push that recurrence into disparate forms, assemblages and combine paintings that are wholly American inventions: as different from Dada projects as they were from nineteenth century norms. Recurring themes include American nationalism, Rivers' civil war veterans, Rauschenberg's eagle, and Johns' flag. But the meaning of these themes is no longer an anti-war or anti-bourgeois rhetoric as exemplified by George Grosz or Otto Dix; their meaning shifts to a ground of meditation and desire, characterized by an awe of its situation and an energy to engender change.

Boundaries; Breakage and Precision

That change is manifested through breakages of boundaries and shifts against deterministic precisions. The James Rosenquist billboard is no longer a billboard. Johns' *Flag* is not a flag. The boundary breaks are conceptual markers that indicate a change in aesthetics: a change in what can be understood as

170

beautiful or sublime, a change in the aesthetic dimension which becomes a social dimension and an indication of a development in Western consciousness. The latter entails a new synthesis in which are combined an understanding of the human condition in much of its complexity and a new order of possibility involving both mass communication and quantitative increases in geographical knowledge and access. What in retrospect appears over-optimistic became for many in the 1960s a new vista of potentials. If one axial plane of the aesthetic dimension can be simplified as carrying both semiotic and pragmatic potentials for comprehension, the pragmatic edge had been subsumed by an art-historical journalism that put its emphasis upon the the semiotic of artistic products – their form and content – to the detriment of understanding their actual practice and aesthetic function. A brief summary of part of the practice exemplified by some of the products may start to make this clear.

It will be useful to begin by distinguishing different groups of activity. The first group defined a boundary, such as a picture edge or frame, and then proceeded to use it as part of the construction. Another group produced similar boundaries and used them to contain apparently disorderly marks and shapes, or a 'floating' paint mass, within the ordered limits of the edge or frame. A third group defined boundaries or frames set inside a larger frame, and produced a variety of disruptions within the range of smaller confined spaces with occasional forays across the limits. The first group of practices has the most direct relationship to European *papier collé* and collage in as much as it relies on the frame edge to produce tensions, weights and lifts. The second and third groups relate to American assemblage and collage in which the 'Open Field' and series are the two more evident aesthetic norms.

Franz Kline's practice conforms to the first group. His study of the black and white techniques of the late nineteenth century British cartoonists Phil May and Charles Keene, and of the contemporary James Whistler, is concealed by Kline's refusal of figurative reference (at least in the works made after the 1940s). His 1957 *Black and White* (65) displays an overlapping series of torn black and white sheets pasted into the near-centre of the rectangular picture plane and visually held there by the vertical tension produced by stripes that are broken by the top and bottom edges, a third band that proceeds to the left edge, and a bar of black that extends vertically against the right edge from the corner to a third of the distance from the top. Taking the paint marks to edges and leaving part of the plane free of paint is part of Kline's aesthetic practice and links his work directly to a European tradition of figure drawing in which a figure, for example, may be depicted off-balance, the figure's arm outstretched giving it support against the vertical edge. Another example in this tradition depicts the weight of a sitter by linking the sitter to the base via a set of darker marks. This European tradition also relates to both the Expressionist practice of Paul Klee and some of the Constructivist practices of El Lissitsky.

Use of the edge as a tension or a dynamic tie is evident in many of the paintings made by Americans like de Kooning, Jack Tworkov and Kline. Another example of the practice can be seen in Lee Krasner's 1955 *Blue Level* (66) (in which the darker torn sheets almost float down the picture plane but are held in tension by the lighter greys in a vertical tangle that 'pins' the inner shape to the top edge). Michael Goldberg's 1960 *Murder, Inc.* (67) (in which the main group of marks is held on a horizon from left to right and then lifted, so-to-speak, by a band the edges of which blur into a spray of splashed, paint marks from the top left edge) shows an understanding of Kline's Constructionist practice and immediately recalls Kline's 1951 *Painting No.11* (68). The latter uses a Whistler-like bridge and two columns held stable horizontally and lifted by the column that cuts the top edge. In Kline's 1956 *Mahoning* (69) (in the Whitney Museum of Art) the depicted collapse of structure in most of the work is held in balance, in suspension, by the horizontal links to the left and right edges. This constructionist norm was already evident in David Smith's 1950 work *The Letter* (70), with its frame and horizontal lines upon which the 'letters' sit in parody of written correspondence, accompanied by 'long-hand' indications from the left edge at the top and to the right edge at the bottom. The technique of hanging from the top edge in some of the work by Clifford Still (for example his 1953 *Untitled* (71) with its blue violet surface interrupted by the dropping yellow and base-line reds) is paralleled in the period by Kline's practice and developed differently by Rauschenberg and others. Rauschenberg's construction in his 1959 *Bypass* (72) displays a top heavy, multiple image area held aloft by a hard black horizontal band that centres on a wider white band cutting the left edge just below the centre line. This is balanced, in Paul Klee's sense of colour-weight, by a red rectangle against the right edge and base corner.

The use of edge dynamics is an American Constructionist norm derived from earlier Constructivist and Expressionist practices. In significant contrast to the former, a second group of artists in the 1950s use the rectangular norm to provide a field, an apparently endless spacetime, in which the tensions are Hans Hofmann's 'push and pull' (towards and away from the viewer effected by the use of colour) and de Kooning's Dionysus alive in undefined freedom. In de Kooning's famous *Woman I*, particularly in the early state photographed in about 1950 (reproduced as plate 314 in Janis and Blesh's *Collage* (1967)), the marks and cut edges depicting the figure are surrounded by extensions of these marks and further cut edges: a depiction of activity without boundary or, rather, without definition. The painted field is itself surrounded in the main by unpainted ground interrupted only by the splashes and runs from the central image and radically shifted by the depiction of a window in the upper right that almost echoes a construction by Franz Kline. There is no innuendo here. De Kooning showed Kline both techniques of collage and fragment enlargement. There is a deep affinity between them, but this is an affinity of materials

172

Franz Kline, *Mahoning* (1956). Oil and paper collage on canvas. (203.2 x 254 cm. Collection of the Whitney Museum of American Art. Purchase, with funds from the Friends of the Whitney Museum of American Art. Accession no. 57.10.

and applications, papers, inks and projectors, rather than an affinity of images or techniques.

A third group defines boundaries, frames, or compartments within the larger frame and produces a variety of disruptions within the range of confined spaces, with occasional forays across the limits. Part of this aesthetic practice is emphasized differently by those artists who have returned to the European tradition more directly. Examples would include Jasper Johns' *Flag* series and his 1955 *Target with Plaster Casts*, and Joseph Cornell's boxes. The use of the box in Cornell's work allows the presentation of damage without the unruliness that damage might have signified (the use of damaged materials is a practice developed from such constructionist artists as Kurt Schwitters). In Cornell's 1943 *Habitat Group for a Shooting Gallery* the disarray of bird images and postage stamps behind a missile-broken glass is held in place by the firm wooden box frame. This practice was continued by Edith Schloss, for example in her *Dow Road* (73) of 1958: *'Box of weathered wood, with torn printed page and wallpaper, lace, glass bottle, etc.'* In the 1960s Larry Rivers factured window-framed portraits of Jim Dine and Leroi Jones. The potentials for order of the horizontal line and vertical edge are considerably developed by Johns in his later work, where two-dimensional drawings can be made to meet in three-dimensional forms: kits for a Buckminster Fuller globe or a toroid form. His 1957 *Gray Rectangles* (74) has three rectangular holes cut into the picture plane refilled with the same shapes marginally reduced to fit the holes with a minimum gap around them. His 1955 *Flag* is a square displaying stars held into the top left corner by a range of horizontal stripes (i.e. an American flag). There is a sense of development from Jackson Pollock's 'all-over' painting-collages such as his *Number 2, 1951* (75) to Johns' 'all-over' work *Painting with Two Balls* (76). It is not simply a shift to include objects.

Johns' work involves a reappraisal of the boundaries that had already been shifted away from the European space by Pollock. His use of boundary carries the techniques of collage and 'Open Field' into a re-assessment of simulation. In collage more than one reality produces a visual disruption within the bounds of one picture plane. Johns factures that disruptive potential through the use of single and common (everyday) images. In 'Open Field', in which (to paraphrase Olson) one perception follows directly on another, Johns factures a recurrence of discrete elements through the use of frames within the framing. The single and everyday image from the already reproduced and the recurrence of the already reproduced is made active for the viewer by Johns' ability to convey a complex conceptual activity in harness with an activity that is directly sensual in his application of materials. This constitutes a new phase of middle dispositions that the 1960s explores towards what then appeared to be a new creative endeavour and aesthetic clarity.

174

Conclusion

The consequences of plurality and simulation are not the artifacts of creative production. Creative endeavour's response to the society it is part of is an inevitable participation of that endeavour with its context. Its wish to change the potentials of that context is what its creativity is about. Its endeavour is to incite the will to live. American creative endeavour in the 1950s shows that it is the artists that changed the potential for perceiving the American context; this does not change the fact that it is the responsibility of a society to realize how those potentials are used.

References

Dawn Ades, 'The Transcendental Surrealism of Joseph Cornell', in Kynaston McShine (ed.), *Joseph Cornell* (New York: Museum of Modern Art, 1980).

Dawn Ades, *Dada and Surrealism Reviewed* (London: Arts Council of Great Britain, 1978).

Lawrence Alloway, introduction, *Robert Rauschenberg* (Washington, D.C.: National Collection of Fine Arts, Smithsonian Institution, 1976).

Dore Ashton, *American Art Since 1945* (New York: 1982).

Berlin, Staatliche Kinsthalle, *Robert Rauschenberg, Werke 1950-1980* (Berlin: 1980/81).

Milton W. Brown, *The Modern Spirit, American Painting 1908-1935* (London: Arts Council of Great Britain, 1977).

Michael Crichton, *JASPER JOHNS* (New York: 1978).

Paul Cummings, Jörn Merkert and Claire Stoullig, *Willem de Kooning: Drawings, Paintings, Sculpture, New York, Berlin, Paris* (New York: Whitney Museum of Art, 1983).

Edwin Denby, 'My Friend de Kooning', *Art News Annual [New York], XXIX* (1964).

Max Ernst, *Beyond Painting*, trans. Dorothy Tanning (New York: 1948).

Anthony Everitt, *Abstract Expressionism* (London: 1975).

E.H. Gombrich, *Aby Warburg, An Intellectual Biography* (London: 1970). The Warburg text referred to is translated in Gombrich from '*Grisaille*, Notebook', 1929.

E.C. Goosen, *Stuart Davis* (New York: 1959).

Al Hansen, *A Primer of Happenings and Time/Space Art* (New York: 1965).

Robert Carleton Hobbs and Gail Levin, *Abstract Expressionism, The Formative Years* (Ithica and London: 1978).

Harriet Janis and Rudi Blesh, *COLLAGE, Personalities, Concepts, Techniques* (Philadelphia, New York, and London: 1967).

Michael Kirby, *HAPPENINGS* (New York: 1965).

Michel Leiris with Dawn Ades and David Sylvester, *André Masson: Line unleashed* (London: 1987).

Garnett McCoy (ed.), *DAVID SMITH* (New York: 1973).

Kynaston McShine, see Ades above.

Robert Saltonstall Mattison, *Grace Hartigan, a painter's world* (New York: 1990).

Frank O'Hara, *Robert Motherwell with selections from the artist's writings* (New York: Museum of Modern Art, 1965).

Frank O'Hara, *Jackson Pollock* (New York: 1959).

Frank O'Hara, *Art Chronicles, 1954-1966* (New York: 1975).
H.W. Janson, *History of Art*, rev. by Anthony F. Janson (London: 1986).
Graham Reynolds, *Turner* (London: 1969).
Nan Rosenthal and Ruth Fine, *The Drawings of Jasper Johns* (Washington: National Gallery of Art, 1990).
William Ruben (ed.), *Pablo Picasso, A Retrospective* (New York: Museum of Modern Art, 1980).
Irving Sandler, *The New York School, The Painters and Sculptors of the Fifties* (New York: 1978).
William C. Seitz, *The Art of Assemblage* (New York: Museum of Modern Art, 1961).
Tate Gallery, catalogue, *Robert Rauschenberg* (London: ca. 1980/81).
Daniel Wheeler, *Art Since Mid-Century, 1945 to the Present* (New York: 1991).

List of visual works

1. Jackson Pollock, *Male and Female*, 1942, Philadelphia Museum of Art (O'Hara, plate 5).
2. Adolph Gottlieb, *Forgotten Dream*, 1946, Herbert F. Johnson Museum of Art, Ithica, New York (Hobbs, black and white plate 9).
3. Joseph Cornell, *Untitled (Cork or Varia Box)*, c.1943, Coll. Mr.and Mrs. E.A. Bergman, Chicago (McShine, black and white plate 74).
4. Cornell, *Soap Bubble Set*, four works with this title, made in the period 1947-48 (McShine, plates 81-84).
5. Robert Motherwell, *View from a High Tower*, 1944 (O'Hara, *Motherwell*, black and white, p. 12).
6. Motherwell, *The Tearingness of Collaging*, 1957 (O'Hara, *Motherwell*, black and white, p. 20).
7. Motherwell, *Pyrenean Collage*, 1961 (O'Hara, *Motherwell*, black and white, p. 31).
8. Motherwell, *Elegy to the Spanish Republic XXXIV*, 1953-54, Albright-Knox Art Gallery, Buffalo, New York (O'Hara, *Motherwell*, black and white, p. 34).
9. Nina Leon, Photograph of the 'Irascibles', 1951, from *LIFE* magazine (reproduced in Ashton, plate 16 and O'Hara, *Motherwell*, p. 78).
10. Photograph of Willem de Kooning in his studio, 1950, reproduced in *Art News Annual XXIX* (1964), 92.
11. Willem de Kooning, *Study for Woman I*, 1950, (Cummings, cat. no. 181).
12. De Kooning, *Woman I*, 1950-52, Museum of Modern Art, New York, (Cummings, cat. no. 190).
13. De Kooning, *Untitled (Matchbook)*, ca. 1942 (Cummings, cat. no. 29).
14. De Kooning, *Woman*, c. 1952 (Cummings, cat. no. 62).
15. De Kooning, *Black and White*, 1959-60, a series (examples in Cummings, cat. nos. 76 and 77).
16. De Kooning, *Woman I*, 1961 (Cummings, cat. no. 212).
17. David Smith, *Collage*, ca. 1931 (McCoy, plate 2).
18. Smith, *Medals for Dishonour*, completed 1940 (McCoy, plate 15).
19. Smith, *Blackburn, Song of an Irish Blacksmith*, 1949-50 (McCoy, plate 33).
20. Smith, *Song of a Landscape*, 1950 (McCoy, plate 44).
21. Smith, *Australia*, 1951 (McCoy, plate 46).

22. Smith, *Hudson River Landscape*, 1951 (McCoy, plate 47).
23. Larry Rivers, *Washington Crossing the Delaware*, 1953, Museum of Modern Art, New York (Sandler, black and white, illustration no. 66).
24. Rivers, *The Studio*, 1956, Minneapolis Institute of Art (Sandler, black and white, illustration no. 68).
25. Gustave Courbet, *The Artist's Studio, Real Allegory, determining seven years of artistic and moral life*, *Musée d'Orsay Guide*, (Paris: 1986), pp. 66-67.
26. Albrecht Dürer, *Knight, Death and the Devil*, 1513, engraving, Museum of Fine Art, Boston (Janson, plate 672).
27. Grace Hartigan, *Knight, Death and the Devil* (Mattison, plate 15).
28. Rubens, *The Tribute Money*, Berlin.
29. Hartigan, *The Tribute Money* (Mattison, black and white plate 16).
30. Walter Silver, photograph, Bridal Store Window (reproduced in Mattison).
31. Hartigan, *Grand Street Brides*, 1954, Whitney Museum (Mattison, cat. no. 11).
32. Hartigan, *Giftwares*, 1955, Neuberger Museum, New York (Mattison, cat. no. 13).
33. Robert Rauschenberg, *Untitled*, 1952 (Berlin cat., nos. 81-84).
34. Rauschenberg, *Untitled*, c.1950 (owned by Jasper Johns) (Alloway, black and white photography, cat. no. 3).
35. Rauschenberg, *Red Import*, 1954 (Berlin cat., 4).
36. Rauschenberg, *Red Interior*, 1954 (Tate Gallery cat., 8).
37. Rauschenberg, *Minutiae*, 1954 (Berlin cat., 5).
38. Rauschenberg, *Hymnal*, 1955 (Berlin cat., 7).
39. Rauschenberg, *Rebus*, 1955 (Alloway, black and white photography, cat. no. 35).
40. Rauschenberg, *Bed*, 1955 (Berlin cat., 6).
41. Rauschenberg, *Odalisque*, 1955-58 (Berlin cat., 8).
42. Rauschenberg, *White Painting*, 1951 (Alloway, black and white photograph, cat. nos. 5 and 6).
43. Rauschenberg, *Crucifixion and Reflexion*, 1950 (Sandler, 126).
44. Rauschenberg, *Factum I* and *Factum II*, 1957 (Alloway, black and white nos. 52 and 53).
45. Pollock, *Blue Poles*, 1953, Australian National Gallery (Everitt, plate 10).
46. Rauschenberg, *Wager*, 1957-59 (Berlin cat., 11).
47. Rauschenberg, *Magician II*, 1959 (Berlin cat., 12).
48. Rauschenberg, *Canyon*, 1959 (Berlin cat., 13).
49. Rauschenberg, *Monogram*, 1955-59, various states (Alloway, black and white, cat. nos. 63-68).
50. Rauschenberg, illustrations for Dante's *Inferno* (Berlin cat., pp. 118-255).
51. Rauschenberg, *Street Throng*, 1959 (Berlin cat., 92).
52. Jasper Johns, *Untitled*, c.1953, Coll. Edwin Janss (Crichton, black and white, p.26).
53. Johns, *Figure 5*, 1955 (Crichton, black and white plate 4).
54. Bruce Conners, *Child*, 1959 (Janis, illus. 335).
55. Edward Kienholtz, *John Doe*, 1959 (Seitz, p. 134).
56. Kienholtz, *Illegal Operation*, 1962, *Art and Artists*, 8, 6 (September, 1973), p. 23.
57. Kienholtz, *The Birthday*, 1964, *Art and Artists*, 8, 6 (September, 1973), p.22.
58. Jim Dine, *Car Crash*, 1960 (example photographs in Kirby, pp. 191-199; and Sietz, p. 91).
59. Jean Tinguely, *Homage to New York: A self-constructing and self-destroying work of art*, 1960 (example photographs in Jean Tinguely, *A Magic Stronger Than Death* (Milan: 1987), pp. 73 and 78-83).

60. Robert Whitman, *Mouth*, 1961 (example photographs in Kirby, pp. 148-57).
61. Claes Oldenburg, *The Store*, 1961 (example photographs throughout Claes Oldenburg, *Store Days* (New York: 1967)).
62. Richard Pousette-Dart, *Untitled Collage*, 1948 (Janis, illus. 230A).
63. Jess (Collins), *Nadine*, 1955 (Seitz, p. 111).
64. Johns, *Flag*, 1955, Museum of Modern Art, New York (Crichton, plate 1).
65. Franz Kline, *Black and White*, 1957 (Janis, illus. 199).
66. Lee Krasner, *Blue Level*, 1955 (Janis, illus. 270).
67. Michael Goldberg, *Murder Inc.*, 1960 (Janis, illus. 201).
68. Kline, *Painting No.11*, 1951 (Ashton, plate 13).
69. Kline, *Mahoning*, 1956 (Sandler, illus. 10).
70. David Smith, *The Letter*, 1950, black and white (in Ashton, plate 14).
71. Clifford Still, *Untitled*, 1953 (Ashton, plate 20).
72. Rauschenberg, *Bypass*, 1959 (Ashton, plate 42).
73. Edith Schloss, *Dow Road*, 1958 (Janis, illus. 256).
74. Johns, *Gray Rectangles*, 1957 (Crichton, plate 36).
75. Pollock, *Number 2, 1951* (Janis, illus. 215).
76. Johns, *Painting with Two Balls*, 1960 (Crichton, plate 63).

The Lengthening Shadow: Lewis Hill and the Origins of Listener-Sponsored Broadcasting in America

John Whiting

The Good Old Days

American radio programs of the 1930s and 1940s are easy to get nostalgic about now that the issues they didn't confront and the questions they didn't ask are well behind us. Because each program had a particular sponsor they were all primarily advertisements, and so tried to amuse, excite, even frighten the punters into a state of mind in which they would be susceptible to the Big Sell. To this end, the 'radio voice' was quickly established. It exemplified a norm of intonation, inflection and voice projection which was as absolute in its rules as the BBC's so-called 'standard English'. Deep chest tones, bland assurance, and a total lack of hesitation or error were essential, so as to convey that ineffable, indispensable quality: 'sincerity'. (This exaggerated diction also helped to compensate for the primitive equipment and bad reception in 'fringe' areas.)

The air time on all the network stations was filled by a small number of announcer/actors whose ranks were extremely difficult to break into. As the great radio maverick Henry Morgan explained, 'about thirty of them did ninety percent of the work'.[1] Morgan himself was one of this elite, having worked his way up from page boy to full-time announcer by 1932, and by 1938 to his own comedy show on WOR, New York (which, at the age of seven, I half-listened to only because it occupied, on alternate days, the same time slot as *Superman*). Lewis Hill, the founder of listener-sponsored broadcasting in America, described in 1951 one of the standard audition procedures through which these people got their jobs:

The test consists of three or four paragraphs minutely constructed to avoid conveying any meaning. The words are familiar and every sentence is grammatically sound, but the text is gibberish. The applicant is required to read this text in different voices, as though it meant different things: with solemnity and heavy sincerity, with lighthearted humor, and of course with 'punch'. If the judges award him the job and turn him loose on you, he has succeeded on account of an extraordinary skill in simulating emotions, intentions and beliefs which he does not possess.[2]

Until the mid 1940s, all programs were presented live. In his highly informative memoir, *Due to Circumstances Beyond Our Control....*, Fred Friendly has explained that 'network policy prohibited the use of recordings lest the entire concept of chain broadcasting be destroyed; [this] might lead to such widespread syndication by records that there would be no need of a live interconnected network'.[3] Yet if the objective was network power over local stations (most of which were voluntarily affiliated, not directly owned), the fact of simultaneity was not simply a control mechanism: it also gave radio an immediacy which had never before existed in a mass medium. I can still remember the tingle of a new and strange excitement while listening in 1939 as an eight-year-old to a speech by Adolf Hitler, realizing that he was haranguing a crowd half-way around the world at that very moment and catching, even through the totally strange lingo, something of the hypnotic mass hysteria.

There were also live 'documentaries' such as *The March of Time* which from 1931 onwards dramatized contemporary history with actors playing the world's leaders (Art Carney and Agnes Moorhead, whose later acting careers would epitomize comedy and melodrama respectively, were Franklin and Eleanor Roosevelt!).[4] An inattentive listener might not have known whether he was hearing fact or artefact. In general, however, the audience believed that what was presented as fact had indeed taken place. The depth of this conviction was demonstrated in 1938 by the hysterical public reaction to Orson Welles's legendary *The War of the Worlds*, to which many listeners had tuned in too late to catch the opening disclaimer. (In its competitive hysteria, commercial television is now regressing to this 'faction' technique which Welles was spoofing, and which radio would soon outgrow.)

Left wing political controversy had to be avoided at all costs. Not that newscasters were required to be objective; rather, their prejudices were expected to reflect those of their bosses and sponsors. The most popular commentators were those with a gimmick: Gabriel Heater always opened with 'there's good news tonight!', Edwin C. Hill presented 'the human side of the news', Fulton Lewis Jr. closed with 'and that's the top of the news as it looks from here', and Drew Pearson was introduced as the commentator 'whose predictions have proved to be eighty four per cent accurate'.[5] (The latter was an old-fashioned muckraker whose revelations continued to make politicians squirm well into the 1960s.)

Like all organized crafts, arts and professions, radio produced a small hand-

180

ful of practitioners who sought to burst the straitjacket. Orson Welles, whose influence on early radio was so profound, broke the conventions in many ways – not least through his delivery, which projected a wry, laid-back irony which distinguished him immediately from his fellow-announcers while at the same time preserving a smooth perfection which affirmed his credentials. Henry Morgan chose satire, sending up his sponsors' advertising techniques until he exhausted, one by one, their bemused tolerance (I remember him delivering in the early 1940s, as Scarface, a testimonial for Schick Injector razors). Morgan didn't get away with this forever and no one else got away with it at all (except, a dozen years later, Stan Freberg). It would be decades before sponsors would allow self-satire to become a cliché.

As radio grew more respectable, occasional programs and even series were given the opportunity to rise above the mediocre. This happened mostly in the areas of music and drama. The still-running Metropolitan Opera broadcasts, sponsored by Texaco, started as early as 1931. In 1936 NBC (National Broadcasting Company) even founded its own symphony orchestra, calling Toscanini out of retirement to conduct it. The orchestra was given its own unique 'floating' studio in Rockefeller Center. (This construction technique, in which the studio is built as a totally self-contained spring- and rubber-suspended box, is now common, but at the time it was revolutionary. The man responsible was the visionary David Sarnoff, a Russian emigre who had become President of RCA in 1930.)[6]

There was also an occasional one-off event of total strangeness, such as the 1947 broadcast of the Gertrude Stein/Virgil Thomson opera, *Four Saints in Three Acts*. While normal life went on downstairs, I sat glued to the little radio in my father's study, having tuned in by chance to a strange hypnotic happening which bore no relationship to either life or art as I knew it. (Years later, in the music archives at University of California, Berkeley, I would discover a complete recording of the event, privately taken off the air on to 78 rpm disks. The collector's motto is: 'Everything exists!')

Radio drama, however, was more interesting than radio music. The technology of sound transmission had not yet evolved to the point where radio music was anything more than a crude approximation of the real thing, but in radio drama the use of sound effects enabled a rapidity and complexity of montage previously possible only in film, and at a tiny fraction of the cost. Furthermore, radio had two advantages over film: it was still 'live' and therefore immediate, like the theatre; and, relying on imagination, as an anonymous child succinctly put it, 'the scenery is better'.

We are indebted to Orson Welles for realizing, evolving and perfecting most of the techniques which radio drama has been using ever since. He bluffed his way into the Dublin Gate Theatre in 1931 at the age of sixteen; two years later he went to New York; within five years, during which he also captured Broadway, he had blagged himself to the top of network radio.[7] His work, first with *Columbia Workshop* from 1936, and then with his own *Mercury Theater on the Air* from 1938, set standards which have been equalled but never exceeded.[8] Anyone intimate with radio drama who listens to Welles's films with their eyes closed will immediately spot the uniquely meticulous craftsmanship of his sound tracks.

Other important writers and directors included, most notably, Norman Corwin, Archibald MacLeish and Arch Oboler. So far as I've been able to determine, Thornton Wilder didn't write for radio; but his most famous play, *Our Town*, cannot but have been influenced by radio drama, and is very effective in that medium with hardly any changes. Performed on a bare stage, it depends on the stage manager's descriptions to set the scenes, and most of the action is carried by dialog. It is questionable whether any of these playwrights could have done their best work without the example, and sometimes the collaboration, of Orson Welles.

In the domain of radio news, the Second World War forced two major revolutions. Firstly, the development late in the war of wire and tape recorders made it impossible to maintain the ban on delayed broadcast, since both convenience and recording quality were far in advance of 78 rpm disk transcription. Fiction documentaries were quickly superseded, since it was now possible to record actual events. Secondly, the seriousness of events in Europe produced a new, more responsible breed of newscaster who spoke to a nation gradually forced out of isolation and narcissism. One of the most notable of these was Edward R. Murrow who, in collaboration with Fred Friendly, would later transform television as well as radio public affairs programing.[9]

Aside from a few good comedy series and a sizeable body of excellent war coverage, however, the scripts of all the outstanding radio programs heard in America during the three decades up to 1950 would today make up a rather small library. Radio broadcasters of all kinds spent most of their professional lives innocuously filling air time, which meant that radio had very little to say to the intelligent listener. Eleanor McKinney, along with Lewis Hill a founder member of Pacifica Radio, anecdotally encapsulated the total frustration of the serious broadcaster:

> I had had quite a career in San Francisco with broadcasting as a writer/director. This was when NBC had about a hundred and twenty people on staff for drama and music and sound effects – I mean it was really a place in those days! I had done a really exciting drama which I wrote on juvenile delinquency and race relations and civil liberties. We recorded it with an NBC orchestra and the sound department and the whole works. Then they called in all the big corporations to come and audition it. They all said, this is fabulous – but I wouldn't touch it with a ten-foot pole! In those days they were considered controversial subjects.[10]

A Gleam in the Eye

Like the BBC under Lord Reith, Pacifica Radio from its foundation in 1949 may fairly be described as the lengthening shadow of one man: a pacifist and poet named Lewis Hill. Both his principles and his character, integrally incorporated into Pacifica's structure, determined its name and history and subsequently, through his direct intervention, the history of Public Broadcasting in America.

I had known Lew Hill slightly in the early 1950s, and later knew many people who had worked closely with him for several years; but when I attempted to assemble a short biography I came up against a blank wall. Several informants could outline in precise detail his opinions about pacifism, free speech and the public media, but none could tell me when or where he was born, who his parents were, where he had gone to school or college, what radio experience he had had, or what conscientious objectors' work camp he had been held in. Further questioning elicited a concensus that he 'didn't talk much about his background, but mostly about ideas'.[11] There was additional agreement that, as Robert Schutz and Morris Horowitz concurred, 'he was essentially a lonely person, because it was difficult for him to reach out to others. To simple people he was an unknown quantity and this made him feel lonely and he could never overcome it'.[12]

Horowitz, a fellow conscientious objector, tells an illuminating story involving Bayard Rustin, one of the leaders of the pacifist movement during World War Two and later of the civil rights movement:

> I met Bayard in Washington once and he asked me 'Hey, do you happen to know Lew Hill?' and I said I did. He said 'they say that you can't understand what he's talking about' [laughter]. I said 'that's not true at all. He's a very intelligent, very interesting talker but he speaks in a formal, complicated way and you have to pay attention'. He was an intellectual and he couldn't attain the common touch even if he tried.[13]

After a long search, it was from Joy Hill, Lewis's widow, that I was finally able to learn the basic biographical details that few of his colleagues seem to have been aware of. They are best told in her own words:

> He was born in Kansas City, Kansas, on May 1st, 1919. His father was an attorney; his grandfather had been a Missouri doctor. His father told the story of having been in law school at the University of Missouri at Columbia. After the first semester, which he 'aced', he went to the Dean when spring came and said 'I don't think I can stand to keep my shoes on any longer. Can I do my studying at home and come back for the finals?' The Dean said yes, and he went home.
>
> His father made a million dollars selling an oil company to J.P. Morgan (he was the lawyer on the deal). Lew's mother's family was the Phillips family of Phillips Petroleum (Frank Phillips was her older brother). Lew's father then bought a small foundering insurance company in Tulsa, where they moved, and built it up and later went into politics. He was in the state legislature and for a part of one term he was Speaker of the

Oklahoma State Legislature. But he had made a campaign pledge to clear out a graft situation in the school textbook purchasing division. He lost the reform bill by one vote, so he resigned because he had made this promise.

Lew was sent off to military school because he was too bright for the public school, and he hated it, just despised it. He completed his first two years of college there, at Wentworth Military Academy. He was also Missouri state doubles tennis champion. But he injured his back playing football, and I really think in the long run that's what killed him.

He went to Stanford University and he was in what they called the 'university program'. There were four or five really brilliant people who were working directly for their doctorate, which was for him unfortunate: when the war came along he had completed his thesis, which was on printers' changes in *Troilus and Cressida* between the fourth and fifth folios, but he hadn't taken his orals, so he ended up with never having a degree, even though he had about six years of college.[14]

While at Stanford, Hill was introduced to the teachings of the Quakers and became a pacifist. When he was drafted in 1941 he registered as a conscientious objector and quickly moved to the top of the organization representing all objectors throughout America.[15]

The exact chronology is hard to determine, but in 1942 and 1943 he spent about fifteen months at a compulsory work camp for conscientious objectors at Coleville, California, 'moving rocks from one side of the road to the other', as he put it. Between then and 1944 he was Director of the National Committee for Conscientious Objectors, and in that capacity he travelled extensively among the CO camps on the west coast, meeting like-minded people he would later ask to help him in his great radio project. He also worked for the American Civil Liberties Union in Washington D.C., where he met his wife-to-be:

I graduated from college in '43 and worked for about a year in Watertown and then I came to Washington. I got a job doing copy and public relations for a small radio station, and it was there I met Lew, who had just been hired as a news announcer. He had been in Washington to do ACLU work for a couple of weeks or so, but he had to get a job to pay the rent and feed his face! He was also writing a book. He went back to radio as the simplest thing to do. The station asked me to interview him to do a little magazine article. He said he didn't think he ought to because he had done just one summer of radio when he was in college.... Lew had a wonderful radio voice. This was one of the reasons why the little radio station wondered why he'd come to work for them. The reason was he didn't have confidence enough to go to a network![16]

Several sources testify that it was between 1944 and early 1946 that Lewis Hill began to formulate plans for a non-commercial radio station for the specific purpose of promoting peace, both interpersonal and international, by means of ethical, intellectual and artistic integrity. (Eleanor McKinney had tried it in commercial radio in San Francisco in the early 1940s and decided it was 'like trying to teach non-violence in the army!').[17] In his brief, pungent history of Pacifica, Christopher Koch pinpoints the conception of Hill's brainchild to a day in January 1946 when Hill was asked to read on the air a news report which he knew from first-hand experience to be untrue. He promptly resigned and headed for California to start his own station.[18] Other versions, not quite so dramatic, are not essentially contradictory. Joy Hill reports that 'he said that when he got to the point where they were talking about liver-*flavored* cat food, he had reached the bottom!'[19] Eleanor McKinney recalls: 'He went up to one of the Japanese relocation camps and saw all kinds of things which he tried to put on the air and was refused permission to do so. So he knew this was not the field he wanted to be in, where censorship prevented one from telling the truth.'[20] Chronology aside, all three versions are probably true and complementary. Everyone agrees that Lewis Hill came to San Francisco in 1946 with the first of a series of constantly evolving, highly detailed prospectuses for a non-commercial radio station whose twin principles would be pacifism and civil liberties. (Contrary to a common misperception, the name 'Pacifica' related to pacifism, not to the station's geographical location.)

Hill, of course, knew San Francisco from his years at Stanford. The intellectual and artistic climate he found when he returned in 1946 is vividly captured in a few deft brush strokes by Hill's immediate friend and collaborator Kenneth Rexroth in a 1966 BBC lecture on the Beat Generation:

San Francisco was the one community in the United States which had a regional literature and art at variance with the prevailing pattern.... During the war, work camps for conscientious objectors were established throughout the mountains and forests of California. These boys came down to San Francisco on their leaves. They made contact with San Francisco writers and artists who had been active in the Red Thirties but who had become ... anarchists and pacifists. During the war, meetings of pacifist and anarchist organizations continued to be well attended. Immediately on the war's end a group of San Francisco writers and artists began an Anarchist Circle.... From this group and from the artists' C.O. camp at Waldport, Oregon, came a large percentage of cultural activities in San Francisco which have lasted to the present time – *a radio station* [emphasis mine], three little theatres, a succession of magazines, and a number of people who are considered the leading writers and artists of the community today.[21]

Although Lew Hill was in touch with San Francisco bohemia from the very beginning, he seems to have already fixed on Berkeley as the ideal location for his radio station. Gertrude Chiarito, who together with her husband Americo (Rick) was among the first staff members, says that Hill 'felt that Berkeley would be the only place that it could possibly happen, that it would be accepted, that there would be cooperation. It was a kind of universal place because of the University, and because the people at that particular university came from such widely scattered areas'.[22] Rick became the first Music Director and Gert would be in charge of the subscription department for many years. The Chiaritos were the only people on record whom Hill brought in from outside the Bay Area. Rick had been in a CO camp in Elkton, Oregon, which Hill had visited a few times, and Gert was the local 'postmaster'. In our conversation she recalled, with a chuckle:

> We drove down here from Portland to meet with a few people and we met up with Lew and then we didn't hear much from him until about February of 1949, when we got a special delivery letter from him asking us to come down immediately! So we arrived in Berkeley on March 13th, 1949. [Gert's computer-like memory has been indispensable in piecing together KPFA's pre-history.] We worked the next month at the station getting everything together – it was a hodgepodge! And then, with great fear in our hearts, we went on the air....[23]

The Chiaritos' immediate response to Hill's peremptory summons exemplifies his mesmeric ability to attract and hold support for his project. But of course he had more in his favor than mere charisma: the prospect of a mass medium becoming a genuine art form and a means of profound communication fired the imagination of everyone he canvassed.

It took Lewis Hill from 1946 to 1949 to assemble the staff and raise the money he needed to obtain a license and go on the air. His two overlapping pools of talent and information were the University at Berkeley and the bohemian enclaves of North Beach in San Francisco. One major figure who was equally at home in both was Thomas Parkinson, Professor of English at the University, whose influence in bringing the best of the Bay Area writers to KPFA, and thence to the whole of America, can hardly be exaggerated. Of equal importance was the poet, essayist and critic Kenneth Rexroth, whose drawling, unedited, primitively home-recorded monologs, like an endless proliferation of Krapp's Last Tapes, captivated or infuriated listeners for many years. (Their end product, in print, constitutes some of America's most vivid cultural and personal history.) In the area of Public Affairs, the greatest single influence on Pacifica's founders was Alexander Meiklejohn, an educator (President of Amherst, 1912-24) and jurist who in the 1950s was to become the most noted defender and interpreter of the First Amendment to the U.S. Constitution, guaranteeing freedom of speech. This was both the 'core of the constitution', as Meiklejohn defined it, and also, together with pacifism, the core of Pacifica's broadcasting theory and practice.

At the University, Hill particularly sought out intellectuals with ideas appropriate to his chosen medium. Robert Schutz, who was to become an early Director of Public Affairs and later Hill's second-in-command, was an early recruit:

> In 1948 I was going to school at Cal, getting a Ph.D and very interested in the idea of getting public exposure to the ideas which I thought were important for promoting peace in the world, so I put together a program that I thought would be a 'situation comedy', got a lot of people involved with it, including professors at the University of California and people at the International House where I lived. Hill heard about this and contacted me and I decided that, although it was a pretty small operation, at least it was something to start with and so I joined up with him.[24]

186

Like other members of Pacifica's extended family, Schutz would be alternatively one of Lew Hill's most indispensable helpers and one of his severest critics.

Although Hill's own radio experience was not extensive, professionalism was to be one of his guiding principles. An invaluable collaborator in this effort was Eleanor McKinney, who would go on to help build and document Pacifica Radio for many years:

> I was one of the founding members from late 1946 and was KPFA's first Program Director. I had been in broadcasting in San Francisco, with NBC and later with an advertising agency where I did programs with all the local stations of ABC, NBC and CBS. I had done a number of dramas through NBC there, so I knew a lot of the actors and musicians in the area. When Lew Hill came out from the east, there was a gathering of people we already knew in the fields of poetry and literature.
>
> He had a prospectus already of this idea he had when he was back east. He was frustrated with commercial broadcasting. He had a party and Tom Parkinson and Richard Moore [who would himself later be head of Public Broadcasting Service stations in San Francisco and Minneapolis/St. Paul] and myself went to this party and that's where I met them – or perhaps it was in Richard Moore's apartment on Post Street in San Francisco, where we had several meetings of poetry and anarchist philosophy – I think that's the *first* time I met Lew and Joy. That would be in 1946.[25]

Another member of the original team, according to Schutz, was Bill Trieste. Previously with the only independent classical music station in the Bay Area, KSMO in San Mateo, he would later be one of the many KPFA alumni who moved on to KQED, San Francisco, the first listener-supported TV-FM affiliation in America. The other original staff members, so far as I can determine, were John Lewis and Edward Meese. Meese was the station's engineer for many years. Lewis was the first Public Affairs Director and a member of the board before the station began broadcasting although, according to Eleanor McKinney, he wasn't there for long: 'he had a hard time financially and a family and he couldn't stick it out.'[26] Over the years, many staff would leave for the same reason.

It is difficult to identify those who were staff and those who were volunteers in those early days. Even sources who were with the station from the very beginning differ among themselves as to how many actual staff members there were. Pacifica's own fortieth anniversary souvenir pamphlet identifies both Eleanor McKinney and Richard Moore, on different pages, as KPFA's first Program Director.[27] Some volunteers worked as hard and were as omnipresent as staff, and no program participants were ever paid for their appearances on the air, so that even payrolls are misleading.

A sequence of technical and social changes had to occur for this unlikely project to take to the air. When Lew and Joy Hill came to the Bay Area, they assumed that they would be starting an AM station, and they worked from that premise for some time. But they came up against the financial realities of media control:

We anticipated getting on the air a lot sooner than we did. Our son was born in March 1947 and we were hoping to get on the air around his birth time, but were not able to. There was an AM channel available, but we did not qualify for it because we didn't have the money for it. This was a great blow and we had in effect to start over.... Perhaps the hardest part of the whole thing was switching from AM to FM, which was brand new and no one had access to it.[28]

FM radio was just being launched in America. Therefore there were open channels available which were not yet worth a great deal of money, since there were very few receivers and only a small audience. The new medium was particularly suited to the high technical, intellectual and artistic broadcasting standards Hill sought to achieve. A few years earlier there would have been only low-fidelity AM channels, prohibitively expensive to acquire; a few years later FM would also become expensive, though not in the same league as AM, whose broadcast radius and therefore audience were much greater. In the meantime the asset, a green-field site, would also become a liability as KPFA struggled to promote both the message and the medium.

FM was so new that, like some primitive witchcraft, its technical parameters were still clouded by superstition. Gert Chiarito reports that, incredibly,

the original plan was for the transmitter to be at Point Isabel in Richmond. That was because at that time they thought that FM transmitters had to have their feet in salt water, and Point Isabel was the ideal location to reach all sides of the Bay Area. If we had been able to get property at Point Isabel, which would have been very cheap, we probably would have tried to build something there or use some trailers.[29]

The location finally chosen and successfully negotiated was in Berkeley at the top of the Koerber Building, a six-story structure at 2050 University Avenue. As Eleanor McKinney reports in *The Exacting Ear*:

The studios and control room were custom built, mostly from used equipment. Friends and strangers heard about the new venture and came up to help stuff sound-proofing materials into the studio walls, hammer on sound tile, help with the carpentry and painting.... The offices were jammed with different groups rehearsing programs, with carpenters, engineers and staff members trying to be everywhere at once.

One night the first signals of the new transmitter were tested. At home, in the early morning, we turned on a radio. There came the familiar voice of our engineer. The thing actually worked. It was a miracle. At three o'clock in the afternoon on April 15th, 1949, Lew Hill stepped to the microphone, and the workmen, hammering down the carpet at the last minute, paused at their work. The rest of us were busy pounding out program copy and continuity on typewriters nearby. He announced for the first time: 'This is KPFA, listener-sponsored radio in Berkeley'. For a moment the typewriter copy blurred before our eyes – and the project was underway. (*Exacting Ear*, pp. 11-12)

The Medium

Going on the air was a remarkable achievement, but it was only the first step. The continuing problem, as Lewis Hill knew, was how the station was to be supported. In spite of the dangers, limited advertising was at first considered but was soon rejected because it would have prevented the foundation being granted charity status, which was essential for survival. It was also seen to be the worm in the bud, as Eleanor McKinney explains: 'The commercial thing was absolutely woven into the fabric of broadcasting. That's why Lew wanted to disengage listener-sponsored radio from any kind of commercial structure, because it goes into every area: you then have to devote a large percentage of your staff to all kinds of work for commercial ends.'[30]

An alternative to conventional commercial backing therefore had to be found. During KPFA's three years' gestation, several prospectuses appeared which indicate the constantly evolving nature of Hill's thinking, but the most useful source of information is Hill's own book, *Voluntary Listener-Sponsorship*, which he wrote in 1957 as a report on the station's progress. Hill and his associates were aware of earlier experiments in which audience support was solicited:

The idea of obtaining money directly from a radio audience, to help pay broadcasting expenses, has had numerous applications in post-war America. A decade before World War II, in New York City, the idea was anticipated in the first publication of a monthly program bulletin, by a commercial 'good music' station. Here the audience paid a nominal subscription for the bulletin alone, covering its printing and mailing costs. Later years however saw stations of this same type in Washington D.C., New York, Chicago, and Seattle both publishing program bulletins for subscribers and setting aside a particular day's schedule, or a single program series. Other 'good music' stations have resorted to their audiences with random appeals for emergency operating funds, as necessity warranted.

Though many of these arrangements or appeals involved an effort to organize listeners into participating councils with positive cultural objectives, they were generally a last resort of the stations employing them. They marked not a chosen course of listener-oriented broadcasting, but the failure of the specialized station to make its way in the competitive market. Several such stations relying on random audience appeals to supplement advertising revenue were forced to close, or to abandon specialization, after response to the appeals dwindled. So far as is known, no plan embodying a concept of continued listener-payment for operating expenses has survived in commercial radio.

Efforts of this kind to place a measure of responsibility on the listener for what he receives have labored against the fact that the listener was free to receive the program whether or not he helped pay for it.[31]

Hill went on to consider the possibility of 'scrambling' signals so as to make the listener rent an unscrambling device in order to receive them. Such technology, still experimental in the late 1940s, is now commonplace, but Hill's rejection of it would still apply to any medium wishing to reach a large audience of the unconverted: 'A signal excluding non-subscribers from the listening privilege would not have served its purposes. The KPFA signal was to be available to the entire public' (Hill, pp. 3-4).

Lewis Hill arrived at a theory which he set out to prove: that a non-commercial radio station could survive if two percent of its potential audience could be persuaded to pay a voluntary subscription to support it. This 'two percent theory', as Hill formulated it, was to be one of the philosophical as well as economic cornerstones of Pacifica Radio. He was convinced from the beginning that the *paying* audience would be predominantly middle-to-upper-class liberals:

> Here [is] perhaps the most profound implication of the theory of listener-sponsorship. As a general rule, it is persons of education, mental ability, or cultural heritage equating roughly with the sources of intellectual leadership in the community who tend to become voluntary listener-sponsors. In the KPFA experiment this correspondence was empirically unmistakable, although the subscribing audience apparently touched every economic stratum. It is thus clear that the 2% theory, when we speak of supporting serious cultural broadcasting by this means, represents also *a way of extending the legitimate functions of social and cultural leadership* [emphasis Hill's]. Obviously, to earn systematic support from the community's intellectual leadership, the listener-sponsored station must give the values and concerns of that leadership an accurate reflection at their highest level.... Because the resulting broadcast service is public, the community at large – no doubt by slow accretion and assimilation – is enabled to participate in the best aspects of its own culture as few communities have done before. (Hill, pp. 13-14)

This is both a statement of intent and of history, for it was written after KPFA had been on the air for eight years. Up to that time, Pacifica had never been remotely proletarian except in sympathy. Although the ends were democratic and egalitarian, the means, and even the broader cultural premises, were unambiguously, unashamedly elitist. The history of Pacifica Radio, and then of National Public Broadcasting in America, is a saga of conflict among those who wished to shift the emphasis towards one pole or the other.

Six years earlier in 1951, after two cliff-hanging years of success and failure, Lewis Hill had discussed the theory of listener-sponsored radio in a broadcast talk. It rested, he said, upon two assumptions: 'First, that radio can and should be used for significant communication and art; and second, that since broadcasting is an act of communication, it ought to be subject to the same aesthetic and ethical principles as we apply to any communicative act, including the most personal' (*Exacting Ear*, p. 20). Hill was aware that within the context of commercial radio such assumptions are utopian:

> The purpose of commercial radio is to induce mass sales. For mass sales there must be a mass norm, and the activity must be conducted as nearly as possible without risk of departure from the norm.... By suppressing the individual, the unique, the industry reduces the risk of failure (abnormality) and assures itself a standard product for mass consumption.... This is the first problem that listener sponsorship sets out to solve – to

give the genuine artist and thinker a possible, even a desirable, place to work in radio. (*Exacting Ear*, pp. 21-22)

Paradoxically, the problem was part of the solution. Pacifica could never have afforded to pay the hundreds of program participants that appeared on the air, but the very fact of commercial radio's awfulness meant that they were prepared to work for nothing, simply in order to find a mass audience for the things they were unable to say and do in the commercial media:

> America is well supplied with remarkably talented writers, musicians, philosophers, and scientists whose work will survive for some centuries. Such people have no relation whatever to our greatest communication medium.... [This] is actually so notorious in the whole tradition and atmosphere of our radio that it precludes anyone of serious talent and reasonable sanity from offering material for broadcast, much less joining a staff. The country's best minds, like one mind, shun the medium unless the possessor happens to be running for public office. Yet if we want an improvement in radio worth the trouble, it is these people whose talent the medium must attract. (*Exacting Ear*, p. 22)

So far Lewis Hill might have been writing a prospectus for a government-sponsored public service like the BBC. But he and his fellow-founders set out to establish a degree of self-regulation which would have been impossible in a quasi-official institution:

> The people who actually do the broadcasting should also be responsible for what and why they broadcast. In short, they must control the policy which determines their actions.... Whatever else may happen, we thus assign to the participating individual the responsibility, artistic integrity, freedom of expression, and the like, which in conventional radio are normally denied him. KPFA is operated literally on this principle. (*Exacting Ear*, p. 23)

Hill anticipated that autocracy would be tempered by 'market forces':

> Some self-determining group of broadcasters might find that no one ... gave a hang for their product.... What then? Then ... there would be no radio station ... and the various individualists involved could go scratch for a living. But it is the reverse possibility that explains what is most important about listener sponsorship. When we imagine the opposite situation, we are compelled to account for some conscious flow of influences, some creative tension between broadcaster and audience that constantly reaffirms their mutual relevance. (*Exacting Ear*, p. 24)

Listener subscription was therefore intended to be more than just a means of meeting expenses. Unlike the BBC, access to whose output was predicated in legal terms on compulsory license fee payment, subscription to KPFA was to be voluntary. Anyone could listen for nothing; it was up to the staff and the excellence of the programs themselves to persuade the listeners to contribute financial support. Subscribers to the station received the *Folio*, then a biweekly (later monthly) publication which listed and described the programs. But Hill emphasized that they were subscribing, not to the periodical, but to the station itself: 'Actually sending in the subscription, which one does not have to send in unless one particularly wants to, implies the kind of cultural engagement, as some French philosophers call it, that is surely indispensable for the sake of the whole culture' (*Exacting Ear*, p. 25).

So far the audience has been an abstraction: it has not been defined or described. Before beginning in detail an analysis of Pacifica's programming, we should give our attention to the prospective audience as Lewis Hill perceived it. Rather than attempt to imagine and then address a 'typical' listener, Hill tore up the advertising manuals and started from a totally different premise:

> The audience was believed to consist of an individual, whose intention was to listen. The listening individual was assumed to have an alertness, an intelligence, an interest and an attention-span commensurate with those of the persons preparing and airing the program. There was no wish to persuade persons in the audience to listen beyond the range of their interests or at the sacrifice of their preconceptions. The number of persons who might be expected to listen to a given program at a given hour was not a governing criterion for either its method of presentation or its scheduling. The station was frankly against the idea of 'background' programming, especially in music, and urged its audience to listen with complete selectivity. It was, in fact, a hopeful assumption that the radio would be turned off, or to another frequency, when KPFA's particular program had less than a compelling value for an audience of one. (Hill, p. 44)

Having established two totally revolutionary principles – absence of commercial sponsorship and indifference to a mass audience – Hill went on to describe in detail some of the attributes of a broadcasting medium which would conform to these criteria. The very fact of non-commercial broadcasting led at once to two interlocking principles: broadcasting time was not *owned* and there was no need for commercial breaks: 'On examination of the tradition and uses of second-hand timing in commercial radio, it appeared that this practice had an entirely economic origin and meaning. Since at best it poses an obstacle to programming freedom, there appeared no reason whatever for its continuance in educational radio not engaged in the sale of time segments' (Hill, p. 53). There were two highly pragmatic consequences: firstly, the absence of commercial breaks meant that broadcasts could assume whatever attention span was required by the subject matter; secondly, this principle could be extended to its logical conclusion. A program could therefore be as long as necessary or appropriate. This was particularly important in accommodating the live broadcasts which were an integral part of Pacifica's programming policy. These factors may not be remarkable to those familiar with the BBC Third Programme (now Radio Three), but the Third Programme had only been on the air since 1946, by which time Hill was already beginning to formulate his plans. Within the context of American commercial radio they were revolutionary.

In order to give flexibility to programs listed in the *Folio* but not yet timed or timeable, 'miscellany' slots were scattered through the day:

The occasional ... use of a Miscellany period denotes KPFA's particular approach to this old and vexing problem in broadcasting.... Its length, as scheduled, varied from 5 to 15 minutes. A variety of reading matter and brief music selections was kept on hand for use as ... the announcer on duty thought interesting and appropriate to occupy the time before the next scheduled program. (Hill, p. 53)

Another important factor in communicating with the audience in a totally different manner was the use of voices on the air which did not sound like the typical radio announcer described in Lew Hill's ironic summary of a standard audition. Instead, KPFA attempted to broadcast at all times as one intelligent person talking to another. 'Theme music', although not prohibited, was not encouraged and rarely occurred: 'Programs were put on the air with a simple announcement of their content or purpose.... It was not thought necessary to lure the listener with titles, or in any way to attempt to disguise the fact that an event of broadcasting was taking place, as distinguished from an event of the lecture-hall, auditorium or theater' (Hill, p. 54).

In these and other ways, then, the attributes of commercial radio were examined one by one and for the most part rejected. All these factors taken together meant that a listener could tune in the station at any time and *instantly* determine that he had arrived at something unique. It is no wonder that KPFA quickly gathered an enthusiastic audience whose members had little in common except discrimination and intelligence.

The Message

The cornerstone of Pacifica's structure was Ghandian pacifism/non-violence; this was intended to be not only the content of its programing but also the guiding principle of its organization. Its successes and failures were to be a microcosm of human history. As Eleanor McKinney remembers: 'I've seen comparisons in Pacifica's history with all kinds of things since, even America and Russia. It is *the* human story. Our bylaws said that: we were to study causes of conflict among individuals and nations, and ways to resolve those conflicts.'[32]

As important as non-violence, and integrally related to it, was allegiance to the First Amendment to the U.S. Constitution guaranteeing freedom of speech. It was no accident that Alexander Miekeljohn was one of KPFA's first and most influential advisers. In a famous speech which he gave first before a congressional committee and later as a prize-winning radio broadcast at the height of the McCarthy witch-hunt in 1953, Miekeljohn set forth the principles which more than any other were to unite Pacifica's broadcasters:

> In our popular discussions unwise ideas must have a hearing as well as wise ones, dangerous ideas as well as safe, un-American as well as American.... To be afraid of ideas, of any idea, is to be unfit for self-government. Any such suppression of ideas about the common good the First Amendment condemns with its absolute disapproval. The freedom of ideas shall not be abridged. (*Exacting Ear*, pp. 131, 137)

Their pursuit of this ideal – and more specifically their regular airing of avowed and suspected radicals – was to keep the Pacifica stations in constant trouble via incessant right-wing attack and occasional government investigation. But Pacifica's scrupulous civil libertarian principles also gave air time to the very forces that were attacking them. Caspar Weinberger, who would become President Reagan's bellicose Secretary of Defense, was a regular KPFA commentator and supporter in the 1960s. I also remember the elegant precision with which Byron Bryant, a public affairs programmer for KPFA in the 1950s, interviewed two principal leaders of the American Nazi Party. KPFA's balance was in its totality, not within any single program. As Elsa Knight Thompson, the station's most long-serving public affairs director, was to put it laconically in the early 1960s, balanced programing did not consist of having someone say yes every time someone else said no.

But there was another aspect of program balance which Hallock Hoffman, a later President of Pacifica Foundation, was to set forth during an investigation by the Senate Internal Security Subcommittee in 1963:

> In my opinion, Pacifica should lean toward programs that present either opinions or information not available elsewhere.... I think Pacifica serves the ideal of balance if it spends little time reinforcing popular beliefs.... I feel Pacifica should be on the lookout for information that is hard for people to get from other sources.... I believe Pacifica should regard its audiences as composed of mature, intelligent, and responsible adults, who can be trusted to make up their own minds.... I do not believe Pacifica should tell its audience what to think about the content of its programs.... (*Exacting Ear*, pp. 32-33)

Lewis Hill's intention was to address a series of minority audiences which would not necessarily overlap. The principles and predilections of Pacifica's broadcasters evolved into a list of program categories, each supervised by a departmental director. As set forth by Hill in 1957, these provide an accurate overview of approximately the first fifteen years of KPFA's programing. (I have added some personal comments in brackets, as well as percentage figures for each category taken from elsewhere in Hill's book.)

> **Music**, including ethnic and folk music and studies in the jazz genre, but with the principal emphasis on serious music, 'classical' and contemporary. So-called semi-classical or light music, and popular dance music of the day, were not used. [Pop music was not yet taken seriously.] The analysis of music forms and history was part of this category. [48%]

Public affairs, through individual commentaries and group discussions incorporating as broad an opinion spectrum as possible, and with the deliberate intention of enabling minority views on important issues to be heard alongside the more orthodox. [By the early 1960s, the battery-operated tape recorder would add one of Pacifica's most distinctive and distinguished formats, the public affairs documentary.] It was meant to include in this program category the broadcasting of news compiled and edited from sources not usually brought together for radio. [18%]

Literature and Drama, again with particular attention to contemporary work in these fields, but drawing also upon the excellent work of the BBC in classical drama. [As serious drama gradually faded from commercial radio, Pacifica's productions would gain national attention.] The station aimed to function as a direct outlet for new poetry and the presentation of contemporary poets [which it achieved with great distinction]. Reviews and lectures were included. [16%]

Philosophy and Science, the latter viewed also in its philosophical ramifications. Technical lectures in science were not part of the format, but considerable emphasis was given the relationship of modern scientific thought to traditional western philosophies. Oriental philosophy, particularly the variants of Buddhism, had considerable treatment [thanks principally to Alan Watts, as we shall see]. In addition to a relatively few programs formally oriented to topics in these fields, there was a general intention to relate discussions on public affairs to questions of fundamental philosophical import. [7%] [As this low figure indicates, there were not enough programs to justify a specialist department, and they were subsumed under Public Affairs and, in some cases, Drama and Literature.]

Programs for Children, ranging through the subject matter of the four categories mentioned. The emphasis fell on pre-school programs with some instructional value, although material in this category was often conceived simply as an effort to provide wholesome entertainment alternatives [then, as now, a losing battle in American commercial broadcasting]. Programs designed specifically for children were scheduled in the hour between 5 and 6 p.m. [10%] (Hill, pp. 41-42, 50)

From the very beginning, program participants included names which were or would become familiar throughout the country. Some extracts from the sample week's programs which Hill included in *Voluntary Listener-Sponsorship* are worth reprinting here because they present more of the flavor of KPFA's broadcasting than any means short of listening to the programs themselves. Several of the names merit expository footnotes.

9:00 ORCHESTRAL CONCERT. Galuppi, Overture #2; Prokoviev, Piano Concerto #3; Beethoven, Symphony #3, E♭ Major.

10:30 BOOKS. A review and discussion of newly published literature by the poet, editor and dramatist Kenneth Rexroth.[1]

11:00 THE CRAGMONT REPORT II. An open roundtable discussion in which parents of the Cragmont (public) school of Berkeley, who drew up a report criticizing the educational practices of the school system, argue the issues with representatives of the public schools, with listeners participating via telephoned questions.

11:45 MISCELLANY.

12:00 JAZZ REVIEW. A survey and discussion, with illustrations, of current trends and recordings in jazz literature, by Philip Elwood.[2]

1:30 FRANK O'CONNOR: 'The Mirror in the Roadway'. A talk given at the University of California by the Irish writer and poet.

2:45 MUSIC OF SOUTH AMERICA. Sixth in a series of illustrated talks on Latin-American music, by Robert Garfias.

3:10 FIDELIO. Beethoven's opera performed by the Vienna State Opera Company conducted by Karl Bohm.
Florestan: Torsten Ralf
Leonore: Hilde Konetzni
Marcellina: Irmgard Seefried
Jacquino: Peter Klein
Pizarro: Paul Schoeffler
Rocco: Herbert Alsen
Don Fernando: Tomislav Neralic

5:15 KIDNAPPED. Robert Louis Stevenson's story of the wanderings of David Balfour in the year 1751, adapted and narrated by Charles Levy and Virginia Maynard. Part XV: 'I Go in Quest of My Inheritance'.[3]

5:45 CHAMBER MUSIC. Composers and performers closely associated with KPFA's first seven years on the air. Milhaud, Quartet #12, performed by the Quartetto Italiano[4]; Sessions, Sonata #, performed by Bernhard Abramo-

---

[1] As we have already noted, Kenneth Rexroth was associated with KPFA from the very beginning and many of his writings originated as KPFA broadcasts.

[2] Philip Ellwood was responsible for KPFA's encyclopaedic jazz coverage for almost forty years, including *Jazz Review* (a weekly survey of live concerts and new records), *Jazz Archives* (each devoted to a single classic musician or group), and *Modern Jazz Scene* (a similarly detailed analysis of contemporary jazz).

[3] Charles Levy and Virginia Maynard were jointly responsible for most of KPFA's original radio drama during its first decade.

[4] Darius Milhaud, during the years he taught at Mills College, Oakland, was a regular contributor.

witsc[5]; Mozart, Quintet in G Minor, K. 516, performed by the Griller Quartet, Gilbert assisting.[6]

7:20   MISCELLANY.

7:30   GOLDEN VOICES. A series conducted weekly by Anthony Boucher since KPFA's first day on the air.[7] John McCormack, tenor (1884-1945), second of three programs: art songs (recordings of 1911-1940).

8:00   KPFA's SEVENTH BIRTHDAY. A documentary by the station's staff on the history of the project since its first broadcast day, April 15, 1949.

8:30   MISCELLANY.

8:45   RENAISSANCE CHORAL MUSIC. Works by Dufay, Josquin des Pres, Lassus, and Vittoria, performed by the New York Musica Antiqua.

9:30   PHILOSOPHY EAST AND WEST. Lectures comparing Oriental thought with the main traditions of Western philosophy, by Alan Watts, Dean of the American Academy of Asian Studies.[8]

10:00 ETHNIC MUSIC. A regular series examining and illustrating the indigenous music of different cultures, prepared and presented by Henry Jacobs.[9]

10:30 THE FILM. A discussion, with appropriate guests, of recent developments in the art form of the film, and a criticism of current films; conducted by Pauline Kael, film critic for *Partisan Review*.[10]

11:00 SIGN-OFF

---

[5] Bernard Abramowitsc, one of the Bay Area's most distinguished pianists, gave a number of live and recorded concerts for KPFA, including memorable Beethoven and Schubert cycles.

[6] The Griller String Quartet, while in residence at the University of California at Berkeley, often appeared on KPFA.

[7] Anthony Boucher, one of America's most prolific and influential mystery and science fiction editors and authors, also shared his enormous collection of early operatic records with KPFA's audiences for almost forty years.

[8] Alan Watts, world-famous for his writings on Buddhism, recorded many programs for KPFA which are still regularly rebroadcast.

[9] Henry Jacobs was an early exponent of ethnic music and experimenter with *musique concrète*.

[10] Pauline Kael, recently retired as perhaps the world's most powerful film critic, launched her career on KPFA.

MONDAY

3:00   HAYDN. Symphony #49, F Minor; Harpsichord Concerto, F Major; Philemon and Baucis.

4:30   BRITISH WEEKLIES. A review from the BBC.

4:45   MISCELLANY.

5:00   STORIES AND MUSIC. A program for pre-school children by Natalie Lessinger.

5:15   THE LITTLE HOUSE SERIES. Stories read by Virginia Maynard.

5:35   YOUNG PEOPLE'S CONCERT. Offenbach, Helen of Troy.

5:45   POETRY. A children's anthology, with notes; prepared and read by Olive Wong.

6:00   ORCHESTRAL CONCERT. Manfredini, Concerto Grosso: String Orch. Krueger; Mozart, Flute-Harp Concerto, C Major: Stuttgart Orch., Lund; Schmidt, Symphony #4: Vienna Symphony, Moralt.

7:20   NEWS. A survey of the day's press wire and other news sources, prepared by a staff member.

7:35   COMMENTATOR SERIES: Views on current affairs. Trevor Thomas, Executive Secretary, Friends Committee on Legislation of Northern California.

7:50   MISCELLANY.

8:00   SYMPHONY CRITIQUE. Alan Rich (KPFA Musical Director) discusses last week's concert by the San Francisco Symphony Orchestra.[11]

8:15   STUDIO CONCERT. Judy Maas, mezzo, and Helen Sizer, piano, in a program of songs by Paisiello, Vivaldi, Wolf, Debussy, Mendelssohn, Schubert, Brahms, and Poulenc.

9:00   INLAND, WESTERN SEA. First of a series of readings from the works of Nathan Asch. The reader is Virginia Maynard.

9:40   SCHUBERT'S C MAJOR QUINTET. A discussion and analysis of the work by Alan Rich, followed by a performance by the Hollywood Quartet, with Kurt Reher, second cello.

11:00   SIGN-OFF.

* * * * *

FRIDAY

3:00   ORCHESTRAL CONCERT. Mozart, Divertimento, C Major, K. 187; Handel, Water Music; Stravinsky, Symphony, C Major.

4:20   JAZZ ARCHIVES. Philip F. Elwood. Last Wednesday's program rebroadcast.

5:00   FOLK TALES OF MANY LANDS. Selected and read, for young people, by Don Therence.

5:15   JOSEPHINE GARDNER. The Irish storyteller in her regular KPFA program for children.

5:30   YOUNG PEOPLE'S CONCERT. Respighi, Ancient Airs and Dances.

---

[11] Alan Rich, one of KPFA's first and most popular music directors, went on to write for the *New York Herald Tribune*, *New York Magazine*, *Newsweek*, and *The Los Angeles Chronicle*.

5:45	FOREST LORE. A talk on plants and animals, by Jack Parker, naturalist for the East Bay Regional Parks.
6:00	CHAMBER MUSIC. Mozart, Quartet, G Major, K. 387; Barylli Quartet; Respighi, Quartetto Dorico; Quartetto della Scalla; Beethoven, Quartet, Bb Major, Op. 130: Budapest Quartet.
7:20	NEWS. Review and summary by a staff member.
7:35	COMMENTATOR SERIES. Robert Tideman, Executive Secretary, Henry George School of Social Science.
7:50	MISCELLANY.
8:00	INDIANS IN CALIFORNIA: 'What Do Indians Say?' The series by Frank Quinn; rebroadcast of last Tuesday's program.
8:30	THE LITTLE SYMPHONY ORCHESTRA.[12] A concert broadcast direct from the Berkeley Little Theater, Gregory Millar, Conductor. Handel, The Great Elopement; Hindemith, Concerto for Woodwinds, Harp and Orchestra; Haydn, Cello Concerto, D Major, Gabor Rejto, soloist; Milhaud, Concerto for Percussion and Orchestra, Meyer Slivka, soloist; Mozart, Symphony #41, C Major.
10:20	MEET THE CANDIDATE. State Senator Richard Richards, seeking the Democratic nomination for U.S. Senator from California, is interviewed by Trevor Thomas, Herbert Hanley, and Robert Schutz.
11:00	SIGN-OFF.

SATURDAY

9:00	COMMENTATOR SERIES REBROADCAST. From the week's commentaries on current affairs.
9:30	MISCELLANY.
9:45	PHILOSOPHY, EAST AND WEST. The talk by Alan Watts rebroadcast from last Sunday.
10:15	THE WORLD OF SCIENCE. By Janet Nickelsburg. Last Wednesday's program in this series rebroadcast.
10:30	CHAMBER MUSIC. Beethoven, Quartet, Bb Major, Op. 18, #6; Brahms, Quintet, G Major, Op. 111.
11:30	THE REAL RESPONSIBILITIES OF THE SCIENTIST. The article of this title by J. Bronowski, published in the January 1956 issue of the *Bulletin of the Atomic Scientists*; read by Robert Schutz.
12:30	ORCHESTRAL CONCERT. Dohnany, Suite, F# Minor: London Symphony, Sargent; Thomson, Cello Concerto: Silva, with the Janssen Symphony; Delius, Closing scene from 'Koanga': soloists and orchestra conducted by Beecham.
1:00	CLASSICAL RECORD REVIEW. Alan Rich discusses, with illustrations, significant new releases.
1:30	THE FILM. Last Sunday's program by Pauline Kael, rebroadcast.
2:00	CHORAL CONCERT. Brahms, Song, for Women's Chorus: Wiener Kammerchor, Schmid; Schubert, Gesang der Geister: Akademie

---

[12] The Little Symphony Orchestra under Gregory Millar was one of America's first uncompromisingly classical chamber orchestras and was heard regularly on KPFA.

Kammerchor, Kraus; Debussy, Le Martyre de St. Sebastien: Danco, Chorus & Orch., conducted by Ansermet.

4:00   MISCELLANY.

4:20   AN ECONOMIC COMPARISON OF AUSTRALIA AND SWEDEN. Erik Lundberg, Professor of Economics, University of Stockholm, Sweden, in a talk given at the University of California.

5:15   POETRY. Selected, read and discussed for young people, by Olive Wong.

5:30   FOLK SONGS. Sung with guitar by Barry Olivier and Merritt Herring.

5:45   PROGRAM FOR YOUNG PEOPLE. Selected recordings, varying from early Edison recording to contemporary musical and dramatic records.

6:00   CHAMBER MUSIC. Malipiero, Quartet #7: Quartetto della Scala; Franck, Piano Quintet, F Minor: Aller, Hollywood Quartet; Beethoven, String Quartet, C Major, Op. 29: Huebner, Barylli Quartet.

7:20   COMMENTATOR SERIES. Virginia Davis, sociologist.

7:35   MISCELLANY.

7:55   THE MYSTERY STORY. An interview on this species of modern writing, with Hillary Waugh.

8:25   MISCELLANY.

9:00   JUNO AND THE PAYCOCK. By Sean O'Casey. Recorded in Dublin, with an introduction by the author.

11:00   SIGN-OFF.

These extracts from the sample week date from 15 April 1956 (KPFA's seventh birthday) to 21 April. When KPFA first went on the air, it broadcast from 3 to 6 p.m., shut down for an hour and a half for dinner (!), and then continued from 7:30 to 10:00 or 10:30. As Gert Chiarito recalls, this curious schedule was partly determined by a legal requirement to broadcast at least three hours before and three hours after sundown.[33] When the station moved to new studios two years later the hours were extended, first to fill the dinner hour, then in October 1956 backward to 9 a.m., and subsequently in October 1958 to 7 a.m. Not until the early 1970s would all-night broadcasting become a regular feature, and that corresponded with a change in programing and audience as well as fortune.[34]

This recurring cycle of serious and ethnic music, lengthy discussion and interview, poetry and drama, and earnest exhortation would continue virtually unchanged well into the 1960s. From then on, as Pacifica's minority audiences became increasingly defined by their ethnic, social, and sexual divisions, and deconstruction led to the abolition of cultural and intellectual hierarchies, so the once-firm guidelines by which Pacifica differentiated itself from the outer fringes of commercial radio would themselves be deconstructed.

Complication and Denouement

If the crucial decision to go on the air had been controlled by accountants, Pacifica's audience would still be waiting for the big moment. Eleanor McKinney wrote in 1962:

> Funds ... were placed in trust. If enough money could not be raised ... all the funds would be returned to the donors.... The group had a critical decision to make. The $15,000 in the bank was enough to build a station and operate it for about a month. Yet there was little prospect of raising more money without an operating radio station to demonstrate what could actually be done. A meeting was held to decide whether to return the money to the donors and give up the project, or to take a leap in the dark and begin the experiment.... Finally Lewis Hill reminded us 'In a crisis – grow. That's the only creative possibility – take a risk and expand'. The phrase was to become the key to many decisions in the future. (*Exacting Ear*, p. 11)

The station remained on the air for about fifteen months. Christopher Koch, prize-winning public affairs producer and chronicler of KPFA's history, wrote in 1968:

> Over six hundred different program participants in drama and literature, public affairs, music and children's programs took part in KPFA's broadcasting in the next five months. They volunteered their services. Listeners too, who dropped into the station, found themselves commissioned to type letters, write continuity and stuff envelopes, and a large volunteer staff soon sprung up next to the paid professional one. By such expedients KPFA kept its operating budget to about $4,000 a month.... Summarizing programming after five months, Hill referred to its success 'in obtaining a large and intensely interested audience for the public affairs broadcasts on controversial subjects....'[35]

Other writers and broadcasters reported the new venture with admiration, traces of envy, and doubts as to its staying power. Their scepticism appeared to be confirmed when on 6 August 1950 KPFA shut down its transmitter. As Koch explains, 'with only 270 subscribers, it was forced to suspend broadcasting to devote full time to fund-raising. The exhausted staff – who were all paid the same, regardless of their position – hadn't received a salary for weeks and many had to leave to find regular employment elsewhere to support their families.'[36] But the station's threatened demise goaded the community into action. Eleanor McKinney writes:

> When the staff announced over the air that KPFA was to stop broadcasting, the telephones began to ring and listeners came to plead that the station continue. At their suggestion, a public meeting of KPFA listeners was announced. To the discouraged staff it was an overwhelming experience to see the meeting place crowded with listeners who valued the station so much that they were determined to give their own energies and money to its survival. A working fund of $2,300 was raised immediately. Vigorous committees and volunteer workers plunged into fund-raising and getting subscription pledges

for a new KPFA, and carried on the intensive campaign for nine months. Strangers to each other, but joined in a common bond of interest, they worked together – some ten hours a day, six days a week during the nine months the station was silent. (*Exacting Ear*, p. 14)

So by the middle of 1951 KPFA was back on the air with an expanded schedule and a more powerful transmitter. Seeking additional space to accommodate the growing army of staff and volunteers, at the beginning of 1952 the station moved to larger premises at 2207 Shattuck Avenue (where it was to remain until 1991).

The immediate future was secured a few months later by a Ford Foundation grant for $150,000 administered through the Fund for Adult Education and spread over three years. Lewis Hill's final report to the Fund was not intended to be merely a justification of the investment, but more importantly, a handbook for other potential community stations. Both Hill's and the Foundation's interests went far beyond the survival of a single FM station: they wished to explore the feasibility of a whole network of stations, television as well as radio, each supported by Hill's two percent theory. The formula has worked in many communities, although the magic two percent has never been reached.

While the continued existence of the station was guaranteed for a while, the security of the staff was not. Hill's attention was fixed on the realization of his dream, and the very qualities that made this possible also estranged him from many of those who had joined his crusade. Robert Schutz recalls: 'Lew had the ability to put things together and to be persuasive. He could go to a widow and get $20,000 out of her without much trouble, but he would wait until salaries had not been paid for a couple of months before he did that.'[37] This may accurately describe the staff's perception of the financial situation, but it could not have been easy for Hill to go about with the begging bowl. Neither did his schedule allow time for fund-raising. His widow Joy Hill points out: 'Reaching charitable-minded wealthy people took contacts and time. Often he returned from a laboriously-arranged interview feeling hopeful, only to get a note from [the prospective donor's] financial advisor saying, in effect, "we don't encourage such far-fetched ideas!"'[38] If Hill was less concerned than others about where the money was coming from, there was a simple explanation. Joy Hill acknowledges:

We would go ages with little or no salary, although we were I think in a better situation than many because his father had given us some stock in the company, so we did have quarterly checks and we would juggle bills and keep everything not more than two months in arrears. I don't know how the kids that didn't have checks coming in survived, I really don't.[39]

But there were deeper problems than money. According to Schutz:

He was also pretty persuasive with the staff; and yet his manner of being so persuasive and right all the time was grinding and grating on people.... A small example of Lew's personal relations: money was very short and somebody dreamed up a kind of letterhead, and everybody was using it. Lew came in with utter scorn for its lack of style.[40]

Hill had gone to great lengths to set up a structure which would guarantee that the staff would retain collective control of the station. Vera Hopkins, who has functioned for many years as Pacifica's quasi-official historian, unwinds the tangled skein with great precision in her indispensable 1987 pamphlet, 'Growing Pains':

> Hill was an idealist who established KPFA on egalitarian principles of equal pay and equal voting. The ultimate governing body, the Executive Membership, met twice a year. It was composed wholly of staff members. Originally it served to bring full staff opinion to bear on the decisions of the Committee of Directors. The Directors were five staff elected by the Executive Membership to run the station and conduct the business of Pacifica Foundation including KPFA. The Directors could replace their number if vacancies occurred, subject to later approval by the Executive Membership. (Hopkins, p. 4)

But the very fact of staff autonomy meant that there were no checks and balances, no external sanctions. The integrity of the community depended entirely on the integrity of the people who composed it. Eleanor McKinney reflects: 'I think Lew's saddest experience was that he could attract so few men of quality and intelligence and capabilities to be in a community of artists and workers and broadcasters who would share the delight in each other's skills and diversity.'[41]

In June 1953 there was a palace revolution and Lew Hill resigned as chairman of the station he had conceived and brought into existence. Vera Hopkins offers so much detail that it is necessary to know the protagonists to appreciate the agonies and ironies of each conflict of conscience, personality, or ambition. Well-documented as her history is, a panel of survivors would even now come no closer to agreement on the facts than they did when the wounds were open.

I think that Eleanor McKinney in conversation caught the essence of the conflict, both its causes and its atmosphere, in words that can be grasped without footnotes because they interlock with what we already know of human frailty:

> There was a difference between people who had been there from the beginning and the next generation who had different ideas. It was a series of almost accidental circumstances, disagreements in the board meetings. From my standpoint it was a difference between young people with not very tested theories and the older ones who had experimented.... They [the younger ones] called Lew, Dick [Moore], and me 'The Triumvirate'! Lew was a poet, and yet he could run the mimeograph machine and do carpentry and fund-raising and poetry and drama and so on – a kind of renaissance man who aroused a lot of competitiveness in men especially, and I think that was at the root of it....

Everybody resigned except me; I have a tenacity, I was determined to hang on.... When they got in trouble some months later they called me and asked if I would help them (that is, the other side) from going under. I had this terrible dilemma: do you help the individual or do you seek the continuity of the institution? I was heartbroken: I turned him down and I never got over it. I always felt that I had betrayed the personal, which in the long run is what matters....

I kept being a thorn in their side. I said 'Pacifica was designed to present every point of view and to be exactly the resolution of these kinds of conflicts. If you don't embody that in your very being as a foundation, how can you embody that on the air?'

The whole point of Pacifica was that the people who made the policies carried them out. We didn't have an absentee board; the *staff* were the board. I said 'You're shedding the very principle of what Pacifica is about'. Alan Watts leapt to his feet and came over glowering and thrust his face into mine – like a monster, trembling with rage. He shouted 'Principles are all very well and good until they don't work and then you throw them out!'

In later years this was one of the big jokes of all time. I'm afraid he opportunistically picked up the pieces and started going with the other side. But that's Perennial Philosophy. He and Lew Hill had some fascinating debates at Asilomar on exactly these subjects: the difference between Ethical and Perennial Philosophy, where everything is relative.[42]

Once he was no longer occupied with the daily management of the station, Hill had time for lengthy reflection on what had gone wrong and how it might be corrected. In September 1953 he wrote to Edward Howden:

There were two principles employed in forming Pacifica Foundation which underlie KPFA's difficulties. The first of these was the limitation of Pacifica's Executive Membership to ... staff personnel of KPFA.... A second principle was that of equality: all persons working for KPFA were to receive the same wage....

There is much to be said about the failure of such ideals, and I will confine myself to the painfully obvious. Over the years it emerged sadly and often violently that people burdened with policy responsibilities which their working hours will not permit them to fulfill are frustrated.... In many of the group there was a general predisposition toward distrust and suspicion, which I am afraid is inseparable from the very idealistic anarcho-pacifist viewpoint ... what was conceived as a mutually evolving fellowship became, in much of the operation, a mutually thwarted competition of personalities....

I felt at the time [June 1953] that my resignation would remove a focus of controversy and permit the equalitarian principles of the organization to assert themselves more positively. Certainly my own rather prideful reluctance as the originator to admit the unworkability of this organization was a major cause of the present chaos. (Hopkins, pp. 6-7)

In the meantime the remaining staff, torn by internecine warfare, also put the blame on defective organization rather than their own intractable behavior. By November, a non-staff Study Committee of respected local figures had been set up to examine alternative patterns of organization: 'One of the listed assumptions on which all of the interested parties agree: in order to assure the station's continuance, it is necessary to remove organizational difficulties

204

which have caused serious controversy' (Hopkins, p. 7). One of the lessons of human history is that any group of eminent people offered even more power and prestige will seize it with both hands:

> The thrust of the Study Committee Plan was to reduce staff participation in the governing of Pacifica. They proposed the immediate addition of two non-staff persons to the Committee of Directors, increasing the number from 5 to 7, and electing non-staff persons to the Executive Membership which eventually should have no more than one-third staff members. This was the beginning of a trend. The Committee of Directors in future years was increased to 11, then to 15. The Executive Membership increased the percentage of non-staff and eventually had 33 members. Its importance within Pacifica decreased until it became superfluous and voted itself out of existence.... (Hopkins, p. 8)

Thus, the cornerstone of Pacifica was finally to be eroded.

Ironically, the process was aided and abetted by Lewis Hill for his own purposes, though with the best of motives. Eleanor McKinney feels that:

> The reason Lew Hill separated the Board of Directors from the staff was that he felt that ... in an ideal world people could be objective ... but in the real world, as we'd experienced disastrously, people could not be objective about themselves, their own salaries, their own positions. He had hoped idealistically to attract mature enough people to deal with the few areas where you have to deal with yourselves as a board, but he didn't get enough mature people. That was his conclusion.[43]

But Lew Hill's organizational solution, though ostensibly opening Pacifica to external guidance, was to offer himself as the *de jure* as well as the *de facto* final arbiter:

> They have tackled successfully the organizational problem of staff participation in membership.... The Committee has not, however, offered any solution to the problem of executive authority.... What Pacifica needs is a President ... [who] should be elected by the Committee of Directors. He should have authority to hire and fire, including the Station Directors. (Hopkins, p. 9)

The bait was taken. In August 1954 the Executive Membership offered Hill the Presidency on his own terms, influenced no doubt by the fact that the station had been a shambles without him. According to Eleanor McKinney, Gert Chiarito, Chuck Levy, and Bob Schutz, who had voted against Hill at the time of his resignation, switched back to support him, and Schutz went to Hill's home in Duncan's Mills to ask him to return as the new President.[44]

'The magic of Hill's personality brought peace for a time' (Hopkins, p. 10). But the old problems remained. Financial pressures were constant, and Hill was forced to plead regularly with individuals and foundations to make up the difference between expenses and subscriptions. KPFA's economic problems were in fact reflected throughout the national FM market:

By the end of 1954, three years after commencement of the experiment ... KPFA was the only independent FM station still in operation in the San Francisco region. The others had either vanished or become affiliated as duplicating transmitters with AM outlets....
This ... was in parallel with the general decline of FM broadcasting throughout the country. In San Francisco [it] amounted practically to a complete collapse in FM's significance for the general public.... The station was [thus] obliged to divert both funds and staff into the manufacture and distribution of FM sets under its own auspices, in an effort to circumvent the national industry decline.... These units were offered at regular retail prices but with a KPFA subscription included. (Hill, pp. 86-87)

In addition to dealing with internal crises, therefore, Hill was forced to bear the whole Bay Area FM market upon his shoulders. By July 1956 he had to ask for a three-month leave of absence, and appointed Schutz Executive Director (Hopkins, p. 11).

There was yet another major element in Lew Hill's gradual exhaustion, and it is a measure of his strength of will that it was almost never mentioned. His widow, Joy, explains:

He injured his back playing football [at college], and I really think in the long run that's what killed him. By the time I met him when he was twenty-four, he couldn't sit on the ground with his legs in front of him at a picnic.... His back bothered him all his life, increasingly, and there were many nights when he couldn't turn over in bed and he'd have to wake me to turn him over.... Once he almost got arrested for being drunk on the street in Berkeley because he had staggered and was clutching a lamppost when the cop saw him. He had to explain that his leg went out from under him at times. He lived with pain all the time, and the cortisone that they were pumping into him when they didn't know what they were doing made an enormous number of changes in his life....
He wasn't the sort of person who talked about it. He didn't even like to be asked how he was feeling – I learned very quickly not to say anything. He just hated to be reminded of it.[45]

It is inconceivable that this life-long struggle between pride and frailty did not affect his personal relationships. As Vera Hopkins reports:

Through 1957 the papers in the archive reflect ambivalence on the part of Hill. He needed to lighten his burden. At one point he wrote to a friend that he was 'fed up and tuckered out'. He needed to earn more money for his family than KPFA provided. He had needed a partial absence for reasons of health, yet he had found it difficult to delegate decision-making. In particular he cherished the right to hire and fire. (Hopkins, p. 14)

Towards the end of his life there was a temporary release before the final plunge into terminal depression. Eleanor McKinney watched it happen:

Lew had rheumatoid arthritis and was given cortisone, but they hadn't tested it fully. They gave him massive doses which worked wonders, but later there were studies that showed that a number of people that were given cortisone became alcoholics and committed suicide.... They taught him to inject himself. He was dancing around with freedom, but there were terrible side effects. I think that was the basic thing, because during the last months of his life he changed a great deal. He drank, which he had never done before. He didn't become a drunkard, but he had never used alcohol as a crutch. His drinking was occasional, not all the time, because he continued to do his work. But he was deeply exhausted, he was still struggling to support that place. There were financial problems and I think he was just exhausted in his soul.[46]

Robert Schutz continued as Executive Director after Hill returned from his leave of absence, but in April 1957 Hill dismissed him for associating 'very closely with ... a small minority ... which expresses extreme opposition to the existing management of the project' (Hopkins, p. 11).

By this point it is difficult to distinguish treachery from paranoia. In the Committee of Directors charge and countercharge were hurled, with the majority of voters still backing Hill. Another major protagonist, Felix Greene, had entered the fray. A popular and ambitious program producer, he was one of the new breed of directors invited to solve Pacifica's problems. Once put in charge of a sub-committee to examine the staffing budget, he attempted to take over the station, producing a lengthy professional-looking report and firing off damaging letters to Pacifica's benefactors. He was sent packing within a year.

At the same time, eleven staff members were petitioning for Hill's resignation. They were mostly new and inexperienced, not ideologically close to the founding pacifists, and easily blown about in the tempests that now swept the station. From without, a subscriber pressure group was demanding official representation. Robert Schutz's final defection – he declared to the Committee of Directors in April 1957 that Hill was unfit for office – must have felt like the stab of Brutus. Sadly, by this time Schutz was probably right. Sinking into depression, Hill withdrew more and more to his distant home in Duncan's Mills (Hopkins, pp. 13-15).

On 1 August 1957 Lewis Hill committed suicide. His wife had seen it coming:

I don't know what else he could have done, he was really at the end of his rope. We were going through the same problems for the second time and we had just been to a nursery in Gurneyville up on the Russian River. There was somebody working in the gardens there who had this rheumatoid arthritis of the spine that Lew had, and he was bent over double so that his back was parallel with the ground and he dug things up crab-like. I felt that awful chill that went through Lew. His parents talked at one time of sending him to the Mayo Clinic where they would have frozen his back upright. This would mean he'd never be able to bend again except very stiffly. There were some pretty damned unpleasant choices he had to look at. I think he ran out of strength to do it, that's all.[47]

Lewis Hill's character, and the staff whom he attracted, are epitomized in an incident related by Rick Chiarito, who had been with him from the very beginning:

A few months back, KPFA was responsible for a broadcast in which a program participant was made the object of a very subtle kind of ridicule and insult by one of the staff
members. The participant was a Republican and a Daughter of the American Revolution,
and therefore a 'safe' target, at least from the point of view of KPFA's many 'liberal'
listeners. But throughout the broadcast Lewis Hill paced the corridors with a troubled
expression. Shortly after the broadcast was over, Lew himself went on the air and, on
behalf of the entire staff, he apologized to the woman ... for the personal indignity she
had suffered. Later the staff pointed out to Lew that he did not have the 'right' to
apologize on its behalf without prior consultation in a truly democratic fashion. I was
among those who thought Lew's action presumptuous. But Lew then raised a question,
the substance of which was this: 'If, as chief officer of this organization, I cannot assume
a common concern for the essential dignity of the individual, what can I assume?' In the
interval that has elapsed since this incident, I have asked myself this question many times
and have been led to agree with the justness of Lew's action. (Hopkins, p. 8)

The Legacy

In spite of staff conflict, Lewis Hill had established such a strong tradition and
organization that his death did not bring about any immediate changes. Eleanor
McKinney, his closest associate, was named General Manager *Pro Tem* (Hopkins, p. 19). But by October 1957 the new permanent President of Pacifica and
Station Manager of KPFA was Harold Winkler, who, not surprisingly, had
been a member of the Study Committee formed in 1953 to overhaul the organizational structure. Thus the precedent was established (and then entrenched)
in which broadcasters were set against directors: the solution which would
become the problem. Thenceforth many of the major crises at Pacifica's stations would be conflicts between those who broadcast and those who commanded: the very dichotomy which Lew Hill in his early wisdom had set out
to eliminate.

But Hill's influence extended beyond Pacifica Radio. He was a founder of
the Broadcasting Foundation of America (BFA), a precursor of the Public
Broadcasting System (PBS), which made possible the whole network of
listener-supported radio and television in America. Eleanor McKinney testifies:

He had created the Broadcasting Foundation of America, which was [intended] to take
KPFA and other programs and send them abroad and bring programs from abroad to this
country [only the latter was actually accomplished]. He thought of it and established a
board and worked with George Probst in New York and helped it come into existence.

I later worked for a decade with PBS and the thing that I noticed was how much
KPFA influenced all of public broadcasting. It was the nucleus of all sorts of things. For
instance, our theory was that words were just as repeatable as good music...[48]

Joy Hill echoes and amplifies these observations:

I don't know if anyone knows that Lew was [influential] when public television was just starting. They were doing just educational programs and all these channels were going to be given to colleges; when there were too many colleges in a town like San Francisco they were supposed to allot the time.... Lew, I think (and I know Eleanor agrees with me), changed that whole direction by pointing out the need for a balance to commercial broadcasting. He came up with the fund-raising idea, and all the magazines that they put out to send to their subscribers ... [are] a spin-off from the KPFA *Folio*. Lew laid out the whole original public appeal for funds for these stations, through KQED [TV, San Francisco].[49]

Hill's greatest legacy was, however, to found an institution in which people of talent and intelligence could develop their skills and address the public without any prior restraint other than the laws of libel and obscenity. KPFA, followed by the other Pacifica stations, has been a forcing ground of unparalleled fertility. In the 1960s influential KPFA alumni in New York included Pauline Kael, film critic for the *New Yorker*; John Leonard, editor of the Sunday *New York Times Book Review*; Alan Rich, music critic for the *Herald Tribune* and then *New York* magazine; Jack Nessel, managing editor of *New York*; and Eleanor McKinney, Executive Director of the Broadcasting Foundation of America. The advantage they all shared was having worked in a medium in which they were allowed the unfettered though impecunious freedom of artists in a garret.

Our concentration on Lewis Hill is in danger of making the subsequent history of Pacifica sound like a long twilight. But even those most devoted to Hill and most opposed to the subsequent changes would readily agree that, compared with most of American radio, Pacifica's output has remained often spectacular.

KPFA's present Music Director, Charles Amirkhanian, has held the post for twenty-five years, during which he has interviewed and broadcast just about every composer of any importance. From the beginning, KPFA championed modern music. During the 1960s it shared studio space in an old Wobbly (Industrial Workers of the World) Hall at 321 Divisadero Street with the Ann Halpern Dance Company and the San Francisco Tape Music Center. The latter was a major meeting place and training ground for America's musical avant-garde, including Terry Riley, La Monte Young, Steve Reich, Pauline Oliveros, and Morton Sobotnik. (The technical requirements of this inventive group led in turn to the Buchla synthesizers, Nady radio microphones, Meyer loudspeaker systems, and other state-of-the-art sound equipment.)

Until his retirement last year drama and literature were under the direction of another twenty-five year veteran, Erik Bauersfeld, who established close links with German radio in Cologne and has produced for radio all the plays of Eugene O'Neill directed by Jose Quintero. Like Amirkhanian he has interviewed and presented most of the important contemporary poets (including another contributor to this volume, Eric Mottram). The tradition goes back to the

209

beginning, when the leaders of the San Francisco literary scene were heard regularly. Lawrence Ferlinghetti speaks for them all:

> KPFA was really a focal point for a lot of the underground.... When I arrived [in San Francisco] in 1951, it was in full force. It was the center of the intellectual community right up on through the early sixties. There were regular commentators and programs that gave me a complete education that was much better than anything I got out of college.[50]

In short, the last forty years of the San Francisco cultural scene without KPFA are unthinkable.

But perhaps the most remarkable feature of Pacifica's output has been its public affairs programming. Its stations have, in fact, been unique among America's surviving broadcasters in their coverage of political controversy. One of the most important figures in this field was Elsa Knight Thompson, Public Affairs Director from 1957 until her retirement in 1974. She came to KPFA from an already distinguished career as director of international affairs broadcasts for the BBC Overseas Service during World War II (she was the first radio broadcaster to break stories of Hitler's death camps). At KPFA she trained a whole generation of radio producers who won prizes (and made influential enemies) at Pacifica's other stations.[51] One of her associates was Dale Minor, who was in Birmingham, Alabama in 1963 when forty days of protest led by Martin Luther Ring Jr. culminated in racist riots and the arrest of more than three thousand demonstrators. The resulting program, 'Freedom Now', was American radio's documentary entry that year for the Prix Italia. Two years later, when rioting broke out in Watts, Los Angeles, Pacifica's black reporters went into the thick of it and came out with the sort of recordings the mass media's overwhelmingly white staff couldn't get.

Pacifica's coverage of the student free speech and civil rights revolt was encyclopedic. In 1960, KPFA recorded the San Francisco hearings of the House Un-American Affairs Committee and was able to document the events leading to the violent confrontation between police and student demonstrators on the steps of City Hall. In 1964, when Berkeley students revolted against an administrative prohibition of on-campus fund-raising for civil rights, KPFA, only a few blocks away, was able to keep staff and volunteer reporters on the scene around the clock. Hours of air time were devoted to interviews, discussions, and recordings of public meetings, demonstrations, and the night of mass arrests in Sproul Hall. (There could be no argument about police brutality and student non-violence: it was all on tape. The official reports were mostly lies. A major step in my education was seeing the police drag the students down the steps by their heels, their heads bouncing off the stones.) Pacifica also provided live all-day coverage of the Vietnam Teach-In at Berkeley in 1965, enlivened by Norman Mailer's speech included a year later in *Cannibals and Christians*. (I still recall my fury at being ordered to take it off the air because of its obscenity, although in retrospect the station may be forgiven its caution:

it had almost lost its license over a broadcast of Edward Albee's *The Zoo Story*.)

Indifference to official and commercial pressures put Pacifica years ahead in covering black militancy, urban and rural poverty, student discontent, the Vietnam War, Hoover's administration of the FBI, the military-industrial complex, censorship, government control of the universities, drug laws, conscientious objection to the draft, feminism, gay rights, and other controversial issues. It is part of the enduring legacy of Pacifica Radio that its tapes continue to be among the most valuable documents of recent history.

Such unorthodox broadcasting might be expected to have landed the stations in trouble. It has. From the beginning there were accusations of communism and subversion, due in part to the fact that in the United States belief in unfettered expression is usually in itself a left-wing conviction. Nor has survival been made easier by the staff's attempts to penetrate official secrecy. In 1963 the Pacifica Foundation was investigated by the Senate Internal Security Sub-Committee to determine possible Communist infiltration. 'Informed sources' suggested that the investigation was perhaps not unrelated to interviews broadcast the previous year with two former FBI agents whose anecdotes about J. Edgar Hoover had been unflattering. At the same time, the Pacifica stations' licenses came up for renewal by the Federal Communications Commission and, although the decision was ultimately favorable, the procedure was rather less routine than usual.

None of this prevented Lewis Hill's dream of a network of Pacifica stations becoming reality: KPFK, Los Angeles, established in 1959; WBAI, New York, given to Pacifica by philanthropist Louis Schweitzer in 1960; KPFT, Houston, started in 1970; and WPFW, Washington, D.C., 1977. Nor has it prevented Pacifica's tradition of distinguished reporting continuing to the present. Launched in 1968, the Pacifica Radio News service in Washington D.C. has been available to all of public radio since 1978. In 1987 Larry Bensky's coverage from this facility of the Iran-Contra affair won the George Polk Award. A mere summary of other awards and commendations would double the length of this chapter.

The fight continues. In April 1989 David Salniker, Executive Director of Pacifica, wrote:

While Pacifica received bomb threats at KPFA because of its reading of Salman Rushdie's *The Satanic Verses*, the Federal Communications Commission and [Sen. Jesse] Helms required us to censor sections of the book that contained language offensive to the FCC. It is ironic that on the same day the Bush administration decried the ayatollah's threat to the First Amendment, it was in federal court defending legislation censoring what little literature you can find on the air.[52]

A recurring lament of KPFA alumni has been the corruption of standards and the desertion of principles. On 26 September 1991, KPFA moved into new state-of-the-art $2,250,000 purpose-built studios. While some cried 'sell-out!' the *Folio* for that month listed a newly-commissioned piece by Lou Harrison; the West Coast premiere of Busoni's opera, *Arlecchino*; a Washington report from Larry Bensky on the Robert Gates/CIA hearings; a celebration of the sixtieth birthday of Gary Snyder; one-and-a-half hours of interviews with Kurt Vonnegut; eyewitness testimony on US war crimes in the Persian Gulf; and an entire day devoted to President Bush's 'New World Order' which included contributions from Noam Chomsky, Michael Parenti, Daniel Sheehan, and Alexander Cockburn.

Not bad for a sell-out. Although Pacifica's format, style, and even content have changed over the years, Lewis Hill's legacy continues to yield a dividend. Like the co-operatives, the Living Theatre, Black Mountain College, the civil rights movement in the early 1960s, and certain segments of the underground press, Pacifica Radio has been a salutary experiment in democratizing the sort of institution which is usually controlled from above. Even since the establishment of an external board of directors, interference with the act of broadcasting has been minimal compared with any other privately or publicly owned media outlets whatsoever. The results are sometimes mediocre, but occasionally spectacular: not because Pacifica's staff have been uniquely talented, but because they could afford the luxury of habitual integrity. They have helped to demonstrate that the most important facts about any source of information are who runs it and what they stand to gain.

Direct listener support provides a reliable assurance that the audience is not being manipulated for unspecified ends, be they commercial, political, or even paternally altruistic. In a time of increasingly centralized information control, such an assurance is precious indeed.

Notes

1. Frank Buxton and Bill Owen, *The Big Broadcast, 1920-1950* (New York: Flare/Avon, 1973), p. vii.
2. Eleanor McKinney (ed.), *The Exacting Ear: The Story of Listener-Sponsored Radio, and an Anthology of Programs from KPFA, KPFR, and WBAI* (New York: Pantheon/ Random House, 1966), p. 21. Further references are incorporated in the main text.
3. Fred Friendly, *Due to Circumstances Beyond Our Control....* (London: MacGibbon and Kee, 1967), pp. xiv-xv. Friendly was public affairs producer for CBS [Columbia Broadcasting System] Television between 1954 and 1964; and President of CBS News between 1964 and 1966.
4. Buxton and Owen, p. 153; Friendly, p. xiv.
5. Buxton and Owen, pp. 172-3.
6. Buxton and Owen, pp. 159, 171.
7. Barbara Leaming, *Orson Welles: a Biography* (New York: Viking, 1985), pp. 50ff.
8. Buxton and Owen, pp. 56, 158.
9. Friendly, p. xvi.

10. Telephone interview with Eleanor McKinney [now Sowande], 30 January 1992.
11. Telephone interview with Morris Horowitz, 7 October 1991.
12. Telephone interview with Robert Schultz, 8 October 1991; Horowitz interview.
13. Horowitz interview.
14. Telephone interview with Joy Hill, 28 January 1992.
15. *Pacifica: Radio With Vision since 1949* (Berkeley: Pacifica Foundation, 1989), p. 8.
16. Hill interview.
17. McKinney interview.
18. Christopher Koch, 'Pacifica' (1968). Reprinted in the KPFA *Folio*, February 1972.
19. Hill interview.
20. McKinney interview.
21. Kenneth Rexroth, 'The Beat Generation', BBC Radio Third Programme, October 1966.
22. Telephone interview with Gertrude Chiarito, 8 October 1991.
23. Chiarito interview.
24. Schutz interview.
25. McKinney interview. Eleanor McKinney has also edited *The Exacting Ear: The Story of Listener-Sponsored Radio, and an Anthology of Programs from KPFA, KPFR, and WBAI* (New York: Pantheon/Random House, 1966), an anthology of representative program transcripts and the only book devoted to this seminal cultural phenomenon.
26. McKinney interview.
27. *Pacifica: Radio With Vision*, pp. 1, 8.
28. Hill interview.
29. Chiarito interview.
30. McKinney interview.
31. Lewis Hill, *Voluntary Listener-Sponsorship: A Report to Educational Broadcasters on the Experiment at KPFA, Berkeley, California* (Berkeley, Ca.: Pacifica Foundation, 1958) pp. 1-2. Further references are incorporated in the main text.
32. McKinney interview.
33. Chiarito interview.
34. Vera Hopkins, 'Growing Pains, with Special Reference to KPFA', unpublished monograph, 1987. Further references are incorporated in the main text.
35. Koch, p. 12.
36. Koch, p. 12.
37. Schutz interview.
38. Hill interview.
39. Hill interview.
40. Schutz interview.
41. McKinney interview.
42. McKinney interview.
43. McKinney interview.
44. Schutz interview.
45. Hill interview.
46. McKinney interview.
47. Hill interview.
48. McKinney interview.
49. Hill interview.
50. David Armstrong, 'Little Network That Could', *San Francisco Examiner*, April 1989.
51. Elsa Knight Thompson, obituary, *San Francisco Sunday Examiner and Chronicle*, 13 February 1983.
52. Armstrong, 'Little Network That Could'.

Don't Knock the Rock: Race, Business, and Society in the Rise of Rock'n'Roll

Jody Pennington

Part One

Forty Miles of Bad Road

From the beginning, rock'n'roll was geared for movement, for dancing: it sounded best in a car, cruising down the highway or cutting down the boulevard. You could buy the record and play it at home above the din of parents yelling 'turn that crap down!' or 'you call that music?' But that was never the same as hearing it suddenly on the car radio (even if for the tenth time in the same day) when some cool disc jockey dropped the needle in the groove. The music was everywhere: blaring out of every apartment, a radio in every car, turned on all the time. In 1956, the year rock'n'roll peaked, it was the perfect accompaniment for bombing around in a '49 Ford or a new '55 Chevy: raked and flamed, decked and lowered, chopped and channeled with fins and tails on a Saturday night; burning rubber zero to sixty to the first red light and then on to the next, looking for another chump with overhead cams, a 4.56 rear end to cut out.

Cars and kids came together in the 1950s, and rock'n'roll was best man at the wedding. This was the latest generation of American Huck Finns running from routine and convention. Their rivers were the roads, highways, boulevards, avenues, and streets of America's big cities and small towns. Their rafts were their cars, and their Nigger Jim was the latest hit on the radio. The night was all beginning and without end.

Mobility meant escape: from the rigidity of home, from high school, from authority. Suburban mothers abhorred deviant behavior in their children and had little patience with wild rock'n'rollers who threatened their own interests or the creeds and symbols they cherished. Dad wanted stability and order on the home front so he could go about his daily bread-winning tasks. Parents restrained their kids with 'restriction', a form of Levittown house arrest meant to quash any interest in music, dancing, motorcycles, souped–up cars, violence, and sex.

Rock'n'roll reflected the interests and needs of its young public; it moved them. This raucous new music appeared in young people's lives at the crucial intersection of the dependency of puberty and the autonomy of the post-teen years. To millions at this age, sitting with the family around the tube watching Milton Berle or Sid Caesar was a drag. Instead they kept to themselves in their own rooms, listening to the hi-fi or radio, with posters of Little Richard, Elvis, and Buddy Holly on the wall; or they went to concerts or dated or hung out with friends at diners and juke joints. Whatever they did, they got away from parents; wherever they went, rock'n'roll was there: reinforcing and enhancing the sensation of independence. Mom and Dad stayed home, secure in their own opinions, values, and standards of conduct. They knew bikers, greasers, and rock'n'rollers who flouted them were ignorant or wicked.

The attitudes embodied by the music were rebellious and provocative.[1] That in itself was nothing new. Jitterbuggers in the 1930s had had their music labeled 'syncopated savagery'. Now as parents, twenty years later, these former savages were shocked at how seriously their offspring took rock'n'roll. Parents saw in rock'n'roll a destructive force, not just a symptom of awkward adolescence. Partly because the kids of the postwar era had wealth like none before them, however, the generational conflict sharpened as never before. As Greil Marcus would later write: 'it's a sad fact that most of those over thirty cannot be a part of it [rock'n'roll], and it cannot be a part of them.'[2] Who, then, were these parents, these over-thirty enemies of rock'n'roll?

Squaresville

Following their victory over fascist Germany and Japan, returning vets felt like national heroes. It was now time to earn a little money, have a family, and prosper. Commuting along the paved highways of the golden fifties in MG-TCs, ex-GIs basked perkily in the suburban afterglow of battlefield heroism. The world was theirs for the conquering: a promotion here, a new house there; a barbecue grill, 2.5 kids who would some day go to college, a wife at home enjoying – or enduring – what Betty Friedan would later call the feminine mystique. Heroes made good neighbors: conservative, a bit artificial, and stiff. Jumpy at the mention of Alger Hiss and Whittaker Chambers, communist spies and Congressional committees, good Americans wore loyalty oaths on their sleeves.

These good Americans went to work in a world very different from that which had existed before the war. In the first place, after a period of some-times difficult personal adjustment and economic reconversion, Dad found a job to go to. In addition, partly because of the modernization of production processes during the war and partly because of the availability of work, his cultural preoccupations shifted from the sphere of work to that of leisure. As David Riesman suggested in *The Lonely Crowd* (1950), in the postwar-world personal fulfillment, sense of purpose, and individual values were now increasingly identified with life beyond the workplace. If the ideals of Suburban Man shifted increasingly towards leisure, moreover, the process extended well beyond suburbia as the consumer society grew in size and scope.

Leisure and consumption, consumption and leisure: congruent ideals which together would breed fulfillment. For most Americans, this was an age of abundance and waste, as the era's characteristic images of Davy Crockett hats, hoola-hoops, polo shots, Salem cigarettes, and Comet suggest. It was also the Golden Age of television. As television sets increased in number (ten thousand new ones installed every day during the mid-1950s), the interests of manufacturers in advertising via the new medium combined with the mood of the times to exert pressure on producers and directors not to offend, which in turn led to restrictions on the kind of material deemed acceptable. *The Honeymooners* and *Sergeant Bilko* met the standards. *Captain Kangaroo* was just beginning (along with Mr. Green Jeans, Dancing Bear, and Bun Rabbit) as were *Wyatt Earp* and *Gunsmoke*, the first television westerns. By the middle of the decade – with Stalin dead, the Korean War over, and McCarthy discredited – the Red Scare had been absorbed by a 'prosperity can cure any ill' mentality. Nobody in 1955 thought this world would ever change. The children of the middle class were, however, about to turn it on its head.

High School Confidential

High school: educational institution and model of life. A world all its own, filled with pep rallies and glee clubs, dress codes and demerits, school papers and assembly programs, field trips and drill teams; a complex of hall passes and phi-deltas, cheerleaders and team spirit, Big-Man-on-Campus and jocks, clicks and outsiders; a realm where one dressed for success in letter jackets, chinos, and penny loafers. Students were groomed to compete in the toughest of schools: popularity. You were either neat or gross, peachy keen or spastic. Lose in this game and you were a creep, a turkey, a *nothing*.

In many small towns and city neighborhoods, school was the focus of students' social lives. They were whipped into enthusiastic abandon by the marching band and wooed by the majorettes at the Friday night football games in the Fall under stadium lights or wowed by the cheerleaders at basketball games. There were hockey games, track meets, and the wrestling team, as well as a plethora of cultural activities, from car washes and banquets to brownie sells and parades. To cap it off there were the high school balls: Homecoming, the sock hops, and the Senior Prom, the culmination of four exciting, memorable years. Amidst all this there was still time for classes. Governed by the conservative norms and mores of the middle class, these were simulations of 'real life' designed to transfigure zitty-faced kids into government or company employees, replicas of what William H. Whyte's 1956 volume dubbed *The Organization Man*. Character was molded by disciplinary measures like restrictions and demerits, but the emphasis was always on the individual. American high schools in the 1950s churned out good citizens: members of the Key Club or the Beta Club, trained in the habits of good citizenship; good employees: members of VICA, prepared to enter the world of work, or DECCA, the future marketing leaders of America; and good wives: members of the Future Homemakers of America, a credit to their sex. Still bolstered by the legacy of McCarthyism, moreover, schools had little problem dishing out their version of the 'American Way'. More than any other age-group, teenagers felt under pressure to conform and to become achievers in a society preoccupied with belonging and success.

Off campus, teenagers were flooded with enticements to consume. If they turned on the television or the radio, flipped through a magazine, or went to the movies, they found themselves barraged with endless images of a stimulating world, one which appeared as the virtual antithesis of high school's drab halls, lockers, and desks. Hedonism beckoned, and teenagers from middle-class families responded with indulgence: girls filled their hope chests with the basics for a good marriage; boys filled the tanks of their cars. They bought radios, cameras, hoola-hoops, frisbees, pogo sticks, television sets, swim suits, clothes, i.d. bracelets, deo, 'greasy kid stuff' – anything that brought them pleasure.

Rock'n'roll hit this world like a bomb. The ultimate safety valve, the ultimate escape for anyone destined for a nine-to-five office job, it was music for the moment (it barely lasted longer). For two or three minutes anybody could be a rebel: speed the car up, hang an arm out the window, cop an attitude, moon a cop, *anything*. The best tracks could obliterate time, creating a world you could vanish into, lose yourself in, and then return from with the help of the disc jockey's patter. Maybe the nine-to-five world could serve as a means to an end: consumption. But it couldn't give life a purpose.

Rock'n'roll fit perfectly into the conflict between the new patterns of the consumer society and the traditional Puritan work ethic of abstinence and industriousness. For these well-to-do teenagers the day was divided between the two worlds: in the classroom teachers propagated the traditional values; in their free time teenagers lived a life of impulse shopping. Just as the stop-and-jerk pace of Chuck Berry's 'Sweet Little Sixteen' swings the young girl from pretty young wild thing to Daddy's little girl, so their lives oscillated between obedience and indulgence. Through the works of writers like Jerry Leiber and Mike Stoller (who wrote 'Hound Dog' and 'Jailhouse Rock' for Elvis Presley, and all the Coasters' hits); Felice and Boudleaux Bryant (who penned hits for the

Everly Brothers); and especially rock'n'roll poet laureate Chuck Berry, rock'n'roll spoke to these teenagers: it dealt with their problems and frustrations, their dancing and dates, their likes, dislikes, and obsessions.

That'll Be the Day

As much medium as message, rock'n'roll was one of the first strokes of cultural self-awareness to blossom in the 1950s. Maybe the lyrics were sometimes as trite or nonsensical as Tin Pan Alley's, maybe white kids had problems understanding the singing, but rock'n'roll – with its solid backbeat and driving eighth-note rhythm – fit the pace and rhythm of a world which had grown modern during the war and which was now coming to grips with its modernity: coast-to-coast broadcasts, transatlantic jet flights, super highways, fast cars, transistors, the Bomb, roller derbies, instant coffee, Sputnik, desegregation, *Playboy*, the rat race, frisbees, and Sugar Ray Robinson. Let Mom and Pop Suburbia condemn the noise and the meaningless babble, let them fox-trot and cha-cha to Frank Sinatra and Rosemary Clooney: what a slow burn! For Junior, it was slow dancing with a rise in his Levis and a tale to take back to the guys: get much?

From the start rock'n'roll had its prophets of doom: 'it'll never last' went the wisdom of schmaltz, and it seemed sound enough. This was, after all, *Leave it to Beaver*-land: fads came, fads went. In fact, rock'n'roll never dominated the charts or musical tastes. As Charlie Gillet points out in *The Sound of the City*, even during its heyday 'from 1955 through 1959, just under half of the top ten hits ... could be classified as rock'n'roll'.[3] During those years, according to Serge Denisoff, rock'n'roll 'did not constitute all of popular music, and even in the heyday of Elvis Presley not all teenagers were into his music, as many rock histories seem to imply'.[4] Nonetheless rock'n'roll endured. It was exclusive and well-guarded, with a strong sense of awareness that the music was something special; it was almost elitist in its sense of being reserved for those hip enough to *dig it*. Rock'n'roll was a fever, a craze; and a lot of kids in the 1950s were on the edge of a fighting mood: 'Your ass is grass! Get bent! You're cruisin' for a bruisin'! Don't give me any grief.' Rock'n'roll caught the mood – 'Blue Suede Shoes', 'That'll Be the Day', 'Too Much Monkey Business', 'Hound Dog', 'Rip it Up'. Chuck Berry summed up the new generation's disdain for the older: 'Roll Over Beethoven.'

Rock'n'roll alone did not induce the new teenage behavioral patterns in the 1950s. Prosperity, new forms of distribution, the portable radio, and television made their presence felt. Still, something in the music sparked fires where cinders glowed. Rock'n'roll was the matrix inside which middle-class teenagers played out fantasies of rebellion within the context of family, home, and future career. With rock'n'roll's distribution through radio, television, and film, these kids became the standard image of teenagers' lives and values for the entire social spectrum. With the appearance of Elvis, *they* – white, American, middle-class teenagers – could dream of performing the music as well. Elvis expressed the inner conflict between conservative and rebellious forces for high school teenagers who wanted to rebel against their parents yet still grow up to be them.

Graceland

If rock'n'roll was the dominant music of white teenagers during the second half of the 1950s, then the key was the King: Elvis Presley. An outsider and a success, he summed up and incarnated the contradictions of the teenager's world. He was one of them: white and young. He had rejected the adult world and sneered his way to the pinnacle of stardom. Elvis not only got the Cadillac; Elvis was bigger and better than a Cadillac. In his music, in his stage act, in his voice, he demanded – and got – respect. As Peter Wicke puts it, he 'embodied the uncertain and consuming desire of American high school teenagers in the fifties, the desire somehow to escape the oppressive ordinariness which surrounded them without having to pay the bitter price of conformity. His quick success seemed to be the proof that, in principle, escape was possible'.[5]

For parents and high school principals in an era when these words still meant something, Elvis Presley was sinful and wicked. He set a bad example. He was a hood, with his long sideburns, ducktail haircut, and curled upper lip. His blatant sexuality, aggressiveness, and bumping and grinding troubled adults. Inside the music industry, though, Elvis was King. From late April 1956, when 'Heartbreak Hotel' dethroned Nelson Riddle's 'Lisbon Antigua' and Les Baxter's 'The Poor People of Paris' at the top of the charts (remaining there for eight weeks), to his late March 1958 induction into the U.S. Army, Elvis ruled the hit parade.[6] He had the number one single in no less than fifty-five out of one hundred and four weeks: 'I Want You, I Need You, I Love You'; 'Don't Be Cruel' and 'Hound Dog' (eleven weeks at number one); 'Love Me Tender' (five weeks); 'Too Much' (three weeks); 'All Shook Up' (nine weeks); 'Teddy Bear' and 'Jailhouse Rock' (seven weeks); and 'Don't' (five weeks).

Although his manager, 'Colonel' Tom Parker, and his record label, RCA, orchestrated his ascent to the top of the pop world, Elvis himself ultimately deserves credit. He had the charisma, the style, the personality, the voice, and (in contrast to Jerry Lee Lewis, who still hasn't lost his rough edges) he could adapt. Elvis had it all. As Greil Marcus would write: 'The version of the American dream that is Elvis's performance is blown up again and again, to contain more history, more people, more music, more hopes; the air gets thin but the bubble does not burst, nor will it ever. This is America when it has outstripped itself, in all of its extravagance.'[7]

Part Two

Train I Ride

Memphis, Tennessee. Home of the Beale Street blues, an African-American gospel tradition, and a hillbilly style of country music. Home of the first African-American-run radio station in the USA and of Hillbilly Cat Sam Phillips' Sun Records at 706 Union Ave. Home, too, of Elvis Aaron Presley: red pants, green coat, pink shirt and socks, sneer, sideburns, and greasy hair. The Pelvis. The King. Home, finally, of rockabilly – Carl Perkins, Warren Smith, Roy Orbison, Johnny Cash, Conway Twitty, Charlie Rich – and 'The Killer', Jerry Lee Lewis.

Rockabilly was played loose, a shuffle in swing eighths. Instead of brass and harmony vocals, bluesy licks on the guitar filled the spaces between the vocals while a walking bass locked into a groove with the bass drum to carry the song forward. The singers were confessors, violent and unpredictable for the times. Elvis wailed breathlessly, patience used up: full of confidence and wanting to go somewhere – though who knew where when he said 'let's get real, real gone' before cutting 'Milkcow Blues Boogie' in the Sun sessions. A hustler, people said, *a white man singing like a nigger* on tracks such as 'That's All Right, Mama' and 'Mystery Train'. Elvis did not sell many records when he recorded for Sam Phillips: he was not a hit outside the South. Only after their Southern Area A&R man Steve Scholes saw Elvis at a disc jockeys' convention in Miami (and risked his job getting Elvis signed) did RCA pay up-and-coming Holiday Inn magnate Sam Phillips $30,000 and put Elvis in a pink Cadillac. Now under contract with RCA, recorded by Chet Atkins, and booked on the Jackie Gleason and Ed Sullivan television shows, Elvis started flooding the top ten with records. By that time the music was no longer rockabilly; it was rock'n'roll.

Phillips stayed on in the business after he had let Elvis go. He helped his singers develop new rhythmic patterns, vocal inflections, and song material that Southern whites didn't much care for. Rockabilly received national attention after Perkins made it with 'Blue Suede Shoes' and Cash followed up with 'I Walk the Line' followed by Jerry Lee with 'Whole Lotta Shakin' Goin' On'. Jerry Lee, who always knew that rock'n'roll was the devil's business, knew too that Sam was the devil's man. The aggression, the violent release which gave vent to pent-up feelings that perhaps only Pentecostal Holy Rollers could truly understand, Phillips now helped to render accessible to a larger audience. (Ironically, although he played the wild man on stage, Lewis himself was rather conservative, as were most of the Southern rock'n'rollers.) Rockabilly combined the conservatism of country music and the rebellious energy of rhythm and blues and in doing so captured the essence of rock'n'roll.

The poverty and rural attitudes that were a part of life in the postwar South influenced the course of rock'n'roll's development. Although the population of the Deep South has shifted during the twentieth century from ninety per cent rural to more than fifty per cent urban, transplanted bumpkins like the Presleys, who had themselves only recently moved to Memphis from Tupelo, Mississippi, stayed 'country'. They did so, moreover, in spite of an increase in their standard of living. (The New Deal and World War Two had been important stimuli to economic growth in the South, but by the 1950s the region's average per capita income was still only half that of the national average).[8] Like country truck driver Elvis, rock'n'roll reflected this migration from the farm to the city. Elvis's first single had a blues number on the A-side and a country song on the flip side. Bill Haley had his roots in Texas and Oklahoma country swing in the tradition of Bob Wills. Jerry Lee (as well as Elvis and the other Sun label stars) had his roots in country swing and white gospel. The Everly Brothers had theirs in bluegrass and the country duet singing of Charlie and Ira Louvin and the Delmore Brothers.

Both the R&B and the country elements of rock'n'roll have origins in the folk music traditions of the outsiders and outcasts of twentieth century America: on the one hand, the African-Americans who picked the cotton; on the other, the so-called 'white trash' who worked it through the cotton mills. The folk blues, typically in a first-person voice, express the experience of African-Americans living in the South during the first half of the twentieth century. The vocabulary is minimal and filled with images of traveling and country roads, field workers and prisoners. Although the dialect and diction are slightly different, the lyrics of country music deal with the realities of rural and city life in the South and the West, again in simple, straightforward language that incorporates the colloquialisms of these regions. Images of truck stops and sunsets, honky-tonks and fields, gamblers and drinkers, cheating and working tell the sentimental stories of taxing, emotional circumstances. The lyrics, sentiments, and, frequently, religious undertones common to both country blues and country and western reflected the inanity of segregation: Southerners of any race had more in common with each other than with anyone from other regions of the USA. Both forms feature expressive vocals: on the one hand, the sharp, nasal sound of country; on the other, the minor pentatonic sound of the blues. An original American sound was heard in the meeting of the two: first in minstrels and then in the songs of Stephen Foster, who was influenced not only by the minstrels but by the music of the African-American churches as well. Generations later, rock'n'roll would emerge as a sort of electrified Stephen Foster in the unlikely form of Bill Haley.

Although both blues and country had long been commercialized when they merged in the guise of rock'n'roll, Decca was taking a chance on Haley. And while the label enjoyed great success – at his first session with Decca, Haley recorded both 'Rock Around the Clock' and 'Shake, Rattle and Roll' – taking chances was not the norm for the majors. Their standard operating procedure had long been to churn out 'cover versions' of songs that had already been recorded by someone else. In the 1950s, however, the majors gave cover versions a new twist. Just as in the 1920s Paul Whiteman's orchestra had set out, in his words, to 'make a lady' of hot jazz, so thirty years later the industry recast R&B in an all-white form: performed by whites (such as Steve Lawrence, Andy Williams, Pat Boone, or the Fontane Sisters), recorded by whites, sold by whites, bought by whites, and profited from by whites. (Otherwise rejecting African-American music, the majors would at best record so-called 'black sepias' like Nat King Cole, who appealed to the white mainstream with sentimental, melodramatic crooning.)

As part of this tactic, the majors thus recorded white artists covering R&B tunes originally cut by African-American artists for the independent labels or 'indies'. These white versions were arranged and performed to sound like banal pop music, with a unique beat but always in a simple 'sing-along' form that would be music to white ears. Working on assumptions derived from European classical music traditions, producers like Mitch Miller considered their cover versions to be an improvement on the originals, which they thought sounded like primitive jungle music: harsh, low-down, and dirty. Such assumptions were broadly shared by the white record-buying public. In mainstream America, Bill Haley was thought of as having introduced a new music, a new rhythm; hardly anyone bothered to mention that 'his sound came from the music of the black population, a people whose "great sense of rhythm" had always been admired, but who, white America insisted, otherwise had nothing non-physical to contribute'.[9]

A Choice of Colors

Cultural interaction between African-Americans and the white majority was never strictly a matter of black *or* white. An irreducible component of Southern culture was the mutual influence of the races upon one another. At shows in towns like Macon, Georgia, white kids would sneak in (behind the backs of their parents and white authorities) and slip upstairs to see the African-American kids down on the dance floor. At first, the white kids would just sit and watch. In the end, however, they were bound to come down and dance. When some young white performers – like Jerry Lee Lewis, sneaking into the 'nigra' clubs in Ferriday, Louisiana, with his cousin Jimmy Lee Swaggart to hear artists like B.B. King – took the music at face value, they helped transform popular music and thereby American youth culture.

Sometimes these Southern rockers covered R&B hits, but more often they brought elements of R&B into their own tunes. Instead of adapting African-

American styles to white tastes, they tried to imitate the originals as closely as they could, as when Elvis covered Big Mama Thornton's 'Hound Dog'. Perhaps the swing disappeared in these white attempts at R&B: simplified in rock'n'roll to a more rigid, basic rhythm under the influence of Hank Williams and the hard-driving style of country pickers like Merle Travis, Joe Maphis, and James Burton. Still, rock'n'roll was noisy and aggressive because these musicians had been singing and playing that way all along. The rock'n'roll played by their native sons, rockabilly, frightened white Southerners most. Long in touch with African-American music, these musicians had sufficient spirit to sell records in the R&B, country, and pop markets. Since they were white, moreover, they could get away with it to such a degree that by 1956 even genuine R&B records started to gain acceptance in the mainstream pop market, much to the horror of many white Southerners.

It was no surprise, therefore, that 'the most extreme and bizarre expressions of antagonism towards rock'n'roll tended to take place in the South. In April 1956, the *New York Times* reported several attempts by white Southern church groups to have rock'n'roll suppressed. The whole movement towards rock'n' roll, the church groups revealed, was part of a plot by the NAACP to corrupt white Southern youth'.[10] A stepchild of R&B, the music was known dismissively in the South during those years as 'nigger music'. Rock'n'roll was music played by and for *niggers* (African-American or white): Little Richard, Fats Domino, and Chuck Berry; Elvis Presley, Jerry Lee Lewis, Carl Perkins, and Buddy Holly. Renegade rednecks in the best Southern tradition, the white rock'n'rollers were the very stuff of Southern nightmares. For although white Southerners deemed African-Americans rarely capable of attaining the same level of rectitude, white descent into blackness had to be averted. For decades Southern whites had drawn arms against an unseen enemy, evincing a distrust of both mulattoes (who *looked* white) and whites who behaved 'black'. Whites who, like the Southern rock'n'rollers, strayed too close to African-Americans were known as 'white niggers': genetically white but 'black' in their behavior. The music they played, rock'n'roll, which sounded like R&B, was the 'jungle music' of burr–heads, blue–skins, tar-pots, spics, jigaboos, darkies, and shines.

The white South's image of African-Americans in the 1950s was much as it had been since the turn of the century. Generations had grown up believing Booker T. Washington to have spoken for all African-Americans and spoken the truth: that they were content to 'cast down their buckets' where they were, chop cotton, lay rails, and work, work, work until Saturday night. By the 1950s, Booker T. was long dead, but in white minds Sambo continued to shuffle contentedly along, bucket in hand. Even while insisting that 'our Nigras are good Nigras', white Southerners had nonetheless devised dogmas and institutions that assured the greatest possible distance between the races. Known collectively as Jim Crow, these had consisted of both legal and extralegal means designed to keep African-Americans in their place and to compel them to behave 'properly' in the presence of whites. The legal measures – the poll tax, stiff residency requirements, literacy tests, and 'grandfather clauses' – kept African-Americans away from the polls and thus ensured the stability of a caste system which governed all aspects of African-American life. Extralegal steps helped guarantee the invisibility of most African-Americans and made those who were visible the Sambos whites needed to see: gullible children in grown–up bodies who slapped their knees, jumped, and turned, and whom whites could allow to run free within their own world without constant guidance after work on Saturday – as long as they showed up at work on Monday morning.

The white South's ability to sustain the system was, of course, challenged on a city bus in Montgomery, Alabama, on 1 December 1955, when Rosa Parks refused to yield her seat to a white man. Although it took years to secure its greatest gains (after Montgomery there was a lull), with Martin Luther King, Jr. more than rising to the occasion the civil rights movement was in the ascendant.

From the Station to the Train

By the time of the civil rights movement, another movement, primarily geographical and cultural rather than social and political, had long since begun: the exodus of millions of African-Americans from the countryside to the nation's cities. Prompted partly by the decline and subsequent mechanization of Southern agriculture, partly by the attraction of often military-spawned jobs, and partly by the dream of a better life beyond Jim Crow, this vast folk migration took hundreds of thousands to Northern industrial cities like New York, Chicago, and Detroit and, to a lesser degree, Southern cities like Memphis and New Orleans. Between 1860 and 1960 the African-American share of the total Southern population dwindled from almost fifty per cent to twenty-nine per cent.

Musical forms born and raised in the South – the blues, jazz, gospel, R&B, and soul – also traveled. On the road, gospel waited alongside the blues in bus depots; jazz and R&B rode together on trains. The movement to the cities helped turn the blue note electric, and African-American radio stations pumped it out. By the early 1950s, R&B stations dotted the urban landscape. Fans had only to turn their tuning knobs to hear the dance blues of singers like Amos Milburn, Roy Brown, Fats Domino, and Lloyd Price, and the 'hot' style of disc jockeys like Hamp Swain in Macon, Georgia, Zenas 'Big Daddy' Sears and 'Jockey Jack' Gibson in Atlanta, and 'Sugar Daddy' in Birmingham. Meanwhile, Alan Freed at WINS in New York set a precedent for white disc jockeys playing R&B; those who followed his lead included Al Benson in Chicago, Hunter Hancock in Los Angeles, and 'Poppa Stoppa' in New Orleans.[11]

These and other artists and disc jockeys gave a voice to a nation of wanderers looking for home: a tricky concept, as James Brown once pointed out, for a people who had been told to move along for a century and a half.[12] Newly-urbanized African-Americans faced a world very different from the one they had known before, but when it came to the question of color, they found themselves on familiar ground. Not surprisingly, when confronted by the racial prejudice of the North and West, they survived just as they and their predecessors had done in the South: by building up their community, families, clubs, and churches. Whether in the North or South, then, home was cut off from white society. White people may have heard R&B as it made its way across the air waves. What their ears didn't hear, what their eyes didn't see, what they wanted neither to hear nor to see, was the distinct *community* which it addressed, a largely self-contained world created by American apartheid: the chitlin' circuit.

The continuing interaction of African-American culture and community was evident through the spreading of gospel music. In the 1940s, after Sister Rosetta Tharpe had taken the music out of the church and carried it to Cab Calloway and the Cotton Club in Harlem, gospel became very big on the chitlin' circuit. It spread through the music of groups like the Sensational Nightingales, the Golden Gate Quartet, the Swan Silvertones, the Soul Stirrers, and the Dixie Hummingbirds; and soloists like Willie Mae Ford Smith, Mahalia Jackson, and the Reverend James Cleveland. It hit storefronts, churches, school gyms, and tents as a myriad of roadshows and revivals passed through down-home neighborhoods where no signs were needed to keep whites out, where white women didn't come around except to pick up the maid; neighborhoods where there was nothing for a white man, where a white man had no business.

Gospel music spoke for and sustained a distinct community, retaining collective and communal features which expressed something of the suppression which so many in that community had experienced. It also helped to transform that community. It did so partly through its influence on rhythm and blues.

Boogie at Midnight

Cacophonous vocals shouted explicit lyrics; loud saxophones, pianos, and guitars honked, rolled, and wailed while drums banged out the heavy rhythm; delirious artists expressed emotions and ideas which exhilarated their audience. Until 1949, when Jerry Wexler gave it the more sophisticated name 'rhythm and blues' while writing for *Billboard*, the white music industry branded all this 'race music'. The lines between urban blues and R&B were tenuous (as are all popular musical categories), and the early R&B charts looked like a blues who's-who: John Lee Hooker's 'Boogie Chillen', Lonnie Johnson's

'Tomorrow Night', shouter Wynonie Harris's 'Good Rockin' Tonight', as well as tunes by Howlin' Wolf, Charles Brown, Muddy Waters, Bull Moose Jackson, and Ivory Joe Hunter.

R&B was updated and mellowed as the influence of gospel smoothed over its rougher edges. Technology played a crucial part. Although different radio stations programmed specific genres, listeners were not so constrained; as a result gospel singles crossed over to the R&B charts: in 1950, for example, the Five Blind Boys' 'Our Father' was chasing Wynonie Harris's 'I Like My Baby's Pudding' up the charts. Quartet singing, long a crossover area for artists like the Mills Brothers and the Ink Spots, was the springboard for the 'bird groups' (the Ravens and the Orioles), who in turn inspired groups like the Clovers and the Dominoes. Founded in 1950 by Billy Ward, the Dominoes built their sound around the gospel-style vocals of Clyde McPhatter. Race restricted the success of songs like 'Do Something for Me' and 'Have Mercy Baby' to the R&B charts, until the appearance of rock'n'roll enabled an R&B group, Frankie Lymon and the Teenagers, to hit the charts for sixteen weeks in 1956, peaking at number six, with 'Why Do Fools Fall In Love?' The original did better than the cover versions by the Diamonds and Gale Storm. The Platters, who had charted in 1955 with 'Only You' released three Top Ten pop and R&B hits in 1956. Many of the R&B acts that followed went on to become rock'n'roll, rather than soul, stars. Imperial artist Fats Domino rode 'Blueberry Hill' and 'I'm in Love Again' into the Top Ten. Two other 'R&B' artists, Chuck Berry and Little Richard, hit the charts with 'Maybellene', 'School Days', and 'Sweet Little Sixteen'; and 'Tutti–Fruitti', 'Long Tall Sally', and 'Rip it Up', respectively.

White listeners started to develop a better feeling for the music: they heard R&B differently. As it became familiar, it became acceptable on its own terms. In its initial cross over into white culture, R&B attracted a cult following among college and high school students. Its rhythm and forbidden thrills, though still contrasting sharply with the milquetoast sounds of Perry Como and company, had been made more palatable by gospel. White R&B fans could now accept the real thing, not covers.

Even though more and more people came to prefer R&B, the majors could not and did not start promoting the product; they seemed scarcely aware of the market. The indies – often using singers with regional appeal in a regional market – detected the trend more quickly. Largely through their efforts, some juke boxes began stocking R&B records, while white dance bands started to incorporate R&B hits in their sets. Whether through the efforts of the majors or the indies, singers and musicians like Chuck Berry, Bo Diddley, and Little Richard found themselves able to play African-American music *as* African-American music: no crooning sepia nonsense. Racial barriers were dissolving as sons of slaves and sons of Pilgrims broke sonic barriers to create the sound of rebellion and deliverance: rock'n'roll.

Whatever their race, these artists were dependent upon the various media to get their music to the widest possible audience. The people who played rock'n' roll could not have known they were making history, but they did know they were on to something new, something that broke with musical traditions. These early rock'n'rollers were no navel-gazers: they were carnival sideshow entertainers with a product to sell and a get-rich-quick scheme: a number one record. The world of rock'n'roll was not only a cultural and social expression but also a commercial network of musical commodities – singles and albums – which had to be recorded, distributed, and promoted.

Part Three

Have You Heard the News?

The music industry has survived despite the appearance of successive new media that at one time or another seemed capable of subjugating it. Radio initially made the need to buy records appear obsolete – until swing music became so popular in the 1930s that a rush on records ensued. Later, television appeared to threaten the industry. Again, however, it endured (most recently by becoming a part of television through MTV). Recorded music has survived because of its unique ability to create an emotional bond between the listener and recorded sound. Everything else – the technology, the marketing, the profits – have resulted from that bond and its basic power.[13]

During and after World War Two, the record industry, radio, and television all experienced changes that together radically altered the modes of musical production: new recording techniques and small-group recording budgets; new companies and a redefinition of the target audience; reductions in record prices; and a new affiliation with broadcast radio. The shift from 78 revolutions per minute to the 33⅓ and 45 rpm speeds, a change in the sizes of records, the substitution of shellac by vinyl, and television's influence on radio station programming – each had an impact on the industry. Although its story cannot be reduced solely to technical innovations, rock'n'roll did evolve out of and along with the technology of these media. What was new about rock'n' roll was its relationship with the means of mass communication: record, radio, television, and film. American rock'n'roll depended on the existence of these media and accepted them without compromise as a condition of artistic creativity.[14]

This Year's Model

Notable technological improvements associated with the introduction of magnetic tape resulted in recording techniques which were not only inexpensive but which made both overdubbing (with remarkably improved microphones) and the correcting of mistakes possible. One pioneer was guitarist Les Paul, who by 1947 had started making 'sound-on-sound' recordings. Real multitrack recording was first used in 1954. Employing just two tracks, it was far from today's sixty-four track digital studios; the basic principle of studio music production – sound-on-sound – nevertheless remains unaltered. Multitrack technology was to influence both the sound and the structure of rock music, since a producer could now assemble the music from individually recorded parts in a final mix instead of reproducing a single take of a song: records no longer needed to be exact copies of live performances, rendering the large rooms previously employed for recording big band orchestras unnecessary.

The modern engineer had to coax the artist into cutting a usable track washed in crude reverb and slapback, which could be overdubbed and then spliced with a razor into the latest hit. Some of the most accomplished East Coast engineers were Tom Dowd, Bobby Fein, Al Weintraub, and Irv Joel. In California, Bunny Robyn and Bones Howe were experts in capturing the rock 'n'roll feel. In the South, Sam Phillips created his own sound at Sun Studios in Memphis, while Cosimo Matassa did the same at his own J & M Studio in New Orleans.

As recording procedures became more specialized, a new creature emerged: the independent producer. Among the most significant of the early independent producers were Leiber and Stoller, Lee Hazelwood, Bob Crewe, Phil Spector (who created the 'wall of sound'), and Bert Berns. Another was Norman Petty, who produced Buddy Holly. These men were responsible for the final mix, for giving the music the big sound that worked on AM radio. By compressing and boosting the recording level a couple of decibels above the original recorded level when mixing to the master deck, for example, the songs could be made to boom out of the dashboard of a car or a transistor. Independent producers were jacks-of-all-trades who wrote or found material for the stars, and financed and supervised the recording sessions.

Behind the stars of rock'n'roll – on stage and in the studios – also stood the backing groups. The guitar riffs, the bass lines, the piano playing, the drumming on the classic records: all were played by musicians unknown outside the business itself. Many rock'n'rollers insisted on using their own bands (a key element in Elvis Presley's 'Sun' sound was the playing of Scotty Moore and Bill Black), but it was not unusual for the studio musicians at rock'n'roll sessions to be blues or R&B players. Recording Chuck Berry, Chess used blues men like Willie Dixon (bass) and Johnny Johnson (piano). Atlantic Records used pianists and session leaders Jesse Stone, Howard Biggs, and Henry Van Walls; guitarist Mickey Baker; and saxophonists King Curtis and Sam Taylor on albums by a variety of their artists. Other African-American musicians who played important roles in producing the sounds of rock'n'roll include drummers Cornelius Coleman and Earl Palmer (Little Richard and Fats

Domino); arranger-musicians like pianist Ernie Freeman; guitarist Rene Hall; tenor sax players Plas Johnson and Lee Allen; and all-round utility men H.B. Barnum and Harold Battiste. These musicians formed the core of the top session band on the West Coast during the rock'n'roll period (many also played for Dave Bartholomew in New Orleans).

When the majors finally realized that rock'n'roll was here to stay, they restructured their A&R departments and hired men who had a better feel for the sound and who understood the new standards. From this point on, the A&R men from the majors picked from the same flock of producers, song writers, arrangers, and session men as the indies.

Listen to my 45s

The most conspicuous technological innovation triggered the 'Battle of the Speeds'. By 1948 CBS engineer Peter Goldmark had perfected the high fidelity long-playing record (LP), which reduced the playing speed from 78 to 33⅓ rpm. With their low noise characteristics and extended duration, LPs transformed not only recording studios and the contents of records themselves, but also the industry's hierarchy, as Columbia first stole the lead on RCA only to see the latter respond with 45 rpm singles. The ascent of rock'n'roll paralleled that of the 45 rpm single (along with the portable radio). Until the emergence of rock'n'roll, and especially Elvis Presley, the 45 rpm single's role in popular music had been minimal. Aimed at the new teenage market and priced within reach of teenagers' pocket money, however, its popularity rose quickly.

Radio, radio

Until rock'n'roll appeared in the 1950s, radio programming had changed very little since the 1930s, when the friendly, conversational microphone styles of Al Jarvis at KFWB in Los Angeles, Martin Block at WNEW in New York, and Arthur Godfrey had first raised announcers to the status of 'personalities', who received as much attention from their listeners as the music they played. Jarvis pioneered the 'Make Believe Ballroom' format, which simulated the atmosphere of a ballroom through the use of real or contrived conversations with the performers and dancers. Block's use of this framework would engender *Your Hit Parade* and *Lucky Lager Dance Time*. Godfrey's irreverent style helped make the radio disc jockey someone not to be treated lightly; his early morning show attracted many listeners and thus numerous sponsors. Such sponsorship represented a commercialization of radio that would have profound consequences. When the American Tobacco Company started sponsoring *The Lucky Strike Hit Parade* nationwide, records began to be ranked according to their popularity. Air play became the most effective type of direct marketing.

By the end of World War Two most singers, musicians, record companies, and sheet music publishers had become aware of the interaction between sales and air play. Record sales and taste trends increasingly engendered and reflected one another: each at once parasite on and host for the other; both having a symbiotic relationship with the charts (particularly *Billboard*'s). A song could become a hit because a lot of people liked it and bought the record, and a lot of people liked a song and bought the record because it was a hit.

Since television during the 1950s rapidly took over the family entertainment role once held by radio, and since programs like *Monitor* (a weekend program of interviews, satire, and news features) proved failures, radio programming other than news broadcasts returned to the hands of station owners, who responded to the challenge of television by converting their stations to a 'Top-Forty' format in order to survive. Top-Forty programs shaped teenagers' perceptions of rock'n'roll: music was ranked, and hits were important. Cheap, battery-driven portable radios made possible by transistor technology came on the market in 1954. Rock'n'roll developed within a technological milieu increasingly beyond parental control. Teenagers' relative independence in deciding what they liked and what they wanted to listen to resulted in an age–specific audience, and rock'n'roll developed on its audience's terms.

Picture This

In the early 1950s the burgeoning television networks, slowly perfecting the means to transmit signals from coast to coast, attracted radio and film stars like Bob Hope, Groucho Marx, Lucille Ball, Fred Allen, Jack Benny, Edgar Bergen, George Burns, and Gracie Allen. As many of their biggest names abandoned the medium, radio by the middle of the decade had disappeared as a way of life with much the same speed that it had appeared in the 1920s and 1930s. Television not only sped the conversion of radio into a Top-Forty, music-dominated medium, it also brought new modes of music distribution. This might not have been evident on the surface. For the established moguls of television, rock'n'roll was in one sense dangerous, or at least undesirable. Their earliest attempts at presenting rock'n'roll tamed it as much as possible: Elvis Presley in tuxedo singing 'Hound Dog' to a pedestal-mounted bassett hound on the Steve Allen show was typical of the approach. With programs like *Your Hit Parade, The Big Record*, and especially *American Bandstand* (started in 1952 in Philadelphia by WFIL-TV and from 1957 transmitted every Saturday morning across the whole country by ABC), the networks cashed in on – and in the process expanded the market for – rock'n'roll. Television gave rock'n'roll a face for millions of viewers who had never gone to concerts.

Suffering, like radio, from the rise of television, Hollywood also responded to the young audience bored with the family ritual in front of the television. A cycle of rock'n'roll films revolving around the rock'n'roll stars and their songs had an additional impact on that element of the American population which made up an increasing proportion of the total film audience: teenagers. Hollywood was also able to foster the success of rock'n'roll directly. 'Rock Around the Clock', for example, did not succeed when first released, but it took off when featured in *The Blackboard Jungle* in 1955.

Living in the Material World

Between 1954 and 1959 the record industry increased its sales from $213,000,000 to $603,000,000. A large proportion of the increase in sales accrued to the indies, who made their break into the market by providing assorted kinds of rock'n'roll. After the majors had dropped their 'race' and 'new jazz' artists during World War Two, the indies had moved into the 'race' market and begun recording rhythm and blues. In 1954 they extended their market to white kids as they developed distribution networks sufficient to give them as good a chance of having a hit with a new record as any of the majors; once they saw the possibilities of profit in rock'n'roll, they recorded almost anybody singing almost anything and put all their energy and money into promoting those records that seemed to stand a chance. The independents doubled their number of Top Ten hits between 1955 and 1956, then doubled them again by 1957.[15] They succeeded in spotting and responding to the grass-roots signs of rock'n'roll's popularity partly because, unlike the majors, the indies often signed singers with regional or local appeal.

Another reason the indies had rock'n'roll to themselves was the reluctance of the majors to gamble on the new music genre. Believing it to be a passing fad that would soon disappear, the majors generally failed to respond to rock 'n'roll before 1956: Columbia, RCA, and Capitol all either ignored it or simply made token recordings of novelty songs. The lone exception was Decca, who signed Bill Haley and let him record his brand of rock'n'roll. (Decca was the best placed company to understand the appeal of rock'n'roll as a result of the long-standing interest in African-American dance music of the company's founder, Jack Kapp.)[16] None of the rock'n'roll pioneers would thus have had a vehicle for exposure had it not been for the postwar development of the indies. In the words of Charlie Gillet:

> The executives of the independents ... had every reason to promote rock'n'roll, the more singers and records the better. Several of them already had the music in their catalogues, classified until now as rhythm and blues; for these it was easy enough to modify the arrangements, simplify the beat, and promote rhythm and blues as rock'n'roll. Imperial with Fats Domino, King with Bill Doggett, and Aladdin with Shirley and Lee made the pop lists this way.[17]

Other indie releases included Buddy Holly on Brunswick and Coral, Chuck Berry on Chess in Chicago, Jerry Lee Lewis and Carl Perkins on Sun, and Little Richard on Specialty in Los Angeles. By the early 1950s more than one hundred independent companies had sprung up. As Gillet explains:

> Many of the companies had built themselves up from humble beginnings immediately after World War Two, when garages served as recording studios and the boots of the owner's cars were the companies' only form of distribution. Unlike the majors, overlaid with conventional corporation structures of administration and decision-making, the independents relied almost entirely on the ingenuity of their owners, who functioned as their own talent scouts, producers, and distributors, as well as the makers of all policy decisions.[18]

Although lacking the sales figures, budgets, and distribution facilities of the major music publishers, record companies, and radio networks, the indies nevertheless changed the direction of popular music and the structure of the record industry.

The indies had produced twice as many hits by the end of the decade as the majors, yet the struggle for survival never eased up. Few would survive the 1960s. Plagued by competition from bootleggers (who pirated copies of their hits) and always fighting to collect from their distributors, indie labels still had to pay 'consultancy fees' to disc jockeys, and the monthly overheads of staff and offices, on top of the costs of pressings. Sometimes their wisest move was to license a likely hit to larger companies like Mercury, ABC, or Dot (all of whom formed fruitful relationships with independent producers).[19]

Through their influence over distribution networks, the majors effectively controlled most record stores, juke boxes, sheet music sales, and radio airplay. Slow to realize the closing of the American racial gap which accompanied and followed World War Two, the majors thus adopted a conservative strategy, deploying their sizeable resources to fight for the success of their established performers, mostly older artists from the dance band era still under five year contracts. The singers who operated under such contracts had to be musical chameleons and appeal to just about anyone (unlike rock'n'roll madmen like Little Richard and Jerry Lee Lewis who were, by contrast, anything but malleable). The majors used their contract singers for the cover versions recorded, released, and promoted hot on the tail of R&B hits. The majors did renovate their commercial policy by releasing singles more quickly, while strengthening their promotion work by marketing from coast to coast. Confident in their market domination, however, they underestimated the ways in which a few radio disc jockeys who appreciated the power of rhythm and blues (such as Danny 'Cat Man' Stiles, Hal Jackson, and George 'Hound Dog' Lorenz) could penetrate the cracks of segregation and discrimination by playing it to anyone who would listen.

The majors slowly came to understand teenage record buyers, drop their traditional sales categories of popular music and rhythm and blues, and call anything that appealed to teenage record buyers 'rock'n'roll'. When the majors finally acted, rock'n'roll devolved into teenybopper music, designed for and chiefly bought by people between the ages of nine and twenty four, who determined what the record charts looked like by the manner in which they spent their own or their parents' money. When some seventeen-year-old Peggy Sue bought the latest hit single by the King, she cared little about the technology or money that had gone into its production and had little interest in knowing that she was dancing to a product made to be marketed and consumed for profit. She simply bought a record she *liked*. Her reasons for picking this particular record were, of course, influenced by many things – her age, gender, race, and social background as well as the forces of advertising and peer group pressure – which may have had little to do with the song itself. Later, as she grew older, the music would nevertheless bring back memories of those halcyon days and the experiences she and her friends had shared with a rock'n' roll backdrop.

As the music industry itself matured, styles would change: from heavy to folk, from country to soft, from bubble gum to disco, from glitter to glam; all, however, were variations on the basic rock'n'roll theme, products of industry attempts to sustain old or develop new markets, while kids tried to find a new sound that fit their world and their experiences. Musicians starting out as kids looking for new sounds came into the industry and developed new styles in the lacuna between the industry's creating and following trends. As a result, the various genres of rock music through the ages – and especially the records that came with them – had (and continue to have) one thing in common: what James Von Schilling has called the ability to 'capture in time a unique combination of music, performance, and artistry and then enable us to make this "timepiece" part of our personal experience'.[20]

Afterword: Funeral Dirge

American Pie

Legend has it that rock'n'roll died. Estimates of the precise date differ, but most agree that at some point in the late 1950s rock'n'roll passed away, only to be reborn as 'rock' in 1964 when the Beatles arrived in New York and Dylan went electric. Elvis switched roles from hoodlum to GI, Jerry Lee disappeared in disgrace into the backwoods of Louisiana with his fourteen-year-old cousin-cum-wife, Chuck Berry was thrown in jail for violations of the Mann Act, and Little Richard threw all his jewelry into the sea and joined the ministry. As for Buddy Holly: he couldn't even pay his rent. Norman Petty had Buddy's money tied up in a bank account and was trying to force Holly to come back into his stable. Angry and broke, Buddy went on tour with a back-up band he called the Crickets, even though he didn't have the legal rights to the name. It was winter, cold as hell, the buses were lousy, and Buddy rented a plane. Whether or when exactly rock'n'roll died may be unclear; Buddy Holly went down in February 1959.

Tears weren't shed among the majors the day the music died. In a cultural sense, if nothing else, industry executives hated rock'n'roll. It was cheap music, the product of illiterate, moody Southerners, like moonshine and stock car racing. If the calypso craze couldn't kill off rock'n'roll, then the commercial predicates of rock'n'roll itself could at least domesticate it. As the media conglomerates developed stronger economic bases and better promotional skills, they were able to put rock'n'roll in their hip pocket and make it play by their rules. The music became more mainstream: less 'black' and more 'white' in sound. The majors hired producers based in their New York, Philadelphia, and Los Angeles strongholds. These men replaced the strong regional dialects of an Elvis or Little Richard, the self-penned songs of a Chuck Berry, and the simple small group arrangements and spontaneity of the indie studios with indistinguishable television faces singing songs they couldn't sing. The charts and airwaves were given over to songs whose lyrics substituted self-pity for self-assertion, and whose beat, or what was left of it, was backed by strings and celestial choruses.

The best example of the shift was evident in Philadelphia, from which city Dick Clark's *American Bandstand* beamed into teenage television land a version of 'rock'n'roll' unlikely to offend anyone. Boys with dark complexions were turned into singing stars if their pictures looked right on the screen and in teen fan magazines. Producers backed these young Valentinos with a mechanical beat that made the earlier rock'n'roll numbers seem subtle. The songs were sing-along: Perry Como gone rock in the form of Frankie Avalon and Frankie Avalon clones – teen idols such as Fabian, Bobby Rydell, and (from New York) Paul Anka. The industry had once more discovered the 'cult of personality'. As the multimedia webs of the industry became more tangled, the moguls produced and marketed pompadoured teenage idols and the cashmere-sweatered girl-next-door: the *image* of the artist was selling records, perhaps more than the music or performance itself. Sales climbed and climbed for the majors, and companies like Sun or Specialty who failed to adapt disappeared. The majors had regained composure. Once again they believed they knew what people wanted to hear. The remark of pioneer record store owner Sam Goody that he might as well have been selling shoes was taken to its logical corporate extreme.

As for the indies, 'they brought [rock'n'roll] to life in 1953, force-fed it for five years, and left it for dead in 1958. Yet if they thought they could outlive the music which put them shoulder-to-shoulder with the majors, they were to discover that nothing was so easy; within five years, most of the indies had themselves followed rock'n'roll to an early grave'.[21] Radio stations, meanwhile, stopped programming records with wild sounds and suggestive lyrics. For teenagers, these lyrics had reflected their lives in city streets, juke joints, and school dances. Now that the music was listened to at home via radio, television, and disc, and Mom and Pop Suburbia had started paying attention to what their kids were listening to, program directors picked tunes with a beat for the kids without lyrics that would irritate the parents. The novelty had worn off: hip was tame, and tame was now hip.

Too Much Monkey Business

A sideshow at the funeral of rock'n'roll was the much publicized 1960 Congressional investigation into the bribing of radio disc jockeys by industry promotions men to secure airplay for new releases, a practice known as 'payola'. Payola had its roots in the free 'exclusive record' technique pioneered by Capitol after World War Two. With over two hundred records being released each week, the 'exclusive' was an industry ploy to break into *Billboard*'s Top Twenty-five. Because the major markets were in large cities like Los Angeles, New York, Cleveland, Boston, and Detroit, disc jockeys at radio stations in these markets found themselves primary targets: airplay on their stations could guarantee entrance into the *Billboard* Hot One Hundred, which in turn meant airplay across the rest of the nation. Payola gave the labels a degree of control over their product by ensuring that their records would be brought before as wide an audience as possible.

Two types of payola were widespread before the scandal broke: the 'consultancy' and 'play for pay'. In the former, and more common of the two, labels working through local distributors allegedly paid big–name disc jockeys under-the-counter fees to listen to their records. Both labels and disc jockeys were equal party to any crime that might have been committed. As James Von Schilling points out, however:

> the big losers in the scandal weren't the major record companies but the free-wheeling rock'n'roll disc jockeys who had played such key roles in the rise of the new music, especially Alan Freed, whose career and personal life crumbled after the hearings. The indies themselves suffered, too, losing whatever respectability they might have gained during the 1950s. Also, any curtailment of payola activities hurt the indies more than the majors, who could still rely on their own extensive distribution systems and, in the case of RCA and Columbia, their own nationwide home record clubs.[22]

Payola may have furnished a small number of Congressmen and the Tin Pan Alley old guard at the American Society of Composers, Artists and Performers (ASCAP) with an outlet for vengeance against rock'n'roll, but its negative influence on teenagers was negligible. Perhaps some parents believed rock'n'roll

235

had 'bought its way into the hearts of the teenagers, but very few fans took this accusation seriously'.[23]

Along with payola, further nails in the coffin of the wild, free-willed disc jockeys and their records were provided, on the one hand, by the introduction of demographics to musical opinion polling and, on the other, by the introduction of Top-Forty radio in 1955 by Todd Storz at WTIX in New Orleans (and applied throughout the station's chain, owned by a Southern pharmaceutical company). Standardization of playlists became the norm as program directors increasingly kept to songs found on the *Billboard* chart. Format replaced originality – and it worked.

You Go Your Way (and I'll Go Mine)

Perhaps time was the final nail in rock'n'roll's coffin. Technology advanced to the point that the reproduction of sound demanded and enabled greater creativity; musicians' techniques improved greatly between 1956 and 1964 as a younger generation absorbed and built on the accumulated knowledge of the primordial rock'n'rollers. As techniques improved, experimentation with rhythm, melody, harmony, meter, and instrumentation grew. The musicians simply outgrew rock'n'roll, although the music's essential formula remained the basis of popular music (and still does to this day).

Change extended beyond the realm of popular music. American culture and society were in the throes of upheavals with which rock'n'roll could not cope. The music was too simple for the sixties, and the original rock'n'rollers were insufficiently flexible in their musical styles to adapt. The forms of popular music that evolved out of rock'n'roll and R&B – rock and soul, respectively – spoke to a new generation of teenagers just as rock'n'roll had spoken to the previous one. Soul music had appeared as early as the mid-1950s, offering an alternative to the lightweight fare of Mitch Miller's Hit Parade radio. By 1960 it had displaced R&B (with the help of rock'n'roll) and around the middle of the 1960s would cross over to the white mainstream. Rock and soul were themselves both to evolve into, and to a degree be replaced by, new forms. The development continues today as rap, house, punk, and techno fill the charts of the early 1990s. Music exists within the context of diverse social processes, and the elements that engender the sound of popular music at any given time change constantly. New styles, new teen idols, new guitar heroes, new technologies come and go. 'Nonetheless', writes Gerri Hirshey in *Nowhere to Run*:

> mainstream American pop cruises along, still trading on the restlessness that moved all those gospel journey songs, that spurred travelling bluesmen and lonesome hillbillies and, later, those car-crazy fifties rockers. After all, riding steerage was the first rock and roll experience for millions of would-be Americans. By the eighties, Bruce Springsteen

236

topped the charts by dipping back into that bag of American journey yarns, stating his belief in 'The Promised Land', then lamenting 'The Price You Pay'.[24]

Notes

1. Thanks in part to Hollywood, rock'n'roll was perceived by many as part of an overt rebellion. Headlines in Los Angeles and New York that accompanied showings of *Blackboard Jungle* linked rock'n'roll to juvenile delinquency. With its theme song, Bill Haley's 'Rock Around the Clock', the movie gave (presumably male) teenagers an anthem that fit their status as rebels within a tradition that would include, amongst others, Marlon Brando, James Dean, and Montgomery Clift.
2. Greil Marcus, ed., *Rock and Roll Will Stand* (Boston: 1969), p. 8.
3. Charlie Gillet, *The Sound of the City: The Rise of Rock and Roll*, rev. ed. (London: 1983), p. 64.
4. R. Serge Denisoff, *Tarnished Gold: The Record Industry Revisited* (Oxford: 1986), p. 8.
5. Peter Wicke, *Rock Music: Culture, Aesthetics and Sociology*, trans. Rachel Fogg (Cambridge: 1990), p. 42.
6. All chart information in this chapter has been culled from Joel Whitburn, *The Billboard Book of Top 40 Hits* (New York: 1989).
7. Quoted in Wicke, p. 23.
8. Neal R. Peirce, *The Deep South States of America: People, Politics, and Power in the Seven Deep South States* (New York: 1974), p. 38.
9. Jonathan Kamin, 'Taking the Roll out of Rock'n'Roll: Reverse Acculturation', *Popular Music and Society*, 1, 1 (Fall, 1972), 6-7.
10. Gillet, p. 17
11. In one sense radio might be described as the midwife of rock'n'roll. Rock'n'roll was born when musicians brought together country, straight R&B, and its gospel-inspired offshoots, and when the majors and indies lumped these musical styles and their mongrel product under the same rubric in response to their teenage audience, which now had access to any style on the radio and listened to whatever particular music suited it. The majors were given their branch to swing on when Alan Freed called the music he was playing 'rock'n'roll', a name which he claimed to have but in truth had not coined.
12. Gerri Hershey, *Nowhere to Run* (New York: 1984), xiv.
13. James Von Schilling, 'Records and the Recording Industry', in Thomas M. Inge, ed., *Concise Histories of American Popular Culture* (Westport, Connecticut: 1982), p. 314.
14. Wicke, p. 4.
15. Gillet, p. 39.
16. Gillet, p. 50.
17. Gillet, p. 42.
18. Gillet, pp. 67-68.
19. Gillet, p. 96.
20. Von Schilling, p. 314.
21. Gillet, p. 65.
22. Von Schilling, pp. 319-320.
23. Denisoff, p. 16.
24. Hirshey, xvi.

The American Comedian as Social Critic, 1950-1970

Eric Mottram

William Claude Dukenfield, alias W.C. Fields, died in 1946, a classic comedian of survival in a society assumed to be totally competitive, which he analyzed and criticized, directly or by implication, in practically every sketch and gag. In the war between the sexes, as it used to be (and perhaps in some quarters still is) called, he is contemporary with the great American comic writer James Thurber (1894-1961), equally a survivor and a satirist. Fields had the advantage of being an actor, and having his performance recorded for posterity on film and video, so that every detail of his social position, his gender programme, and his location within vaudeville traditions is visible as well as audible. We also have tapes of his later radio materials through which to appreciate his gifts of language, his use of repartee as a weapon of survival. Through rough wit and sleight of mind, a logic is constructed to defeat a victim into speechlessness and mere gesture or spluttering. Except on video, however, the superb flinch, the particular nose and eyes cannot be experienced as part of his aggression – an aggression always at the edge of defence. Fields says: there is a limit to interference and turning the other cheek, and this is it. The performance of vulnerability and superiority opens into disclosures of the hidden and taboo, the causes of laughter that entertains anxieties: 'That neurotic coldness or embarrassment before disclosure, or intensity, which is one reason for so many jokes and so much tragedy in our lives.' The words are Muriel Rukeyser's, a major American poet and social critic who so much enjoyed British comedians, especially Tony Hancock and the Goon Show.[1] Mark Twain offers a related insight in *Following the Equator*: 'Everything human is pathetic. The secret source of humour itself is not joy but sorrow. There is no humour in heaven.' The comedian-social critic sets up a location of exposure and laughter, an interface with intricate functions, or (using recently-fashionable jargon itself ripe for satire) an intertextuality between entertainment and the disturbance of habits within what the media establishment and its controlled consumers insist is leisure experience.

238

The assumed impermanence of performance arts has long since been relegated by recording techniques, most recently the video tape and laser disc. At least more of the comedian's performance may be experienced, even something of the sociality of an act that is essentially responsive. Laughter is usually at some act, human or animal. Laughing at trees could be manic. Henri Bergson is firm in his 1900 essay *Laughter*: its social use deters inflexibility:

> To understand laughter, we must put it back into its natural environment, which is society, and above all we must determine the utility of its function, which is a social one....
>
> The comic will come into being, it appears, whenever a group of men concentrate their attention on one of their number, imposing silence on their emotions and calling into play nothing but their intelligence....
>
> The laughable element ... consists of a certain *mechanical* inelasticity, just where one would expect to find a wideawake adaptability and the living pliableness of a human being....
>
> Society will be suspicious of all inelasticity of character, of mind and even of body, because it is the possible sign of slumbering activity as well as of an activity with separatist tendencies, that inclines to swerve from the common centre around which society gravitates: in short, because it is the sign of an eccentricity....
>
> A gesture, therefore, will be [society's] reply. Laughter must be something of this kind, a sort of *social gesture*. By the fear which it inspires, it restrains eccentricity, keeps constantly awake....
>
> Laughter, then, does not belong to the province of aesthetics alone, since unconsciously (and even immorally in many particular instances) it pursues a utilitarian aim of general improvement. And yet there is something aesthetic about it, since the comic comes into being just when society and the individual freed from the worry of self preservation, begin to regard themselves as works of art....
>
> Automatism, inelasticity, the habit that has been contracted and maintained, are clearly the causes why a face makes a laugh.[2]

The comedian can expose the interior motivational structure of the habitual, a split between unconscious and conscious motivation, between physiological processes and social constraints – to use Julia Kristeva's terms for the action of a 'speaking subject'. This is part of the reason why most of the American comedians under consideration use dramas rather than jokes – short dramatic scenes rather than small jokes, or gags. We can recall Kristeva's use of the term 'jouissance' for that totality of enjoyment which can include ecstasy whether sexual, spiritual or conceptual: a total joy.[3] Hobbes's definition of humour as a triumph (in chapter eleven of *Leviathan*) is too restrictive, necessarily within his vision of life as systems of dominance and submission:

> *Joy*, rising from imagination of a man's power and ability, is that exultation of the mind which is called GLORYING: which if grounded upon the experience of his own former actions, is the same with *confidence*....

> *Sudden glory*, is the passion which maketh those grimaces called LAUGHTER; the apprehension of some deformed thing in another, by comparison whereof they suddenly applaud themselves.

But, he adds, 'of great minds, one of the proper works is, to help and free others from scorn; and compare themselves only with the most able.'

Such liberations are probably true but over-selective and one-sided. Laughter is in practice much more varied and graduated. The comedian's discourse is heterogeneous: the subjects keep disintegrating and re-forming, in the presence of semi-improvizational methods and responses from an audience. It is nearer to what Deleuze and Guattari call lines of flight or flows, and acts of deterritorialization and recovery.

The laugh for a comedian as social critic is not only a surplus relief; it may well be troubled, and troubling, in the presence of the unfamiliar, the taboo, the risking edge: '*Laugh* through saturated-striated meaning, through affirmed-rhythmic identity. Laugh into a void composed of logical, syntactic, and narrative surplus. An unfamiliar, troubling, undefinable laugh.'[4] Kristeva also refers to 'Swift's furious, disillusioned, and cruel wit, unearthing hell under social harmony and proving to Man that he is "Lilliputian"':

> All networks of possible meaning must be exhausted beneath common sense, banal, obvious meaning, or cruel, threatening, and aggressive meaning – before we can understand that they are ungraspable, that they adhere to no axis, that they are 'arbitrary' just like the sign, the name, and the utterance, but also pleasure and jouissance ... the arbitrariness of the break establishing meaning, which is itself squarely against the flow of rhythm, intonation, and music, that provokes this laughter. We do not laugh because of what makes sense or because of what does not. We laugh because of possible meaning, because of the *attitude* that causes us to enunciate signification as it brings us jouissance....
>
> We do not laugh, then, in order to judge the position that gives meaning; even less so in order to put ourselves out of judgment's reach, in some surreality where everything is equal. We laugh on account of the limit assumed in the very moment that enroots and uproots finitude within an endlessly centered and yet decentered process. Laughter of language, laughter of sociality itself.

Laughter is troubled especially if entrenched positions on morality, religion, sex and taste (in behaviour *and* in language) are subjected to exposure, ridicule, offence. Kristeva refers to 'the Rabelaisian joy shaking up science, esotericism, marriage and Spirit, based on a full, recovered, promising body – the laughter of gigantic Man'; and she adds 'with Voltaire and Diderot, laughter dethrones'.

It follows that the comedian as social critic de-mystifies the authoritarian, the taboo, the rigid and the mechanical, the assumed sacred. He can draw attention to exhausted meaning – in Kristeva's words: 'laughter is black with burnt up meaning: Jarry, Roussel, Chaplin...' Or he can undermine pleasure and jouissance into bitterness, disillusion, nihilism, pulverization. Laughter as a language discourse may move towards uprooting and the void. Comedians are dangerous to those who obey and those who dominate, to gods and those on their knees before gods and rulers. Laughter emerges in the authoritarian situation, but may not alleviate it. The helpless situation may remain. It emerges in the chaos – often states of humiliation and bewilderment – which James Thurber invokes for us to laugh at. In the preface to *My Life and Hard Times* he wrote: 'the little wheels of comedy are set in motion by the damp hand of melancholy ... the claw of the sea-puss gets us all in the end.' Mark Twain's comic faith in the capabilities of human beings to moderate themselves and love each other moves increasingly towards the edge of hysteria. His writing as controlled hysteria and his public speeches move into depression and secrecy. His descendants include Nathanael West, whose situation in the 1930s responds to the murderous futilities and hypocrisies of American capitalism, with its centres in both politics and the entertainment and publishing spheres. *Miss Lonelyhearts* parodies Roosevelt's New Deal promotions as the limitations of advice to be gained from an agony column. Concurrently, Thurber emerges in the *New Yorker* magazine as both writer and cartoonist. His basic criterion was: 'The line is thinly drawn between American comedy and American insanity.' West drew on French Dada and surrealist sources, and André Breton's *Humeur Noir* anthology remains both a resource book and a collection of recognitions of black comedy from Swift through to de Sade, de Quincey and Poe, and then from Lewis Carroll and Nietzsche to Roussel, Kafka, Duchamp and Dali. It was first published in 1939 and revised in 1966. In the 1950s and 1960s, a powerful group of fictional styles emerged in America as 'black humour', and included those of Terry Southern, Bruce J. Friedman, Stanley Elkin and William Burroughs. These were the critical comedians in prose fiction for the violent decades of the Korean and Southeast Asian wars, the civil rights movement, and the Beat and Free Speech protest movements.

In the 1950s certain American comedians broke into those domains official authority and its supporters needed to keep from radical enquiry: the Korean and Southeast Asian wars, drug addiction, malnutrition, nuclear fall-out, unorthodox sexuality, disease, international political insanity, urban violence, obsessive consumerism, and the rest. Faith in the state could barely be maintained for many Americans exposed to these locations. Comedians might have to confront such situations, and some with the sense that their audience might be less than supportive. Jack Leonard used to greet his audiences with 'Good evening opponents!' Certainly the unease continued when women comedians began to imitate the men's routines in the 1980s. Lenny Bruce probed further than any. One of his routines concerned the power of television and exposed the desires of the audience and the producers for sacrifice: 'I'd like to kill myself on TV. That would be a real first. Of course, the producer would be nervous: "You're not going to say anything dirty?" "No, it's a very clean act.

I just take four little pills and die." "Okay, as long as you don't do anything dirty."'

Parody and satire, especially as elements of black humour, edge into the fruitful region of morbidity, bad taste and cruelty. But, then, so does religious, political and legal authority, although it tries to pretend otherwise, especially since it is fearful of irreverence towards areas of the violently sacred and the sacrificial. Mort Sahl, a major political satirist, nearer to the effects of the cartoonist Jules Feiffer than Bruce, came on fairly nervous about such infringements, insisting on his 'ethical standpoint' within open 'discussion':

> license imposes discretion. It doesn't permit anarchy. There are some words and subjects that are too harsh, and I won't use them. Some of the things that have happened in America in recent years were due not only to intellectual cowardice but also to lack of heart. I have no time for people who are trying to make us even more heartless....

Yet the comedian as social critic is not usually concerned with issues of anarchy and discretion, but rather with establishing an integrity of penetration and a language of witty surprise for his audience: an integrity of dissent, a fervent basic tradition in the United States. This is present in Sahl's claim: 'I was just a product of my time. This license was lying around waiting for someone to pick it up.' It is not surprising that many of the 1950s and 1960s comedians were urban and either Jewish or black. Some of the reasons lie in one of Goebbels' condemnations of Jews in 1938: 'the destruction methods of a Jewish-infected minority, the jokes that cease to be jokes when they touch on the holiest matters of national life.' James Thurber worried about the very foundations of critical humour: 'Humour makes its own balances and patterns out of the disorganization of life around it, but disorganization has been wiped out by organization, statistics, surveys, group action, program, platform, imperatives, and the like. These are good for satire, but they put a strait jacket on humour.'

But the comedian's performance is essentially a regular confrontation with an audience he must make laugh – and with those provisos Walter Benjamin suggests in his book on Brecht 'there is no better starting point for thought than laughter; speaking more precisely, spasms of the diaphragm generally offer better chances of thought than spasms of the soul'.[5] He is writing on the occasions for laughter in epic theatre, the theatre of alienation, and part of that action is the performance art of the comedian.

But the spasm explodes in the body as a social occasion, however private and helpless the actual act of laughter. In a 1928 essay entitled 'Humour', Freud writes that 'pleasure derived from humour ... proceeds from a saving in expenditure of effect' – and the comedians presented here are essentially verbally neat within whatever exuberances of stance and audience control they use.[6] Humorous satisfaction demonstrates confidence in handling the event, at least verbally, as a volatile articulation of what the audience does and does not know. To be *socially* effective, it cannot be over-satisfying, unless the comedian needs to reassure the audience that all is well and that he represents authority as its jester. Maurice Solotow tells how after a show at the University of Kentucky football game, Bob Hope is walking with him along a dark, deserted street in Lexington, when a young girl gets out of a white Mustang, cries 'Oh, Mr. Hope', and could she please hug and kiss him...? Hope complies and soon there is a pile-up in the middle of the night with Hope signing scraps of paper and doing his act, and being repeatedly kissed like a presidential candidate. Hope's the name and hope's the object. It is not on record that any *men* kissed him, or tried to. It is unlikely that in any way this event could have happened to a comedian as unreassuring as Lenny Bruce.[7]

Smug self-satisfaction, knowingness, in both comedian and audience, are certainly part of the routines of the Hope category. Concentrated analysis, cutting through assumption and dispersed information, provides another kind of relief, for another kind of audience: relief in recognition that someone can articulate catastrophe or a lying myth. Through the exit always lies the full performance: society, generally taken to be infinitely disastrous. Inside the performance there is another exit: a resourceful confrontation after analysis and increased information.

The routine of the comedians here contains their ability to lead into a situation through a small drama which depends on a knowledgeable audience, and in most cases a white middle class audience turning up to a comedian for a known set of purposes. This comes across even on recordings of performance, and, in some cases, even on a studio record. The comedian leads in, and then changes expectation. Customary social response, group response, is made to absorb official response, official trained attitudes in the public. Perhaps the audience is unaware – at least at the time – of the degree of subversion in the surprises. The performance is a concentration of energy alerts rather than comforts, although being alerted can be both comforting and flattering. But the refusal of cliché is salutary – especially in Lenny Bruce's miniature dramas parodying the prison movie, or the Lone Ranger outlaw complacency, and in Murray Roman's Dracula movie parody.

The comedian as social critic has at least to dare entry into the mined, forbidden fields of mass belief: politics, sex, law and race, and the confines known as 'good taste'. The 'liberating effect' spurs up here, together with the need to 'spare oneself the affects to which the situation would give rise' by overriding 'with a jest the possibility of such an emotional display'. Freud adds that this leads to a possible drama he calls 'the triumph of narcissism, the ego's victorious assertion of its own vulnerability. It refuses to be hurt by the arrows of reality or to be compelled to suffer'.[8] Once again the repressed returns as a kind of history, an historical analysis. Humour for Freud, rather humourlessly, is therefore among 'the great series of methods devised by the mind of man for evading the compulsion to suffer – a series which begins with neurosis and culminates in delusions, and includes intoxication, self-induced states of abstraction and ecstasy'.

But the comedian's essential movement towards the edge of rationality, upholding the pleasure principle 'without quitting the ground of mental sanity', cannot be subjugated to such negative psychologizing, such a model of mechanistic passivities. Socially critical humour includes disobedience of the super-ego or parental or state authority. The end, however temporary, is not entirely or at all subordination, and this is particularly clear during the 1950s and 1960s in the United States. The critical comedians do not simply enact the drama of child versus adult in their versions of challenge to the authoritarian. Authority is in fact displaced. Energy is transferred from one kind of obedience to another in the characteristic procedures of art. Repeatedly the energy of performance and response emerges from a mutual paranoia. The paranoid appeal takes up the fear that all is connected by hidden power. The comedian can play on this partial suppression by identifying the power. He grows increasingly paranoid and combative against that power, and as the finest comic writer of the decades since 1950, William S. Burroughs, says, the paranoid is the person in possession of all the facts. A sense of persecution invades the comedians as these decades proceed. Persecution links both Lenny Bruce and Mort Sahl to their audiences, and in the black comedians it is a foundation which does not have to be stated. Repeatedly within their dramas, the vulnerable man uses what weapons he can to expose oppressive forces which, given his gross conservatism, Freud can only simplify into a personalist psychic condition arising from childhood suppression.

But this action stops short of ideologically determined conclusions: the invitation to cut through complex social occasions to a *solutionary* understanding within such terms is disallowed. A certain security binds comedian to audience. It is not crossing the taboos of taste which worries but the recognition – frequently obvious to a detached position if not to the audience on the occasion – that the ideal society from which criticism is made could only be achieved by revolutionary changes, changes which neither the comedian nor his audience could contemplate. 'Spasms of the diaphragm' may 'offer better chances for thought' but if the thought is that radical, the humour can in effect *cause* suppression to the point of repression. This seems to have occurred in that American situation described as a *military* society by Gore Vidal in '*Some* Jews and *the* Gays' (two focuses of humour which are endemic in these decades), one of the funniest and most penetrating analyses of homosexuality in America ever to have been written. Vidal's context is ignorance of facts: 'Our therapists, journalists and clergy are seldom very learned. They seem not to realize that most military societies on the rise tend to encourage same-sex activities for reasons that should be obvious to anyone who has not grown up ass-backward, as most Americans have.'[9] Here is an ideal situation for a comedian – especially for a comedian who is Jewish *and* homosexual –

but Vidal just recalls an exchange between Christopher Isherwood and a young Jewish movie producer: '"After all," said Isherwood, "Hitler killed 600,000 homosexuals." But the young man was not impressed. "But Hitler killed six *million* Jews," he said sternly. "What are you?" asked Isherwood. "In real estate?"'

The issue is: who makes jokes about whom and what? Later in his essay, Vidal reminds us that 'all despised minorities are quick to make rather good jokes about themselves before the hostile majority does. Certainly Jewish humour, from the Book of Job (a laff-riot) to pre-*auteur* Woody Allen, is based on this'. But then the issue becomes: who makes jokes about the majority's lives and to whom? The inference in social critic comedians is largely that the majority under authority are a barn-door target. 'Loyal workers and consumers', to use Vidal's phrase, would be unlikely to listen to Mort Sahl, Bruce or Tom Lehrer with total allegiance, let alone conviction; and appreciation of the art of the critical comedian in itself requires a degree of detachment remote from spectatorism. The comedian works with logic – a logical process sometimes so fanatical it appears surreal – in a category distinct from both reality and pleasure principle. The world of most people is illogical – and Vidal has no difficulty in demolishing his main target in this essay, a peculiar member of the Jewish intellectual 'new right' called Midge Decter, wife, apparently, of the editor of *Commentary*.

As a black American, Ralph Ellison would necessarily be alert to the spasmodic theatre of humour – in fact, his 1958 essay 'Change the Joke and Slip the Yoke' is a classic analysis of the strategies of minority humour in a hostile society, and concludes that 'when American life is most American it is apt to be most theatrical.... America is a land of masking jokers. We wear the mask for purposes of aggression as well as for defense; when we are projecting the future and preserving the past. In short, the motives hidden behind the mask are as numerous as the ambiguities the mask conceals'.[10] Beyond being able to conceive and carry out strategies of survival lies a possible silence: Baudelaire's poverty-stricken clown in the *Spleen of Paris*:

> Everywhere joy, profit and dissoluteness; everywhere the assurance of bread for tomorrow; everywhere the frenzied explosion of vigour. But here absolute poverty, poverty bedecked, as a crowning horror, with comic rags, where need, much more than art, had introduced contrast. The wretch did not laugh! He did not weep or dance or gesticulate or shout; he sang neither a gay nor a sad song, he did not supplicate. He had given up, he had abdicated. His destiny was over.[11]

From about 1950 onwards into the 1960s, a number of American comedians moved within the social protest movement; those that did not overtly do so – Tom Lehrer, Bob Newhart, Burns and Schreiber, Shelley Berman, Murray Roman and others – worked within the context and spirit of analysis that moved into riot, civil disobedience and authoritarian suppression. White and black comedians – the latter including Godfrey Cambridge and (in those days) Bill Cosby – played mostly on the anxieties of a largely middle-class clientele, nervous about racism, about violence, about the rat-race, and about criticizing the Eisenhower-Nixon-McCarthy mess and what followed. They began before the Beats, before the campus revolts and before much of the street protest for civil rights and against the draft for Southeast Asian wars. Later, the counter-culture would include them. They are anarchists without dogmatic ideology, crossing taboos and exposing illogical assumptions; their allies are the contemporary practitioners of 'black humour', who extend and develop the controlled hysteria of Twain, West, Thurber and Ring Lardner.[12] Their humour originates in the state of the nation they share. They do not have their routines written by paid teams of professionals with an eye on the market; they do not wear funny hats, open with 'a funny thing happened to me on my way to the theatre', except in mockery, or close with 'singing you all a little [and usually comforting] song entitled ...' Nor do they talk down to the audience, even if that audience frequently has to be quick on the uptake, and may on occasion need a jolting reminder. Of course, since the humour is local and topical in its immediacies, whatever the metaphysics beneath, it can date and become un-intelligible without special knowledge. But, not surprisingly, little of it has dated yet.

Groucho Marx criticized S.J. Perelman's use of *The Merry Widow* in a piece of writing (Perelman was one of the scriptwriters for Marx Brothers films): 'How can an audience laugh at a joke about something they never even heard of?'[13] Jimmy Durante, the long-nosed comedian, used to say how he remem-bered the midwife at his birth saying 'Dis ain't da baby – it's da stork'. This is probably a joke for everyone in 'the West'. It is doubtful whether there are in fact universal jokes. The research has yet to be done. 'The comedy of dis-sent' is the title of a 1960 article by *San Francisco Chronicle* columnist Ralph Gleason.[14] He registers reaction to a tranquillizing humour of conformity, the sense that post-Bomb humour – not to speak of post-Dachau, post-Depression humour – could be funny, grotesque and gruesome, the humour of the McCarthy witch-hunts against anyone. Satire needled the culture of consent, and significantly Mort Sahl, the San Francisco pioneer humorist, began as an angry college student in the Eisenhower-Nixon-McCarthy years. In a 1958 article called 'The Unrocked Boat' Vidal called for a certain work to be done: 'If one can make the cautious laugh by clowning, half the work is done, for laughing is the satirist's anaesthetic; he can then make his incision, darting on before the audience knows what has been done to it. But he must be swift and engaging or the laughter will turn to indifferent silence, the ultimate censor-ship...'[15] But he then adds: 'Where can the American satirist operate today? Not on television, seldom if ever in the movies, and on the stage only if he is willing to play the buffoon.' Vidal had missed the jazz club culture of younger Americans in the 1950s, already damned by reactionaries and their police, who

246

refused to understand the nature of shock therapy and necessary irreverence. The charge of obscenity, so frequently made, had become absurd in modern society itself so essentially obscene. In 1965 Lenny Bruce wrote in his auto-biography *How to Talk Dirty and Influence People*: 'What does it mean for a man to be found obscene in New York? This is the most sophisticated city in the country.... If anyone is the first person to be found obscene in New York, he must feel utterly depraved.'[16]

This is the precise point at which the law will intervene to represent the church and state, the assumed stability of an instable society, the mask. Bruce's response was to engage with law to the point of virtually becoming a lawyer:

> I was so sure I could reach those judges if they'd just let me tell them what I try to do. It was like I was on trial for rape and there I was crying, 'But, Judge, I can't rape any-body. I haven't got the wherewithal,' but nobody was listening, and my lawyers were saying, 'Don't worry, Lenny, you got a right to rape anyone you please, we'll beat 'em in the appellate court.'

But the function of the law is to mask instability by judgment and punishment. In his 'Religions Incorporated' sketch, Bruce pointed out that religious ad-vertizing exceeds entertainment advertizing in the weekend papers, and had an evangelist claiming 'This year we've got a tie-in with Oldsmobile. Now I don't ask you to hard-sell Oldsmobile from the pulpit. Just zing it in there now and then ... DRIVE THE CAR HE DRIVES'. But this is barely an amplifica-tion of the facts. Gleason cites a press-release from a New York firm:

> The Ask Mr. Foster Travel Service received word from their representative in Rome that a group travelling under their direction presented Pope John XXIII with a $12,000 Cadillac limousine.
> Reportedly Pope John told the group at the presentation 'We'll meet again at the Gates of Paradise. I bless this car and also all your cars – I assume you all have cars.' He con-tinued: 'A benediction to all of you, with or without cars.'

Such a Christian sanction of capitalist enterprise for profit called for exposure in the tradition of Twain and West, although whether Satan in Twain's *The Mysterious Stranger* is correct to believe that 'against the assault of laughter nothing can stand' is highly doubtful. Most of America's finest comedians re-main Jews and Blacks, with a smattering of homosexuals; and their targets – class, cash, sex and race – have not changed since Twain's immediate ante-cedents.

Dick Gregory reached major popularity in 1961 at the age of 28 through rou-tines which projected race jokes to an essentially white audience.[17] But, like Bruce, he was bound to extend his range to sex, war and politics. He begins one series with atomic submarines – 'they come every eight years, just long enough to get the fellas re-enlisted' – which leads to the sexual conservative edginess of Americans – 'you're in a submarine *eight years*! You'd *better* find a friend!' – which leads to his own army experience and the debunking of an old mythical responsibility: 'I lost my rifle in the army and it cost me eighty-five dollars. And people wonder why the captain goes down with the ship!' This leads onto the presidency, the southern vice-president and the racist South: 'the President wanted to build a great cross on the lawn of the White House, but he was afraid the Vice-President would burn it' – which leads to racism in general and in the Army, the nation's weapon of righteous defensive aggression: 'They told me it was integrated. That meant *I* had to sleep with Puerto Ricans.' A comment on the embezzlement and robbery endemic in capitalism becomes a statement of the black condition of the utmost seriousness: 'I'm damned sick and tired of being robbed from the inside.' At a time when it was widely supposed that integration was the aim, and was coming on steadily, Gregory voiced the proper scepticism: 'I sat at a lunch counter down South for eleven months and when it finally integrated, they didn't have what I wanted.'

Gregory's night club circuit image was at that time conventional: smartish suit, not too well-fitted; a camouflage, like his slightly ungrammatical language, a comfort to an audience who wanted him funny but not socially mobile. He chain-smoked fastidiously. His gestures were an economically poked finger, a slightly raised arm, a few steps, a bit of a grin, a disguise of charm for the white middle class. Earlier, on the Chicago southside, it is reported, he had another style. He attacked blacks who wanted to climb within the system, and who yielded to hair-straighteners and long Cadillacs. For the whites with whom he became famous, he takes up the stereotypes that Ellison examines: the feared dark side, the taboo, of America, at night in a night-club with the day and its black problem slicing into leisure.[18] The routine becomes part of civil disobedience, a way of handling imposed silences, poverty, degradation, and the manipulations of sports and the Army. He takes up the entertainment occasion and undermines it. A fruitful nervous tension is raised between recognition and explosion. In the early 1960s he was already receiving mail from the South congratulating him on his success – this before the urban protests in Watts and Harlem in 1965 and 1966, before Selma and the assassination of Malcolm X. He had his own record label, had appeared with Dizzy Gillespie, and was managed by Broadcast Management, a top system.

Some origins emerge from his autobiography, *Nigger*, published in 1964. The title itself signifies the ambiguity of his position, nervously seized in the dedication to his mother: 'Wherever you are, if ever you hear the word "nigger" again, remember they are advertizing my book.'[19] His astonishing performance before white southern college students, at the height of the civil rights protest, has its roots in the Depression and the rough St. Louis life of a black in 1932 who gained a high school sports scholarship to Southern

Illinois University (where he set a half-mile record and majored in business administration). He discovered his comedian's talent in the Army, worked as a mail clerk in the Post Office, and was fired for 'flippin' letters addressed to Mississippi in the "Overseas" slot'. He took over an m.c. job at a night club; then an ABC man caught his act in Chicago and taped it for a television show called 'Cast the First Stone' which was well-known for its use of race problems. He then appeared on the Jack Paar and David Susskind talk shows, and at the Chicago Playboy Club and the Blue Angel in New York. His 1961 earnings reached the $100,000 level. His popularity lay partly in his focusing of guilt and repressed assault, especially at a time when both black revolt and white court decisions against blacks were mounting. Chicago's history of race riots showed that policing was ineffective, and that city housing and park plans were expensive and useless. Cheap mill and foundry labour and ghetto life governed – and this was an era of northward exodus for southern blacks. There had been a United Nations riot over the Lumumba murder, and sit-ins in the South. The 'Invisible Man' of 1952 had become partly visible, and audible. A figure like Gregory could no longer be dubbed 'Negro comic' to imply safety status, the location of Amos 'n' Andy, Stepin Fetchit, and that long line of comedians, dancers, actors in Imamu Amiri Baraka's 'A Poem for Willie Best' – Best's Hollywood name was Sleep 'n' Eat – and 'Black Dada Nihilismus'.[20]

Even within the black communities, comedians played out routines on stereotypes of laziness, drunkenness, infidelity and so on: Negro jokes for Negroes, like Jewish jokes for Jews, a certain in-group permission not granted to whites and gentiles. From 1950, blacks trained in America's wars, and the 1954 Supreme Court decision against public school segregation, began to generate new television comics like Nipsy Russell and Slappy White. Routine material expanded. James Baldwin's 'Do we really want to integrate with *them*?' is a basic in Gregory. When the latter returned to Chicago to receive a City Council citation, he addressed the assemblage through his new power: 'Things are getting so rough for Kennedy; I heard Nixon flew into town the other day and stopped the recount. I voted for Kennedy myself. He was my second choice. My first choice was Lincoln. If it hadn't been for him I'd still be on the open-market.'[21] When he was once asked if a Negro should be sent into space, Gregory replied: 'The man they sent was coloured. He *turned* white when he found out what he volunteered for.... When I do land on the moon, a little four-headed, six-legged, green-complected man is sure to come up and tell me he don't want *me* marryin' *his* sister.' That same year he reminded the whites that emancipation had failed: 'People make a fuss over this being the Centennial of the Civil War. All that means to me is one hundred years of separate toilets.' In 1962 he told a New York audience: 'Take my home town – Chicago. When the Negroes move into one large area, and it looks like we might control the votes, they don't say anything to us – they have a slum clearance.'

Gregory's insinuating voice played North against South, white against black, black against black, beyond abuse and irritants. He had little of Bruce's penetration into the more taboo areas of sex and power but he had a wider audience – even if the Chicago *Tribune* could only call him the black Mort Sahl. In 1966 he financed his own trip to visit American prisoners in North Vietnam (arranged by Bertrand Russell and North Vietnamese in London).[22] The civil disobedience pacifist claimed it was simply to entertain the men, and when asked why not the soldiers fighting in the South, he replied:

These prisoners are without a government, they are paying their debt for the war like North Vietnam captives are paying theirs. I wouldn't entertain anyone who is engaged in killing his fellow man.... Look, I entertain in jails all over the country, these guys were murderers, rapists, and bank robbers, but now they are paying back. I don't tell jokes at bank robbers' convention.

By this time he would tell his harangued white audience: 'We all have our troubles, baby. May nature be good to you.' During his mayoral campaign in Chicago he told an interviewer: 'I have 400,000 votes in my hip pocket, and that is more than enough to destroy the Daley machine. I would consider that a personal victory.' Asked about State Department pressure and the dangers of being in North Vietnam, he replied: 'I will probably have 16 CIA agents and two workers from SNCC trailing me. Those guys from SNCC want to make sure I don't go Uncle Tom over there.... I'm going to be where Ho is and that has to be the safest place in that country.'[23]

Gregory the comedian had moved into another kind of politics. In 1968 he became presidential candidate for the Peace and Freedom Party, based in California, and gained a large vote. Earlier he had fasted in protests against the Southeast Asian war and then in 1976, at the age of 44, he ran from Los Angeles to New York protesting world hunger, commenting: 'Fifty miles every day, and you talk about pain and hardship and blood.' From 20 April until the beginning of September 1980 he fasted in Teheran to pacify the tensions, including the hostages issue, and then returned to America to walk from the United Nations in New York to the White House to fast in vigil on President Carter's porch. He believed that the Iranians had responded: 'their feeling towards American blacks is like that of black folks in America towards Indians.'[24] He talked with the hostages' student captors and the Ayatollah, and replaced a government minister who could not make a speech: 'I gave them two hours of peace and love.' He left when he needed acupuncture in Boston for infected teeth: 'I did not want to become an embarrassment to the Iranian government with my illness.' He believed that a solution to the situation would be for the United States to apologize and then buy back some useless military equipment. The old Gregory appeared through the new idealism when he told an interviewer who commented on his thinness and skull-like face: 'I want to look really dramatic.' He added that his motive began with 'resentment':

I've been trying to be nice to pay the world back for what I was able to break out of – poverty. It's really like paying you back with revenge. Was I really against the war in Vietnam as much as I was against America and its racist tactics? Sometimes you catch yourself being against one and pulling for the other. That cannot be truly peace ... being against America and pulling for the Vietnamese.

His alternative was drawn from a firm American tradition, black and white, since the seventeenth century:

Let's pray, let's take a shot at it. We got a power in God, let's use it. Let's say to that bunch of old men that no longer will you determine our fate or destiny ... a nation is a reflection of its people. [Prayer] changes people ... opens [them to] see the same beauty in Queen Elizabeth or the President of France or Muhammad Ali or Jimmy Carter or a wino or a drug addict.

By 1980 Gregory had got religion, but part of his power still drew on his ability to penetrate hypocrisy and apparent deadlock, and shame Americans into mobility.

Gregory first appeared at the hungri i, the pioneering basement café in San Francisco, in 1958. Mort Sahl opened there on 23 December 1953, just as the 'San Francisco renaissance' was beginning to intensify the indigenous anarchism through Beat generation writers from the East. Sahl, too, responded to the Eisenhower regime, and drew on the newspaper he carried in his act, referring to it as his security symbol. By 1958, when he was thirty, Sahl had become the star satirist in the Age of Conformity, probing into the cracks in its superficial hardness and self-righteousness. Playing on the anxieties of a knowledgeable middle class white audience, he could condense large schemes of material and say, for instance, 'we're welcoming back Dr. Robert Oppenheimer this week. He's been given an amnesty. And he's taking a quick course in German so he can join our country's defense'. Television banned him when industry tycoons heard his work, but he could still confidently call his New York Broadway show *The Next President* and attack Senator McCarthy as 'The Investigator'. His first record reached black market prices under the counter. He therefore had the power to say: 'NBC had me under contract, but nothing much happened. They suspected me of being an intellectual. But it's not true. I just *know* an intellectual. Guilt by association. And I have a library card – that's enough right there.' Sahl mocked Eisenhower and Dulles, the primary instigators of the imperialist disasters of the 1960s, from the left of the Democratic Party. But when Kennedy came to power he declined and could not recover, even when it became clear that his friend JFK masked the continuation of the prior regime under a boyish myth of public sincerity, nailed by Paul Goodman in his *New Reformation: Notes of a Neolithic Conservative*:

To have commanded the Moon landing was the only action of John Kennedy that rightly fitted his adolescent mentality, and therefore it had grace. Contrast the inappropriateness of his adolescent poker-playing during the Cuban missile crisis or his adolescent moral cowardice during the Bay of Pigs. It's too bad that he didn't live to bask in the Moon glory.[25]

Sahl's method in 1958 included a total excoriation of the Korean War and subsequent escapades: 'I'd like to be on the *avant-garde* trip – get in there, land, on the beach, be there thirteen minutes and say – "Is the PRO station set up yet? Has the Coca-Cola arrived or have the folks at home forgotten us?"'[26] In 1961, Sahl's records sold nearly a million copies; he was thirty four.[27] He became the first comedian on long-playing records, the first to perform in college concerts, to address the National Press Club in Washington, to be profiled in the *New Yorker*, *The Reporter*, *Playboy*, *Esquire* and *Holiday* magazines, and the first to make the cover of *Time*.

After an early childhood in Canada, he grew up in California, majoring in engineering and city administration at the University of Southern California. His humour emerged from the events and idioms of the campus during the 1950s: Korea, McCarthyism, the hypocrisies and guilts of the Affluent Society. A Canadian-born Jewish American whose youth was spent in early 'Beat' San Francisco and around Berkeley, Sahl had advantages in undermining the Bob Hope routines of the complacent. But the dinner jacket circuit was hard to break into. In 1953, Enrico Banducci, owner of the hungri i, a student and intellectuals' hang-out, hired him; he played to what he called his 'group', and his image was theirs: sweater, open-necked shirt, slacks. His jokes were not shocking to them. His one about the Army jacket with the McCarthy flap which zips across the mouth became almost a museum-piece of the period. Sahl's basic method, heavily imitated, resembled an oral strip cartoon of types and figures in scenes, with (compared with Bruce) a minimum effort to distinguish voices. His theme was the dangerous absurdity of current politics, delivered, like Bruce, as jazz improvisation on chords and phrases, and at more or less breakneck speed. Eisenhower was the senile golfer; Adlai Stevenson the egghead paralyzed with indecision – and on McCarthy: 'You might not agree with what he has to say, gang; but at least he's definitive.' Sahl's method was to say he didn't know whether the approaching unidentified aircraft was going to drop a hydrogen bomb or spell out 'Pepsi-Cola'; to blink through the nightclub fumes and say 'It's smokey in here. Fallout. Anyway, onward'; to say of the racist Governor Faubus of Arkansas, 'I guess he's all right – but how'd you like him to marry your sister?'; to say of teenagers studying Buddhism in a coffee bar, 'They said that Western religions have failed them.'

Sahl's heyday was the Eisenhower regime; while the 'New Frontier' supplied him with materials for a while, it became a matter of clothes, cars, cameras, hi-fi equipment, stainless steel Christmas trees, travel, the all-night delicatessen where Edward Hopper people brooded in insomnia and minimal social reassurance. He picked up the late 1950s hi-fi craze and analyzed it as a McLuhan or Tom Wolfe might:

Can't get too many crazy sounds. There's this company, they don't record music, just sounds. Sports cars at Sebring, riveting on the Indiana toll road, mixing cement, workers eating their lunch. If you're a purist, you're not really interested in records anyway. The big thing is to be able to turn on the pre-amp and watch the tubes light up. Put a couple of pre-amps together and split the sound quadrangle. With a jack in each ear? You know, 'Hello, Earth' – that kind of thing.

He changed Eisenhower's slogan as the man who kept us out of war to 'kept us out of Mars'. His hero was an anonymous American who went around the nation writing on walls the strange word 'No'. On his wartime life Sahl remarked: 'I was so close to MacArthur I got radiation burns.'[28] His targets included huge car tail fins, George Washington's preoccupation with the overlapping golf grip, Trotskyite girls who 'won't let him walk on the outside', and cool jazz so modern it is not music. On the issue of integration, Sahl could compete with Gregory: 'Eisenhower says we should approach the problem moderately. But Stevenson says we should approach the problem gradually. Now if we could just hit a compromise between these two extremes ...'

His routines rescued the audience from impositions of official language and the policies of various controllers. His questioning rhetoric organized argument so that the audience could go along *with* him, and his free-association methods resemble those of the psychiatric couch: not free but compulsive improvizatory monologuing. His athletic connectiveness is a manic syntax of anxiety within confident artistry. Unlike Bruce, however, he has a safety area. He told his night-spot people that their suspicions were right, earned more than $7,500 a week for doing so in 1961, and appeared on the cover of *Time* magazine – for exposing the White House occupants and their cronies and saying that Korea was World War 2.4. A comedian may gain success for massaging, even whipping, guilt and worry. He may come on as the defiant but likeable citizen, brandishing the newspaper as the symbol of daily vicarious anguish, using his favourite phrase 'social mores', shouting 'Onward!', and reaching into the dark areas of Bruce only with remarks like: 'Nice little Studebaker. This car was used just once. In a suicide pact. There's just a little lipstick on the exhaust pipe.'

Sahl is neither Marxist nor anarchist nor nihilist, nor barely Jewish. He began imagining news commentaries as a child; now he treats the news as a surreal farce in serial form. In the richer night-clubs of New York and Miami, audiences were reactionary and hostile; hecklers shouted 'Commie!' and 'Don't talk so fast!' Not surprisingly, he wore two wrist-watches, one set permanently to Los Angeles time. The key is his remark 'I have never uttered a negative statement about the status of man'. In a 1961 profile he even said 'It's in the United States tradition, we can laugh at things and also hold them dear'.[29] So on cigarette advertisements: 'They have this rugged, masculine bid going. The ultimate will be an ape, smoking.' And, most classic of all Sahl's routines for his group:

I am against analysis, along with the Church and the Communist Party, because it turns you against your folks. On the other hand, I always enjoy Arthur Miller because before the second act is over I get a chance to hit my father. The best thing about analysts is that if you don't make it with them, they'll refer you to another analyst. They call it rehabilitation referral motivation therapy. We call it fee-splitting.[30]

A passage in his autobiography *Heartland* penetrates to a darker side of Sahl's work: 'I know that there are those of you out there who are going to say, "Well, I've seen people helped by psychology." I've seen cannibals helped by Christianity. Listen, it's really endless.' But this is 1976 and he has been thoroughly attacked by official America. His close association with President Kennedy is detailed in the book, as well as his attack on the reporting of the Kennedy assassination and the subsequent Warren Commission report, in the middle of 'the most obscene event in American history ... the Vietnam War'. He was blacklisted: 'You can't bring me back. I never left.... If you state your own case, it's paranoia; if they state it for you, it becomes social justice.' In 1971 and 1972 'all venues were cut off for me except the colleges. I must have played five hundred'. The FBI, CIA and police harassed him, accusing him of drugs, communism and the rest: 'Of course, now it's paranoia to talk about it.' He did not gain a new television show until 1975. Sahl held the first national interview with Jim Garrison, the New Orleans DA: ninety minutes on Channel 11. Arriving in the city, the cabby refused to drive to Garrison's house, since rumour had it a machine-gun was pointed at his door. Sahl reports the state of 'the most influential columnist' in Chicago, Kupcinet, once his friend: 'After a show in Chicago, when I finally found a way to make the Chicago audience not only look at the Warren report but laugh at it, he said to me that I should stop mentioning that – it was indecent. It's the first time I heard that a columnist tried to edit me.'

On the other hand, Mr. Justice William O. Douglas came to see Sahl in New York in 1974:

He told me I must bend every effort to look into the fact that the CIA has a former telephone company executive administering its funds for a dollar a year and that one of the things he knows about is that other agencies' funds can be diverted into the CIA.... 'You've got to do it, Mort. There isn't anyone else.' Now, I ask you, fellow Americans, are you worried now?

Meanwhile Sahl had two 'strange car accidents' and his back broken twice.

The CIA was the active arm of our foreign policy and it was not responsible to Congress. We had an army dominated by ambivalences and sustained by narcotics. A generation had gone on a lifetime sit-down strike. The American dollar was thinning.... How many more have to die before some Americans realize murder is not a way of life? ... America's poet Don Mclean reminds us, 'Just because you're paranoid doesn't mean they're not out to get you.'[31]

254

Mort Sahl did not turn to law like Bruce, or civil disobedience like Gregory, He was ready to return sharply when the Watergate scandal blew up.

In 1945 Lenny Bruce, then aged twenty and not yet discharged from the Navy, won a prize for conventional one-line joke comedian routines. But he could not find work except as an m.c. for burlesque shows. In 1971, five years after his death, the American Historical Association devoted a special session to his work.[32] He had become one of America's most penetrating critics of hypocritical power in religion, politics, drug legislation, sexuality and freedom of speech issues, and above all, of that majority self-righteous ignorance and cowardice in these and kindred matters. *Playboy* serialized his autobiography and published it in book form in 1965. It was edited by Paul Krassner, the founding editor of *The Realist*, a unique satirical magazine launched in 1958, who also published Bruce's articles and stood for the same kinds of convention- and law-breaking assault as the comedian did. During the 1950s Bruce gained notice, beginning with a 1957 appearance in San Francisco; he was no longer a joke-telling comedian but a social critic with an evangelistic rhetoric, using a routine of short dramatic scenes linked by direct questions and statements to the involved audience. His analyses and humour already edged into a wit that excluded open laughter. With his Jewish upbringing, in fact, it became clear to some of his Jewish admirers that he was rabbinical, within a strong tradition of moral story-telling. Towards the end of his life, in his rare public appearances, he wore what he called his 'Chinese rabbi suit', a black priestly modification of a Chairman Mao tunic.

Between 1960 and his death he was repeatedly arrested for drug-possession and obscene language, and repeatedly cleared. But he was banned from Australia and Britain, and club, café and theatre proprietors in America increasingly refused him engagements. In October 1965 he filed suit as a pauper in a US District Court, and pleaded for an injunction against police harassment that had cost him his livelihood. He had not worked for two months. He had even been refused advertisements in trade journals. In August the following year he was found dead in his home. In the words of John Judnich, who occupied a room in Bruce's house and found his body: 'the spike was in his right arm.'

In the mid-1950s, his routines in southern Californian burlesque clubs increasingly became attacks on all authoritarian controls, exposing in particular religious, sexual and legal restriction and hypocrisy. But in a period of protest and demonstration in the United States, this is exactly what the liberal, critical public needed: licence to laugh with a risk-taking jester, who broke the taboos, and every night came before them as an outlaw. While initially rooted in his time and place, Bruce's humour and criticism remain valid in so far as his targets remain the necessary targets: the police, the law, religion, politicians, censorship, the anti-sexuality perverts, all those who enforce their own beliefs at the expense of others to the point of violation. So he ended his life as outlaw engaged in compulsive analyses of law, giving his life-energy to law-books, sacrificing his talents to the effort of finding a way for Americans through the labyrinths of court oppression.

In particular, he needed bases for resisting court criticism of his necessary uses of language to expose hypocrisy. His linguistic versatility used words like 'hotel' and 'trailer' as dirty inferences – and he once observed 'in fifty years, coffee will be another dirty word'.[33] His criticism of the obscenities of racism, capital punishment, police violence and oppression against homosexuals necessarily had to involve obscene language and inference. When the leisure entertainment sites of the night-club, café and theatre were denied, he turned, like Mort Sahl, to the universities, where Beat Generation writers had also performed. It was at the Berkeley campus of the University of California that his most exemplary late law session was recorded in the mid-1960s (it was produced by Frank Zappa and others and later issued as a double album). On campus, he could be less restricted by the demand to entertain, and could exercise his new self-assumed function as lawyer. His gifts for language changed as he became obsessed with the definition of terms in law books concerning obscenity and freedom of speech – what, for example, he called 'the dirty word problem'. There is one expert routine in which he parodies the words 'to come', including their erotic meaning, exposing the censor's stupidity. A San Francisco District Attorney who had convicted Bruce later admitted his mistake: 'He used words as weapons to hit (the audience) – to hit 'em over the head with ... clearly not for the purposes of entertaining.' But Bruce's violence was not designed to bludgeon; the analogue is wrong, and typical of ignorant law-enforcers. As the British theatre-writer Kenneth Tynan wrote, introducing Bruce's autobiography in 1965:

> The very existence of comedy like his is evidence of unease in the body politic. Class chafes against class, ignorance against intelligence, puritanism against pleasure, majority against minority, easy hypocrisy against hard sincerity, white against black, jingoism against internationalism, price against value, sale against service, suspicion against trust, death against life – .... The message he bears is simple and basic: whatever releases people and brings them together is good, and whatever confines and separates them is bad. The worst drag of all is war; in didactic moments Bruce likes to remind his audience that 'Thou shall not kill' *means just that*.[34]

In the 1950s and 1960s trust in the efficacy of some Americans to resist institutional and state authority allowed Bruce an audience he could trust with distrust, that he could challenge on the spot to feel secure if they dared, and could rely on to be triggered into energies they had perhaps kept under control in their work and at home, if they were not themselves to become outlaws, criminals, Beats, nonconformists. The audiences needed Bruce and other comedians as social consciences. Black humorists participated in what Norman Mailer in his 1957 *Dissent* essay 'The White Negro' termed 'a psychic blood-letting' – blood-letting against the pressures of tranquillization and towards possibilities of 'a psychically armed rebellion'. Mailer's 'hipster' is no liberal since 'what the liberal cannot bear to admit is the hatred beneath the skin or a society so unjust that the amount of collective violence buried in people is perhaps incapable of being contained'.[35]

But there is a further element in Bruce, as Frank Kofsky very well explains: that of the Jewish teacher using a story and a joke to 'make a point with power'.[36] As Charles Marowitz, one of the most brilliant American theatre men of the 1960s and 1970s, wrote in 1967:

> When asked how much of his act was autobiographical, Bruce admitted 'All of it'.... He uses comedy as confessional, he *is* what he *says*.... His delivery suggests the free-wheeling delivery of *On the Road*; his form, the deliberate discontinuity of William Burroughs; his mordant satire finds parallels in Ginsberg's, and in his psychotic drive, sexual preoccupation and ornery compulsiveness, could almost be Norman Mailer transplanted.... With Bruce the homosexual reference is much more telling as it takes into account the subversive connotation of homosexuality in America. (One of the biggest Eisenhower Administration scandals was the discovery of homosexuals in the State Department. In the Armed Services, suspected homosexuals are frequently mustered out with a Dishonorable Discharge). The homosexual and the Ideal American stand in the same ratio as the War Hero and the Draft Dodger. The homo is about as un-red-white-and-blue as you can get. He doesn't take part in sports; he doesn't whore; he doesn't eat Wheaties; he is never found in a painting by Norman Rockwell. He is all arty and sensitive instead of being practical and level-headed.
>
> That is why the demasculinization of a character like The Lone Ranger (prototype of the American He-Man; a kind of Boy Scout Emeritus) is so devastating. In Bruce, the queer is used to mock the brawny, heterosexual vision of the world which, in America and elsewhere, is in itself a desperately-maintained fiction.[37]

A fiction, indeed, which remain a major cause of sexual unhappiness and the resort to competitiveness and lethal weapons. Bruce unpacks the social-sexual energy inside American myths, especially those continually reproduced by Hollywood, television, comic books and 'the military-industrial complex'. He had to be arrested repeatedly on any charge because he *analyzed*, and, as chapter ten (entitled 'Persecution') of Albert Goldman's biography shows, Bruce's performance had to take place within the police and law performance – theatre within theatre of cruelty.[38]

By 1962 he had constructed his image: black 'Chinese rabbi' tunic, nervous pacing with the microphone, a sense of haunting and being haunted, hunting and being hunted, the classic stance of the charismatic outlaw spokesman. He attacked communists and liberals as much as the right – partly because they fed off each other and therefore kept the whole system going; and he probed the bigotry in those who came to his performances to laugh reassured at their own enemies and dislikes. Who did *not* smart under his humour? Yet the signatories who supported him against obscenity charges in New York included Theodore Reik, Reinhold Niebuhr, Lionel Trilling, Mailer, William Styron and James Baldwin. They knew Bruce was a national asset. Here, the attitude of the conventional moralist Malcolm Muggeridge is apposite. After witnessing Bruce's act in 1962, he wrote condescendingly but usefully:

> He is essentially a moralist; a sort of beat Savonarola or delinquent John Knox. The poor fellow's disgust at the age we live in and at the flesh he wears is pitiable to behold. It seemed quite heartless to laugh at him. The audience of seemingly prosperous Chicagoans laughed conscientiously at the appropriate times, but were, I thought, somewhat subdued. A short distance away, in the notorious Cicero district, the strip-tease joints were in full swing. Pretty well every sort of vice is available in Chicago, with the usual array of pornographic and sadistic literature. It remains a town of violence, which has certainly not been eased by the influx of a large coloured population. In these circumstances, there was something ineffably funny in the authorities fastening on Bruce.[39]

But, as Graham Greene wrote of Charlie Chaplin: 'The man who falls down must suffer if we are to laugh; the waiter who breaks a plate must be in danger of dismissal.'

Chicago's Catholic-dominated administration and police department side-stepped sexuality, both in and out of Bruce's performance. To them obscenity meant criticism of the Church. At Bruce's 1963 trial the jury, judge, prosecuting attorney and the latter's assistant were Catholic, and appeared in court on Ash Wednesday with ash on their foreheads. They won. In 1963-64 in Los Angeles the charge was 'narcotics' violation, but the cop whose testimony convicted Bruce was under suspicion, and was afterwards sentenced to five years for importing narcotics; a court doctor who also testified against Bruce had been dismissed from a Tennessee hospital for castrating a patient and 'other forms of incompetence'.[40] Ignoring expert witness testimony that Bruce was not addicted to heroin, the judge gave him ten years instead of the possible two. American authority determined to prevent Bruce performing at all. By October 1965 he was bankrupt. Small wonder that he held Wilhelm Reich's belief that authoritarian behaviour caused and fostered irrational and repressive laws maintaining such behaviour. In one routine he imagines the hypocrisy of taking some kids to their first dirty movie – not a clean one like Hitchcock's *Psycho* but one showing an ordinary couple caressing and kissing before sex.[41] As Tynan observed, unlike Sahl, Bruce's criticisms remained valid whichever group was in power, 'even if a little reading of Marx might have sharpened his political acumen'.[42] His routine exposing Stanley Kramer's liberal integrationist movie of 1958, *The Defiant Ones*, is both a kind of ideal film criticism (a black escaped convict sacrifices freedom for his white buddy) and a good example of how, in the words of C. Wright Mills' *The Power Elite* (1956), the celebration of civil liberties, even their defence, had become 'a safe way of diverting intellectual effort from the sphere of political reflection and demand'. Mills adds: 'The defensive posture of postwar liberals has also involved them in the very nervous center of elite and plebian anxieties about the position of America in the world today' – and that is the point at which Bruce works.[43]

His Jewish upbringing cuts through both liberalism and conservatism. For him Jack Ruby was a Jew in Texas and therefore trying to prove himself to male Christians by killing the guy that killed the President.[44] But when Leslie Fiedler, contributor to *Encounter* (a journal published with CIA money through the Congress for Cultural Freedom), supported the guilty verdict against the Rosenbergs, Bruce could also use that scene for repeated performance. What a jazz musician creates in the changes Bruce called *'extensions* of realism' rather than 'realism in a representational form'.[45] 'Father Flotsky's Triumph', rightly Kofsky's main subject of analysis, is excellent because it holds together so beautifully so many of Bruce's themes and methods. This time the exposed myth is the prison revolt movie: the conventions of prison chaplain and prison governor authority, the suppression of prison sexuality, the brutality of the chair. When the condemned prisoner cries out 'And there's that door! I don' wanna go in there – I don' know what to do, I don' know what to do!' – and the black prisoner replies: 'Don' siddown, massuh!' – Bruce's victory is artist-ically and morally complete.[46] As the waiter at the Off Broadway club shouted the night Bruce returned to San Francisco after the Los Angeles trial, 'Lenny, you're honest!'[47] As S.J. Perelman said, of himself: 'Before they made S.J. Perelman, they broke the mould.'

Thurber believed that 'humour is counterbalance'.[48] Kofsky believes that Bruce was 'a catalyst in accelerating ... changes' – changes in opinion which could change the state.[49] Certainly, critical humour is directed towards what is absent: a gap or a lack, a missing factor in the nation's construction. Laughter may bring you to the edge of revolt, but it remains part of a critique. As Richard Pryor informs his audience for *Live on Sunset Strip* in 1982: 'I am no day at the beach.' Yet for Arthur Koestler, laughter's 'only function seems to be to provide relief from tension'.[50] But surely therapy usually infers adjust-ment to a norm – which is rather different from being secure in what R.D. Laing calls an 'unquestionable self-validating certainty'.[51] Humour is like any other art: its effects and affects can be part of hope for both re-tension and change; it may be a reinforcement of the desire to reinforce a continuing, end-less tension and relief oscillation. It may also be a desire for explosion. Any discussion of laughter and humour had better bear in mind Mrs. Henry Adams' remark that Henry James chewed more than he bit off.

Notes

1. Muriel Rukeyser, *The Life of Poetry* (New York: Current Books, 1940), p. 46.
2. Henri Bergson, 'Laughter', in Wylie Sypher, ed., *Comedy*, (New York: Anchor Books, 1956), pp. 65-73.
3. Julia Kristeva, *Desire in Language*, ed., Leon S. Roudiez (New York: Columbia University Press, 1980), introduction and p. 16.

4. This and the following quotations are taken from Julia Kristeva, 'The Novel as Polyglot', in Kristeva, pp. 181-2.
5. Walter Benjamin, *Understanding Brecht* (1966; London: New Left Books, 1973), p. 101.
6. Sigmund Freud, 'Humour', in Philip Rieff, ed., *Freud: Character and Culture* (New York: Collier Books, 1963), pp. 263-9.
7. Maurice Solotow, 'On the Road with Bob Hope', *Reader's Digest*, April, 1981, p. 106.
8. Quotations here and in the next paragraph from Freud in Rieff.
9. Gore Vidal, '*Some* Jews and *the* Gays', *The Nation* [New York], 14 November 1981.
10. Ralph Ellison, *Shadow and Act* (New York: Random House, 1965), pp. 54-5.
11. Charles Baudelaire, *Flowers of Evil and Other Works*, ed. and trans. Wallace Fowlie (New York: Bantam Books, 1964), p. 135.
12. See also William Burroughs, *The Naked Lunch* (1959); Terry Southern, *The Magic Christian* (1960); Bruce J. Friedman, *Stern* (1962); Stanley Elkin, *Boswell* (1964).
13. Alan Brien, 'The Man in the Ironic Mask: S.J. Perelman', *Dialogue* [Washington, D.C.], 12, 3, (1979), p. 38.
14. Ralph Gleason, 'The Comedy of Dissent', *The Paper*, part 1, October 8; part 2, October 15 (Chicago: 1960) – reprinted from *Contact* magazine.
15. Gore Vidal, 'The Unrocked Boat', *The Nation*, 26 April 1958.
16. Lenny Bruce, *How to Talk Dirty and Influence People* (Chicago: Playboy Press, 1965), p. 195.
17. John A. Williams, 'Dick Gregory: Desegregated Comic', *Swank*, 8, 4 (1961).
18. Ralph Ellison, 'Twentieth-Century Fiction and the Black Mask of Humanity' (1946-53) in *Shadow and Act*.
19. Dick Gregory, *Nigger* (New York: Dutton, 1964; Cardinal: 1965).
20. LeRoi Jones, *The Dead Lecturer* (New York: Grove Press, 1965).
21. Arthur Steuer, 'The Space for Race in Humor', *Esquire* (November, 1961).
22. Joe Flaherty, 'To North Vietnam: Dick Gregory on his Way to Entertain the Jailed', *Village Voice* [New York], 6 December 1966.
23. SNCC: Student Non-violent Coordinating Committee; Ho: Ho Chi Minh, president of North Vietnam.
24. Matthew Hoffmann, 'Taking Himself Hostage', *Time Out*, 15-25 September 1980, p. 23.
25. Paul Goodman, *New Reformation* (New York: Random House, 1970), pp. 26-7.
26. 'The Sound and Foolery of Mort Sahl', *Esquire* (January, 1959).
27. Jonathan Miller, 'Beyond the New Frontier', *New Statesman*, 21 July 1961.
28. Bruce Rothwell, 'The Egghead Hits Back', *News Chronicle*, 12 May 1958.
29. 'Profile of Mort Sahl', *The Observer* [London], 16 July 1961.
30. 'The Sound and Foolery of Mort Sahl', *Esquire* (January, 1959).
31. Mort Sahl, *Heartland* (New York and London: Harcourt Brace Jovanovich, 1976), pp. 37, 101-2, 139, 155, 116, 125-6, 146, 149, 153-4, 156.
32. Frank Kofsky, *Lenny Bruce: The Comedian as Social Critic and Secular Moralist* (New York: Monad Press, 1974), p. 9.
33. Bruce, *How to Talk Dirty*, pp. 130-1.
34. Kenneth Tynan, 'Foreword' in Bruce, *How to Talk Dirty*, p. vi.
35. Norman Mailer, 'The White Negro', in *Advertisements for Myself* (New York: New American Library, 1960).
36. Kofsky, p. 90.
37. Charles Marowitz, 'The Confessions of Lenny Bruce', *Encore* [London], July-August, 1962.

38. Albert Goldman, *Ladies and Gentlemen, Lenny Bruce!!* (1971: New York: Ballantine, 1974), pp. 510-575.
39. *New Statesman* (December, 1962).
40. Kofsky, pp. 57-58.
41. Bruce, *How to Talk Dirty*, ch. 23.
42. Tynan in Bruce, *How to Talk Dirty*, p. ix.
43. C. Wright Mills, *The Power Elite* (New York: Oxford University Press, 1956), p. 334.
44. Lenny Bruce, *The Berkeley Concert*, Transatlantic Records, TRA 195, 1969.
45. Bruce, *How to Talk Dirty*, p. 46.
46. Lenny Bruce, *Lenny Bruce's Interviews of Our Time*, Fantasy, UAL 29076, 1969; Lenny Bruce, *Lenny Bruce: American*, Fantasy Records, Fantasy 7011, n.d. (unexpurgated version).
47. Ralph J. Gleason, sleeve note for Bruce, *The Berkeley Concert*.
48. Helen Thurber and Edward Weeks, eds., *Selected Letters of James Thurber* (Boston: Little Brown, 1981).
49. Kofsky, p. 62.
50. Reprinted from the *Encyclopedia Britannica* (1974) in *Dialogue*, 8, 3-4 (1975), p. 96.
51. R.D. Laing, 'Ontological Insecurity', *The Divided Self* (Harmondsworth: Penguin, 1965).

The Contributors

Marzia Balzani teaches at the Roehampton Institute of Higher Education in London. She took a first class honours degree in French and Classics at King's College, London in 1984, and then switched fields to study for a D. Phil in anthropology at Wolfson College, Oxford, winning the Wolfson Award in the process. She is currently working on her thesis: 'The Legitimation of Power with Reference to the Institution of Monarchy in Hindu South Asia.' Marzia Balzani is also an editor of *Talus*, an interdisciplinary cultural studies journal published at the University of York.

Clive Bush is Reader in American Literature at the Department of English, King's College, University of London. The author of *The Dream of Reason: American Consciousness and Cultural Achievement from Independence to the Civil War* (1977) and *Halfway to Revolution: Investigation and Crisis in the Work of Henry Adams, William James and Gertrude Stein* (1991), as well as many articles on American literature and culture, he is also editor of the American Studies journal *Democratic Vistas*. The most recent of his three published volumes of poetry, *shifts in undreamt time*, appeared in 1989.

Dale Carter lectures in American Studies at the Department of English, University of Aarhus, Denmark. A graduate of the University of Warwick, the Institute of United States Studies, and King's College, University of London, he is the author of *The Final Frontier: The Rise and Fall of the American Rocket State* (1988) and various articles on twentieth century America. He is currently working on a study of human/machine interactions in post-war American culture and society.

Allen Fisher is a poet, painter and theoretician. Having studied art and science in London before taking an M.A. at the University of Essex, he is currently Curriculum Coordinator at Hereford College of Art and Design in England. He has published over ninety volumes of poetry and documentation, including *Unpolished Mirrors* (1985), *Brixton Fractals* (1985) and *Buzzards and Bees* (1987). His work has also appeared more recently in Gillian Allnutt, *The New British Poetry* (1988) and the first of Paladin's contemporary British poetry anthologies: Brian Catling, Allen Fisher and Bill Griffiths, *Future Exiles* (1992). He includes in his list of activities 'researching the imaginary, complexity, beauty and consciousness'.

Elsebeth Hurup graduated from the University of Aarhus, Denmark, in 1984 with an M.A. in English and History of Art. The author of *Milk and Honey*.... (1985) and *The Great Gatsby: En Analyse* (1985), she was Lecturer in Danish at the University of Michigan, Ann Arbor, between 1987 and 1989. More recently, she has taught English language and American Studies at the universities of Aarhus and Odense, Denmark. She is currently Research Fellow at the Department of English, University of Aarhus, working on manifestations of nostalgia in American film and television during the Carter presidency.

Peter Ling currently lectures on the civil rights movement at the undergraduate and postgraduate levels at the Department of American and Canadian Studies, University of Nottingham, England. The author of *America and the Automobile* (1990), he has also written about the role of transportation in the civil rights movement and is now working on a study of the political education activities of Septima Clark's Citizenship Schools and the Mississippi Freedom Schools.

Callum MacDonald is Reader in History at the Department of History and Joint School of Comparative American Studies, University of Warwick, England. The author of *The United States, Britain and Appeasement, 1936-1939* (1981), *Korea: The War Before Vietnam* (1986), *The Death of SS Obergruppenführer Reinhard Heydrich* (1989), and *Britain and the Korean War* (1990), he specializes in American foreign relations. His latest work, a study of the Battle of Crete during World War Two, is to be published in 1993.

Eric Mottram retired in 1991 as Professor of English and American Literature at the Department of English, King's College, University of London. He has lectured widely in Britain, the United States and elsewhere, and was during the autumn of 1992 Visiting Professor of Poetry at the State University of New York at Buffalo. The author of *William Burroughs: The Algebra of Need* (1977), *Blood on the Nash Ambassador: Investigations in American Culture* (1989), and many other works, Professor Mottram has also published more than one hundred articles on diverse aspects of British and American culture and over twenty volumes of poetry.

Jody Pennington is working towards a master's degree in English and Mass Communications at the University of Aarhus, Denmark, having previously received a bachelor's degree in English from Georgia Southwestern College, Americus, Georgia. His current thesis research focuses on the relationship between basic American beliefs and values, political rhetoric, the political economy, and what he calls 'the American genius for not dealing seriously with its growing social problems'.

Karl-Heinz Westarp is Associate Professor in English at the Department of English, University of Aarhus, Denmark, and has a particular interest in theatre studies. His recent publications (as author, editor or co-editor) include *Flannery O'Connor: The Growing Craft* (1992), *Where?: Place in Recent North American Fictions* (1991), *Walker Percy: Philosopher and Novelist* (1991), *Realist of Distances: Flannery O'Connor Revisited* (1987), and *British Drama in the Eighties: Texts and Contexts* (1987).

John Whiting is a freelance sound engineer and recordist based in London and working throughout Europe and America. The holder of an M.A. from the Institute of United States Studies, University of London, he was in the 1960s a volunteer and then Production Director/Program Producer at KPFA in Berkeley, California, where his happy memories include technical direction for Erik Bauersfeld's now-legendary series *Black Mass*. He is currently working on a full-length study of KPFA.

Abstracts

The Paradox of Power: Eisenhower and the 'New Look'
(Callum MacDonald)

President Dwight Eisenhower's security policies were a reaction to NSC-68 and the Korean War. Sharing with right-wing Republicans a belief that NSC-68 threatened the American economy by promoting an open-ended arms race, the president attempted to reduce costs while deterring the Soviet Union by giving nuclear weapons a key role in his 'New Look'. Despite the rhetoric of 'massive retaliation', however, Eisenhower was careful to avoid pushing the Russians to the brink.

The central paradox of his administration was that nuclear weapons were so destructive that war was no longer a rational option – the United States and the Soviet Union shared a common interest in survival. In this period the first moves towards a nuclear test-ban treaty were taken. By contrast, Eisenhower pursued brinkmanship with China to please the Republican right and drive a wedge into the Sino-Soviet alliance. While this approach may have accelerated a Sino-Soviet split, it also convinced Mao that China had to have the bomb. Finally, while seeking to decrease nuclear tension with the Russians, the Eisenhower administration also engaged in a struggle with third world nationalism in which, crucially in Vietnam, North-South issues were confused with East-West ones.

Evasive Action: War, Peace and Security in the Fifties (Dale Carter)

In the wake of the Axis collapse in 1945 and the development of radically new forms of weaponry, the nature of warfare in advanced industrial societies underwent complex changes. With ultimate victory in any military sense no longer possible, the United States during the 1950s witnessed the development of other forms of conflict in which new sorts of armies developed and perfected novel strategies and tactics. In place of war and peace there came the dream of national security; instead of victory or defeat there proliferated evasive action.

This chapter documents and analyses some of the major expressions of that action. Drawing on a diverse range of sources – from the novels of Norman Mailer, Thomas Pynchon and Sloan Wilson to the era's feature films, from studies of the red scare to government statistics – it discusses the logic of suburbanization, the growth of consumerism, the culture of religious belief, and the struggle for relaxation. Conceptualizing this complex of social and cultural phenomena in terms of the metaphor of evasive action, the chapter concludes with a discussion of the image of communism in public thought and popular imagination. More than any other single concept or phenomenon, 'communism' became a phrase to which was attached whatever suburban America resented, felt guilty about, or found distasteful. Ironically, and in keeping with the broader theme of evasive action, what was thereby projected was very often the necessary underside of the suburban dream.

Bridge Over Troubled Water: Nostalgia for the Fifties in Movies of the Seventies and Eighties (Elsebeth Hurup)

Since the early 1970s, Hollywood has turned out numerous movies set in the 1950s, most of which focus on teenagers and issues related to growing up. This article seeks to shed light on the nature of the nostalgia expressed in three of these movies – *American Graffiti* (1973), *Grease* (1978), and *Peggy Sue Got Married* (1987) – as well as to explain the continuing fascination with the 1950s.

Rather than merely expressing a wistful longing for days gone by, these movies question our nostalgic perception of the 1950s. They thus serve to bridge the gap between then and now, in the process reestablishing our sense of identity which (according to sociologist Fred Davis) is the function of nostalgia. The conclusion to be drawn from each of the movies is that the 1950s may be a nice place to visit but not somewhere to live. Due to the events and changes that have taken place since then, the 1950s now seem light years away. Through the collective search for identity and the effort to regain a sense of continuity and stability in the midst of chaos, they have become a cultural icon, our perceptions being filtered through the stylizing lens of Hollywood. Just as the individual's youth, with time, takes on mythical qualities, so too have the 1950s in the collective consciousness.

Dusk and Dawn: Black Protest in the Fifties and Forties (Peter Ling)

As the civil rights battles of the 1955-1965 period become more distant events, scholars have begun to develop new perspectives on the origins and significance of the civil rights movement. This article looks at two such perspectives. The first, derived from the 'new labour history', builds upon community studies of unionization and radicalism at the local level to advance the argument that during the Depression and war years a bi-racial popular movement was formed that provided the springboard for the later more celebrated move-

266

ment. Significantly, this earlier movement had a more radical class-based programme than its successor.

The second perspective, derived from black nationalism, also sees hopeful signs of black solidarity in the 1940s and suggests that the civil rights movement was fatefully deluded by the appeal of integrationism and non-economic liberalism in the 1950s. As a result, the necessity of organizing African-Americans into a cohesive social and economic entity to compete in America's pluralistic political economy was neglected. A consideration of these contending race and class-conscious visions serve to illuminate the complex etiology of the civil rights movement.

Is He a Bedouin? Post-War American and French Responses to North Africa in the Work of Paul Bowles and Albert Camus
(Marzia Balzani and Clive Bush)

This chapter compares Albert Camus's and Paul Bowles's responses to North Africa in the fifteen or more years after the end of the Second World War. It contrasts the complexities of the Frenchman's and the American's cultural and political positions in the 1950s against the background of decolonization. The immediate political and literary contexts of both cultures are examined in historical terms, and the contrasts and convergences of their literary production are seen to be legitimized by the actual interest many French and American writers of the period had in each other.

While both writers are shown to face their own 'displacements' in terms often borrowed from the others' culture, political differences between the two writers and their cultures are emphasized, and the effects highlighted in their respective books. Camus's relation to the struggle for Algerian independence and Bowles's critique of British imperialism in Kenya are invoked to fill out the comparison in more detail. Both writers' 'construction' of a 'North Africa' are detailed with reference to their writings; their 'nostalgias' for a fugitive past are also described and compared.

The article contributes to an ongoing debate about 'orientalism' and 'colonization', taking up issues about the construction of the 'other' within colonialist discourses. Bowles's novels are presented as more radical than his political pronouncements might indicate; the four major novels examined illustrate this proposition. The article concludes by suggesting that Bowles's North Africa becomes a prototype of the space of 'interzone', a cityscape of post-modernity which will fascinate American writers from the 1950s onwards.

Conscience of a Decade: Arthur Miller (Karl-Heinz Westarp)

Arthur Miller's fundamental convictions about human freedom of expression came into particular focus through his own struggle for artistic freedom during the anticommunist-inflamed 1950s. Though deeply involved personally, Miller was able to distance himself sufficiently both to identify and dissect critically the mistakes and shortcomings of his society. At considerable cost, he fought relentlessly for a renewed sense of personal dignity. His works contributed to the creation of a new level of awareness of such values. He became in this sense the conscience of the decade.

This article first discusses Miller's own development during the 1950s. It then addresses his characters' struggle towards a recognition of their duty to society as a means of achieving personal dignity. *The Crucible* is presented as a study of the close interrelationship between powerful social mechanisms and the individual's fight for personal freedom. Taking a stand in accordance with one's conscience when confronted with centralized state manipulation is essential: this was Miller's seminal message, not only for the 1950s but also the 1960s.

San Francisco: Arts in the City that Defies Fate (Eric Mottram)

Cities or regions in the United States from Chicago to New York have periodically acted as focal points for cultural interaction and renaissance. During the 1940s and, more visibly, the 1950s, as this paper explains, San Francisco and its environs flourished as such a centre.

Stimulated by the painting of Mark Tobey, Morris Graves and Clyfford Still; the poetry and prose of Henry Miller, Kenneth Rexroth, Robert Duncan and Kenneth Patchen; and the jazz of Miles Davis, Gerry Mulligan, and Stan Getz, the San Francisco renaissance witnessed an articulation of developments in literature, music and the fine arts. Institutions ranging from the California School of Fine Arts to the San Francisco State College Poetry Centre, from KPFA subscription radio to clubs like the Black Hawk and Jimbo's Bop City, contributed to the growth and maintenance of a cultural complex within which creative artists could work and engender an audience. Manifestations of the renaissance were diverse: public poetry readings by writers drawn to the city like Allen Ginsberg, Lawrence Ferlinghetti and Gregory Corso; the City Lights Press and bookshop; a thriving theatre scene; literary circles and little magazines.

Even as it flourished, the renaissance was confronted by counter-forces (from the House UnAmerican Activities Committee to local customs and police forces) which felt threatened by its values and practices. In the movement from Beat to both beatnik and protest, its temporary coherence dissolved. The renaissance had never involved a single, unified community: it was personally and culturally diverse; yet its multiple groups shared a resistance to official culture whose values and achievements remain vital.

Plurality and the Reproduced: A Selective Approach to American Visual Arts in the 1950s (Allen Fisher)

This chapter investigates American visual arts of the 1950s, emphasizing a number of characteristics found in the period's art and discussing implications for the art that has followed. The characteristics chosen include gesture and figuration, collage and disruption, and recurrence and simulation. There is also a discussion of the issue of boundaries. The text incorporates practical summaries of these characteristics and offers detailed analyses of selected works by, amongst others, Jackson Pollock, Robert Motherwell, David Smith, Larry Rivers, Willem deKooning, Robert Rauschenberg, Jasper Johns and Franz Kline.

The Lengthening Shadow: Lewis Hill and the Origins of Listener-Sponsored Broadcasting in America (John Whiting)

Before the 1950s the dominance of commercialism meant that relatively little of worth was transmitted by American radio stations. As this chapter shows, however, the opening in 1949 of the Pacifica Foundation's KPFA radio station brought about valuable new developments in broadcasting whose influences are evident to this day.

Conceived of during and after World War Two by pacifist Lewis Hill, KPFA set out to provide programming determined not by commercial criteria but by standards of intellectual and artistic excellence. Emphasizing freedom of speech and committed to the peaceful resolution of conflict, the station drew on the human resources of its Berkeley, California setting – university staff, Bay Area artists and intellectuals, pacifists and others – to produce a wide range of programs presenting a broad spectrum of thought: from public affairs to music (classical, folk, ethnic), from literature to philosophy. Dependence on financing provided by voluntary listener-subscription, donations and foundation grants (rather than advertising) made survival difficult, but allowed KPFA a flexibility in programming and format unthinkable for most commercial stations.

In addition to financial constraints, both disputes over administration and generational tensions during the 1950s led to power struggles and resignations (including, temporarily, Lewis Hill's own). In spite of attacks by reactionary interests and his own exhaustion and early death, however, Hill's pioneering efforts in FM radio led to significant gains, not least the growth of public television broadcasting. Today KPFA continues to operate as part of the public radio network Hill had anticipated, while its archives now constitute a unique resource for local and national history.

Don't Knock the Rock: Race, Business and Society in the Rise of Rock'n' Roll (Jody Pennington)

When Emerson called out for 'men of elastic, men of moral mind, men who can live in the moment and take a step forward', he had Little Richard, Chuck Berry and Elvis Presley in mind. He was just too soon to know it. It was no coincidence that these early rock'n'rollers were southerners: the form their music took, its appearance in the mid-1950s, and its demise a few years later were intimately connected not only with the fate of the music's heroes – including Jerry Lee Lewis and Buddy Holly as well as Presley, Berry and Little Richard – but also with the changing texture of the region's racial relationships. The music's roots lay in the emergence of African-American musical forms (rhythm and blues, gospel) at the same time as white country music. The merging of elements from these distinct traditions resulted in rock'n'roll. Only the technological development of the various media connected with the music's production and distribution, particularly radio, lacked this uniquely southern dimension.

Rock'n'roll's ethereal hits were well suited to an America more concerned with experience than meaning: the songs came and went – so long as the radio kept on playing. While rock'n'roll radio articulated the open-ended futuristic dreams shared by much of the nation, the music specifically reflected the daily life of an increasingly affluent sector of the population: white middle-class teenagers. Notwithstanding its premature 'death' in the late 1950s, its appeal has ensured that rock'n'roll has become just as much a part of the American landscape as the Manhattan skyline, Fords and gas stations.

The American Comedian as Social Critic, 1950-1970 (Eric Mottram)

Humour does not have to be mere entertainment or diversion or a source of personal reassurance or victory in a competitive society. It may be unnerving and troubling (and at the same time socially liberating), particularly if it confronts official taboos and fixations relating to morality, religion, sex, race, law or taste. Drawing on and challenging the ideas of writers as diverse as Hobbes, Freud, Kristeva, and Bergson, this essay discusses how, during the 1950s and 1960s, the comedian as social critic offered a hazardous but necessary challenge to authoritarian, rigid and mechanical beliefs and practices in America.

In different ways the careers of Dick Gregory, Mort Sahl and Lenny Bruce illustrate the means by which the comedian as social critic demystified hypocritical power. Creating dramas rather than one-line gags in a fashion quite distinct from the reassuring routines of a Bob Hope, they offered non-ideological critiques which challenged sacred assumptions and exposed the interior structures of public motivation. Risking popular hostility and official suppression, they engendered analysis and dissent. Dick Gregory focused on race relations and white guilt in a context of rising challenges to prejudice; Mort Sahl satirized the Age of Conformity and its political agents; Lenny Bruce extended the range of criticism to hypocrisy in all fields. All three experienced fame and fortune but also condemnation and persecution. In Bruce's case, the results included bankruptcy and premature death: indices less of his obscenity than of the accuracy and importance of his humour and the degradation of the society it engaged.